Foundations of Communication
Library Edition

Editor
Roland Posner

# Evidence and Argumentation in Linguistics

Edited by
Thomas A. Perry

W
DE
G

Walter de Gruyter · Berlin · New York
1980

303248

_U_

*CIP-Kurztitelaufnahme der Deutschen Bibliothek*

**Evidence and argumentation in linguistics** / ed. by Thomas A.
Perry. — Berlin, New York: de Gruyter, 1979.
  ([Grundlagen der Kommunikation: Bibliotheksausgabe.]
  Foundations of communication: Library ed.).

  ISBN 3-11-007272-6

NE: Perry, Thomas A. [Hrsg.]

Satz und Druck: Heenemann GmbH & Co, Berlin
Buchbinder: Lüderitz & Bauer, Berlin

# Preface

The present volume offers a variety of contributions addressed to argumentation, research methods, evaluation of evidence, and identification of goals in linguistic research. They were not chosen from a particular coherent tradition within linguistics, nor were they necessarily chosen for coherence of theme or mutual comparability. Some are comprehensive, others are sharply focused on particular issues or works. Some are exploratory and make a particular claim of interest; others are illustrative and, while not necessarily reaching a conclusion of broad philosophical import, demonstrate or analyze a point that can be profitably fit into a broader context. The collection is by no means exhaustive, but is intended to contribute to the continuing discussion of the issues addressed by the papers presented here.

There is a share of disagreement evident here, both between individual contributions here and with work outside the book. This is an intentional, but passionless result of the collection. There are no ulterior motives, no conspiracies reflected in the selection of papers here. Disagreement exists, is interesting, and should be reflected in print. This book is only a vehicle for putting research before the interested public, on the premise that any serious effort to grapple with linguistic reality should not be ignored. It does not have to be accepted.

The introduction is an essay intended to set off the collection rather than review or summarize its content.

Thomas A. Perry

Table of Contents

# Acknowledgements

Sidney Greenbaum, "Syntactic frequency and acceptability," *Lingua* 40 (1976), reprinted by permission of the publisher, North-Holland Publishing Co.

Jon D. Ringen, "Linguistic facts: a study of the empirical scientific status of transformational generative grammars," in D. Cohen and J. Wirth, *Testing Linguistic Hypotheses,* reprinted by permission of the publisher, Hemisphere Publishing Corporation

# Introduction

Thomas A. Perry

Any discipline like linguistics that proposes to investigate objective subject matter should provide for a process of continuous critical evaluation of ongoing research programs using the analytic tools of logic and the philosophy of science. In more developed sciences this process is somewhat less important than in less established disciplines — and linguistics must be counted in this group — where the objects and means of research cannot be presumed to be definitively identified. Linguistics is in just such a state despite, and to no small degree because of, the influential work of Noam Chomsky. Although his work has gone a long way toward delineating a plausible, coherent, and well-specified research program for linguistics, it has by no means closed the discussion around even the most primary questions of importance to the discipline. Indeed it has had the effect of opening serious debate on the methodological status of linguistics. Much of the contemporary discussion surrounding the formulation and import of theories of language, and the collection and use of data as evidence in such theories, is keyed to issues raised in Chomsky's work. This discussion should continue — at all levels of inquiry — even and perhaps especially with respect to the question of what kind of science linguistics is or should be, if it is one at all.

The contributions to this volume all explore in one way or another arguments, research procedures, methodological assumptions, or the nature of linguistic evidence which bear on some aspect of the open question of the scientific status of linguistics (although many do not address this question directly). It will be seen in the present volume and related work cited here that it is not at all agreed whether linguistics is i) an independent empirical science, or ii) an autonomous branch of an independent empirical science, or iii) a non-autonomous branch of an independent empirical science or iv) a non-empirical, or formal science.[1] In what follows, some of the broad issues involved in determining the status of linguistics in terms of i) — iv) will be reviewed, after a prefatory discussion of the formulation of research goals and the structure of a theory.

---

[1] For discussion of the terms *independent* and *autonomous*, see below and related discussion in Sanders 1970, this volume and Derwing 1973, this volume.

Any methodological discussion, whether with regard to a formal or an empirical science, has as its eventual aim some ultimate degree of effectiveness with which that science reaches the goals set out for it. Successful inquiry can be frustrated as much by setting the wrong goals as it can by fallacious inferences or bad data. An evaluation of the appropriateness and import of any particular set of research goals is necessary prerequisite to the discussion of specific methodological questions. Goals set too high can lead to necessary methodological indeterminacy, i.e., it is possible to select a goal for which there is *no* effective research procedure for realizing the program. This criticism has been directed at Chomsky's goal of investigating competence independently of performance, for example.[2] On the other hand, too narrowly-defined goals lead to results of little or no import. The American structuralist dictum limiting descriptive goals to what can be obtained by segmentation and classification over an observed corpus has been criticized in this way.[3]

The twin issues of appropriateness and import of goals grow out of the questions: What should we find out? and: how much would these projected results advance our knowledge of the world? The first of these (the appropriateness question) is logically prior to the second (the import question). Their answers jointly permit a reasoned judgement as to whether a particular line of inquiry is worthwhile. Both are therefore logically prior to the question: how do we go about finding out what we have set out to find out?[4] It is important to distinguish the two goal questions from the latter strategy question, which refers to the development of research procedures. Research procedures within a given science always develop relative to particular goals of inquiry, and can subsequently be judged as either effective or ineffective toward the realization of these goals. The effectiveness of research procedures can be computed with analytic tools provided by a general theory of methodology (such measures of conclusiveness as statistical significance, experimental controls, logical consistency, etc.). The proposal of an appropriate goal can only be put forward by the researcher in the form

---

[2]   See Derwing (1973), Linell (1974), and others. Arguments to the effect that Chomsky approached his goal ineffectively address another question. Goals which are *in principle* out of reach are grossly inappropriate, of course, since pragmatic principles would ordinarily forbid undertaking endeavors with no possible yield.

[3]   See the well-known arguments in Chomsky 1964, 1966, or Postal 1968, among others. Notice that this research goal of American structuralism is defined by the contemplated research procedure. This state of affairs is backwards, since the adoption of goals is logically prior to the adoption of research procedures to realize them.

[4]   This question is distinct from the appropriateness question, since the researcher typically makes judgments of feasibility without knowing specific means of reaching a given goal. It is possible to set out to find a cure for cancer, for example, without a specific idea of how to go about it.

of a belief statement based on the researcher's insights, conjectures, and interests. The question of the import of goals can only be based on an evaluation of the usefulness of the results of research in some larger context (consequences for other research programs or disciplines, social consequences, and the like). The judgment of import is therefore also subjective.

It is of little interest to attack the belief statements offered as a basis for some particular research goal. It is, on the other hand, important to evaluate the effectiveness of research procedures critically to find out whether they are adequate to deliver the answers called for by the statement of research goals. This, in turn, requires an examination the use of evidence and structure of arguments characteristic of a given research program. This examination includes, in a fundamental way, the determination of the scientific status of the research program — as it is practiced — within the logically possible states of affairs i) — iv) above. Indeed, much of the methodological discussion currently under way in linguistics is connected with this determination, directly or indirectly (which is something no longer true in a 'central' science like physics, for example). It is therefore useful to examine the states of affairs i) — iv) more closely.

Determining the status of a linguistic theory with respect to the properties of empiricalness, independence, and autonomy is easier if we adopt some uniform conception of 'theory' of some standard sort. Let us assume, then, that all theories are ideally conceived as axiomatic systems[5] providing well-defined primitive terms and a means of making predications on those terms. We can call this the *axiomatic base* of the theory. Such a theory *is about* or *refers to* some set of individual constants in its *domain*, representing real objects. Employing rules of inference governing the theory in conjunction with the axiomatic base and given initial conditions, we can derive assertions about the members of the domain. An unproved assertion of this kind is a hypothesis, a proved one is a theorem. A linguistic theory might generate an assertion of the following sort: "If S is a sentence of English, then if S has a direct object O, the verb in S precedes O." Such terms as 'sentence,' 'direct object,' 'precedes,' etc. are provided by the axiomatic base, S is a member of the domain, the predications 'S is a sentence of English' and 'S has a direct object' describe initial conditions, and the if-then form of the assertion is hypothesis, this can be shown to be a valid theorem by showing that there are no members of the domain for which the initial conditions are true but not the assertion 'the verb in S precedes O.'

---

[5]   See also Hutchinson (1974, this volume).

Given the above characterization of a theory, we can now say that the nature of the domain is crucial to determinig the empirical status of any theory. If the members of the set constituting the domain represent *contingently real objects*, then we say the theory in *empirical*. 'Contingently real object' can be contrasted with 'definitionally real object,' which characterizes the members of the domain of a non-empirical, or formal theory. Contingently real objects — the set of all coniferous trees, for example — do not necessarily exist, and are ordinarily thought of being contingent on spatiotemporal reality.[6] Definitionally real objects — the set of natural numbers, for example — exist necessarily with respect to a given theory, and hence can be arbitrarily defined. Such a theory can never be false, insofar as it is well-formed. The correspondence between the set of constants of the domain and the real objects represented by these constants in an empirical theory cannot be arbitrary in this way.

The testing of empirical theories, in this view, consists in examining the consistency of the assertions about the domain of the theory with the state of affairs in the world. (In a formal theory, this correspondence is guaranteed by definition.) This procedure requires a methodology which can specify research procedures appropriate to the nature of the real objects represented in the domain of the theory. Identifying a domain for a theory is thus a fundamental step (see the discussion with respect to linguistics in Sanders 1970, this volume, Wirth, this volume, and Berdan, this volume). The question of which research procedures respresent the best instruments for examining the nature of the domain of a given purportedly empirical linguistic theory represents a classical point of disagreement in linguistics. Chomsky's use of intuitional judgments in a research procedure for examinig the grammatical status of sentences remains highly controversial (cf. Chomsky 1965, Ringen, this volume, Itkonen 1974, 1976, 1978, and this volume). Attempts to control the reliability of such judgments with more effective research techniques (cf. Greenbaum 1970, this volume; Elliot, Legum, and Thompson 1969) do not in themselves guarantee that the testing of linguistic hypotheses on the basis of intuitional judgments will be more secure, since it is logically possible that the objects taken to be in the domain of the theory (in this case, the competence of ideal speaker-hearers) are not contingently real at all. If that were the case, no amount of testing would be sufficient to show anything about the domain of the

---

[6]  This statement is not intended to preclude the possibility tht something can be a contingently real object but not spatiotemporally contingent. Given an appropriate methodology for indirect observation, such objects might be accessible by their relationship to spatiotemporally contingent objects. Energy, as far as I know, is not itself spatiotemporally contingent, but is with certainty contingently real.

theory, and the theory would be non-empirical (cf. Ringen, this volume, Dahl, this volume, and Itkonen, this volume).

Finally, we can address the questions of independence and autonomy. A science can be said to be *independent,* as construed here, if it has a unique domain and axiomatic base, i.e., if its axiomatic base and domain are not properly included in those of some other theory. Sanders (1970, 1972) has argued for the independence of a particular formulation of a linguistic theory (and this is apparently the only such argument for linguistics of any detail). Chomsky (1965, 1968 and elsewhere) has explicitly assumed the non-independence of transformational-generative grammar, asserting that it is a branch of cognitive psychology. In fact, elements of the axiomatic base of Chomskian linguistics, such as concepts like tacit knowledge, learning, cognitive development, and so forth are obviously of more general import within cognitive psychology.

The weaker status of *autonomy* can be attributed to a field of research if it is non-independent but has a unique domain. In practice, this means that a theory with this status can be constructed and tested independently of any other theory, while drawing on the axiomatic base of another theory. Such is the relationship posited by Chomsky between a competence theory in linguistics and a general theory of cognitive psychology. Derwing (1973, this volume) has argued directly against this view, claiming that if we construe the domain of a linguistic theory as an empirical domain (cf. the preceding paragraph), then it is not unique, but constitutes the domain of a more general theory of linguistic behavior, including performance. The ajudication of such claims and counterclaims, it should be clear, is essential if we expect to arrive at a clear understanding of what kind of discipline linguistics is, or should be.

It has been claimed here that the fundamental questions about the empirical status, independence, and autonomy of linguistics need to be discussed further. This does not mean that all linguistic research must stop until these questions have been thoroughly examined. Indeed, the practices typical of ongoing research give valuable feedback for the discussion of methodological questions, since practice is often a more accurate reflection of the status of a discipline than intent. It may well be that linguistics, upon closer examination, is an unfortunate amalgam of sub-disciplines of quite disparate methodological orientations. Especially if this is so, it is indispensible to know what one is doing when one does it. Such clarity is rare in linguistics, given its present state of affairs.

6 Thomas A. Perry

## Bibliography

Berdan, R. This volume. "Idealizations in the development of a sociolinguistic theory."

Chomsky, N. 1964. "Current issues in linguistic theory" in: J. Fodor and J. J. Katz *The Structure of Language* Englewood Cliffs: Prentice-Hall.

— 1965. *Aspects of the Theory of Syntax* Cambridge: MIT Press.

— 1966. *Topics in the Theory of Generative Grammar* The Hague: Mouton.

— 1968. *Language and Mind* New York: Harcourt Brace Jovanovich.

Dahl, Ö. This volume. "Is linguistics empirical? a critique of Esa Itkonen's *Linguistics and Metascience.*"

Elliot, D., Legum, S., and Thompson, S. A. 1969. "Syntactic variation as linguistic data." Papers from the Fifth Regional Meeting of the Chicago Linguistic Society.

Greenbaum. 1970. *Elicitation Experiments in English* London: Longman.

Hutchinson, L. G. 1974. "Grammar as theory" in: D. Cohen (ed.) *Explaining Linguistic Phenomena* Washington D. C.: Hemisphere Publishing.

— This volume. "Axiom, theorem, and rule."

Itkonen, E. 1974. *Linguistics and Metascience* Kokemäki: Studia Philosophica Turkuensia, Fasc. II.

— 1976. "Linguistics and Empiricalness: Answers to Criticisms." Helsinki: University of Helsinki, Department of General Linguistics working paper No. 4.

— 1978. *Grammatical Theory and Metascience* Amsterdam: Benjamins.

Itkonen, E. This volume. "Reply to Dahl."

Linell, P. 1974. *Problems of Psychological Reality in Generative Phonology* Reports from the Uppsala University Department of Linguistics No. 4.

Postal, P. 1968. *Aspects of Phonological Theory* New York: Harper & Row.

Ringen, J. This volume. "Linguistic facts: a study of the empirical scientific status of Transformational Generative Grammars."

Sanders, G. A. 1970. "On the natural domain of grammar." *Linguistics* 63: 51—123.

— 1972. *Equational Grammar* The Hague: Mouton.

— This volume. "Linguistically-significant attributes of linguistic objects."

Wirth, J. This volume. "Discourse grammars and conversational principles."

# I. The Domain of Linguistic Theory

# Linguistically-Significant Attributes of Linguistic Objects

Gerald A. Sanders

## 0. Introduction

The domain of an empirical science is determined by the properties and relations that are predicable of some set of real objects by interpretation of the valid theorems of some scientific theory.[1] The possible domains for scientific theories are doubly unbounded, since both the set of real objects and the set of real properties and relations of each individual object are infinitely large and heterogeneous. It is clear, though, that only a very minute subset of this infinite set of possible domains will consist of reasonable or natural domains for actual scientific inquiry — domains which partition the universe in such a way as to facilitate rather than hinder our efforts to understand it. In many cases, our ordinary unformalized knowledge of the world tells us immediately that certain possible domains, like the tails of Siamese cats, or the words of English, are grossly unnatural, and that others, like the domain of all animals, or that of all discourses of all languages, are much more natural than the former, and much more amenable to systematic investigation and informative analysis. It is one of the primary tasks of the scientist in any field to provide a formal explication and extension of this knowledge of relative naturalness by contributing to the construction of a set of theories with natural domains, which thereby serve to account for the significant similarities and differences between subparts of the known universe, while jointly providing an optimally general and systematic account of its known characteristics. The scientist will be concerned, moreover, not merely with the *achievement* of maximal naturalness, but rather with its *principled* achievement, since it is the principles that determine natural domains that provide their only real definitions and the only real explanation for their significant distinctiveness.

---

[1]   This paper was first presented on May 12, 1972 at the First Annual UWM Linguistics Symposium, "On Limiting the Domain of Linguistics," appearing subsequently also in the mimeographed Proceedings of the symposium, edited by D. Cohen, distributed during the summer of 1972 by the Department of Linguistics, University of Wisconsin-Milwaukee. A number of the matters discussed here are dealt with in somewhat greater detail in Sanders (1970) and Sanders (1972), where the fundamental metaconstraints and notational conventions of universal grammars and equational theories are explicitly stated and much more extensively exemplified.

This paper will be concerned with some of the primary formal bases for the principled achievement of a natural domain of natural language grammar. The first part of the paper will be devoted to an informal consideration of some of the fundamental distinguishing characteristics of all natural scientific domains and the natural theories that determine them. Three of these essential characteristics will be seen to be domain-independent and fully determined by the general metascientific non-reducibility condition for naturalness. The two remaining characteristics, which have to do with the significance of the objects that are characterized by a theory and with the significance of the attributes that it predicates of those objects, will be seen to be determinable only by domain-specific metaconstraints on the formal properties of the theories that determine specific domains. The second part of the paper will be concerned with the linguistic bases for the principled achievement of object-significance in linguistic theories. The final section of the paper will be concerned with the principled achievement of attribute-significance for such theories. It will be suggested that while object-significance is determined by power-reducing constraints on the form, content, scope, and inferential use of grammatical axioms, attribute-significance is determined wholly by formal constraints on the theorem-interpretation rules of linguistic theories. These constraints will be seen to serve both as a formal definition of the linguistically-significant attributes of linguistic objects and as an empirical hypothesis about the nature and functions of the systems of human knowledge that underlie their distinctively human uses.

## 1. The Characterization and Determination of Natural Domains

Natural domains are informally distinguishable from non-natural ones by the *coherence, exhaustiveness, exclusiveness,* and systematic *significance* of the properties and relations that determine them.

A theory has a *coherent* domain if the attributes that are predicated by its interpreted theorems can all be appropriately predicated of the same types of objects. Thus, for example, a theory whose interpreted theorems predicate analyticity and specific gravity does not have a coherent domain, since specific gravity attributes can be appropriately predicated only of physical objects, while analyticity can be appropriately predicated only of linguistic objects, which are non-physical pairings of sounds and meanings. On the other hand, a theory that generates predications of analyticity and synonymy has a coherent domain, since both of these attributes can be appropriately predicated of linguistic objects.

A theory has an *exhaustive* domain if the attributes which it predicates of the objects in its domain cannot be truly predicated of any object outside of its domain. Thus, for example, a theory which predicts the specific gravities of metals but not non-metals does not have an exhaustive domain, since specific gravity attributes can be truly predicated not only of metals but also of substances which are not metals. Similarly, a theory that predicts synonymy of sentences but not of discourses has a domain that is not exhaustive, and hence not natural, since synonymy can be truly predicated not only with respect to pairs of sentences like (1 a) and (1 b), but also with respect to pairs of non-sentential discourses, such as the dialogues (2 a) and (2 b).

(1) (a) I let out the cat at ten o'clock
    (b) I let the cat out at ten o'clock
(2) (a) When did you let out the cat?
        I let out the cat at ten o'clock
    (b) When did you let out the cat?
        I let it out at ten o'clock

An equally unnatural domain would be generated by any theory that characterizes synonymy non-exhaustively with respect to languages — e.g. by predicting synonymy relations between English sentences but not between French sentences, or not between English sentences and French sentences.

A theory has an *exclusive* domain if the attributes of objects which it predicts are not predictable for those objects by the interpretable theorems of any other theory presently known or conceivable. Thus, for example, a linguistic theory that predicts that there are no phonetic renditions of linguistic objects in which voicing is initiated after it has been terminated within the same syllable[2] would have a non-exclusive domain, since the same predication would apparently be generated for these as well as many other non-linguistic articulatory objects by any adequate theory of human physiology. In other words, since the impossibility of tautosyllabic revoicing apparently follows from independent principles of physiological theories, there cannot be any natural theory of language that generates this same prediction, or any more specific assertion that follows from it — such as the prediction that [kæpz] cannot be the fine phonetic representation of the plural of "cap" in English. Similarly, since the relative oddity of the speaker's beliefs or presuppositions associated with a sentence like "My cat said that it was going to rain today" would presumably be fully characterized by the

---

[2]  The existence and linguistic implications of this important extralinguistic generalization were apparently first noted by Robert Harms in his paper "Some Non-Rules of English" (1972). Harms also discusses a number of other physiological constraints of the same general type.

relation between the assertions 'The speaker assumes (or presumes) that cats can speak' and 'Cats can't speak,' where the latter presumably will follow from any adequate theory about cats or animals, there can be no natural theory of language which itself generates attributions of oddity to such sentences or to the belief or presupposition statements that are linguistically associated with them. It can be readily seen, in fact, that such oddity attributions can be generated only by the joint assertion of certain attributes of linguistic objects and certain attributes of the extra-linguistic universe. Such attributes thus fall within the domain of no scientific theory less general than the ultimate theory of everything. Pending the development of such a theory, therefore, all attributes of this sort must be systematically excluded from the domains of all scientific theories.

I have suggested in my paper "On the Natural Domain of Grammar" (1970) that the intuitively-recognized naturalness or non-naturalness of scientific domains can be at least partially characterized and explicated by the formal relations of reducibility and non-reducibility between theories. Thus the domain of a given theory will have the properties of coherence, exclusiveness, and exhaustiveness which are characteristic of all natural domains only if that theory is not reducible to any other theory presently known or conceivable, where, roughly, one theory is reducible to another if and only if every interpreted theorem of the first theory is an interpreted theorem of the second theory, and the axiomatic basis of the second theory is smaller than the sum of the bases of both theories.[3] Given this general non-reducibility criterion for naturalness, it was then shown with particular reference to linguistics that there are no natural domains of phonology, syntax, semantics, words, sentences, or particular languages, and that the only presently-defensible domain for a science of linguistics is that determined by theories which generate universal grammars for the discourses of all possible natural languages. It was shown that such universal theories of discourse grammar are sufficiently general to account for all facts of traditional interest to linguists, psycholinguists, and students of empirical logic — including all facts about the constant and variable attributes of natural languages, their systematic ontogenetic and phylogenetic changes, and their uses for the communication of information, arguments, requests, etc. It was also suggested that such theories are not reducible to any other theories presently known or proximately foreseeable, and that their ultimate reduction would appear to be possible only with respect to a general theory of human knowledge, which is actually that theory which reduces all scien-

---

[3]   This, of course, represents the conditions for theory reduction in a considerably over-simplified way. For a more detailed discussion of some of the fundamental problems of reduction, see Sanders (1970) and the references cited there.

tific theories to one ultimate and scientifically terminal explanation of the universe.

The reduction of sentence grammars and grammars of particular languages to the universal discourse grammars that subsume them can be justified and practically achieved in an almost trivially simple way.[4] However, though such reduction represents a necessary step towards the determination of a natural domain for linguistic theories, it is clearly grossly insufficient for the full achievement of such a determination. The primary reason for this is that the non-reducibility condition is a necessary but not sufficient condition for naturalness, since the properties of coherence, exhaustiveness, and exclusiveness that it determines are not sufficient to distinguish all intuitively natural domains from all intuitively non-natural ones. What has been left out, of course, is the essential property of significance, which is the most difficult of all domain-properties to characterize, but also the one which is philosophically and empirically most interesting, and which is perhaps most critical of all with respect to the achievement of a conceptually and explanatorily useful partitioning of the universe.

The insufficiency of the non-reducibility criterion can be shown most easily by showing that there are domains which clearly differ as to relative naturalness but not in the coherence, exhaustiveness, or exclusiveness of their attribute sets. I will give two examples of this situation here, which will also serve to illustrate the two senses of scientific significance that I will be presently concerned with.

Consider, first, the following three theories of biology:

(1) a theory that characterizes ordinary real animals like dogs, cats, aardvarks, and dinosaurs; this can be called the real animal theory.

(2) a theory that characterizes everything that the real animal theory characterizes, and, in addition, characterizes such things as unicorns, griffins, centaurs, and sea-serpents; this could be called the theory of real and mythical animals.

(3) a theory that characterizes everything that is characterized by the second theory, and, in addition, such things as the following: a type of animal that is just like a cat except that it has the capacity to acquire and use the language of the human community that shares its habitat; an animal that is just like a cow except that it has the bodily shape of an ameoba; an animal that is just like a human being except that it has no bodily shape and cannot die;

---

[4] Algorithms for the reduction of particular grammars to universal grammars and for the expansion of any well-formed universal grammar into the set of particular grammars that it subsumes were presented in my dissertation (1967). A slightly modified version of the reduction algorithm appears in Sanders (1970, p 97).

this might be called the theory of real, mythical, and metaphysical animals.

Now it is clear that the third theory is grossly less natural than the first, and that *any* theory which fails to distinguish between real and metaphysical animals cannot be a scientifically significant theory at all. Yet the third theory could easily be non-reducible with respect to any other known or readily conceivable scientific theory, and there is no reason to suppose that the attributes which it predicts would be any less coherent, exhaustive, or exclusive than those predicted by the first quite natural theory of real animals. In fact, given only the non-reducibility condition, we would be forced to conclude that theory (3) is more natural than theory (1), since the latter is apparently reducible to the former, but not vice versa. But this conclusion is clearly false, which shows that the non-reducibility condition is clearly non-sufficient for the determination of natural domains.

The status of theory (2), whose domain includes real and mythical animals, but not metaphysical ones, is less clear, but could nevertheless be reasonably claimed to be less natural than that of theory (1) and more natural than that of theory (3). Again, the non-reducibility condition alone would generate the opposite ranking.

I would like to call the difference between these three theories a difference in the significance of their respective domains. Thus any partitioning of the universe that distinguishes the set of all real animals from all other contents of the universe will thereby provide a more significant conceptual and explanatory basis for scientific inquiry than could be provided by any alternative partitioning that fails to distinguish real animals from metaphysical and mythical ones. Theory (1) is a more natural theory, therefore, because its domain is scientifically more significant than those of the other two theories.

It is easy to find linguistic counterparts of mythical and metaphysical animals, and to see that most of the actual theories of language that have been proposed thus far are more comparable in naturalness and significance to the third of the three hypothetical theories of biology rather than to the first or second. Thus, the linguistic counterpart of a ghost animal or an ameoba-shaped cow might be, for example, something that is just like a natural language except that none of its sentences express entailments or presuppositions of any other sentence, or something that is natural-language-like except for the fact that every sentence that begins with $p$ is ambiguous. A linguistic counterpart of a mythical animal like a unicorn or centaur might be something like a language without any anaphoric or elliptical reductions, or a language generated by a conjunction of the phonological rules of English and the non-phonological rules of Kabardian or Upper Chehalis. In the realm of linguistics, as in the realms of biology and all other sciences, the distinctions between real, mythical, and metaphysical objects are sometimes intuitively unclear, of course, but any theory that fails to account for all clear cases of typological identity and non-identity will fail to provide any basis at all for the analysis of unclear cases or for the attainment of real systematic understanding of anything.

The type of significance that has been involved in the preceding illustration concerns the significance of the set of objects that are delimited by a given theory. I will thus refer to this scalar attribute of scientific domains and theories as *object-significance,* and will say, for example, that the reason why the three cited theories of biology differ in naturalness is because they differ in object-significance, the first theory having more object-significance than the second, and the second having more than the third. Object-significance is intimately related to the notions of type and essence, and to the relative explanatory and conceptual utility of alternative classifications of the overwhelmingly varied collection of objects and events which comprise the actual universe. There is another type of significance, however, which has nothing to do with objects or classes of objects themselves, but rather with the particular set of attributes that are explicity predicated of these objects by the theories that characterize them. This type of significance, which I will call *attribute-significance,* is an equally essential characteristic of all natural scientific theories and their domains, and any theory that fails to achieve attribute-significance will thereby fail to differentiate the essential and accidental properties of its characterized objects and will provide no real insight into their nature and relationship to other objects in the universe.

Thus, for example, consider a theory about real animals which includes among its theorem-interpretation schemata a schema that generates predications of the attribute of "hirsupodality" to biological species, where an animal is "hirsupodal" if and only if the mean number of hairs on its limbs is at least 42 percent of the mean number of hairs on the rest of its body. It would be obvious, I assume, to any biologist, and probably to most other normally-experienced human beings as well, that this is simply not a significant property of real animals, and that any theory of the sort described will be grossly unnatural, and certainly not something that could be seriously counted as a scientifically significant theory about real animals.

The intuitively recognized unnaturalness of this theory, however, cannot be accounted for in terms of any deficiency with respect to the coherence, exclusiveness, exhaustiveness, or object-significance of its domain. Thus it is quite possible that hirsupodality might be truly predicable only of objects which also have the attributes of self-control, reproducibility, etc., and that this attribute is not predicable of such objects by means of any other known scientific theory. It is quite possible, therefore, that this theory might satisfy not only the condition of non-reducibility, but also the condition of maximal object-significance — since hirsupodality is clearly just as much a real and empirically determinable attribute of real animals as the ordinary biological attributes of having a three-chambered heart, or giving birth to live young. To account for the intuitive unnaturalness of this theory, therefore, and to provide a principled basis for its exclusion from the set of possible scientifically significant theories, it is necessary to impose as an additional metaconstraint on all empirical theories the requirement that they have domains that satisfy the condition of attribute-significance. A theory will thus be a natural and empirically-defensible scientific theory only if it has a domain satisfying not only the condition of non-reducibility but also the conditions of object-significance and attribute-significance. It is possible that these may be both the necessary and the sufficient conditions for naturalness. Their necessity, in any event, is presumably fully established.

While the properties of coherence, exclusiveness, and exhaustiveness can be characterized in a very general and relatively easily formalized way through explicit domain-independent relations between the elements, axioms, and interpretation rules of different theories, the significance or non-significance of a scientific domain cannot be determined except by reference to domain-specific characteristics of that domain and the theory or metatheory that determines it. This is due, of course, to the fact that nothing can be significant or non-significant absolutely or by virtue of itself. Significance, in other words, is a strictly relative notion, and something can be significant only *for* or *with respect to* something *else.* Thus while the absolute characteristics of coherence, exclusiveness, and exhaustiveness can be assured for theories about X, Y, and Z by a metascientific non-reducibility condition that is wholly independent of any particular features of X, Y, or Z, it is impossible to assure the significance of these theories except by separately assuring that the objects and object-attributes of X are X-significant, that those of Y are Y-significant, and that those of Z are Z-significant. The principled achievement of significance for any given domain is thus determined by the principles of the theory that determines that domain. In the following section we will consider some of the types of linguistic principles that contribute to the achievement of object-significance for the domain of linguistic objects. In the final section, we will consider some linguistic principles for the achievement of attribute-significance in this domain.

## 2. Object-Significance in Linguistic Theories

The object-significance of an otherwise natural theory is directly proportional to the degree of homogeneity or typological distinctness of the set of objects that it characterizes, and the closeness of fit between this set and the set of objects that includes all intuitively clear instances of a given object-type and no intuitively clear non-instances. A theory may thus fail to achieve object-significance by virtue of either insufficiency or excessiveness of generative capacity, or characterization power. Though all theories that fail to achieve object-significance are non-natural, those that fail by virtue of excessive power will generally be much more seriously defective than those that fail because of insufficient power. It is largely for this reason that productive research in linguistics and all other sciences must be directed largely toward the progressive achievement of principled reductions in the characterization powers of theories, and hence in the heterogeneity or range of possible variation in the sets of objects that are generated by these theories.

A theory will have insufficient power if there are real objects of the type that it characterizes which are not characterized by that theory. A theory will have excessive power if it characterizes unattested objects that are clearly not of the same type as the attested objects in its domain. Though many actual theories depart from object-significance in both of these ways, the counterproductive effects of excessive power are generally much greater and less easily corrected than those resulting from insufficient power. In fact, I think it is reasonable to say that while all departures from object-significance constitute departures from naturalness, theories which are excessively powerful are not only unnatural but false.

Thus, for example, consider the following two theories: (1) a theory that characterizes all known natural languages except Upper Chehalis; (2) a theory that characterizes all known natural languages and in addition a language in which all negative sentences are phonetic mirror images of their corresponding affirmatives. Though both theories are unnatural with respect to object-significance, it seems to me that the second theory is clearly much less natural than the first. Moreover, while the first theory is strictly not a theory about all natural languages, it *is* nevertheless a theory about *something* — namely, the set of all types of natural languages other than the Upper Chehalis type. The second theory, on the other hand, seems to be simply not a theory about anything at all. In fact, since every theory formally defines an object-type and asserts that all objects that it characterizes are of that type, and since it is known intuitively and prior to any theory construction here that things with mirror-image relations between negatives and affirmatives are not instances of the object-type known as natural language, the second theory is false by virtue of the falsity of its typological assertion, and it cannot possibly contribute anything to our understanding of the nature of human language or anything else in the universe. Thus where an insufficiently powerful theory can nevertheless tell us something about a natural domain by characterizing one of its proper parts, an excessively powerful theory cannot tell us anything about the universe at all, since its domain will necessarily be not only non-natural itself but also not included in any possible domain that is natural.

Not all departures from object-significance are equally serious, therefore, and those resulting from excessive power would appear to be different in kind as well as in degree from those resulting from insufficient power. These differences are correlated with differences in the nature and extent of the corrective changes in a theory that are required in order to overcome its deficiencies in object-significance. Thus, while all excessively powerful theories require non-trivial changes in their basic assumptions about the possible statements, elements, element-interpretations, and principles of valid inference and proof for the given domain, there is at least one type of insufficiently powerful theory which can be corrected without any modification at all with respect to fundamental assumptions of this sort. This very common type of insufficiency is in fact not really due to any deficiency in the theory itself but simply to its assertion of one rather than another set of possible associations between certain possible statements generated by the theory and certain possible scope or provenance elements that are also generated by the theory. In such cases, therefore, the theory has no inherent deficiencies in object-significance at all, and its empirical incompleteness is only an accidental consequence of a particular selection of contingent statements, which can be trivially overcome by the selection of a different set, where each such selection simply makes a different claim about which set of possible objects in the domain of the theory happen as an accidental and purely contingent fact to actually exist in the present real world.

Thus, consider again the case of insufficient power exemplified previously. It is logically possible that this theory fails to account for Upper Chehalis while accounting for all other known languages because the proof of theorems characterizing Upper Chehalis requires the assumption of some element, statement-type, or principle of inference that is not required for the proof of characterization theorems for any other known language. The likelihood of this actually being the case, however, is close to zero, and it would almost certainly be the case here simply that one rather than another of the infinite set of possible universal grammars generated by the theory has been found to be the correct one for the present world. There is of course nothing about natural language that makes it essential or necessary that a language like Upper

Chehalis should exist in the actual world. In fact, any theory that is inherently incapable of generating universal grammars for universes that do not include Upper Chehalis, and for those that do not include any of the languages of this world, would be clearly incorrect, since such a theory would be falsely claiming that the existence of certain particular languages is linguistically essential and follows necessarily from some intrinsic property of natural language. This would be like a theory of biology claiming that the existence of animals entails the existence of elephants.

To achieve object-significance, therefore, all that is required of a theory is that it generate a set of possible object-universes such that one of these is consistent with the facts about this world, and such that each of the others is consistent with the facts about another world that is no less possible than this one. If such a theory fails to correctly specify the one object-universe that happens to be appropriate to this world, its deficiency can be eliminated simply by the purely contingent selection of another member of the set of object-universes that it generates. No such intrinsic self-correctability is possible in the case of theories that are excessively powerful. Such a theory can be corrected, in fact, only by being replaced by another theory, since the characterization power of a theory can be reduced only by making at least one addition, deletion, or substitution in its axiom set.

Excessively powerful theories are typically false, moreover, not only by virtue of their failure to achieve object-significance, but also on the related but still more serious grounds of internal inconsistency. Thus any theory that is too powerful will generate object-characterizations that are empirically unnecessary and that cannot be justified on the basis of any known facts about its subject-matter or any reasonable extrapolations from these facts. Where such an overabundance of characterizations is found, however, it nearly always involves attested objects as well as unattested ones. An excessively powerful theory will thus usually generate not only indefensible characterizations of objects outside of its proper domain, but also multiple characterizations of objects within that domain, where such characterizations are mutually incompatible but equally consistent with all empirical data and equally valued by all reasonable criteria for generality and conceptual or explanatory utility. A theory that generates inherently undecidable alternative explanations of the characteristics of any object is false by virtue of internal inconsistency, and hence not a real theory of anything at all. Evidence of such inconsistency can be cited for all of the known standard theories of natural language grammar, whose deficiencies in object-significance are also fully evident and quite well documented.[5] Such inconsistencies are

---

[5] Some examples of such inconsistencies were presented in my Linguistic Society of America papers "Precedence Relations in Language" (summer meeting, 1970) and

eliminated, moreover, by precisely the same power-reducing changes as required for the achievement of increased object-significance.

We will thus take the task of achieving object-significance in a scientific discipline to be primarily the task of effecting by principled means a progressive reduction in the characterization powers of its theories.

The principled achievement of object-significance for a scientific domain is effected by the assertion of object-independent metaconstraints on the form and content of axioms and theorems and on the system of inference which defines valid proofs for all theories that characterize that domain. Since my concern here is more with the attribute-significance of linguistic theories than with their object-significance, I will restrict my discussion of the latter property chiefly to an indication of the general types of metaconstraints that are relevant to the achievement of object-significance in linguistics, and the general metatheoretical framework that is prerequisite for the expression of such metaconstraints. I will then turn to the question of attribute-significance, which will be shown to be attainable apparently only by means of a metaconstraint of a quite different character from those which contribute to the achievement of object-significance.

It has been seen that the general non-reducibility condition for naturalness is sufficient to assure that all scientifically-defensible linguistic theories must be theories that generate universal discourse grammars for all possible sets of natural languages. This has certain automatic favorable consequences with respect to object-significance, since there can be no principled basis or means for the expression of constraints on the distribution and cooccurence of statements in the grammars of particular languages unless such particular grammars are non-primitive sets which are derived from the statements of universal grammars by general principles of the governing theory of grammar. It is not simply that the explicit reduction of all grammars to universal grammars makes multilingual or universal rules possible and permits an explicit formal evaluation of alternative grammars in terms of the relative universality of their statement-sets. Much more importantly, such reduction would appear to provide a necessary but otherwise unavailable basis for the expression of metaconstraints which contribute to object-significance in a particularly direct way by prohibiting the joint use of certain well-formed statements for the proof of linguistic theorems, or, in other words, by excluding certain sets of well-formed statements from the set of possible grammars of particular languages. It is impossible to express such principles without making essential reference to variables for the provenance speci-

---

"Some Evidence for the Hypothesis of Simplex-Feature Representation" (winter meeting, 1971). Expanded versions of these have now been published in *Foundations of Language* 11 (1974), 361—400, and *Glossa* 8 (1974), 141—92, respectively.

fications, or language-identification markers, of grammatical statements, and it is only for the statements of universal grammars that such specifications are not only possible but independently necessary.

Thus in a universal grammar all statements must necessarily be of the form (Q, S), where S expresses a relation between linguistic representations and Q expresses a (possibly null) restriction on the scope or provenance of S, that is, a restriction that delimits the set of purported proofs for which S can be appropriately used in determining their validity or invalidity.[6] This is necessary, of course, in order to distinguish between real-world linguistic objects like (3 a—c) and mythical linguistic objects like (3 d), and in order to characterize the obviously significant relations of "being in the same language", which holds between the pair of sentences (3 a) and (3 b), and "being in different languages", which holds for all the other sentence pairings in (3).

(3) (a) It's hot today
    (b) Cleopatra floated down the Nile
    (c) Il fait chaud aujourd'hui
    (d) It fait hot aujourd'hui

All monolingual linguistic objects in a given universe will thus be formally characterized by the distinctive property of having characterization theorems whose proofs are validated by statements with non-distinct provenance restrictions.[7] In contrast, every polylingual or centaur-like object such as (3 d) will have no valid characterization theorem that is not validated by statements bearing at least two distinct provenance restrictions. Similarly, for any linguistic objects A and B, A and B are members of the same language if and only if the characterization theorems for A and B are both validated by statements with non-distinct provenance restrictions, and they are members of different languages if and only if the provenance restriction of the validating statements for A is distinct from that of the validating statements for B.

A number of questions concerning the formal expression of provenance restrictions and their range of explanatory functions have been

---

[6] Provenance restrictions are not conditions on the *truth* of statements, of course, since a true principle of English grammar, for example, will obviously be equally true at all times and places and in all possible worlds. Rather, such restrictions express (probabilistic) directions to the most efficient locations for *testing* the truth of statements in terms of the truth or falsity of the theorem-interpretations that follow from them. Thus while it is *possible* that a claim about the synonymy of two sentences in contemporary Minneapolis English might be appropriately testable in Chicago, Periclean Athens, or even, with luck, on the moon, the conditions for testing are clearly most *likely* to be satisfied only in contemporary Minneapolis.
[7] Two provenance restrictions are distinct if and only if they include non-null non-negative language-identification specifications that are not identical, or if one includes a specification (Pm, Tn) and the other includes the specification ~ (Pm, Tn).

discussed in detail in Sanders (1967) and Sanders (1970). It was suggested there, for example, that there is a natural basis for expressing provenance restrictions affirmatively for lexical axioms and negatively for all non-lexical grammatical statements. This makes for an empirically-appropriate correspondence between the restrictedness or peculiarity of grammatical statements and the formal complexity of their provenance restrictions, and provides the necessary internal justification for the postulation of metatheoretical redundancy rules which predict all or part of certain provenance restrictions for certain statements from the formal properties and relations of those statements.

It was also shown that provenance restrictions are most appropriately represented not by means of unanalyzable language-identification elements such as $L_1$, $L_2$, etc., or VEDIC-SANSKRIT, 1972-CHICAGO-ENGLISH, etc., but rather by pairings of independently variable place and time specifications of the form (P, T), where P is potentially interpretable into a statement identifying the geographical locus or range-center of a possible individual or group, and T is potentially interpretable into a specification of absolute or relative time, stated either in terms of calendar time or age from birth or both.[8] The motivations for this sort of analysis of language-identification markers are precisely parallel to those that motivate the analysis of morphological and phonological segments into their constituent independently-interpretable minimal features. In both cases the analysis results in an enormous simplification in the theory's rules of interpretation, and provides the requisite principled basis for the formulation of lawlike generalizations that predict certain structural elements from certain others. Each of these predictive principles is internally justifiable in terms of its function with respect to the metascientific goal of optimal simplification of the axiomatic bases of all theories. Each principle also makes a direct externally verifiable claim about the nature and variability of all possible object-sets in the domain of the theory. To the extent that such claims are correct, therefore, for the set of known languages, the theory that generates them is successful in providing a *principled* language-independent *explanation* of certain observed delimiting characteristics of this set of actual languages.

Every predictive principle, or redundancy-rule, for provenance specifications could be expressed as a special case of the statement-schema (4),

(4)  $(G) [G = ((Q_1, S_1), X)] \rightarrow [G = ((Q_2, S_1) X)]$

---

[8]  It is logically possible that two contemporaneous languages or dialects might have identical ranges and hence identical range centers. To differentiate in such cases, it would be necessary to index statements with respect to a third parameter, perhaps physiological or cultural. Lacking knowledge of any actual cases of identical ranges, however, the restriction to two parameters would appear to be empirically necessary.

where G is a quantifier for all universal grammars, and $Q_1$ and $Q_2$ are specified schemata for provenance restrictions, and $Q_1$ is properly included in $Q_2$, and $S_1$ is a specified schema for grammatical statements, and X is a (possibly null) schema for other grammatical statements and /or provenance restrictions. Each such predicative principle thus justifies the substitution of a more fully specified provenance restriction for a less fully specified one in a given class of grammar contexts.

A given instance of this schema can then be considered to be an internally, or metascientifically, justified axiom of some theory if and only if the number of specified elements in the statement-instance is less than the product of the element-difference between $Q_1$ and $Q_2$ and the number of statements in the theory of the form $S_1$ whose fully-specified provenance restriction includes $Q_2$.[9]

Each internally-justified provenance-prediction statement thus serves to project certain characteristics of a given set of languages to all sets that properly include it. Each statement of this sort is thus vulnerable to direct empirical falsification on the basis of any actual linguistic facts that are not included in the original data-base for its internal justification. To the extent that such falsification attempts fail, the statement stands as a true principle of natural language grammar, and the characteristics that it imposes on all possible sets of languages are shown to be essential characteristics of natural language rather than accidental ones. Provenance prediction statements are thus one of the basic means by which otherwise natural linguistic theories can achieve a principled increase in naturalness by virtue of principled power reductions and the gains in object-significance that they determine.

The subtypes of provenance prediction statements illustrated in Sanders (1970) were presented in support of the claim that such statements are necessary and sufficient for the expression of all possibly-true explanatory generalizations about the typological variability of natural languages and about their systematic phylogenetic and ontogenetic patterns of development over time. Thus, for example, if each distinct language in the universe of a universal grammar is associated with a distinct element-pair of the form (Pj, Tk), then the theory that generates that grammar may include internally justified provenance axioms of the types illustrated in (5).

---

[9] This criterion is very similar to that proposed by Halle (1962) for the justification of phonological redundancy rules. The requirement of axiomatic simplification as a condition on the postulation of redundancy rules was shown by Halle to provide a principled differentiation of accidental and systematic gaps in the set of morpheme or word sounds of a language. With respect to redundancy rules for provenance specifications, the same requirement provides for an equally principled differentiation of accidental and systematic gaps in the set of languages in any universe.

(5) (a) If G includes provenance-restricted statements [(Pj,Tk) (XYZ)] and [(Pj, Tn) (XZ)], then $k \neq n + 1$; i.e., for any given P, the T-index of a relatively less general statement can never be the next greater successor of the T-index of any relatively more general statement that it properly includes.

  (b) If G includes [(Pj, Tk) (X)], then G does not include [(Pj, Tk + 1) (Y)], i.e., for any given P, there can be no pair of languages with adjacent T-indices such that the language with the lesser T-index has a rule of the form X and the one with the immediately greater T-index has a rule of the form Y.

  (c) If G includes [(Pj, Tk) (X)] and [(Pj, Tn) (Y)] and $n$ is greater than $k$, then G must also include a provenance-restricted statement [(Pj, Tm) (Z)], where $m$ is greater than $k$ but less than $n$; i.e., for any given P, a language with rule Y can have a greater T-index than that of a language with rule X only if there is another language that has rule Z and that has a T-index that is intermediate with respect to those of the other two languages.

  (d) If G includes [(Pj, Tk) (X)] and [(Pj, Tk + 1) (Y)], then, for any Pm and any Tn, G does not include both [(Pm, Tn) (Y)] and [(Pm, Tn + 1) (X)]; i.e., if a language with rule X has a T-index immediately less than that of a language with rule Y, then there is no language with X that has a T-index immediately larger than that of any language with Y.

Since the internal justification for any instance of such statements is determined *independently* of any possible observations about language typology or change, each justified statement can be legitimately used for the purpose of *explaining* such observations. Thus by assigning as an empirical interpretation of each distinct P-index a distinct description of a geographical place or locus, and as an empirical interpretation of each distinct T-index a description of some distinct time or age, the internally-justifiable provenance prediction schemata of (5 a—d) would serve to generate the respective empirical law-schemata of (6 a—d):

(6) (a) For any pair of grammatical rules standing in a proper inclusion relation, no language that has the including (i.e. less general) rule can be an immediate descendent of any language that has the included (i.e. more general) rule.

  (b) No language that has a rule of the form Y can be an immediate descendent of any language that has a rule of form X. ((6 a) is a special case of this, namely the case where Y includes X.)

  (c) For any languages Lx with rule X and Ly with rule Y, if Ly is a descendent of Lx, there must be some language Lz with rule Z such that Lz is a descendent of Lx and an ancestor of Ly.

(d) If there is a language with rule Y that is immediately descended from a language with rule X, then there is no language with rule X that is immediately descended from any language with rule Y, i.e. there are certain types of direct linguistic changes that are not directly reversible.

It is clear that all such laws are directly vulnerable to empirical falsification with respect to known facts about the temporal and spatial loci of actual language communities, or in the case of ontogenetic laws, the actual ages or age ranges at which given idiolects are used. To the extent that they remain unfalsified, therefore, the internally-justified provenance statements that generate such laws constitute true explanatory principles of language change and diversification. Each restriction that they impose on the structure of universal grammars also provides an empirically-motivated restriction of the generative power of the including theory and thereby serves to increase its object-significance and naturalness.

There are many other types of internally-justifiable provenance statements which have no direct implications with respect to language change but which nevertheless serve an equally important role in the achievement of maximal object-significance for linguistic theories. Thus, for example, consider the two statements in (7).

(7) (a) For any universe of languages whatever, any grammar for that universe must include at least one (non-lexical) statement S such that the fully-specified provenance restriction of S is null.

(b) For any universe of languages $(L_1, L_2, \ldots, L_{20})$, no grammar for that universe can include any non-lexical statement S such that the fully-specified provenance restriction of S is $[\sim[Pn, Tm]]$.

The first of these statements appears to be clearly true and the second almost certainly so. As expressed, however, they are both quite trivial, and unless a very restricted theory of grammar is assumed to begin with, both would be inherently unfalsifiable and hence scientifically worthless. Thus (7 a) simply asserts that for any universe of languages there is at least one universal rule, and (7 b) asserts that a sample of any twenty languages will be sufficient to reveal the non-language-uniqueness of all non-lexical rules. That *some* grammatical axioms must be universal for the present universe of actual languages is evident from the large number of striking similarities that have been observed between all known members of this universe. What we really want to know, of course, is *which* statements, or really which *types* of statements, are universal and which are not. Similarly, while (7 b) presupposes something about the size and overlaps of the statement-sets characterizing particular languages, we are obviously not interested in the *existence* of such set relations but rather in the grammatical *principles* which *explain* their existence. It is evident, moreover, that there is no way to achieve such explanations, or to make significant use of metaconstraints on provenance restrictions for the maximalization of object-significance in linguistics, without also having a precise characterization of the set of possible statement-types for all universal grammars.

The logical dependence of the provenance principles of a theory upon those principles which delimit its axioms, theorems, and possible proofs explains the general emptiness and untestability of most of the actual proposals that have been made thus far concerning grammatical universals. Consider, first, the various claims of universality that have been made for specific rules — for example, the various universal rules for (phonetically-directed) coordination reduction proposed in Koutsoudas (1971), Postal (1968), Sanders (1967, 1970), Schane (1966), and Tai (1969). That *some* reduction principle of this sort must have a null provenance restriction for the present universe of languages seems fully evident, since there are certain facts about this universe which could not otherwise be explained at all — for example, the fact that every one of its known members has pairs of synonymous sentences which are formally related in precisely the same way, one sentence consisting of two clauses identical except for their (superficial) subjects, the other consisting of one clause with a compound (superficial) subject. But what we are really interested in here is, of course, not *that* there are universal principles of coordination reduction, but rather *what* these principles are, and, still more importantly, *why* they are universal. It is obvious that these questions cannot even be seriously asked, let alone answered, without the prior establishment of some reasonably precise and reasonably restrictive characterization of the possible forms, contents, and inferential functions of all grammatical statements.

Consider, next, the various proposals that have been made concerning the universality not of particular statements but of statement-types. Such proposals are inherently much more significant and much more amenable to empirical testing. Thus where the assertion that a certain principle of coordination reduction is universal really does little more than express the fact that all languages have a phonetically-directed process of coordination reduction, the assertion, for example, that all principles justifying identity deletion are universal goes far beyond any particular collection of observed data, and could serve not only to explain why certain specific known processes like coordination reduction are universal, but also to generate an unbounded set of testable predictions about specific processes that have not yet been discovered. It is clear, though, that all principles specifying the universality or non-universality of a given statement-type necessarily presuppose its precise formal differentiation from all other possible grammatical statement-types. Thus, for example, the proposal in Sanders and Tai (1972) that all non-lexical syntactic rules[10] are universal necessarily presupposes the distinctive formal characterization of syntactic, phonological, and lexical rules, as well as the formal differentiation of syntactic *rules*, which are suggested as being language-invariant, and syntactic *constraints*, at least some of which are asserted to hold for certain languages but not for certain others.

The same is true for all other possible proposals concerning grammatical universals, since all of these must necessarily involve constraints on provenance specifications, and since it is meaningful to talk about such specifications only with respect to statements or statement-types that are *possible* well-formed constituents of the axiomatic basis of some theory.[11] The dependency here is clearly not mutual, moreover, since it is quite meaningful to talk about the possibility of axioms, inferences, and theorems independently of any consideration of their provenances or specific conditions for effective verification. Enormous effects upon the characterization power and object-significance of a theory can thus be achieved simply by the assertion of certain constraints on the form, content, and inferential uses of its axioms rather than certain others. In general, of course, the more restrictive these constraints are, the more restricted and homogeneous the domain of the theory will be. Since such constraints also serve to restrict the set of valid theorems of a theory, their relative restrictiveness affects not only the relative object-significance of a theory but also its relative attribute-significance. In fact, since the attribute-significance of a theory is determined by the restrictions that it imposes on its theorem-interpretation rules, all constraints that restrict the theorem sets that such interpretation rules are defined on will thereby also constitute an important foundation for the achievement of attribute-significance for that theory.

To illustrate this, and to serve as a basis for the subsequent discussion of theorem-interpretation conditions for attribute-significance, I would like to outline the basic domain-restricting principles of the general theory of equational grammar, a theory which I believe achieves a

---

[10] Ordering rules are also assumed to be exempted from universality, but, as shown in Sanders (1972), these are most appropriately viewed as only a special case of lexicalization — namely, the case where the non-phonological member is the sematically-interpreted relational element for (commutative) grouping and the phonological member is the phonetically-interpreted relational element for (non-commutative) linear ordering.

[11] For a quite different view of the characterization and explanatory role of universal grammatical statements, see Bach (1971 a, 1971 b).

28 Gerald A. Sanders

greater degree of object-significance than any other yet-unfalsified theory of natural language grammar. (Detailed discussion and justification of this theory is presented in Sanders (1971, 1972).)

The basic hypothesis of equational grammar asserts that all grammatical statements are assertions of equivalence or non-equivalence between linguistic representations, that all grammatical theorems are assertions of equivalence between a terminal phonetic representation and a terminal semantic representation, and that all valid proofs of such theorems are equation sequences terminating in an identity equation, with all governing principles of inference being strictly universal.[12] The equationality hypothesis thus restricts the content of every universal or particular grammar to a finite set of symmetrical axioms of the form (A = B) or (A ≠ B). Each equivalence axiom of a grammar determines in conjunction with the principle of equal substitution a pair of symmetrical derivational inferences, or directed transformations, which serve as affirmative local conditions on the well-formedness of proofs justified by that grammar. Each non-equivalence axiom of a grammar asserts that a given pair of representation-types cannot be representations of the same linguistic object. Each such statement thus serves as a negative or prohibitive global constraint which characterizes as invalid any otherwise valid proof in which either of the non-equivalent representations is directly or indirectly derived from the other. A theorem will thus have a valid proof with respect to some grammar only if every line can be derived from the preceding line by substitutions justified by equivalence axioms of that grammar and there are no pairs of lines that are non-equivalent as determined by any non-equivalence axiom of the grammar. All other conditions on the validity of proofs are specified by strictly universal principles of the governing theory. Languages and language-universes that are generated by equational theories of grammar will thus differ from each other only to the extent that such differences can follow from the assumption of different sets of equivalence and non-equivalence assertions with respect to possible linguistic representations.[13]

---

[12] Effective procedures for the generation of well-formed theorems and valid proofs are presented in Sanders (1972).

[13] Further restrictions are empirically-necessary, of course, with respect to the internal structure of grammatical axioms and the vocabulary of elements out of which all axioms, theorems, and linguistic representations are constructed. Thus, for example, it was suggested in Sanders (1972) that all facts and significant generalizations about natural languages can be adequately accounted for by theories whose grammatical axioms are restricted wholly to instances of the following four statement-schemata:
(1)   *Redundancy Rules* (justifying adjunction and deletion of constants)
      (X [A] Y) = (X [A, B] Y)

The hypothesis of equational grammar has a wide range of highly restrictive implications concerning the nature and range of variability of all possible linguistic objects, languages, and language-universes. It has been demonstrated in particular (Sanders 1971, 1972) that the set of language-universes generated by an equational theory constitutes a small proper subset of the set of universes generated by any otherwise comparable non-equational theory. Evidence has been presented to show that the known universe of actual natural languages is included in this properly included subset and that there are grossly unnatural universes that are outside this set but within the larger set generated by non-equational theories. Similar evidence of the empirically-motivated restrictive value of the equationality hypothesis has also been presented with respect to the sets of linguistic theorems, proofs, and law-like axioms of theories that differ in their consistency with this hypothesis. It has been shown, in other words, that the hypothesis of equational grammar determines a greater degree of object-significance than can be achieved in any principled way by any theory that is inconsistent with this hypothesis, including in particular such standard theories of non-equational grammar as those of Chomsky (1965, 1971) and Lakoff (1971).

One of the most obvious and most narrowly restrictive implications of the equationality hypothesis is that there can be no non-universal principles of inference for the domain of natural language, and hence no possible pairs of languages that differ only with respect to differences in the direction, order, or necessity of the derivational substitutions justified by any given set of axioms. This follows from the fact that all statements in equational grammars are of the forms $(A = B)$ or $(A \neq B)$, where A and B are linguistic representations, while there is no possible way to express any statement about the directionality, order, or necessity of derivational use of an axiom as an instance of either of these equational statement-types. Since this exclusion of language-variable principles of inference does not follow from either the contrary or the contradictory of the equationality hypothesis, its apparent consistency with the known facts about natural languages would appear to confirm

---

(2)  *Idempotency Rules* (justifying adjunction and deletion of one of two identical variables)

   $(W, X, Y) = (W, X, X, Y)$

(3)  *Lexical Rules* (justifying substitutions between constituents free of terminal phonetic elements, including the phonetic relational element for linear ordering, and constituents free of terminal semantic elements, including the semantic relational element for association or constituent-grouping)

   $(W [x] Y) = (W [Z] Y)$

(4)  *Constraints* (determining the non-validity of otherwise valid proofs)

   $(X) \neq (Y)$

this hypothesis and to disconfirm all theories that are not consistent with it.

The non-expressibility of inference principles by means of equational axioms has been demonstrated in Sanders (1971). Thus to assert that (A → B) is the only appropriate phonetically-directed inferential use of (A = B), it is necessary to assert that there are no well-formed phonetically-directed derivations in which a line including XBY immediately precedes a line including XAY. To assert that (A → B) represents a necessary, or obligatory, phonetically-directed use of (A = B), it is necessary to assert that there are no well-formed phonetically-directed derivations in which there is a line including XAY and an immediately subsequent line that does not include XBY. Similarly, to assert that the directed inference (A → B) is ordered before, or applicationally precedent to, the inference (C → D) in phonetically-directed derivations, it is necessary to assert that there are no well-formed phonetically-directed derivations in which a pair of lines including XAY followed by XBY is preceded by a pair of lines including UCV followed by UDV.[14]

All statements asserting the direction of use, necessity of use, or relative order of use of grammatical axioms will thus be instances of the respective statement-schemata (8 a), (8 b), and (8 c), where P is a variable for some specified set of proofs or derivations.

(8) (a) $(P) (P \neq (..., XBY = Z, XAY = Z, ..., w = w))$
    (b) $(P) (P \neq (..., XAY = Z, \sim (XBY = Z), ..., w = w))$
    (c) $(P) (P \neq (..., UCV = Z, UDV = Z, ...,$
        $XAY = Z, XBY = Z, ..., w = w))$

It is obvious that none of these statement-schemata can be reduced without loss of meaning to either of the equational schemata (A = B) or (A ≠ B), which are the only permitted statement-types in the universal or particular grammars generated by equational theories. It is also obvious that such reduction will be equally impossible for any possible meaning-preserving translation, abbreviation, or otherwise variant expression of the statement-schemata of (8). The theory of equational grammar thus generates the principled claim that there are no non-universal principles of grammatical inference, and hence that there are no facts about natural languages and no significant explanatory generalizations about such languages which require the assumption of any non-

---

[14] There is some measure of oversimplification here, since the schema for extrinsic-ordering constraints that is suggested here, as well as in Lakoff (1971) and Sanders (1971), actually turns out to be neither necessary nor sufficient for the expression of *all* types of extrinsic-ordering relations. For detailed discussion of this question, see my paper "On the Exclusion of Extrinsic-Ordering Constraints" in A. Koutsoudas (ed.), *The Application and Ordering of Grammatical Rules* (The Hague: Mouton, 1976).

universal principle concerning the directionality, necessity, or relative order of derivational use of any statements of any grammar.

There is every reason to believe that this claim is empirically correct. The supporting evidence is particularly strong with respect to directionality and applicational ordering[15] where it has been shown for a large sample of relatively clear data that all empirically-motivated restrictions follow from a small set of universal principles of linguistic inference that apply in an entirely formal and language-independent fashion to any possible set of equational axioms and any possible grammatical derivation or proof. This evidence thus suggests not merely that language-specific directionality and extrinsic ordering constraints are empirically non-necessary in the domain of natural language,[16] but also that any theory which fails to provide a *principled exclusion* of such constraints, regardless of how they are expressed or how their powers are distributed, will necessarily predict a degree of language variability that is grossly inconsistent with everything that is presently known about the actual range of variation of the known set of actual languages. In other words, theories that fail to provide such a principled exclusion will generate objects which are clearly not of the type called natural language, and by virtue of this will fail to achieve object-significance.

Thus, with respect to directionality, it was shown in Sanders (1971, 1972) that any theory that permits grammars to include directed, or non-symmetrical, statements will generate a set of possible grammars

---

[15] For any theory that has the power of language-specific specification that certain rules of grammar are obligatorily applied whenever they can be applied, there would appear to be an at least weakly equivalent theory that no makes such specifications but has the power of invalidating otherwise valid proofs by means of well-formedness constraints on representations or derivations. There is considerable evidence that the power of obligatoriness specification is empirically insufficient, and all known theories that have this power (e.g., those of Chomsky (1965, 1971) and Lakoff (1971)) also make use of the power of invalidation constraints. It would thus appear that language-specific obligatoriness statements are neither necessary nor sufficient in the domain of natural-language grammar, and that the intuitive pretheoretic notions of linguistic optionality and obligatoriness are really non-primitive relational notions that are derivable from the independently-determined validity or non-validity of formally-related proofs. For further discussion, see my paper "On the Notions 'Optional' and 'Obligatory' in Linguistics" in *Minnesota Working Papers in Linguistics and Philosophy of Language*, no. 2 (1974), appearing also now, in revised form, in the journal *Linguistics*.

[16] No arguments of necessity have ever been given for the power of extrinsic-ordering, as far as I can determine. The arguments that have been given all appear rather to be based primarily on the *a priori* assumption that simplifications in the rules of grammars at the expense of an increase in the number of constraints they include is in some sense more desirable than simplification of constraint-sets at the expense of rule-complications. The arguments most often fail, moreover, even on their own question-begging grounds, since the elimination of the purportedly necessary extrinsic ordering constraints often requires no change in the posited rules at all, and apparently never requires any changes resulting in loss of generality, naturalness, or explanatory power.

which includes for any possible directed statement (A → B) two grammars that differ only in that one includes (A → B) while the other
includes (B → A). There certainly appear to be no known languages
whose grammars differ in this way, and no significant resemblance
between the present universe of languages and most of the universes
generated by such non-equational theories. In fact, the evidence that we
have concerning our present universe of languages strongly suggests that
it is *never* the case that there are converse transformations that are
empirically-defensible for proofs terminating in the same interpretable
alphabet. Thus while we find motivation for the phonetically-directed
devoicing of word-final consonants in languages like German or
Russian, we find no motivation in any language for the phonetically-
directed voicing of word-final voiceless consonants.[17] Similarly, while we
find evidence for the postulation of phonetically-directed processes of
anaphora-formation, ellipsis, subject-selection, agreement, clitic-attach-
ment, and predicate amalgamation, the converses of these processes are
invariably found to be empirically-defensible only for semantically-ter-
minated derivations and never for phonetically-terminated ones. No
theory can provide a principled explanation of such facts as these unless
it provides a principled basis for the exclusion of all language-specific
constraints on directionality and for the prediction of all empirically-
motivated conditions on directionality by means of universal principles
that are defined over the set of all linguistic proofs and all symmetri-
cally-related pairs of linguistic representations. Such explanation is
provided by theories that are consistent with the equationality hypothesis, but not, as far as I can determine, by any theory that is not
consistent with this hypothesis.

The facts with respect to the applicational precedence relations of
grammatical rules appear to be precisely parallel to those concerning
their directionality. Thus any theory that has the power of language-
specific extrinsic-ordering constraints will generate pairs of possible
languages that differ only in that the grammar of one includes a statement asserting the applicational precedence of rule A over rule B, while
the grammar of the other includes a statement asserting the precedence
of B over A. There is no evidence that such language pairs exist in the
known universe of natural language, all published attempts to suggest
the contrary (e.g. Halle (1962), Kiparsky (1968), Chomsky and Halle
(1968), Anderson (1969)) being based on data that is insufficient for the
demonstration of anything, and most of the arguments being simply
logically invalid or essentially dependent on the assumption of rules that

---

[17]  The principle involved may actually be somewhat less general than this, however, since
for stops there is some evidence from Dakota of alternations betweeen voiced word-
finals and voiceless medials.

are clearly unnatural or incorrect independently of any questions about their order of application.

Thus, for example, it has been shown by Koutsoudas (1972) that a very large class of purported arguments for the postulation of extrinsic-ordering constraints are simply invalid by virtue of what Koutsoudas calls the Strict Order Fallacy. This is the fallacy of concluding that a constraint asserting the applicational precedence of rule A over rule B is necessary if the assumption of that constraint is consistent with the available facts and the assumption of a constraint specifying the opposite precedence is not consistent with these facts. The fallacy here, of course, is due to the argument's non-consideration of the third alternative for all such cases — namely, that there is *no* constraint on the relative order of application of the two rules — an alternative that clearly must be shown to be false before either of the other alternatives can be demonstrated to be correct. Koutsoudas has shown with respect to a number of published arguments of this sort that the third alternative is in fact not false, and that the very facts which were put forth to argue for the necessity of an extrinsic ordering constraint actually suffice to demonstrate its non-necessity.

The non-necessity of another large class of purportedly necessary extrinsic ordering constraints has been demonstrated by Ringen (1972 a) and Sanders (1974). In the latter paper it was suggested that all empirically-defensible constraints on the applicational precedence of grammatical rules can be correctly determined by a single universal principle of Proper Inclusion Precedence, which asserts that, for any rules A and B and any representation R, A takes applicational precedence over B if and only if the structural description of A properly includes the structural description of B. It was shown in Koutsoudas, Sanders, and Noll (1974) that this universal and the assumption that all obligatory rules must be applied whenever they can be applied constitute a universal theory of rule application that is sufficient for the determination of empirically appropriate rule-applications for a wide range of cases which had been claimed in the literature as requiring the assumption of extrinsic-ordering constraints. It was also shown in this paper that the elimination of extrinsic ordering constraints in favor of universal principles of grammatical inference results in no loss of generality, naturalness, or explanatory power with respect to any of the various synchronic and diachronic facts that are dealt with there, and that such elimination typically leads to axiomatic simplifications and discovery of significant generalizations that are obscured or internally unmotivated as long as the gross power of extrinsic-ordering is available.

Additional evidence of the non-necessity and explanatory non-utility of extrinsic-ordering constraints is presented in recent papers by Iverson (1973), Lehmann (1972), Norman (1972), Perry (1972), and Ringen

(1972 b). These and the other papers cited here provide a strong empirical basis for the claim that the power of extrinsic-ordering is empirically unmotivated for theories of natural language, and that any theory of grammar that fails to exclude this power, regardless of the form or manner in which it is manifested, will fail to achieve a sufficient degree of object-significance with respect to this domain.

The principled exclusion of this and certain other empirically excessive powers was shown to follow from the general principle of equational grammar. It has not been my purpose here, of course, to explore the full range of implications of the equationality hypothesis, or even to attempt to demonstrate that it is a correct principle of natural language grammar. My purpose, rather has been to show how a small number of very general assumptions can serve to severely restrict the characterization power of a linguistic theory and provide a principled basis for its achievement of object-significance and naturalness with respect to the domain of natural language. Even for a highly-restrictive theory of equational grammar, though, optimal naturalness clearly cannot be achieved without the optimal achievement of attribute-significance, which requires much more than the basic equational restriction of theorems to assertions of equivalence between terminal phonetic and semantic representations. What is required is the additional assumption of some very severe restrictions on the interpretation rules for these theorems. The remainder of this paper will be devoted to questions concerning the nature of these principles for the determination of attribute-significance, their formal expression, and their empirical implications with respect to the nature and function of natural language and the principles of human knowledge that underlie it.


3. Attribute-Significance in Linguistics

Every empirical theory must be capable of generating an unbounded set of verifiable assertions about the properties and relations of the objects in its domain. Each of these assertions must be derivable by general principles of interpretation from some set of one or more statements which follow as valid theorems from the axioms and rules of inference of the theory and its governing metatheory. To claim that two different objects have the same property, or that two pairs of objects are related in the same way, it is necessary that there be valid theorems for each object which are analyzable as special cases of the same general theorem-type or theorem-schema, and that there be a universal interpretation specified for all instances of that schema. The set of distinct properties and relations that are characterized by a theory thus stand in a one-to-one relation to the set of distinct theorem-interpretation schemata which are explicitly specified by that theory. Each theorem-interpretation principle thus serves as a formal definition and explication of some property or relation which can be truly predicated of some but not all of the objects in the domain of the theory. The theorem-interpretation statements of a given theory distinguish the set of attributes which that theory claims to be empirically significant for its domain, and thereby constitute its characterization of attribute significance for that domain.

Since the rules of interpretation for any empirical theory must be finite, while the number of actual properties and relations of any given object will always be infinite, no theory can possibly assert everything that could be truly asserted about the objects in its domain. For every theory, in other words, it is necessary that some finite subset of the attributes of its characterized objects be selected out for explicit attribution by means of theorem-interpretation principles, with all other attributes of these objects being left uncharacterized by the theory itself. In this way, every theory of X will necessarily differentiate a finite set of X-significant attributes, which are explicitly predicated by that theory, from an infinite set of X-non-significant attributes, which are not explicitly predicated by the theory, though possibly inferable, of course, by inspection of its theorems or by the interpretation rules of other theories. The selected set of theorem-interpretation rules that are posited by a theory thus serve to define a set of significant attributes for its domain, and the distinguishing properties of these rules provide a formal explication of the notion of attribute-significance with respect to that domain.

In practice, the scientist most often makes this selection of theorem-interpretation principles in an informal and non-systematic way, the general reasonableness of such selections being due to the general reasonableness of the scientist's pretheoretical intuitions about attribute-significance in his field. However, it is one of the primary purposes of scientific theories to explain such intuitions as these, and to provide us with characterizations of attribute-significance which are sufficiently general and explicit to serve as a basis for extending and refining our intuitions and as a source of direction for productive avenues for further inquiry. No theory about natural language can be adequate, therefore, unless it provides an adequate and fully explicit characterization of the set of attributes that are linguistically-significant.

For object-significance and attribute-significance alike, the scientist begins with certain pretheoretically clear cases of significance and non-significance with respect to a given area of inquiry, along with a large number of intuitively unclear cases whose significance can be determined only by the projective powers of theories that are adequate in distinguishing the clear cases. Thus, for example, the linguist begins with his intuitive knowledge that the sentences of English are linguistically-significant objects and that the elephants of Africa are not, that ambiguity is a linguitically-significant attribute of English sentences while their lengths or euphonic properties are not. He then seeks to construct a theory that is sufficiently restrictive to differentiate between all of these clear cases of significance and non-significance. To the extent that the theory is adequate with respect to the clear cases, the claims that it generates for all unclear cases can serve as a principled extension of our intuitions about the nature of natural language and as a source of new knowledge about this domain.

Since a theory can generate empirical claims or predictions about the extratheoretical universe only by interpretations of its valid theorems, the set of possible theorems of a theory will automatically impose an initial upper bound on the set of possible attributes that can be predicated of objects by means of that theory. For all theories of equational grammar, nothing can be a theorem unless it is a statement of the form $(A = b)$, where A is a finite string of elements that are all distinctively interpretable into distinct observation statements about privately-perceptible semantic states, or meanings, and $b$ is a finite string of elements that are all distinctively interpretable into observation statements about publicly-perceptible articulatory gestures or their publicly-perceptible effects in the extraorganic universe.

By thus restricting the set of possible grammatical theorems to statements referring only to a pair of terminal representations out of different terminal alphabets, such theories automatically exclude an enormous number of attributes of linguistic objects from the set of attributes that are predicable of such objects by theories of natural language grammar. Thus, for example, since there are no possible theorems that make reference to representations that are not fully interpretable, there is no possible way for a linguistic theory to generate empirical claims about the non-terminal representations of linguistic objects or about any of their attributes that are definable only with respect to such representations. This means, therefore, that the property, for example, of having thirteen equivalent representations, or thirteen lines in its derivation, cannot be a possible linguistically-significant attribute of any linguistic object. The same is true for such attributes as the property of having an animate subject at the end of the first cycle, or the relation of having identical subjects at the end of the last cycle.

In fact, the basic equationality constraints on theorems clearly suffice to exclude the linguistic generation of any empirical claims about linguistic objects that are dependent on any properties of these objects that are not properties of their meanings or expressions. This restriction appears to be intuitively quite natural, and it will be seen to delimit a set of possible attributes that properly includes all of those that are most clearly linguistically-significant.

The schema that characterizes all possible theorems for equational grammars is itself a schema for theorem-interpretation rules. Thus any valid equation of the required form (A = $b$) can be appropriately interpreted into observation statements asserting that the interpretation of A is a meaning of the interpretation of $b$, that the interpretation of $b$ is a sound or expression of the interpretation of A, or simply that the paired interpretations of A and $b$ constitute a linguistic object for the language-community that is identified by the provenance specifications on the axioms justifying the proof of (A = $b$). All three of these observation statements describe attributes that are clearly linguistically-significant. We can thus assume as the first, most fundamental, and most clearly necessary theorem-interpretation principle for all adequate theories of natural language the interpretation rule for linguistic-objecthood, which is represented in (9) in one type of standard form for the expression of all rules of interpretation.

(9) 'The interpretation of (A, $b$) constitutes a linguistic object for the language community (P, T)' = def
There is a valid theorem [(P, T) (A = $b$)]

This interpretation rule will serve to map the set of valid monolingual theorems of any grammar into a set of determinably true or false assertions about the linguistic-objecthood, or symbolic equivalence, of actual sound-meaning pairs in possible language communities.

Two linguistic objects are distinct if and only if they differ in sound, in meaning, or in both sound and meaning. Thus any set of distinct linguistic objects will stand in a one-to-one relation to a set of distinct equational theorems of the form (A = $b$), and any theory that generates valid proofs of those theorems will thereby effectively enumerate that particular set of linguistic objects. The distinct meanings and distinct sounds of any set of linguistic objects will similarly stand in one-to-one relations to the sets of distinct semantic and phonetic members of the equational theorems that characterize those objects. The valid theorems of an equational theory thus provide an enumeration of all of the linguistic objects and all of the cognitive and articulatory renditions of such objects for all languages and language-universes constituting its domain.

Two distinct linguistic expressions are synonymous, or paraphrases of each other, of they have the same meaning.[18] A linguistic expression is

---

[18] It should be noted that the relation of synonymy is explicitly restricted here to pairs of expressions that are not identical. It is thus taken to be an irreflexive rather than a reflexive relation, which seems to be in accordance with the ordinary usage of the term "synonymy." Thus it would be quite unnatural to say that "Dogs run" is synonymous with "Dogs run." The natural thing that would be said with respect to such pairs would be simply that "Dogs run" and "Dogs run" are two tokens of the same sentence type.

ambiguous if it has two distinct meanings. Every instance of either of these clearly significant linguistic attributes thus entails the existence of a pair of linguistic objects which differ either in their pronunciations (in the case of synonymy), or in their meanings (in the case of ambiguity), but not in both pronunciation and meaning. For any set of valid equational theorems that correctly enumerates the members of some set of linguistic objects, it will thus necessarily be the case that there is a one-to-one relation between the instances of synonymy in that object-set and the set of valid theorem-pairs with identical semantic members and non-identical phonetic members, and a one-to-one relation between all instances of ambiguity and the set of theorem-pairs with identical phonetic members and non-identical semantic members. The appropriate theorem-interpretation rules for synonymy (10 a) and ambiguity (10 b) are thus essentially self-evident, given the ordinary meanings of these attributes and the relatively ordinary conception of a linguistic object as a distinct symbolic pairing of sound and meaning.

(10)  (a)  'The interpretations of $a$ and $b$ are synonymous' $=$ def
            There are valid theorems $(a = C)$ and $(b = C)$ such that
            $a \neq b$
      (b)  'The interpretation of $a$ is ambiguous' $=$ def
            There are valid theorems $(a = B)$ and $(a = C)$ such that
            $B \neq C$

It will be observed that the attributes of being synonymous or ambiguous are ordinarily predicated of the expressions of linguistic objects and not of the objects themselves, a practice that is explicitly observed in the interpretation rules of (10). The theorem-interpretation rule for linguistic-objecthood can be reformulated without loss of information so as to accord with this pattern of attribution with respect to expressions, and I wish to suggest here that this pattern is equally appropriate for the interpretation rules for all other linguistically-significant attributes. It is also evident that there are certain common parts of the interpretation rules in (9) and (10) that would also appear in every other interpretation rule for significant attributes. These common parts — references to validity, interpretations of representations, variables for provenance, etc. — are thus redundant with respect to particular rules and would be most appropriately specified once for all in the theory's general metaconstraint on theorem-interpretation rules. By eliminating such redundancies, with a minor reformulation of (9), and the adoption of the convention that identical and non-identical representation variables must respectively have identical and non-identical values, we can now reformulate the first three basic attribute-generating interpretation rules as in (11).

(11) (a) '*b* is an expression of A' = (A = *b*)
     (b) '*a* and *b* are synonymous' = (*a* = C) and (*b* = C)
     (c) '*a* is ambiguous' = (*a* = B) and (*a* = C)

These interpretation rules are so straightforward and so easily arrived at in comparison to the interpretation rules for other linguistic attributes such as analyticity, contradiction, entailment, and presupposition that one might easily be tempted to consider their formulation to be a trivial endeavor, or their particular formal properties to be logically necessary given the ordinary meanings of the attributes that they serve to predicate. It can readily be shown, however, that this is clearly not the case, certain formal characteristics of the rules of (11) being shared by all other interpretation rules for linguistically-significant attributes but no non-significant ones, and none of their properties being entailed by the meanings of the attributes they characterize.

To determine which of the shared properties of (11 a), (11 b), and (11 c) are criterial for the characterization of linguistically-significant attributes it is of course necessary to investigate the interpretation rules for other such attributes. At this point, therefore, it is sufficient to merely note that all of these basic interpretation rules refer only to constant-free representation-variables for terminal phonetic and semantic representations, that each predicates an attribute with respect to one or two phonetic representations, and that each makes reference to either *one* valid theorem (in the case of the *property* of linguistic-objecthood) or *two* valid theorems (in the case of the *relational* attributes of synonymy and ambiguity). None of these characteristics are logically necessary.

Thus, for example, it is logically possible that there could be a language in which an expression *bcd* is an expression of the meaning EF if and only if the expression *dcb* is an expression of the meaning E. The interpretation rule for linguistic-objecthood for this clearly non-natural language would presumably have to be something like (12):

(12) '*bcd* is an expression of EF and *dcb* is an expression of E' = (EF = *bcd*) and (E = *dcb*)

It is equally possible that there could be language in which an expression is ambiguous if and only if it begins with the sound *k*. The simplest ambiguity rule for this equally artificial language would presumably be (13):

(13) '*kx* is ambiguous' = (A = *kx*)

It would also be possible to construct an artificial language in which two expressions are synonymous if and only if they contain the same words in any order. Unless words are phonetically identifiable in this language, it would, of course, be impossible for an equational theory to generate any claims about synonymy at all here. Moreover, even if its words were phonetically marked, it would appear that any possible theorem-interpretation rule for this strange kind of "synonymy" in this very strange language would not only be radically different in form from the rule for synonymy in natural languages, but would also require certain theoretical vocabulary items and notational conventions that are apparently not required for any other purpose for any of the statements of therories about natural langvages. It is clear in any event that all three of these artificial languages are grossly unnatural, and that the kinds of "linguistic-objecthood," "ambiguity," and "synonymy" that can be attributed to their objects are of a radically different character from the attributes of natural-language objects that are called by these names. These differences are formally revealed by the radical differences in the forms of their respective interpretation rules — most notably here, by the fact that all of the non-natural rules but none of the natural ones must make essential reference to the internal structure of the phonetic representations in their theorem schemata. Any constraint that precludes such reference in any possible theorem-interpretation rule for theories of natural language grammar would thus suffice to exclude the non-natural cases here without excluding the clearly natural ones.

The preceding examples illustrate the case of otherwise significant attributes being predicated of non-significant objects. The non-naturalness of the objects is revealed in such cases not only by the fact that they have interpretation rules that differ from those for all natural objects and hence cannot possibly be predicating the same attributes, but also by the fact that their rules are of a different *type* and hence cannot be predicating even the same *type* of attributes. The second consideration is equally relevant to the much more interesting cases of real but non-significant attributes predicated of significant objects, where the typological relationships between interpretation rules serve as the only possible basis for differentiating between significance and non-significance.

Thus, for example, it its probably true of some linguistic objects in all known natural languages that their expressions begin with a consonant. This attribute of consonant-initiation could be correctly predicted and formally characterized by the theorem-interpretation rule (14).

(14) '[CONS] $x$ is consonant-initiated'
  $= (A = [CONS] \ x)$

Consonant-initiation seems to me to be a very clear case of an attribute of linguistic objects that is not a linguistically-significant attribute. Its non-significance can also be clearly associated with the formal difference between its governing theorem-interpretation rule (14), which makes reference to the internal structure of a linguistic representation, and the governing interpretation rules for the significant attributes of

linguistic-objecthood, synonymy, and ambiguity, which make no reference whatever to the internal structure of representations. The same
formal distinction in interpretation rules would also serve to distinguish
the three significant attributes from such other clearly non-significant
linguistic attributes as rhyme, alliteration, having a primary-stressed
predicate, having oppositely-ordered arguments, etc.

Since the distinctive formal properties of the interpretation-rules for
linguistic-objecthood, synonymy, and ambiguity thus appear to be
clearly significant with respect to the characterization of linguistically-
significant attributes, it would be reasonable as a first step to consider *all*
of their common properties to be significant and to impose complete
conformity with these properties as a metacondition that must be satisfied by all possible theorem-interpretation rules of linguistic theories.
Abstracting the common properties of the rules in (11), and adopting the
convention that non-identical late-letter variables may have either identical or non-identical values, the three rules of (11) are reducible to
special cases of one or the other of the two statement-schemata in (15),
where $x$, $y$, Y, Z are constant-free representation-variables and P is a
variable for predicates of observation statements.

(15)  (a)  '$x$ is P' $= (x = Y)$
      (b)  '$x$ and $y$ are P' $= (x = Y)$ and $(y = Z)$

By use of the standard angle-bracket convention for the conflation of
linguistic statements, (15 a) and (15 b) can then be reduced to a single
statement-schema which could be imposed as a metacondition for all
theorem-interpretation rules by the incorporation of (16) in all theories
of grammar.

(16)  For any linguistic theory T, and any statement S, S is a possible
      interpretation rule of T if and only if either S interprets a single
      constant or S is of the form:

      '$x$ ⟨and $y$⟩ be P' $= (x = Y)$ ⟨and $(y = Z)$⟩

      *where:*  $x$, $y$, Y, Z are constant-free representation-variables
      and P is a variable for predicates of observation state-
      ments

Any theory that is governed by (16) will be capable of predicating all of
the linguistically-significant attributes considered thus far and none of
the non-significant ones. To this extent, therefore, (16) constitutes an
empirically-substantiated formal definition of attribute-significance in
the domain of linguistics.

The definition provided by (16) may actually be too restrictive,
however, since it would exclude from the set of linguistically-significant
attributes a number of particularly interesting properties and relations
that have often been considered just as significant, just as essential to the

nature of natural language as the three basic attributes of grammaticality, synonymy, and ambiguity that are admitted by (16). The attributes in question include such familiar properties and relations as analyticity, contradiction, entailment, and presupposition, which are clearly not characterizable in accordance with the conditions on theorem-interpretation imposed by (16). I wish to suggest, though, that such characterizations could be admitted by a relaxation of only one of these conditions, and that the eventual formal definitions of these and all other additional linguistically-significant attributes would then be expressible in accordance with this slightly less restrictive version of (16).

I have presented arguments elsewhere (Sanders 1970, 1972) to suggest that whatever the correct characterizations of analyticity, contradiction, entailment, and presupposition may be, these characterizations will be expressible as schemata consisting of one or two theorem-schemata defined over the set of all well-formed equational theorems of equational grammars. I attempted to support this claim by presenting certain rough and tentative equational theorem-interpretation rules for each of these attributes, those for analyticity and contradiction being essentially no more than the equational translations of Katz's (1964) interpretation rules for these attributes. These equational interpretation rules are repeated here, with minor modifications, in (17). [19]

(17)  *Analyticity*
      '*a* is (copulatively) analytic'
      $= (a = [[N, X], [PRED, X, Y]])$
      '*a* is (subordinatively) analytic'
      $= (a = [W, X, S [X, Y], Y, Z])$

---

[19]  See Sanders (1972) for detailed discussion of these rules, their inadequacies, and some of the possible bases for eleminating these inadequacies. The notational and vocabulary assumptions that are presupposed here are stated and exemplified rather fully in Sanders (1967, 1970, 1972). It should nevertheless be noted here that these assumptions include the assumption that [A, B] and [B, A] are equivalent representations for the grouping or sister-constituency of A and B; that $(\ldots W/X \ldots Y/Z \ldots)$ is an abbreviatory conflation of $(\ldots W \ldots Y \ldots)$ and $(\ldots X \ldots Z \ldots)$; and that lower-case non-italicized variable letters (which appear in the rule for focal presupposition) stand only for sets of bracket-free single elements. It should also be noted that though the predicates of the interpretation rules here and elsewhere have been left as unanalyzed primitives, this in no sense should be taken to imply that they are not analyzable. Thus, for example, following the general line of presupposition-analysis suggested in Hutchinson (1971), the observation statement schema for focal presupposition could be more precisely formulated as 'a speaker's standard communicative use of *a* in communicating with a given hearer at a given time and place implies that the speaker believes the proposition that is expressed by *b* and also believes at that time that the hearer has no reason to disbelieve that proposition.'

'*a* is (conditionally) analytic'
= (*a* = [[IF, [[N, X, Y], [PRED, W, Z]],
[THEN, [[N, X], [PRED, Z]]]])

*Contradiction*
'*a* is (self-)contradictory'
= (*a* = [[N, [[Ø/NEG], X, Y],
[PRED, [[NEG/Ø], X] Z]]])

*Entailment*
'*a* entails *b*'
= (*a* = [[N, X, Y], [PRED, W, Z] U])
and (*b* = [[N, X], [PRED, Z] U])

*Presupposition*
'*a* (existentially) presupposes *b*'
= (*a* = [X, [THAT, N, W], Y])
and (*b* = [[ONE, RELEVANT, N, W],
[PRED, EXIST]])
'*a* (focally) presupposes *b*'
= (*a* = [W [x, FOCAL, Y] Z])
and (*b* = [W [x] Z])

Though each of these rules is demonstrably inadequate in one or more respects, the common properties that they share with the presumably fully adequate interpretation rules in (11) would seem to be clearly not accidental, and their systematic violations of the constraints imposed by (16) are such that it can reasonably be concluded that the adequate rules that would ultimately replace them would violate (16) in precisely the same way.

Thus each of the interpretation rules in (17) makes essential reference to constant elements in the terminal semantic members of its theorem schemata, thereby violating the constant-free condition for Y and Z in the statement-schema specified in (16). It will also be observed, though, that none of the rules of (17) violate the constant-free condition with respect to terminal phonetic representations, or the restriction that (16) imposes on the number of theorem-schemata that an interpretation rule can refer to. It seems quite clear, moreover, that these things will be equally true for all possible corrective substitutions for the rules of (17), since they simply reflect the fact that analyticity and contradiction are properties, that entailment and presupposition are binary relations, and that all four of these attributes are attributes of given objects solely by virtue of the *meanings* these objects have and never by virtue of their forms.[20]

---

[20] The only attempt that I know of that has been made to characterize any of these attributes in terms of form rather than meaning is Chomsky's (1971) attempt to generate instances of '*a* (focally) presupposes *b*' for English by specifying certain particular

The set of linguistic attributes that can be predicated by linguistic theories could thus be expanded to include these four intrinsically meaning-dependent attributes simply by the assumption of (18) rather than (16) as the metarule for theorem-interpretation statements in all theories of natural-language grammar.

(18)   For any linguistic theory T, and any statement S, S is a possible interpretation rule of T if and only if either S interprets a single constant or S is of the form:

'$x$ ⟨and $y$⟩ be P' $= (x = Y)$ ⟨and $(y = Z)$⟩

*where:*  $x$ and $y$ are constant-free variables for terminal phonetic representations, and Y and Z are either constant-free variables for terminal semantic representations or a combination of such variables with one or more semantically interpretable constants, and P is a variable for predicates of observation statements.

It follows necessarily from this assumption that attributes like linguistic-objecthood, synonymy, ambiguity, analyticity, self-contradiction, entailment, and presupposition, which are all formally definable as instances of its specified statement-schema, can be characterized and generatively enumerated by theories of natural language, while an infinite number of other real attributes of linguistic objects will remain formally uncharacterized by such theories.[21] Any theory that incorporates or is governed by this principle would thus succeed in formally delimiting the class of empirically significant and strictly linguistic attributes of linguistic objects in such a way as to include all those properties and relations which are most obviously and most directly relevant to the function of natural language as an instrument of human communication, while excluding a vast and heterogeneous class of observable attributes that are clearly irrelevant to this function.

---

phonetic and intermediate properties of *a* and *b* in this language. Although Chomsky's generation procedure here has the general characteristics of an interpretation rule, it is difficult to believe that it was really intended as such, since this would require the assumption either that presupposition relations can be correctly predicted by this schema for all other languages (which seems exceedingly improbable) or that there are some languages which have no instances of presupposition (which is simply false). It is thus not clear what Chomsky's schema is really supposed to be doing, or whether it is capable of doing anything at all.

[21]   Not all non-significant attributes are excluded by (16) alone, of course, but those that are not would thus far seem to be always excluded on the basis of general grammatical principles that are motivated independently of such exclusion. Thus, for example, the clearly non-significant attribute of having an odd number of predicates, which could have an interpretation rule that is consistent with (16), is excluded by the fact that its interpretation rule would have to make essential reference to numerical elements and numerical variables, both of which must be excluded on independent grounds from the vocabularies of all possibly-adequate theories of grammar.

Theories that are consistent with (18) would thus provide a principled explanation of the fact that successful communication by means of language in any human community depends essentially on the ability of speakers to determine in a reasonably fast and accurate way what an utterance means, what it presupposes, and what it implies — but not what is rhymes with, or how many words it contains, or whether it includes any nouns of a certain declension class. While it is true that most language-users are capable of recognizing some small subset of the attributes that are excluded by (18), it can in no sense be said that such abilities serve any necessary or even remotely useful *communicative* function, i.e., a function which permits or helps the language-user to give and receive information, commands, requests, promises, etc., by means of the language of his community. The metaconstraint expressed by (18) can thus be appropriately viewed, it seems, both as a formal delimitation of the set of attributes of linguistic objects that are essential to their function as linguistic objects, and as an explanatory model of a certain well-defined aspect of the system of species-universal linguistic knowledge that is acquired and maintained by all competent users of natural languages.

I would like to suggest, therefore, that (18) is a true assumption about the nature of natural language, and that the formal definition that it provides constitutes an empirically correct characterization of the linguistically-significant attributes of linguistic objects.

# References

Anderson, Stephen (1969). *The West Scandinavian Vowel System and the Ordering of Phonological Rules.* M. I. T. doctoral dissertation.

Bach, Emmon (1971 a). "Syntax since *Aspects*." In R. J. O'Brien (ed.), *Monograph Series on Languages and Linguistics,* No. 24, Pp 1—17. Washington: Georgetown University.

— (1971 b). "Questions." *Linguistic Inquiry* 11. 2. 153—66.

Chomsky, Noam (1965). *Aspects of the Theory of Syntax.* Cambridge: M. I. T. Press.

— (1971). "Deep Structure, Surface Structure, and Semantic Interpretation." In Steinberg and Jakobovits, Pp 183—216.

Harms, Robert (1972). "Some Non-Rules of English." Manuscript.

Halle, Morris (1962). "Phonology in Generative Grammar." *Word* 18. 54—72.

Hutchinson, Larry (1971). "Presupposition and Belief-inferences." *Papers from the Seventh Regional Meeting of the Chicago Linguistic Society,* Pp 134—41.

Iverson, Gregory (1973). "Some Phonological Changes that are Not Cases of Rule Recordering." *Minnesota Working Papers in Linguistics and Philosophy of Language* 1. 73—80.

Katz, Jerrold (1964). "Analyticity and Contradiction in Natural Language." In J. Fodor and J. Katz (eds.), *The Structure of Language,* Pp 519—43. Englewood Cliffs: Prentice-Hall.

Kiparsky, Paul (1968). "Linguistic Universals and Linguistic Change." In E. Bach and R.

Harms (eds.), *Universals in Linguistic Theory*, Pp 170—202. New York: Holt, Rinehart and Winston.

Koutsoudas, Andreas (1971). "Gapping, Conjunction Reduction, and Coordinate Deletion." *Foundations of Language* 7. 3. 337—86.

— (1972). "The Strict Order Fallacy." *Language* 48. 88—96.

— Gerald Sanders, and Craig Noll (1974). "The Application of Phonological Rules." *Language* 50. 1—28.

Lakoff, George (1971). "On Generative Semantics." In D. Steinberg and L. Jakobovits (eds.), *Semantics*, Pp 232—96. Cambridge: Cambridge University Press.

Lehmann, Twila (1972). "Some Arguments Against Ordered Rules." *Language* 48. 541—50.

Norman, Linda (1972). "The Insufficiency of Local Ordering." *Papers from the Eighth Regional Meeting of the Chicago Linguistic Society*, Pp 490—503.

Perry, Thomas (1972). "Absolute Neutralization and Unordered Rules." Paper presented at the Winter Meeting of the Linguistic Society of America, Atlanta, Georgia. Mimeographed: Indiana University Linguistics Club.

Postal, Paul (1968). "Coordination Reduction." Yorktown Heights, N. Y.: IBM Research Center.

Ringen, Catherine (1972 a). "On Arguments for Rule Ordering." *Foundations of Language* 8. 2, 266—73.

— (1972 b). *The Ordering of Rule Applications*. M. A. thesis, Indiana University.

Sanders, Gerald (1967). *Some General Grammatical Processes in English*. Indiana University doctoral dissertation. (Mimeographed, Indiana University Linguistics Club, 1968.)

— (1970). "On the Natural Domain of Grammar." *Linguistics* 63. 51—123.

— (1971). "On the Symmetry of Grammatical Constraints" *Papers from the Seventh Regional Meeting of the Chicago Linguistic Society*, Pp 232—41.

— (1972). *Equational Grammar*. The Hague: Mouton.

— (1974). "Precedence Relations in Language." *Foundations of Language* 11. 361—400.

— and James Tai (1972). "Immediate Dominance and Identity Deletion." *Foundations of Language* 8. 2. 161—98.

Schane, Sanford (1966). "A Schema for Sentence Coordination." Bedford Mass.: MITRE Corp.

Tai, James (1969). *Coordination Reduction*. Indiana University doctoral dissertation. Mimeographed: Indiana University Linguistics Club.

# Discourse Grammars and Conversational Principles

Jessica R. Wirth

## I. Introduction

One fact about language that is generally agreed to fall within the domain of linguistics is the fact that speakers are capable of producing and interpreting sequences of sentences (discourse) just as they are capable of producing and interpreting single sentences. Indeed, it has been explicitly argued (e.g., Sanders 1970) that discourse facts (including, but not limited to, single sentences) are the proper domain for the construction of grammars, and that linguists should be in the business of constructing grammars of discourse, not grammars whose domain is just the set of single sentences. A recent article by Grice (1975), which has met with wide acceptance, includes a proposal to account for certain aspects of the speaker's ability to assign (nonliteral) interpretations to sentences in conversation. Grice's proposal appears to be distinct from a discourse grammar *per se*, but there are a number of facts about discourse which, it appears, could be accounted for by either a conversational account or by a discourse grammar. The question then can be raised whether there is complete overlap in the types of facts about sequences of sentences which can be accounted for by discourse grammars (grammars whose domain is discourse) and a theory of conversation.[1]

\* I am very grateful to Edith Moravcsik and Gerald Sanders for extensive discussion and invaluable help in clarifying my thoughts about principles of conversation and discourse grammars, and for reading and commenting on the manuscript. I would also like to thank Masahiro Tanaka for his very careful reflection on the Japanese data in verification of its accuracy. (All errors are mine.)

[1] The same question can be raised concerning the types of facts about the internal properties of sentences (as opposed to sentence sequences) that can be accounted for by both conversational principles and grammars whose domain is single sentences (or that subpart of discourse grammars that would deal exclusively with internal properties of sentences). Much of the discussion in Kempson (1975) and Wilson (1975) reveals that there are many internal properties of sentences which could in principle be accounted for by a grammar or by a set of conversational principles.

The present paper does not treat this question, but the same types of conclusions as those drawn in the present paper can be reached in an attempt to answer this question, because it is possible to construct an argument with respect to internal properties of sentences which is exactly analogous to the one presented here.

In the present paper it is argued that conversational principles as conceived originally by Grice are necessary, but are not sufficient to account for all types of facts about discourse, and that grammars of discourse, conceived of as analogous (in structure and function) to grammars of sentences, are necessary but are not sufficient to account for all types of facts about discourse. The argument will proceed in the following way: First, a summary of the arguments given by Sanders yields some types of facts about discourse that must be accounted for. Next is a discussion, in general terms, of how a discourse grammar, conceived of as analogous to a sentence grammar, would be designed to account for such facts. Third is a consideration of an additional type of fact about discourse (conversational implicatures) and a characterization of the mechanism proposed by Grice (conversational principles) to account for them. It will then be seen that a number of facts about discourse can in principle be accounted for by either a grammar of discourse or a set of principles of conversation. The questions are raised whether grammars of discourse can account for all types of facts about discourse, and whether conversational principles can account for all types of facts about discourse. Next, it is shown that there are certain types of facts (conversational implicatures) that discourse grammars are incapable of accounting for but that conversational principles are capable of accounting for; and conversely, that there are other types of facts that conversational principles are incapable of accounting for but that grammars of discourse are capable of accounting for. It is shown in addition that it is impossible for there to be a *single device* which performs the functions of both a grammar of discourse and a theory of conversation. The conclusion then is that a grammar of discourse and a theory of conversation are each necessary, and each is independent of the other.

## II. Arguments for a Discourse Domain

The arguments given by Sanders for the necessity of discourse as the domain of grammars reveal three general types of facts about discourse:

a) Many attributes of discourse are of the same general types as attributes of sentences (e.g., grammaticality, synonymy, and ambiguity).
b) There are properties of well-formed sentences which are best predicted by principles governing discourse.
c) There is a distinction between potentially complete discourses and necessarily incomplete discourses.

Facts of type a) are summarized in the table below:

| *Facts* | *Examples* |
|---|---|
| Sequences of sentences exhibit a grammatical/ ungrammatical distinction. | 1) Did John go? Yes, he did.<br>2) * Did John go? Yes, they did.<br>3) * Yes, he did. Did John go? |
| Discourses exhibit synonymy with other discourses, and with sentences. | 4) Cleopatra will go to Karnak. Cleopatra will see Caesar at Karnak.<br>5) Cleopatra will go to Karnak. She will see Caesar at Karnak.<br>6) That dog was running. That dog was barking.<br>7) That dog was running and that dog was barking. |
| Discourses exhibit ambiguity. | 8) Cleopatra was seen by Josephine yesterday. She was eating lunch then. |
| Discourses can paraphrase ambiguous sentences. | 9) Flying planes can be dangerous.<br>9′) Some planes fly. Those planes can be dangerous.<br>9″) Some people fly planes. That can be dangerous. |

The conclusion from these is that since discourse properties are of the same general type as sentence properties, they ought to be described and explained by linguistic theory; moreover, even if the linguist's interest lies solely in describing and explaining properties of sentences, grammars designed for that purpose must still have a discourse domain, since the properties of sentences (e.g., paraphrasability, ambiguity) include their relations to discourse (cf. 6), 7), and 9) above).

Facts of type b) include such formal properties of sentences as the distribution of contrastively stressed elements, anaphoric expressions, and definite noun phrases. The fact that such elements (contrastive stress, anaphoric pronouns, and definite noun phrases) are found both in sequences of sentences and single sentences implies that a grammar limited to the domain of single sentences would be incapable of predicting the distribution of those elements in discourse and furthermore would not be able to capture the fact that each of the processes yielding these elements in both single sentences and sequences of sentences is a single, general process.

As for c), sentences like 10) compared with those like 11)

10) It arrived at 6 o'clock.
11) A train arrived at 6 o'clock.

exemplify the fact that there is a distinction between necessarily incomplete discourses (discourse dependent sentences) and potentially complete discourses. The conclusion is that, given that such a distinction ought to be characterized, grammars whose domain is single sentences either fail to characterize the distinction or characterize it arbitrarily by excluding sentences like 10) from the grammar altogether. The general conclusion from the facts of type b) and c) is that grammars whose domain is discourse would give a full, simple, natural account of them whereas sentence grammars would not.[2]

## III. Discourse Grammar

Under the assumption that arguments such as those given by Sanders are correct, it may be concluded that the functions of the mechanism whose domain is discourse would be to characterize and correctly predict the grammaticality, synonymy, and ambiguity of stretches of discourse, and to characterize the distinction between potentially complete and necessarily incomplete discourses. With the exception of the last property of discourse (which, however, is quite analogous to the distinction between complete sentence and sentence fragment), a grammar whose domain is single sentences has exactly the same functions. It is natural, then, to assume that the mechanism which accounts for discourse would be virtually identical in its gross outlines to that which has been proposed to account for single sentences. Thus, to determine the general outlines of what a grammar of discourse would look like, it is necessary to outline the general characteristics of grammars of single sentences.

Grammars of sentences have the following general properties.[3]

I.   They contain
  a) a set of statements which, taken together, effectively specify the full range of possible (well-formed) sentential expressions in the language. Such statements necessarily make reference to linear order and constituent structure of the expressions in the language.
  b) a set of statements which pairs representations of (literal) meanings of sentences ("semantic representations") with

---

[2]   For a more complete discussion, see Sanders (1970).
[3]   The characterization of grammars given here is intended to be neutral with respect to generative semantics, interpretive semantics, etc. It also does not purport to claim that a single statement performs only one function; under the intended interpretation of the characterization given here, it is possible for a single statement, e.g., a transformational rule, to simultaneously specify properties of well-formedness of an expression as well as associate that expression with a semantic representation.

sentential expressions.[4] Such statements necessarily make reference to such notions as semantic representations and constituent structure; the statements may assert that the semantic representations are a function of the constituent structure of the sentence, or the converse, or both.

c) a set of statements which specifies the systematic relations between pairs of formal expressions of the language. Such statements necessarily make reference to the constituent structure and linear order of elements in the expressions.

d) a set of statements which specifies in effect the possible relations between pairs of semantic representations (e.g., entailment, contradiction, etc.) Such statements necessarily make reference to semantic representations.

II. Grammars (via general linguistic theory) are associated with a set of definitions (which make reference to terms in the statement types of a) through d) above) which characterize grammaticality, ambiguity, and synonymy, and make correct predictions about particular sentences with respect to these properties in accordance with those definitions. (Examples might be: a sentence is grammatical just in case it is in the set specified by the statements in set a); an expression is ambiguous just in case it is paired with at least two non-equivalent semantic representations; two expressions are synonymous just in case they have the same semantic representation.[5])

A grammar of discourse could naturally be designed along the same lines as those given above, and the description of its general outlines would be identical to that given above, with the exception that all occurrences of "sentence" and "sentential" would be replaced by "discourse", where "discourse" would mean sequences of one or more sentences. Such a grammar would naturally and simply give a general characterization of grammaticality, ambiguity, and meaning relations (e.g., synonymy) among stretches of discourse, and make predictions about each particular discourse with respect to these properties. An additional definition could be given which would appropriately distinguish potentially complete discourses from necessarily incomplete ones, perhaps by defining necessarily incomplete discourses as those whose derivation

---

[4] Grammars also have access to a specification of the set of semantic representations; that set, however, presumably is made available by universal grammar, logic, or cognitive psychology.

[5] The definitions of synonymy, ambiguity, etc., given here are not the only possible ones; particular definitions vary according to different theories of grammatical form.

would entail certain kinds of violation of the conditions for applying rules which apply across discourse constituent boundaries.[6]


## IV. Conversational Principles

Grice (1975) has pointed out, and proposed another type of mechanism to account for, another fact about discourse, namely, the fact that the utterance of linguistic expressions can be associated with ("implicate") propositions which are not the (literal) meaning of the expressions used. An example illustrative of this is his example introducing the notion of implicature:

> Suppose that A and B are talking about a mutual friend, C, who is now working in a bank. A asks B how C is getting on in his job, and B replies, *Oh quite well, I think; he likes his colleagues, and he hasn't been to prison yet.* At this point, A might well inquire what B was implying, what he was suggesting, or even what he meant by saying that C had not yet been to prison. The answer might be any one of such things as that C is the sort of person likely to yield to the temptation provided by his occupation, that C's colleagues are really very unpleasant and treacherous people, and so forth. It might, of course, be quite unnecessary for A to make such an inquiry of B, the answer to it being, in the context, clear in advance. I think it is clear that whatever B implied, suggested, meant, etc., in this example, is distinct from what B said, which was simply that C had not been to prison yet. (Grice 1975; 43)

A proposition which is conveyed indirectly in this manner ("implicated") Grice names an "implicatum." An implicatum is distinct from the proposition which is conveyed directly ("said"), and in the example above one of the possible implicata is that C is the sort of person likely to yield to the temptations provided by his occupation, whereas what is said is that C has not been to prison yet. Grice distinguishes two types of implicature, conventional and conversational, but the mechanism he proposes (a set of conversational principles) is specifically designed to account for only one type, the conversational implicature. Conventional implicata are those propositions which are conveyed indirectly where the determination of what the implication is takes place solely by virtue of the conventional meaning of the words used[7]; conversational implicata, on the other hand, are those which are determined not only by the conventional meanings of the words used, but also by the conversational context in which the utterance is located.

---

[6] It is irrelevant whether this particular proposal is correct in its details. The thrust of the example is to point out that a definition along these lines would be possible and natural in discourse grammar.

[7] Grice's example of a conventional implicature is an utterance of *He is an Englishman; he is, therefore, brave,* which implicates, but does not specifically say, that if a person is an Englishman then he is brave. The present paper does not address the question of how conventional implicature ought to be accounted for.

Conversational implicatures are associated with a number of properties

a) The particular implicata conveyed by a single expression may vary in accordance with changes in the conversational context (both linguistic and non-linguistic).

b) In some conversational contexts, a single utterance may be indeterminate with respect to which one of a set of possible implicata the speaker intended to convey.

c) A conversational implicature may be cancelled; the speaker may append a clause warning the hearer not to interpret his utterance as conveying a particular implicatum, or the context itself may cancel it.

d) A conversational implicature is generally "nondetachable," i.e., "[i]nsofar as the calculation that a particular conversational implicature is present requires, besides contextual and background information, only a knowledge of what has been said (or of the conventional commitment of the utterance), and insofar as the manner of expression plays no role in the calculation, it will not be possible to find another way of saying the same thing, which simply lacks the implicature in question, except where some special feature of the substituted version is itself relevant to the determination of an implicature . . ." (Grice 1975: 57, 58)

e) That which is conversationally implicated is not a part of the (linguistic) meaning of the expression used in conveying it.

f) The truth of a conversationally implicated proposition is not logically entailed by the truth of what is said; "the implicature is not carried by what is said, but only by the saying of what is said, or by 'putting it that way.' " (Grice 1975: 58)

Grice's proposal to account for conversational implicature hinges on the central assumption that participants in a conversation are acting sincerely in accordance with a general principle governing behavior in conversation, the Cooperative Principle:

Our talk exchanges do not normally consist of a succession of disconnected remarks, and would not be rational if they did. They are characteristically, to some degree at least, cooperative efforts; and each participant recognizes in them, to some extent, a common purpose or set of purposes, or at least a mutually accepted direction. This purpose or direction may be fixed from the start (e.g., by an initial proposal of a question for discussion), or it may evolve during the exchange; it may be fairly definite, or it may be so indefinite as to leave very considerable latitude to the participants (as in a casual conversation). But at each stage, SOME possible conversational moves would be excluded as conversationally unsuitable. We might then formulate a rough general principle which participants will be expected (ceteris paribus) to observe, namely: Make your conversational contribution such as is required, at the stage at which it occurs, by the accepted purpose or direction of the talk exchange in which you are engaged. One might label this the COOPERATIVE PRINCIPLE. (Grice 1975: 45)

In a further (but not fully articulated) elaboration of his proposal,

Grice suggests four categories of conversational principles which any participant obeying the Cooperative Principle is committed to observing.

*Quantity maxims*
1) Make your contribution as informative as is required (for the current purposes of the exchange).
2) Do not make your contribution more informative than is required.

*Quality maxims* (Generally, "Try to make your contribution one that is true.")
1) Do not say what you believe to be false.
2) Do not say that for which you lack adequate evidence.

*Relation maxim* ("Be relevant".)

*Manner maxims*
1) Avoid obscurity of expression.
2) Avoid ambiguity.
3) Be brief (avoid unnecessary prolixity).
4) Be orderly.

Within this framework, the characterization of conversational implicature involves an attempt by the hearer to reconcile the fact that the speaker said what he said with the assumption that the speaker is obeying the Cooperative Principle. The hearer must come up with some proposition that he assumes the speaker to have intended to convey, in order to effect such a reconciliation. The proposition which the hearer comes up with is the conversational implicatum. The calculation of conversational implicature thus involves an argument which is roughly of the following form:

Premise 1:    The speaker is obeying the Cooperative Principle.
Premise 2:    The speaker intends to convey X. (X is the implicatum)
Premise 3:    The speaker knows that the hearer can come up with X.
Premise 4:    (Relevant propositions describing the context of the utterance, the background of the speaker and hearer, maxims obeyed, not obviously obeyed, and/or clearly violated by the speaker in saying that p, etc.)

.
.
.

Premise n:
_____

Conclusion: Speaker might or would say that p.

Thus, for example, an argument which the hearer could construct in the case of Grice's introductory example above might be roughly the following:

Premise 1:    The speaker is obeying the Cooperative Principle.
Premise 2:    The speaker intends to convey that C is likely to yield
              to the temptations provided by his occupation.
Premise 3:    The speaker knows that the hearer can come up with
              the proposition that C is likely to yield to the tempta-
              tions provided by his occupation.
Premise 4:    The speaker's utterance is an apparent violation of the
              maxim of Relation.
Premise 5:    The speaker deems his utterance relevant (from
              premise 1)
Premise 6:    (perhaps some additional background information)
.
.
.
Premise n:
_____
Conclusion: The speaker might or would say that C hasn't been to
            prison yet.

Within this framework, the properties a) through f) of conversational
implicature can be viewed as consequences of a general characterization
of conversational implicature which claims that the presence of an implicature is due to the necessity of constructing an argument containing
premises about the features of the discourse context and principles
governing conversational behavior. Properties a), b), and e) are consequences, since the calculation of the implicature crucially involves reference to the context of the utterance, and the indeterminacy in b) is due
to the possibility of coming up with any number of propositions that the
speaker might have intended to convey in saying that p. Properties c)
and f) are also consequences, since the argument involves making reference to *the speaker saying* something and *the speaker intending* to convey
something; and, because of this, the truth of what is said cannot possibly
*require* that the implicatum be true. Finally, property d), the nondetacha-
bility of the implicature, is a consequence of the characterization, since
the conversational principles generally presuppose that the only aspect
of the utterance itself that is relevant to conversation is the meaning of
the expression used, not the form of the expression used.

Although the theory of conversational principles is by no means fully
elaborated, a general outline of the function of the theory and the type
of mechanism envisioned by Grice can be given. The purpose of the
theory is to give a general characterization of conversational implicature, and presumably,[8] to predict correctly for any meaningful linguistic

_____
[8]  Grice himself does not say explicity that the theory of conversation should have this
     predictive power. But if the theory is to have any explanatory value other than that of
     *post-hoc* explanations it must have this predictive power when fully articulated.

expression in any context what set of conversational implicata, if any, could possibly be assigned to that expression in that context as the message that the speaker intended to convey.

I.   The theory of conversation would contain a set of conversational principles (maxims), which includes:

    a) a set of statements which specifies which of the propositions expressible in the language are appropriate propositions for the speaker to express in any given context.

      i) Some of these statements would include belief predicates and define a relation that must hold among the speaker, the candidate proposition, and the context, in order for the proposition to be expressed in that situation. (Example: the speaker believes p is not false.)[9]

      ii) Other such statements would include (some equivalent of) the predicate "inform" and define a relation that must hold between the context, the candidate proposition, and some increment of information. (Example: the Quantity maxims might be constructed as roughly, "in context x, proposition p informs to degree y".)

    b) a set of statements which specifies how the proposition chosen is to be expressed in that context.

      i) Such statements would define a relation that must hold between the proposition chosen, certain aspects of the form of the expression used to express the proposition, and the context.[10] (Example: expression E unambiguously expresses proposition p in context x.)

II.  The theory gives a general definition of conversational implicature, (which makes reference to terms appearing in the statements of the sort outlined above) which, when applied to particular instances of conversational interaction, correctly predict

---

[9]   Although the maxims are given by Grice in imperative form, which makes them look like rules that actually guide speakers' and hearers' behavior, they can also be construed in a way such that they resemble grammatical rules more closely, and can be considered to be rules specifying a notion of "well-formed conversation," analogous to grammatical rules which specify a notion of "well-formed sentence." Such a reconstrual, which does no injustice to Grice's proposal, facilitates the comparison of conversational principles with principles of discourse grammar.

[10]  It is not clear from Grice's discussion whether the Manner maxims are intended to be constraints on the manner of expressing the proposition chosen, or on the manner of conveying the implicatum, or both; e.g., does "avoid ambiguity" mean

    a)  avoid using a *linguistic expression* that is ambiguous (in this context).

    b)  avoid choosing an expression that might *implicate* more than one implicatum (in this context).

    c)  both a) and b)?

The example given only captures the a) interpretation.

the set of conversational implicata associated with the utterance of the linguistic expression in that context. (e.g., A conversational implicature is the construction of an argument one of whose premises is an assumption that the speaker obeys the Cooperative Principle; another of whose premises is the assumption that the speaker intended to convey X; another of whose premises is that the speaker knows that the hearer can come up with X; other premises representing information about the context, including descriptions of what maxims the speaker is or is not, apparently, obeying; and whose conclusion is the proposition that the speaker might or would say that p.)

## V. The Question of Overlap

It is apparent that the original functions of discourse grammars and conversation principles are distinct, but since each of them seems to have the capacity to explain at least some properties of discourse, the question arises as to whether the sets of discourse facts that they can account for are mutually exclusive or whether the sets of discourse facts that they can account for intersect.

Viewed from the perspective of the types of terms that appear in statements representing conversational principles, it appears to be the case, at least with respect to the types of examples presented here from the arguments put forth by Sanders, that the set of conversational principles could possibly be used to account for facts about the oddity of sequences of sentences, the ambiguity of discourse, and with some slight modification, the synonymy of pairs of stretches of discourse (both single sentence and multi-sentence sequences). It furthermore appears that the conversational principles may be used to embody generalizations about certain properties of discourse which are reflected in single sentences as well as multi-sentence sequences, and that the conversational principles might be able to effectively characterize the difference between potentially complete discourses and necessarily incomplete discourses.

The way in which the conversational principles could be used to account for these types of facts about discourse might be the following:

a) *Constraints on sequences of sentences*

The contrast in examples 1) and 2) with respect to oddity/well-formedness

1)   Did John go? Yes, he did.
2) *Did John go? Yes, they did.

could be construed as a difference between conformity with or violation of the maxims of Relevance and Quantity. The maxims of Quantity could be construed as requiring that appropriate answers be given to questions[11], and that in 2) above, the speaker, by answering with "Yes, they did." has given more information than required by the question, where such information is irrelevant to the question. The oddity of example 3)

    3) *Yes, he did. Did John go?

could also be considered to be a violation of the maxims of Quantity construed as requiring, in effect, that questions precede, not follow, their answers.[11] Under these interpretations of examples 1)—3), the claim would presumably be that the sequences are not ungrammatical, but simply nonsensical or serving no purpose. More generally, presumably the claim would be that, in general, there are no constraints on sequences of sentences in terms of their formal expression, but rather, what constraints there are on sequences of sentences are due to their content; and that in general, only single sentences have constraints on their form (such constraints being specified by (sentence)[12] grammars).

b) *Synonymy*
    The synonymy of examples 4) and 5)

    4) Cleopatra will go to Karnak. Cleopatra will see see Caesar at Karnak.

---

[11] The maxims of Quantity have in fact been construed as requiring that appropriate answers be given to questions, and that questions precede, not follow, their answers. (Kempson 1975: 149, 170)

[12] It is assumed, for the purpose of the present article, that the conversational principles are supplemented by sentence grammars. This is in accord with Kempson's conclusion (1975: 138—141) that a characterization of linguistic meaning is logically independent of, and forms the basis for, a characterization of speaker's meaning. Kempson's conclusion is in direct opposition to an attempt to derive linguistic meaning from a Gricean notion of speaker meaning which is defined in terms of intentions and beliefs without reference to the conventional rules of the language.
The logic of the argument of the present article does not hinge crucially on the assumption that conversational principles are supplemented by sentence grammars; the assumption merely simplifies the explication of how the conversational principles might account for certain types of discourse facts. If Kempson's conclusion is wrong, and linguistic meaning is derivable from a Gricean notion of speaker meaning, then it would still be the case that the conversational principles would in principle be capable of accounting for discourse facts of the sort given in section V; it would just be that those aspects of meaning which are taken as previously specified by sentence grammars would not have been specified by sentence grammars, but rather would have presumably followed from the definition of speaker meaning. In either case, those aspects of meaning could already be given (either by sentence grammars or as consequences of the definition of speaker meaning), so that the conversational principles would be able to make reference to them in an account of facts of the sort discussed in section V.

    5) Cleopatra will go to Karnak. She will see Caesar at Karnak.

could be accounted for as follows. The conversational principles presuppose some specification (presumably provided by a sentence grammar) of the meanings of the words used in an utterance. Part of the meaning of a definite referring expression could be said to be the fact that it has a referent associated with the expression. The proper noun, "Cleopatra," is associated with a referent, and, by the maxim of Relation, the second occurrence of "Cleopatra" must be interpreted as having the same referent as the first occurrence of "Cleopatra." Thus in 4) the same individual is being referred to in both occurences by the use of the noun phrase "Cleopatra." By the same reasoning, since part of the meaning of the pronoun (which is also a definite referring expression) is that it is associated with a referent, its particular referent is determinable again by the maxim of Relation to be that denoted by "Cleopatra." Since the meanings of all the other words in examples 4) and 5) are identical, examples 4) and 5) are correctly predicted to have identical meanings. Examples 6) and 7) are somewhat more complicated,

    6) That dog was running. That dog was barking.
    7) That dog was running and that dog was barking.

but can still be accounted for by the types of statements which would appear as conversational principles. The conversational principles could include some statement to the effect that all propositions expressed by the same speaker are interpreted as associated with the logical connective "&." (Such a statement might be construed to be necessary anyway in order for any participant in a conversation to determine if the speaker has contradicted himself in successive utterances. This would then allow the participant to determine if what the speaker said (or part of what the speaker said) was false, so that the participant could determine if the speaker had obeyed or violated a maxim of Quality.) Given some such statement (which would only make reference to the content of the utterance), since the meanings of the words and sentences in examples 6) and 7) are otherwise identical, the two stretches of discourse would be given the same interpretations.

c) *Ambiguity*
    By the type of reasoning used for examples 4) and 5), the ambiguity of example 8)

    8) Cleopatra was seen by Josephine yesterday. She was eating lunch
       then.

can be naturally accounted for. "Cleopatra" and "Josephine", being definite expressions, are each associated with a particular referent; "she," being also a definite expression, also has a referent. By the maxim of

Relation, the referent of "she" has to be relevant to the context and thus can be either that of "Josephine" or that of "Cleopatra."

The synomymy of 9') and 9") with each of the interpretations of 9) can also be naturally accounted for with the suggestions made above.

9)   Flying planes can be dangerous.
9')  Some planes fly. Those planes can be dangerous.
9")  Some people fly planes. That can be dangerous.

Since the conversational principles presuppose a specification of the meanings of 9) (assigned presumably by a sentence grammar), the specifications of the meanings of 9) are already given. Each pair of propositions in 9') and 9") can be interpreted as associated with the logical connective "&;" by the maxim of Relation which determines the referent of "those planes" in 9') and "that" in 9"), each of the examples 9') and 9") can be interpreted as having the meanings associated with 9).

d) *Principles of discourse which are reflected in single sentences as well as multi-sentence sequences*

i) *Predictability of contrastive stress*

The fact that the placement of contrastive stress in sentences is predictable from discourse context can, it appears, be accounted for with a further elaboration of the conversational principles. Kempson (1975: 191—198) has, in fact, proposed an elaboration of the maxim of Relation (precisely in order to account for constrastive stress) to include a statement to the effect that the form of the expression must be relevant to its content. The reader is referred to her book for the details of her proposal. With an articulation of the conversational principles which is not outrageously inconsistent with the general outlines of the conversational principles (such a modification is akin to I b in the outline of the principles above) it thus seems to be possible to account for the placement of contrastive stress based on (what appears to be) a simple principle of conversation.

ii) *Single processes operating sentence-internally as well as across multi-sentence sequences.*

It should be clear from the discussions in b) and c) in this section that the fact that the same processes are operant in the interpretations of anaphoric pronouns and definite noun phrases between and within sentences can be captured by the conversational principles. Given that definite expressions are associated with referents as a part of their meanings, the interpretations of their particular referents are determinable by a single principle, the maxim of Relation, regardless of whether the definite expressions and their antecedents are in single sentences[13] or in multi-sentence sequences.

f) *Potentially complete versus necessarily incomplete discourses*

It appears that the distinction between potentially complete and necessarily incomplete discourses could be characterized by invoking the principles of conversation. It might be proposed, for example, that the set of potentially complete discourses is that set of utterances which do not violate any of the Quantity or Relation maxims, and the set of necessarily incomplete discourses is that set of utterances which result from a violation of one or more of the Quantity or Relation maxims.[14]

Thus, at least with respect to the examples considered here, it appears that a fuller articulation of the conversational principles could reasonably account for those properties of discourse which motivated the claim that discourse grammars are necessary. Moreover, the elaboration of the conversational principles could be given in the types of terms in which the original set of conversational principles is cast. Thus, although the original function of the conversational principles is distinct from the function of a discourse grammar, it appears that the types of statements which would be used to formulate the principles would not have to be drastically altered in their nature in order to account for the properties that discourse grammars would be designed to account for, because such statements would generally only make reference to the content (and context) of the expression used and not to the particular structural details of the form of the expression used.

It may be concluded then, that the sets of discourse facts that discourse grammars and conversational principles can account for are not mutually exclusive, and do indeed overlap. In fact, it has been seen that, with respect to the particular examples given to illustrate the types of facts which motivate discourse grammars, all of the examples can be accounted for by a theory of conversational principles.

The question now arises whether the sets of discourse facts that discourse grammars and conversational principles can account for are coterminous, i.e., whether they overlap completely. It may be asked then whether all the properties of discourse that conversational principles were designed to account for can in principle be accounted for by discourse grammars as originally conceived; and conversely, it may be asked whether all the properties of discourse that grammars of discourse

---

[13] The possibility that the Relation maxim might be used to account for all cases of anaphora sentence-internally as well as in sentence sequences also raises the question of overlap between conversational principles and (sentence) grammars. (see fn. 1.)

[14] Whether this proposal is correct in its details is irrelevant. Since an incomplete discourse is, intuitively, one which does not fit a context in some way (in particular, has been isolated from, or displaced from, its appropriate context), it seems clear that even if the details of this proposal in the text are not correct, in principle the conversational principles could provide a characterization of the distinction between potentially complete and necessarily incomplete discourses.

were designed to account for can in principle be accounted for by a set of conversational principles as originally conceived.


## VI. The Necessity of Conversational Principles

There are facts about discourse that discourse grammars cannot in principle account for. Grice's introductory example of conversational implicature is a case in point. The fact which the discourse grammar would have to explain is the fact that the utterance of the discourse *Oh quite well, I think; he hasn't been to prison yet,* can convey the message that C is likely to yield to the temptation provided by his occupation. Since there is no obvious *strictly linguistic* connection between the proposition said and the proposition conveyed (e.g., a relation of entailment) the explanation of that fact requires that statements in the explanation make reference to the speaker and his beliefs (the speaker deems X relevant) and intentions (speaker intends to convey X), in addition to the linguistic context (the meaning of the sentence and the preceding question). Since the statements that would appear in discourse grammars do not include reference to speakers, their beliefs, or their intentions,[15] discourse grammars could neither offer a general characterization of conversational implicature nor predict particular implicata that could be conveyed in particular cases.

Moreover, since the particular conversational implicatum varies in accordance with linguistic and non-linguistic context, it is necessary, for the correct prediction of the range of implicata associated with any expression, to make reference to the context in which the expression appears (cf., a) and b) in the list of properties associated with conversational implicature). Since discourse grammars do not contain statements making reference to non-linguistic contexts, discourse grammars could not in principle account for the property of variance of conversational implicata.

Therefore, since any adequate account of the properties associated with conversational implicature must require reference to speakers, their beliefs and intentions, and the linguistic and non-linguistic context of the utterance, discourse grammars could not in principle provide such an account, for they do not contain statements which make reference to speakers, their beliefs and intentions, or non-linguistic context, but a theory of conversation, which does contain such statements, can.

Furthermore, another type of fact about discourse which discourse grammars could not possibly account for is the fact that it is possible for a speaker to lie. The characterization of a lie can be naturally formulated, in the theory of conversation, as a covert violation of the first maxim of Quality. Discourse grammars could not possibly account for lying, since the statements in them make no reference to speaker's beliefs about the truth or falsity of the propositions they express.

It thus appears that the ranges of discourse facts that the theory of conversation and discourse grammars could in principle account for do overlap, but not totally. Since there are at least some discourse facts which a theory of conversational principles in principle could account for but which discourse grammars could not in principle account for, the conclusion is that a theory of conversation is necessary.

Since it appears, from the examples discussed above, that the set of conversational principles could account for the full range of types of discourse facts which motivated the claim that grammars must range over a discourse domain, the question arises whether discourse grammars are necessary at all. The question may now be asked whether all types of facts about discourse can be accounted for by a set of conversational principles as originally conceived.


## VII. The Necessity of Grammars of Discourse

There are properties of discourse involving well-formedness and inter-pretations of discourse (synonymy, ambiguity) which cannot be accounted for in principle by conversational principles but which can naturally be accounted for by discourse grammars. The examples which illustrate these properties of discourse are such that an adequate account of them must necessarily refer to the particular constituent structure properties of the constructions involved and not just the content of the expressions used.

a) *Grammaticality*
On a conversational principle account of examples 12—15)

12)   Did John read the book? Yes, he read it/the book.
  13) *Did John read the book? Yes, he read.
  14)   What did you do with the banana? I ate it/the banana.
  15) *What did you do with the banana? I ate.

it might be suggested that the oddity of 13) and 15) is due to a violation of the Quantity maxim requiring the speaker to give as much informa-tion as is required. But a conversational account fails. First, the informa-tion that the book/banana ("it") is what is being talked about is already known to the participants, so there is no obvious reason why the book/banana ("it") should be mentioned again; that is, it is not at all clear that the oddity of 13) and 15) can reasonably be claimed to be due to a viola-tion of the Quantity maxim. Moreover, even if fthe speaker obeys the Quantity maxim non-linguistically by overtly pointing to the book/banana while uttering "He read"/"I ate", the response would still be ungrammatical as a response. Furthermore, the same discourse rendered in Japanese is grammatical:

16) John   wa     sono  hon   o    yomimašitaka?
             theme this  book  obj.  read-polite-past-ques.
    Hai, (sono hon o) yomimašita.
    yes

(17) ano   banana  wa     dō   šimašitaka?
     that          theme  how  do-polite-past ques.
     (ano banana wa) tabemašita.
                     eat-polite-past

Since it is highly unlikely (and, under a strict Gricean view, impossible) that languages would differ by virtue of the presence or absence of the maxims of Quantity, the well-formedness of the Japanese compared with the ill-formedness of the English examples suffices to show that the oddity is not due to aspects of the content of the responses, but rather to aspects of the particular structural details of the form of of the expression used. In the case at hand, it is a particular structural fact about English (as distinct from Japanese) that objects of non-deleted verbs in sequences of sentences may be represented by pronouns but not by a null expression (deleted). An account of the ill-formedness of 13) and 15) would thus necessarily make reference to aspects of the constituent structure of sequenced sentences. It should be clear that conversational principles as originally conceived do not include statements which make reference to such structural elements as object noun phrases; thus, with respect to the types of elements appearing in statements in such a theory, a theory of conversational principles could not in principle account for such facts about the grammaticality/ungrammaticality of sentence sequences.

Another example which shows the insufficiency of a theory of conversational principles to account for certain cases of grammatical/ ungrammatical sequences of sentences is the following:

18) Where did John go?   He went to a lake.
                         To a lake.
                         ?A lake.
                         *Went to a lake.
                         *To lake.
                         *Lake.
                         *Went lake.

19) *Japanese version*
    John wa doko e ikimašitaka?        mizuumi e ikimašita.
                  mizuumi e.
                  mizuumi.
         where to go-polite-past-ques. lake      to go-polite-past

Although all the responses seem to be in conformity with the conversational principles, not all the responses are well-formed as responses. Moreover, it would not be possible to appeal to any non-discourse alternative such as the possible claim that the ungrammaticality of the responses is due to the fact that the responses are not themselves *sentences,* for some of the grammatical responses are themselves not sentences. Thus, it appears that the only way to account for the grammaticality/ungrammaticality distinction in these cases is by a discourse grammar which containts references (directly, or indirectly by general principles) to such structural elements as subject noun phrase, preposition, postposition, article, etc.

Many examples can be found which exhibit the grammatical/ungrammatical distinction in discourse in languages with agreement and case markings. The sentences can be used in complete compliance with the conversational principles but the sentence sequences are grammatical or ungrammatical due to the particular structural details of the forms of the expression used. A few examples are:

i)   *Agreement*
20)  *French*

| De quelle couleur est cette balle? | What color is this ball? |
|---|---|
| Verte. | Green. |
| *Vert. | |
| De quelle couleur est ce livre? | What color is this book? |
| *Verte. | Green. |
| Vert. | |

21)  *Spanish*

| ?Cómo es María? | What is Maria like? |
|---|---|
| Alta, hermosa ... | Tall, pretty ... |
| *Alto, hermoso ... | |
| ?Cómo es Juan? | What is Juan like? |
| *Alta, hermosa ... | Tall, handsome ... |
| Alto, hermoso ... | |

ii)  *Case marking*
22)  *German*

| Wen hat er gesehen? | Who did he see? The man. |
|---|---|
| Den Mann. | |
| *Der Mann. | |
| Wer hat ihn gesehen? | Who saw him? The man. |
| *Den Mann. | |
| Der Mann. | |

23) *Hungarian*
    Kit látott John?              Whom did John see?
    A fiút.                    The boy.
    *A fiú.
    Ki látta Johnt?             Who saw John? The boy.
    *A fiút.
    A fiú.

It may be concluded then that sequences of sentences are governed by principles that necessarily make reference to such aspects of constituent structure as subject and object noun phrases, prepositions, postpositions, articles, agreement particles, case markings, and so forth. Since the statements of conversational principles do not make reference to such structural properties, conversational principles in their original conception cannot in principle account for these types of facts about the grammaticality of discourses, but discourse grammars, which do make reference to constituent structure, can.

b) *Interpretations of discourse (synonymy and ambiguity)*

It is necessary for the statements representing the principles governing discourse to make reference to the constituent structure of the discourse, not only in order to account for the grammaticality of discourses, but also to account for the meanings that are assigned to stretches of discourse. In Japanese, for example, the pronoun *kare* receives varying interpretations depending on whether *kare* and its possible antecedent are in the same discourse constituent (single sentence, as opposed to clause), or not:

24) John wa hon   o katte,          kare wa empitsu o utta.
            book    buy-conj. form he      pencil    sell-past
    (John bought a book, and he sold a pencil.)      (kare $\neq$ John)
25) John wa hon o katta. Kare wa empitsu o utta.
    (John bought a book. He sold a pencil.)      (1. kare $=$ John)
                                                (2. kare $\neq$ John)

In 24), a single sentence, *kare* cannot refer to John but must refer to someone other than John. In 25), a sequence of sentences, *kare* can refer either to John or to someone else. Since the only difference between 24) and 25) is the difference between one sentence (discourse constituent) or two sentences (discourse constituents), the statements which assign the correct interpretations in these cases must necessarily refer to the constituent structure of the expressions, in particular, to the difference between a single sentence (as distinct from a clause) and two sentences in sequence. It is quite clear that the maxim of Relation, which was capable of assigning the correct referents in the case of examples 4) and 5), would be incapable of assigning the correct interpretations in the cases of 24) and 25), for it would predict that in 24), *John* and *kare* denote the same individual. None of the conversational principles are capable of distinguishing the sets of readings associated with these sentences, again because they do not make reference to details of constituent structure. On the other hand, discourse grammars, whose statements do make reference to structural characteristics of expressions, would be capable in principle of assigning the correct interpretations to 24) and 25). All that is necessary is a (structural) definition of a notion "discourse constituent" (sentence as opposed to clause) in order to state the constraint on semantic interpretations.

Moreover, the addition of another sentence to examples 24) and 25), namely 26),

26) John wa hon o katte, Ø empitsu o utta. (Ø = John)

exemplifies a set of discourse facts analogous to that presented by Sanders in example 9); in this case, however, it is the sentence *sequence* which is ambiguous and each of its readings is paraphrasable by a *single sentence*. Example 25) is ambiguous and each of its readings is paraphrasable by examples 26) and 24). Of particular interest is that in order to account for the synonymy of example 26) with the first reading of 25), the statements which assign meaning to expressions must make reference to the fact that in expressions whose reading is that John is the seller the pronoun is present or absent depending on the constituent structure of the discourse. Thus, even to account for the synonymy of expressions in discourse, reference is necessary to particular structural details of the expressions. The Japanese example also suffices to show that ambiguity is present or absent depending on the constituent structure of the discourse, since 25), a sentence sequence, is ambiguous and 24), a single sentence, is not.

Another example which shows that ambiguity is a function of discourse constituent structure is the following:

(A possible previous statement)
I went to a concert that Bill and Mary were in, which was excellent; the program was good, too — it included, "Ave Maria," which I just love.

(Possible subsequent sentences)
27) Bill played and Mary sang "Ave Maria."     (ambiguous)
28) Bill played. And Mary sang "Ave Maria."     (unambiguous)
29) Bill played. And Mary sang. "Ave Maria."     (ambiguous)

In 27) and 29) the ambiguity involves the two possible readings of *Bill played*. On one reading, Bill played some unspecified piece or instrument; on the other reading, Bill played "Ave Maria." In 28) the only possible reading of *Bill played* is the former. The only thing that differ-

68 Jessica R. Wirth

entiates these examples is whether they are one, two, or three single
sentences; thus the ambiguity/nonambiguity difference can only be
attributed to the constituent structure of the discourse. It is thus clear
that any characterization of the ambiguity/nonambiguity of these examples must make reference to the structural properties of the expressions.

It may be concluded then that there are facts about discourse
involving grammaticality, synonymy and ambiguity in which the well-
formedness and ranges of interpretation are specifically a function of the
constituent structure of the expressions. Clearly, then, any adequate
account of these types of facts must make crucial reference to the constituent structure of the expressions. A theory of conversational principles
does not make reference to such structural properties but discourse
grammars do. Thus a theory of conversational principles as originally
conceived cannot in principle account for certain properties of
discourse, but discourse grammars can. The conclusion then is that
discourse grammars are indeed necessary.

The general conclusions to be drawn from the discussions in sections
VI and VII are 1) that a theory of conversation is necessary, but is not
sufficient to account for all properties of discourse, and 2), that
discourse grammars are necessary, but they are not sufficient to account
for all properties of discourse. A theory of conversational principles,
which contains statements about speakers, their beliefs and intentions,
and the context, is necessary to account for conversational implicature,
but is not sufficient to account for a range of facts about grammaticality,
synonymy and ambiguity of sentence sequences whose characterizations
require reference to constituent structure. Discourse grammars, which
contain statements making reference to constituent structure, are necessary to account for discourse grammaticality, synonymy, and ambiguity,
but are not sufficient to account for conversational implicature, which
requires reference to speakers, their beliefs and intentions, and the
context.

VIII. The Independence of Discourse Grammars and Conversational
Principles

Even if the conversational principles could make reference to specific
constituent structure properties of discourse, a distinct set of principles
governing grammaticality, i.e., discourse grammars, would be necessary;
and conversely, even if discourse grammars could make reference to
speakers, their beliefs and intentions, and the context of utterance, a
distinct set of conversational principles would be necessary.

Suppose, for example, that the theory of conversational principles
took on the function of characterizing and predicting instances of gram-

maticality, synonymy, and ambiguity, as well as its original function of characterizing conversational implicature. Presumably then, some or all of the principles of conversation would constitute the principles governing the grammaticality of discourse expressions in the language. Suppose, in particular, that *all* of the principles of conversation are taken to be principles governing grammaticality. Any expressions used in violation of any one of the conversational principles would presumably then be claimed to be ungrammatical. But the theory of conversational principles also functions to characterize and predict conversational implicature, and many (if not all) instances of conversational implicature are due to the violation of one of the conversational principles. Irony, for example, is a case where a maxim is deliberately and overtly violated to conversationally implicate the exact opposite of what is said:

30) John has been my confidant for years but I just found out he's been telling all to Bill, my arch enemy. John's a fine friend.[15]

*John's a fine friend* is obviously false and the speaker exploits that fact to convey the implicatum that John is not a good friend at all. The prediction would be that this discourse is ungrammatical, which is clearly counterintuitive. Similarly, any cases of expressions that constitute lies, are unclearly stated, are not informative enough, etc., would be claimed to be ungrammatical (for they violate conversational principles); all of such claims would be obviously counterintuitive. Therefore, if intuitions about grammaticality are to be captured, it is impossible for the entire set of conversational principles to simultaneously have the functions of characterizing grammaticality, etc., and conversational implicature.

Suppose, however, that only some of the conversational principles functioned in the charcterization of ungrammaticality, etc., and others functioned in the characterization of conversational implicature. In this case, in order for the theory to correctly predict, in the cases of violations of the principles, whether the violation results in an implicature or simply in ungrammaticality, it would be necessary to mark each principle as being a principle governing grammaticality or implicature. But this amounts to building a distinct discourse grammar into the set of conversational principles. Thus, a distinct component of principles governing grammaticality, i.e., a discourse grammar, is still necessary.

Conversely, suppose that discourse grammars took over the function of the conversational principles, namely, to characterize and predict conversational implicature, as well as its original function of characterizing grammaticality, etc. Then all or some of the principles governing

---

[15] Kempson's (1975: 55—62) discussion of the Lakoffs' treatments of presupposition suggests the conclusion that reference to speakers' beliefs and intentions should not at all be permitted in grammars.

grammaticality, etc., would also be principles governing conversation. Suppose that all of the principles governing grammaticality were also principles governing conversation. Then any deliberate and overt violation of a principle in the discourse grammar would presumably be claimed to have the capacity to give rise to a conversational implicature. It seems highly unlikely that deliberate violations of rules like case marking, for example, would give rise to conversational implicatures. Thus it appears that a requirement that the entire set of grammatical principles of discourse take over the functions of the theory of conversational principles would yield incorrect predictions about the range of possible ways in which implicatures arise. Moreover, to require this would thwart the possibility of explaining the principles of conversation as merely special instances of rational, purposive behavior, which seems a reasonable possibility (Grice: 1975: 47). Since it is highly unlikely that the actual principles governing grammaticality (e.g., a constraint against deletion of objects of verbs in English but not Japanese (cf. 12—17)) could ever be considered to be special instances of rational, purposive behavior, a requirement that the conversational principles be embedded in discourse grammars in the guise of grammatical principles would preclude the possibility of explaining conversational principles as instances of rational behavior.

If only some of the principles governing the structural properties of discourse were claimed to be principles governing conversational implicature, again this would have the consequence of building a distinct set of conversational principles into a discourse grammar. Thus, a distinct component of conversational principles is still necessary.

The conclusion from this discussion is that on grounds of their functions alone, independent of the types of statements which appear in them, discourse grammars and conversational principles cannot be collapsed together without making incorrect predictions about grammaticality or conversational implicature or precluding reasonable explanations of the principles governing conversation. Discourse grammars and conversational principles are each necessary for the performance of specific tasks in the characterization of mutually exclusive attributes of discourse, and they must be independent of one another.

It has been established that a set of conversational principles is necessary and that discourse grammars are necessary. But it has also been established that the sets of facts which each set of principles can account for overlap. In particular, it was seen that examples 1)—9) could be accounted for by means of a discourse grammar or a set of conversational principles. The question of which is the best way to account for

---

[16] This example is from Grice (1975: 53) but has been reformulated here.

each of the facts in 1)—9) is thus left open, and the alternative proposals to account for each of 1)—9) must be individually evaluated for their empirical adequacy and explanatory value.

## IX. Conclusion

It has been seen that, given that discourse facts must be accounted for, there are some discourse facts that can be accounted for by either a discourse grammar or by a theory of conversation. Thus it has been seen that discourse grammars and a theory of conversation overlap in the sets of discourse facts they can account for, a state of affairs which raises the question of whether either mechanism (discourse grammar or conversational principles) is necessary. It has been further shown, however, that each mechanism is necessary, for there are distinct sets of facts which each mechanism, but not the other, can in principle account for, because the two mechanisms differ in the types of statements that they can make. Since conversational principles as originally conceived make reference to speakers, beliefs, and intentions, and the context of utterance, but not to constituent structure, they can in principle account for all the properties of conversational implicature but not all of the properties of grammaticality, synonymy, and ambiguity of discourse. Since discourse grammars make reference to constituent structure of expressions, but not to speakers, their beliefs and intentions, and the context of utterance, discourse grammars as originally conceived can in principle account for all properties of grammaticality, synonymy, and ambiguity of discourse, but cannot account for the properties of conversational implicature. Thus, both discourse grammars and conversational principles are established as necessary. Furthermore, it has been seen that even if discourse grammars could include the types of statements that necessarily appear in conversational principles, and even if conversational principles could include the types of statements which necessarily appear in discourse grammars, it would not be possible for there to be a *single* mechanism which simultaneously has the function of characterizing conversational implicature as well as the function of characterizing grammaticality; such a mechanism would make incorrect predictions about grammaticality or the range of possible conversational implicatures, and could also preclude the possibility of explaining conversational principles as special instances of rational, purposive, behavior. The general conclusion, then, is that discourse grammars and conversational principles are both distinctly necessary and necessarily distinct.

# References

Grice, H. Paul. 1975. Logic and conversation. *Syntax and Semantics, Vol. 3: Speech Acts,* edited by Peter Cole and Jerry Morgan. New York: Academic Press. 41—58.
Kempson, Ruth. 1975. *Presupposition and the Delimitation of Semantics.* Cambridge: Cambridge University Press.
Sanders, Gerald. 1970. On the natural domain of grammar. *Linguistics:* 63, November 1970. 51—123.
Wilson, Deirdre. 1975. *Presuppositions and Non-Truth-Conditional Semantics.* New York: Academic Press.

# Idealizations in the Development of a Sociolinguistic Theory*

Robert Berdan


Nearly a decade ago DeCamp (1970) posed to linguists a question which is still unresolved: "Is a sociolinguistic theory possible?" After delineating some of the issues such a theory must accommodate, DeCamp's response was at that time somewhat indeterminate: a sociolinguistic theory would be highly desirable, both for linguistic and for social reasons; and the time was ripe in terms of general linguistic theory. But the nature of a sociolinguistic theory remained largely undefined. Writing at about the same time, Labov considered the essential social nature of language and raised a somewhat similar question, "In what way, then, can 'sociolinguistics' be considered as something apart from 'linguistics' (1970: 30)?" Labov questioned not the feasibility of constructing a sociolinguistic theory, but whether viable linguistic theories could exist that did not also address the concerns of the sociolinguist.

In the years since these questions were raised, substantial work has been done, amplifying the issues raised by DeCamp and Labov. In the area in which these questions converge, i.e., the nature of sociolinguistic theory and its relation to other linguistic theory, it now seems useful to characterize at least some aspects of a sociolinguistic theory, nascent though it may be. Among the broad range of concerns that have generally fallen within the purview of sociolinguistics, the problems discussed here are chiefly distributional rather than functional. Within this broad dichotomy, however, the distributional problems considered are both microsociolinguistic and macrosociolinguistic. That is, the present concerns are the representation of linguistic variability in a formal grammar for an individual and the representation of the distribution of individual grammars in language communities.

---

* Earlier formulations of some of the ideas developed here were presented in the last chapter of my dissertation (Berdan, 1975) and in a paper read to the 1975 Annual Meeting of the Linguistic Society of America, "The ideal speech community in sociolinguistic research." Portions of the work on which this paper is based were supported by SWRL Educational Research and Development under grant No. OB-NIE-G-78-0109 with the National Institute of Education, Department of Health, Education and Welfare.

Conventional generative transformational linguistic theory as it has developed since *Syntactic Structures* has not addressed certain aspects of language that are of critical interest to sociolinguists. In particular, conventional theory appears to have little, if anything, to say about the use of real languages in real languages communities. Its universe of inquiry was rather neatly circumscribed by Chomsky in the introductory pages of *Aspects*:

> Linguistic theory is concerned primarily with an ideal speaker-listener, in a completely homogeneous speech-community, who knows its language perfectly and is unaffected by such grammatically irrelevant conditions as memory limitations, distractions, shifts of attention and interest, and errors (random or characteristics) in applying his knowledge of the language in actual performance ... To study actual linguistic performance, we must consider the interaction of a variety of factors, of which the underlying competence of the speaker-hearer is only one ...
> Only under the idealization set forth in the preceding paragraph is performance a direct reflection of competence ... A grammar of a language purports to be a description of the ideal speaker-hearer's intrinsic competence (1965: 3—4).

This explicit restriction on linguistic theory has provided a focus which is sufficiently narrow that an impressive amount of cumulative research has evolved. After a decade of this research Chomsky felt that the idealizations were thereby justified:

> It seems to me that the idealization of grammar as a cognitive structure with certain properties and principles, interacting with other structures, is a reasonable working hypothesis, justified by the success in discovering explanatory principles specific to grammar (1975: 86).

Although this limitation on the scope of linguistic inquiry may well have facilitated the development of linguistic theory, it has long been the sticking point in the relationship been sociolinguistics and linguistic theory.

Recent work in sociolinguistics generally falls outside the narrow domain of what Chomsky labelled the "competence" theory of linguistics. Sociolinguists have been more interested in real speakers than they have been in ideal speakers. Rather than being constrained to homogeneous speech communities, the interpersonal variability of real language communities has given substance to much of the sociolinguistic work. Whether this extended inquiry is part of what Chomsky labelled a theory of "performance" is of little interest. The important point is that the set of theoretical entities that sociolinguists use in their inquiry overlaps in very large part with the formal vocabulary of theoretical linguistics. Both find it necessary to use such concepts as "is a sentence," "noun," "object of" or "voicing." The overlap is in fact so great that it is difficult to believe that the two approaches address areas of human experience that are in any meaningful way discrete. This strongly suggests that the hyphenated distinctions drawn within linguistics as an academic discipline are more closely related to the historical development of linguistic theory than they are to any real world dichotomy. This in turn argues for a single theoretical framework to embrace the pursuits of both the theoretical linguist and the sociolinguist.

It is not surprising that sociolinguistics, with its keen interst in observed language behavior, finds the idealizations of competence linguistics somewhat irrelevant. Idealizations, by definition, do not have concrete exemplars. As Rudner observes, "There is no entity, process, or state of affairs to which the idealization stands in designatory or descriptive relation. This is, of course, the reason they are called 'idealizations' (1966: 57)." It does not follow from this, of course, that idealizations have no value, or no potential for explanatory power. Idealizations have been used both in the physical sciences and in the social sciences for the construction of models and theories.

Chomsky's idealizations have been cited by some as sufficient reason to ignore all linguistic variability (e.g., Katz 1966: 117); they are cited by others as sufficient reason to ignore all that is happening in generative linguistics (e.g., Maher 1971: 87). Given the amount of controversy that these idealizations have generated, it is somewhat surprising that there has been so little attention among linguists to the role of idealizations in cognate disciplines and in scientific theories in general.

At least implicit in Chomsky's work is the assumption that his use of idealizations is equivalent to their use in the development of theories in the physical sciences (cf. Chomsky 1965: 4). The comparison is made explicitly by Katz:

> A linguistic description is an idealization in exactly the same sense in which any scientific theory, such as the dynamic theory of gases or the Newtonian theory of mechanics is. Just as these physical theories do not state their laws for the behavior of actual physical objects but instead formulate them in terms of ideal objects under ideal conditions, so the rules of a linguistic description are not stated as a characterization of what any actual speakers tacitly know about their language but are formulated as a characterization of the tacit knowledge of an ideal speaker (1966: 115).

More recently, Katz & Bever reiterate the claim that linguistic idealizations are comparable to those of physics:

> Chomsky's notion of absolute formulations as part of an idealization permits him to exclude from such formulations any factor that should be considered a matter of performance rather than competence by simply considering the former as something to be abstracted away from, the way the physicist excludes friction, air resistance, and so on from the formulation of mechanical laws (1976: 21).

Such comparisons of linguistic idealizations to the use of idealizations in other disciplines seem always to have been directed toward the physical sciences. They seem never to consider idealizations in other disciplines which are more closely related to human behavior, particularly sociology, anthropology and economics. Not all idealizations have the same formal properties, a fact well recognized by Katz in his attack on Carnap's idealized languages. Katz argues that the artificial languages constructed by Carnap (1937) and his colleagues are not idealizations of natural languages. One reason they are not is that:

> The artificial languages developed by Carnap and his followers are, unlike successful idealizations in physics, under no strict empirical controls that determine their adequacy. A scientist who proposes an idealization must demonstrate that it predicts accurately within a reasonable margin of error and that the closer actual conditions approximate the ideal, the smaller this margin of error becomes (1966: 63—64).

This criterion for a successful idealization is well-established in the natural sciences. However, it is not often applied to idealizations in linguistics (but cf Katz 1966: 118).

Idealizations do not purport to describe anything that exists in the real world. It is nonetheless legitimate to inquire what, if anything, distinguishes idealizations in the natural sciences, such as those mentioned, or the ideal gas or instanteous velocity or any of the many others; from idealizations in the social sciences, such as the folk society, perfectly rational man, perfect competition; from those of linguistics, in particular the ideal speaker/listener and the homogeneous speech community. And what distinguishes any or all of these idealizations from other statements which have the same logical form and do not have corresponding true existential statements, such as claims about the nature of the venerable unicorn?

The nature of idealizations and their use across a range of disciplines has been insightfully considered by Hempel (1965). His *Aspects* was published at the same time as Chomsky's and it is useful now to consider Chomsky's idealizations of syntactic theory in the light of Hempel's elaboration of their use in scientific explanation. Hempel observes a fundamental dichotomy between what he terms "theoretical idealizations" and "intuitive idealizations."

The notion of an ideal gas is frequently cited as a theoretical idealization. In the kinetic theory of gases, Boyle's law and Charles' law relating pressure, volume and temperature strictly speaking operate only for a gas with zero volume and zero mass. In the real world, there is of course no such gas, nor could there conceivably be, given conventional notions of atomic structure. However, under certain conditions real gases behave according to these laws with a high degree of approximation, particularly if the molecular weight of the observed real gas approaches that of the ideal. Two things may be observed about this idealization: first, the idealization may be stated in terms of a limiting condition in general kinetic theory; secondly, as this limit is approached in the real world, differences between real observations and theoretical predictions of the idealized laws diminish. These two characteristics, being deducible from more comprehensive theoretical principles, and being capable of approximation in the real world, are essential characteristics of theoretical idealizations for Hempel. These two characteristics may be observed of the many idealizations employed in natural sciences: the ideal lever, perfectly elastic impact, and the perfect vacuum, to name but a few more.

Contrasted with these theoretical idealizations in the natural sciences, Hempel considers as intuitive idealizations some of those used in economics and sociology. Many of these idealizations stem from the early work by Weber developing "ideal types" (1947, 1949), for example, "perfectly free competition" or "economically rational behavior." These latter are not deducible from, or replaceable by, any more general theory of behavior. As Rudner observes,

> We might expect that a general theory of social behavior or a general theory of social action would, were it a viable theory, have variables of behavior such that descriptions of . . . rational behavior . . . could be *derived* by letting those variables take on extreme values. Such a comprehensive theory of social action would, in short subsume economically rational behavior (or sensible behavior) as a special case. Unfortunately, no such comprehensive theory seems at present to be available (1966: 62).

This distinction is not simply a distinction between theories dealing with human behavior and theories of the physical universe. As Hempel (1965: 169) points out, the formula for the mathematical pendulum was discovered empirically by Galileo. However, this did not constitute what Hempel considers a theoretical idealization until much later when more comprehensive hypotheses had been established.

The difference between these latter idealizations in economics and those which have been used in the natural sciences is not in any of their formal logical properties. They may all take the form of a universal conditional:

$$(x) [f(x) \supset g(x)]$$

However, since they are idealizations, and strictly speaking describe nothing in the real world, there are not corresponding true existential statements of the form:

$$(\exists x) [f(x)]$$

Thus they need not assert the existence of anything.

To have any potential of explanatory power, idealizations cannot simply be analytic statements. They must be contingent, capable of disconfirmation. Both theoretical idealizations and intuitive idealizations can be formalized in this logical form. However, only when the idealization is reducible to more comprehensive theoretical generalizations can it be truly explanatory. The difference between theoretical and intuitive idealizations lies in the manner in which they are constituted in theories.

A linguistic or sociolinguistic theory is not of necessity to be faulted for employing intuitive idealizations. They are part of the normal

growth process of theory development. Instantaneous language acquisition may be a useful idealization for linguists, but an expectation of
instantaneous theory development serves no cause. On the other hand,
intuitive idealizations ought not to be touted as a theory's strength. They
are rather an explicit statement that the theory's relation to the rest of
the natural universe is not well understood. As Lopreato & Alston point
out, the use of idealizations leads to an interesting paradox in the development of a theory:

> On the one hand, the idealization simplifies relationships and thus conceals the
> details and complexities of a real situation. On the other hand, it provides a powerful
> thrust toward analysis because of its logical demand that we account systematically for
> discrepancies existing between what the idealization asserts and what observation
> reveals. In the process — and this is the real value of the idealization — it surrounds
> itself with other theoretical propositions which relate to the real situation. In short, a
> theoretical idealization is a focal point of a research program whose execution
> enhances the probability of producing systematic and cumulative theory (1970: 92).

It may thus in this sense seem paradoxical, but the idealizations which
have tended to insulate theoretical linguistics from needs of sociolinguistics also provide the most likely spot for expanding the domain of
linguistic theory. Within Chomsky's discussion of idealizations there are
at least three independent but quite compatible idealizations: (a) the
idealized speaker-hearer, (b) the homogeneous speech community, and
(c) the language generated by a competence grammar. Katz (1966: 115)
asserts that these are equivalent to theoretical idealizations. Nonetheless,
they appear to have much more in common with what Hempel characterized as intuitive idealizations. It is in attempting to reformulate them
as theoretical idealizations that a sociolinguistic theory can begin to take
form.

Of these three idealizations, the idealized speaker-listener is perhaps
closest to what Hempel considers a theoretical idealization. It is also the
least important in terms of present theoretical considerations. The ideal
speaker has a memory which pushes the limit; it is infinite. This idealized
speaker makes no mistakes, is completely symmetrical with respect to
perception and production, and experiences instantaneous language
acquisition.

Each of these parameters on which the speaker-listener is idealized
needs to be considered seriously. It is not enough simply to assert that
there are idealizations in natural sciences and thereby assume that all
conceivable idealizations in linguistics are comparable to them. Each
must be shown to follow from some general principle in established
theory. In the case of the idealized speaker-listener, memory is a notion
that is reasonably well-defined quite apart from its relationships to
grammars. No real person can be endowed, even experimentally, with
infinite memory. However, such simple expedients as pencil and paper

provide, as it were, an extended buffer for memory, and thus noticeably increase the ability to process syntactically complex sentences.

Theories of memory may well be conceived of as employing variables which, when taken to extreme values, allow the processing of indefinitely long sentences. To the extent that this is true the idealization can be considered to be a theoretical idealization. That means that one can appeal to a theory of memory to explain certain problems that real speakers have processing long sentences, rather than building such a mechanism into a theory of language per se.

The second idealization in the *Aspects* paragraph, that of the completely homogeneous speech community, has received considerably less attention than has been given to the idealized speaker-listener. In order to determine the formal status of the idealization of the perfectly homogeneous speech community, it is necessary to state exactly what is being claimed to be homogeneous; what kind of variables are given extreme values in this ideal case.

Katz specifies certain factors which he says may lead to variations from speaker to speaker in actual performance that are irrelevant to the homogeneous ideal: "background, motives, intelligence, characteristic mannerisma, etc. (1966: 117)." If the idealization is well-formed, groups of speakers of similar background, for example, should be linguistically more homogeneous than groups of speakers of diverse backgrounds. Katz does not specify what he means by "background." However, the work in sociolinguistics suggests that it must surely include such things as place of origin, education and social status.

There is no reason to believe, of course, that it would ever be experimentally possible to assemble a group of speakers who are linguistically totally homogeneous. In the first place, existing metrics of such things as social status may be far too imprecise to allow determination of what persons are of exactly identical social status. This in no way detracts from the theoretical importance of the idealization. Secondly, there may in fact not be any two persons who are exactly the same with respect to all the parameters of background, intelligence, and motives. Nonetheless, as one observes speakers who are more and more similar in these respects, the idealization of the homogeneous speech community predicts that they will be linguistically more and more similar.

If, for example, one wanted to test whether the grammar of English contains some Rule Q, but observes that some speakers accept sentences consistent with Q and other speakers do not, one could sample a large number of speakers for their acceptance of Q sentences. One could then begin to cluster speakers who are most similar with respect to social status, age, education, income, sex, area of origin, etc. If the homogeneity idealization is appropriate, these clusters should have less variance with respect to Q than does the entire heterogeneous sample. Some one of the clusters, at least, should be reasonably homogeneous with respect to acceptance of Q.

But, there are problems with this test of Q as a scientific experiment. First, the variance within the groups could decrease significantly from the total variance, only if some of the groups are significantly different from each other with respect to acceptance of Q. That is, there can be homogeneous groups of Q acceptors only if there are also groups with a proportion of Q rejectors greater than that in the total sample. The question then becomes, in which homogeneous group shall Rule Q be tested: a group that accepts it, or a group that rejects it? Obviously if there is to be a true test of Rule Q, determination of the group in which it is to be tested cannot be decided on the basis of the outcome of the test. Some other principled determination of the appropriate group must be made. Unless there is some independent, a priori determination of which homogeneous sociological groups Q is to be tested in, there is no true test.

There is a second problem with this test. In the physical sciences idealizations result from allowing certain factors to take extreme values, e.g., the Boyle-Charles gas laws in which the volume and mass of the molecules of an ideal gas are assumed to be zero. Similarly the linguistic idealization of the homogeneous speech community assumes that interpersonal variation is zero. But what are the extreme values of place of origin, of ethnicity, or of sex? Obviously, there can be no zeroing of these parameters.

Place of origin is not a metrical concept as is the physical concept of molecular weight. The elements can be ranked according to how closely they approximate the idealized value of zero. But how does one rank Topeka, Kansas and Hoboken, New Jersey? That is a problem of a different order from ranking natural groups according to the amount of interpersonal linguistic variation they evidence. One can predict that historically stable rural communities will show less variation than will urban areas with recent immigration. In practice this distinction between homogeneity itself and the parameters by which it is approximated seems to have been overlooked.

An idealization of homogeneity is fundamentally different from an idealization such as a "perfect vacuum." If the homogeneous linguistic community is truly an idealization rather than a reality, as is surely the case, it is a prediction that real populations can be divided into two or more groups that are linguistically different from each other but each internally more homogeneous than the whole. Thus implicit in the idealization is the recognition of interpersonal variation. If the idealization is explicitly stated, as Katz agrees it must be, it predicts that the groups formed by the intersections of the parameters by which it is defined will be linguistically different. In the face of this, empirical pursuit of such notions as "the" grammar of English is doomed to failure for the very simple reason that there is no such thing as "the" English language, at least not in the sense that is capable of being characterized by some one conventional grammar. Katz' (1966: 115) claim that "it no more matters that the speech of some English speakers does not exhibit a distinction represented in the rules of a linguistic description of English than it matters in Newtonian mechanics that objects of certain shapes actually fall faster than do objects of other shapes" is tenable only under one condition. That condition is that the "English" so described is not to be construed as the language of the English speaking world, but as some theoretical language. In the practice of American lingustics it has been contemporary American Standard English.

Standard English is not a dialect or language in the usual or natural sense. It is rather a conventionalized language (Wolfram & Christian 1975: 43). It exists solely as the result of agreement on a set of more less arbitrary conventions. During the time in which linguistic inquiry was confined to what Chomsky (1965: 20) characterized as the "enormous mass of unquestionable data," it was possible to appeal to the conventions of Standard English to determine the extent to which grammars accounted for the relevant facts.

But generative theory proved to be a powerful tool for approaching syntax, and the inquiry soon outstripped the codified system of Standard English. Generative grammarians then appealed to the methodology that had served descriptive linguists so long: the venerable native speaker informant. However, the most sophisticated informants turned out to be the linguists themselves. The notion of the idealized speaker-listener became confounded with that of the real speaker-linguist, and the idealization of homogeneity came unglued.

In the literature two approaches have been taken in the attempt to rescue the homogeneous speech community. One is to deny that the variation is real, or perhaps only to deny that it is relevant. It results only from the vagaries of performance; competence grammars need not deal with it. But there has been a certain unwillingness on the part of some linguists to acquiesce that their own strongest intuitions are only speech errors. And so the current approach has been rather to reduce the concept of the community to equivalence with the individual.

In this reductio ad absurdum approach to the speech community the illusion of homogeneity is maintained only by stripping it of any potential for empirical import or explanatory value. In a community consisting of a single grammar, that grammar must be identical to all grammars in the community, namely itself.

Linguistic theory is now left in a rather uncomfortable position. It seeks to explain the nature of human language (cf Bach 1974: 2). It is in this respect that it maintains its claim to be an empirical pursuit. Human language is found in speech communities, but the theory addresses only individual grammars, the idiolect (cf Ringen, This volume).

Sociolinguists have harbored few illusions of ever discovering a single conventional grammar to account for all of English, or for any other natural language. They have accommodated interpersonal variation by dividing the language community into relatively homogeneous groupings based on sociological and demographic criteria: age, sex, place of residence, place of birth, occupation, education. Grammars are written for each of the resulting groupings. Although not usually thought of in these terms, this research has attempted to identify linguistically homogeneous groups. Unfortunately, the linguistic homogeneity of sociological groups has traditionally been an assumption rather than the conscious object of research. Thus statements of relative homogeneity of groups must be inferred from demonstrable differences between groups. However, the parameters identified by sociolinguists for differentiating groups (age, education, occupation, place of origin, etc.) are surely also among the parameters to be used for idealizing to linguistically homogeneous groups.

Making the parameters more explicit does not, however, in itself give them explanatory power. The lack of necessary relationships between the values of such parameters and any particular grammar makes statements of causal relationships somewhat improbable. This is because such demographic and sociological parameters are in fact not primary in determining the acquisition of any particular grammar. Such primacy must be reserved for the "primary linguistic data," that corpus from which the child acquires its grammar. It is not the fact that certain people share common sociological designations that causes them to speak alike; it is rather that they share a common language acquisition ecology.[1] The extent to which that acquisition ecology is in common across persons correlates highly but not perfectly with homogeneity on the sociological and demographic parameters discussed by sociolinguists.

Seen in this light, the "fundamental problem of linguistic theory" and of any sociolinguistic theory is indeed, as Chomsky (1972: 67) pointed out, to "account for the choice of a particular grammar, given the data available to the language learner." Persons encountering identical sets of primary linguistic data may be assumed to acquire equivalent grammars,

---

[1]   Bloomfield points out that the period of language acquisition has no well-defined termination: "The infant learns to speak like the people around him, but we must not picture this learning as coming to any particular end: there is no hour or day when we can say that a person has finished learning to speak, but, rather to the end of his life, the speaker keeps on doing the very things that make up infantile language learning (1933: 46)." No distinction is made here between the language acquisition ecology of childhood, and subsequent language learning.

i.e., grammars capable of generating the same language.[2] This premise is, of course, an empirical assumption subject to verification or falsification. However, it may not be directly testable, because it may not ever be possible to find any two individuals who have been exposed to exactly the same set of sentences in exactly the same order in the same contexts. Such persons may not exist. Even if they did, the lingust may never be able to identify them, because of the difficulty in knowing *all* the data that have been presented to any person. Nonetheless, the prediction that persons with the most similar language acquisition ecologies acquire the most similar grammars is empirically testable.

If this homogeneity idealization is to be construed as a theoretical idealization it must be possible to approximate it in the real world, not by appealing to conventionalized languages such as Standard English, but by observation of real speakers. Of all conceivable speakers of real languages, the two speakers most likely to provide evidence for identical grammars would be some set of twins who experienced virtually identical language acquisition environments, who have since childhood talked with all the same people.

This first choice is not for any reason of genetic similarity, but because of an at least implicit belief that the grammar which an individual acquires is determined, totally or in part, by what have been called the primary language data with which the learner is confronted. Thus those persons who undergo the most similar language acquisition scene would be those persons who would be most likely to evidence similar grammars. That is an empirically testable claim.

Given this acquisition hypothesis, the idealization of the homogeneous linguistic community has potential to become a theoretical idealization. The idealization can be stated in terms of common language acquisition ecologies: persons who experience identical language acquisition ecologies acquire identical grammars. This follows from a more general theoretical hypothesis about language acquisition: commonality of individual grammars is a function of the commonality

---

[2]   As Peters (1972 b) points out in his discussion of the projection problem, such grammars need not be identical; there may be an infinite set of grammars which could be projected from a single set of data. Nonetheless such grammars may still be at least weakly equivalent. The set of primary linguistic data may not be the only determinate of the grammar which is acquired. In that case the theory would also have to seek to explain the role of such things as intelligence in the acquisition of a grammar. If Carden's randomly distributed dialects can be shown not to correlate with any set of primary linguistic data, it may not constitute a counter example to the premise that persons with common primary linguistic data acquire equivalent grammars. It may be that the set of primary linguistic data does not extend to include the necessary information for the formation of such portions of the grammar.

of language acquisition ecologies. The verification of that hypothesis, in turn, must await a theory of acquisition, or a solution to what Peters (1972 b) termed the "projection problem." A statement that a homogeneous linguistic community is a set of individuals who share a common grammar, would be analytic, following necessarily from the definition of linguistic homogeneity. A statement that they are a set of persons with a common acquisition ecology embodies an empirical claim.

The homogeneity idealization functions to predict that it is not just an accident that children tend to learn the languages, or acquire the grammars, of their parents, and subsequently of their peers. It also predicts that it is not an accident that persons with sociologically similar language acquisition ecologies, but with no direct contact, acquire linguistically similar grammars. It is not an accident, that is, if the parameters of the homogeneity idealization predict that the fundamental factor is the primary linguistic data.

The homogeneity idealization also functions as a constraint on the set of possible grammars to be found in extant social groups. The language acquisition ecologies of such persons are not independent, but overlapping. From this it can be predicted that the resulting grammars will be more closely related than would a random sample from all possible grammars. That is a very weak constraint indeed, but it is nontrivial. Explicit statements of such constraints must be made in any fully specified sociolinguistic theory.

In the absence of any such theory the parameters by which sociolinguists have defined groups (e.g., age, ethnicity, place of origin) have no explanatory value; they are strictly descriptive. They do, however, have predictive value with respect to determining which speakers are likely to have had similar language acquisition experience. Such predictions can be given only in probabilistic terms.

Assumptions of a homogeneous speech community relate to particular grammars. Sociolinguistic theory must attempt to explain differences among such communities, as well as explaining their internal homogeneity. To state that groups that are different have differing acquisition ecologies, may explain why they remain distinct, but does not explain the source of the difference. As Bloomfield (1933: 47) observed, the source of differences could be pushed back generation by generation to the dawn of mankind. Obviously, all of that data is not available. Linguistic theory must provide hypotheses of the causes of diversification.

There is one cause of continuing diversification that has received some attention in studies of bilingualism, but generally has not been considered in generative studies. The primary linguistic data which confronts a child derives from more than one speaker, and thus from more than one idiolectal grammar. There is no necessity that the grammars generating those data be equivalent. Thus a child's mother may understand sentence (1) to mean that none of the dishes has been washed, while the child's father understands (1) to mean that some but not all of them have been washed.

(1) All of the dishes haven't been washed.

How does the child understand such a sentence? Is it ambiguous? Will all children confronting such a situation independently arrive at a single interpretation, and what would it be? A fully specified linguistic theory must be able to make predictions about such situations, just as it must predict for homogeneous situations. Bloomfield claimed that "Every speaker's language, except for personal factors which we must here ignore, is a composite result of what he has heard other people say (1933: 46)." In generative terms this might suggest integration into a single composite grammar. Bailey (1973), on the other hand, predicts that children would distinguish the different sources and develop grammars for discrete lects. The two ideas make different predictions about the nature of language change. At this point there is little empirical evidence for judging between them. A comprehensive sociolinguistic theory, however, must address interpersonal variation as well as interpersonal homogeneity if human language behavior is to be explained.

There have been numerous observations (e.g., Carden 1972, 1973; Elliott, Legum & Thomson 1969) that certain grammatical differences do not appear to be distributed in speech communities according to geographical or social parameters in the way many social dialect features are. It may well be that the critical examples needed to determine some grammar characteristics are not at all present, or not present in sufficient quantity in the primary language data to effect natural language acquisition.

Most of the reported instances of what Carden has called random variation appear to involve features of complex syntax, e.g., the relative scope of quantifiers and negation, or the identity constraints on While-clause reduction. They do not involve, for example, the order of subject and predicate, or the structure of relative clauses, both grammatical features which vary across languages, but are present in abundance in any natural language acquisition ecology. The idealization of the homogeneous speech community suggests as a research strategy that it would be of great interest to determine whether or not these constructions which appear to evidence random variation are in variation across siblings. If differences are found, even between close siblings, what generalizations characterize the linguistic structures that are found to be in variation?

The duality of language as an attribute of the individual and language as an attribute of the community has plagued linguistics for decades. From it comes the dichotomy of *langue* and *parole*, and in some respects that of competence and performance. Rather than attempting to compromise this duality, linguistic theory ought to accept and explain both the individual and the social nature of language.

Within the idealization of the homogeneous language community, nothing stands or falls by determining the locus of a grammar. It matters little whether grammars are predicated of individuals or of the community. In fact, a single grammar can be posited as a grammar for each individual in the community and also for the community in aggregate. This symmetry, however, obtains only under the idealization of homogeneity. Conceptually this can be viewed as a conventional grammar posited for each individual in the community and a set of grammars posited for the community in aggregate. The set has the strong constraint that all member grammars are identical, or at least equivalent. As one moves from idealized homogeneity to reality what changes is the nature of the constraints on membership in the set.

Real language communities are not perfectly homogeneous, but the degree and type of heterogeneity is different in different communities. This suggests two different, but interrelated approaches to empirical research; one primarily linguistic, the other primarily social.

The substantive linguistic problem is to determine the sets of grammars that describe real language communities. The theoretical linguistic problem is to determine the linguistic constraints on such sets. These linguistic problems are not unlike those found in the pursuit of language universals. The important difference is that in this case there is a limiting factor: communication must be possible among the languages generated by the grammars of the set.

The social problem is to determine the social correlates of different degrees of linguistic heterogeneity. Much of current sociolinguistic research attempts to isolate groups that are relatively homogeneous sociologically, and then to characterize the central linguistic tendencies of these groups. Recognition that linguistic homogeneity is an idealization suggests that what is of interest is the nature of the linguistic heterogeneity within such groups. Are such social groups truly more homogeneous than society at large? Given the linguistic differences that are observed among social groups that is certainly the case.

The present, highly fragmented idiolectal approach to theoretical studies of English syntax might suggest that there are no constraints on the set of possible grammars to be found within a language community. However, the grammars evidenced in natural language communities are not just random amalgams of the grammars evidenced by real speakers chosen arbitrarily from the languages of the world. A sociolinguistic theory must seek to formalize the constraints on these sets.

One early attempt to specify constraints on natural sets of grammars was the implicational array, or Guttman scale model (DeCamp 1970, Stolz & Bills 1968). This model, which would arrange in a single linear additive order all grammars of the language community, has provided a model for discussing the sets of grammars of several speech communities. Bailey's (1973) wave model can be viewed as another attempt to formalize such constraints. Variable rules as developed by Labov and elaborated by Cedergren & Sankoff (1974) represent another approach.

The relationship between conventional generative thory and a sociolinguistic theory capable of confronting heterogeneous language communities is fairly straight forward. Under the idealization of homogeneity the constraint on the relationship among member grammars is in a weak sense, equivalence, or in a strong sense, identity. This idealization of homogeneity derives from a theoretical claim about the nature of language acquisition. Equivalence of grammars derives from congruence of language acquisition ecologies. An adequate sociolinguistic theory must ultimately attempt to determine the constraints on sets of individual grammars in real language communities as a function of congruence of real language acquisition ecologies. Only in that case does homogeneity become a theoretical idealization as defined by Hempel.

Redefining homogeneity as a theoretical idealization provides a basis for incorporating the necessary general principles to account for observed linguistic heterogeneity, or interpersonal variation into a sociolinguistic theory. It does not, however, bring the problems of intrapersonal variation within the scope of the theory. As was pointed out earlier, there is substantial commonality across the technical vocabularies of sociolinguistics and conventional theoretical linguistics. There remains, however, one fundamental gap. This is a disagreement over what constitutes the data of language.

Sociolinguists who look at intrapersonal variation draw their data from the actual utterances of speakers of the language community in which they are interested. Theoretical linguists in the Chomskyan tradition use as data the potential utterances of a language. Sociolinguists base their study on sentence tokens; theoretical linguists base their study on sentence types. This distinction is important because it circumscribes the evidence available for disconfirming any theory. As long as the two sub-disciplines use mutually exclusive sources of evidence, there is limited potential for an integrated theoretical base.

The sociolinguistic study of intrapersonal variation has shown that the probabilities with which certain grammatical processes operate, i.e., the number of times a process is predicted to occur out of the number of times that it has opportunity to occur, are themselves linguistically meaningful; they are stable, nonrandom, conditioned by linguistic contexts, subject to natural linguistic processes, and capable of transmission across generations. The notion of probability is not directly interpretable in conventional grammars.[3]

It is not meaningful to speak of rates of variation with respect to language defined as the set of possible sentence types. Consider for example the deletion of postvocalic /r/. In the conventional theory, the set of English sentences contains all the possible /r/-ful sentences, including (2):

(2) It's hard to start the car.

It also contains a set of sentences identical to the set of all possible /r/-ful sentences except that they are all /r/-less as in (3):

(3) It's haɾd to staɾt the caɾ.

And the language also contains a set of sentences identical to a subset of the above, except that they include all the possible combinations of /r/-fulness and /r/-lessness within sentences, including for example (4 a—c):

(4) a. It's hard to start the caɾ.
    b. It's haɾd to staɾt the car.
    c. It's hard to staɾt the car.

If a grammar is a formal theory accounting for the above sets of sentence types, what could it possibly mean to claim that speakers delete or vocalize /r/ more often if it is followed by a consonant than if it is sentence final? Such a claim, if it were true, would yield no insight into the process of /r/ deletion. If would rather be an artifact of English sentences, e.g., most sentences being longer than two words, there are more positions within sentences for /r/ to occur and thus be deleted, than there are sentence-final positions. Or, if one observes Labov's principle of accountability, and gives the relative frequency of deletion in each environment, no difference is possible, since for every /r/-ful sentence, there is another /r/-less sentence (type), given the environments of interest.

The result of this incompability in terms of what constitutes evidence of a theory renders all of the work in probabilistic models meaningless in contemporary generative theory. Chomsky has explicitly and unequivocably rejected probability as an aspect of grammar, but for a different reason:

> ... No sense has ever been given to the notion of 'probabilities or continuum type scales' ... in the domain of grammatical description; and every concrete proposal that has been made has been shown to lead to absurdity. Perhaps the time has come for

---

[3] Berdan (1975) presents a fuller discussion of the role of probabilistic grammars in sociolinguistic theory.

linguists who insist on the importance of such notions to face this simple fact (1966: 36).

One reason for this rejection is that he finds the determination of sentence probabilities incompatible with the possibility of creating novel utterances:

> Since most of the 'normal sentences' of daily life are uttered for the first time in the experience of the speaker-hearer (or in the history of the language, the distinction hardly being important at this level of frequency of occurrence), they will have had probability zero before this utterance was produced and the fact that they are produced and understood will be incomprehensible in terms of a 'probabilistic theory of grammar' (1966: 35).

Even non-novel utterances have a probability that approaches zero, as Chomsky has pointed out subsequently:

> It must be recognized that the notion 'probability of a sentence' is an entirely useless one, under any known interpretation of this term. On empirical grounds, the probability of my producing some given sentence of English — say, this sentence, or the sentence, "Birds fly" or "Tuesday follows Monday" or whatever — is indistinguishable from the probability of my producing a given sentence of Japanese ... except for a trivial set, all such probabilities will be empirically indistingushable on empirical grounds, within or outside of the language (1969: 267, 268).

The problem with the theory of grammar that Chomsky objects to is not that it is a probabilistic model. The problem is rather that the grammatical models referred to claim that the important linguistic relationships in sentences are the contiguities of lexical items and of other surface morphemes. The problem with such Markovian models of language exists independently of any attempt to assign probabilities to the transitions between states (i.e., lexical items). Determination of probabilities of such transitions does not make the models adequate for natural language. By the same token the inadequacy of any conceivable probabilistic mode is not established either. Rather, as Suppes (1970: 99) points out, "The use of a probabilistic grammar in no way entails a commitment to finite Markovian dependencies in the temporal sequence of spoken speech."

Reviewing Chomsky's assessment of probabilistic grammars, Suppes (1971) argues at length that Chomsky has missed the point in his rejection of them, that he "writes without familiarity with the way in which probability concepts are actually used in science (1971: 30)." Suppes agrees that the probability of any actual sentence is close to zero, but points out that so is any particular observed sequence of a thousand flips of a coin ($2^{-1000}$ assuming the coin to be true). Further, if one assumes an infinite number of trials (as the set of English sentences is often assumed to be infinite), the probability of any particular sequence is strictly zero.

From the observation that the probability of any of the infinitely possible sequences is zero, it in no way follows that the probability associated with any particular toss of the coin is of no interest. In the same way one can meaningfully discuss probabilities associated with particular decision points in the grammar (e.g., optional rules) even if the probability of any particular surface string is of no empirical interest.

Rejecting the Markovian probabilistic grammar, however, still does not remove the fundamental incompatibility between conventional grammars and probabilistic grammars of the kind employed by Suppes or those found in the work of Sankoff, Cedergren, and their colleagues. The incompability can be resolved, though, by appealing to the notion of idealization. In his arguments against what he calls "corpus grammars", Chomsky makes it clear that the actual occurrence of particular sentences is of no import to the theory. Thus, no violence is done to conceptualize a generative theory as a theory about languages whose sentences occur at the extreme idealized frequency of zero times. The conceptualization is analogous to the ideal gas that has zero mass. In this idealized theoretical framework, probabilities of sentence occurrence and probabilities of rule application are undefined. The relatioinship of the ideal case to sociolinguistic theory, however, is well-defined. Frequency of occurrence is a metrical concept. When the frequency of occurrence of any utterance increases to one or greater, it functions as evidence not only in an idealized competence theory but also in the broader sociolinguistic framework.

It is this use of idealizations in conventional linguistic theory that results in its classification by Ringen (This volume) as a nonempirical scientific theory. Linguistic theory is comparable in this respect to formal logic or mathematics. The adequacy of conventional generative grammars is not judged on empirical facts, i.e., actual utterances by native speakers. Conventional generative grammars generate not natural languages, but formal languages, consisting of sets of formal sentences, with an utterance frequency of zero. Attempts to assess the congruence of these formal languages generated by formal grammars, and natural languages spoken by real speakers, usually treated under the rubric of "acceptability," regularly go awry because the heterogeneity of real language communities: some speakers find a theoretical sentence to be an acceptable representation of a real sentence and other speakers do not (cf Elliott, et al. 1969, Legum, Elliott & Thompson 1973). Within a sociolinguistic theory that expects real language communities to be represented by sets of grammars. that heterogeneity does not present a problem. It does, however, point up the need for caution in moving between ideal and real levels of the theory.

From this perspective conventional generative theory represents a single, special case within a broader sociolinguistic theory. That relationship, as Chomsky correctly assessed, results from the use of idealizations. In practice, however, the idealized case has not always been distinguished from the use of real language in real language communities.

This confounding of real and ideal has come about because linguistics is and always has been the study of real language, Chomsky's (1965: 3) disclaimer notwithstanding.

When DeCamp first raised has question of whether a sociolinguistic theory were possible, he characterized much of the then current work in sociolinguistics as butterfly collecting. His reference was to what Northrup (1947, cited in Hempel 1965: 139) considered the "natural history stage of inquiry." Clearly, much more butterfly collecting remains to be done before sociolinguistics can proceed to what Northrup characterized as the subsequent "stage of deductively formulated theory." Nonetheless, it is fruitful to speculate about what might ultimately characterize an adequate deductively formulated sociolinguistic theory.

In its narrowest interpretation, sociolinguistic theory idealizes to complete homogeneity. It thus abstracts away from the problems of heterogeneity in order to characterize basic linguistic processes. In its broadest interpretation, a sociolinguistic theory relaxes any constraint of mutual intelligibility on the concept of membership in a language community. Focusing in this way on language as a human phenomenon, the development of language universals provides a mechanism for stating constraints on possible grammars within the set of all human languages. It is the vast area between those limits which now requires theoretical specification. Only by relating constraints on naturally occuring sets of grammar to conguence of language acquisition ecologies can linguistics develop explanations of natural language heterogeneity and of language change.

This sketchy characterization of a sociolinguistic theory argues, as did Labov himself, that sociolinguistics is not something apart from linguistics. However, the relationship between their respective theories is not that which one might infer from their roles in general linguistic practice. A sociolinguistic theory must be far more encompassing of natural language phenomena than is conventional generative-transformational linguistic theory. As shown here, conventional linguistic theory must be deduced from more general theoretical sociolinguistic concepts by the imposition of idealized limits on variation. From this perspective the idealizations specified by Chomsky in *Aspects* are not the place at which sociolinguists and other linguists part company. Rather, they provide a formal mechanism for maintaining the unity of the discipline.

References

Bach, E. 1974. *Syntactic theory*. New York: Holt, Rinehart and Winston.
Bailey, C.-J. N. 1973. *Variation and linguistic theory*. Arlington, Virginia: Center for Applied Linguistics.
Berdan, R. 1975. On the nature of linguistic variation. Unpublished Ph. D. dissertation, University of Texas at Austin.
Bloomfield, L. 1933. *Language*. New York: Holt, Rinehart and Winston.
Carden, G. 1972. Multiple Dialects in multiple negation. In: P. Peranteau, J. B. Levi & G. C. Phares (eds.) *Papers from the Eighth Regional Meeting Chicago Linguistic Society*. Chicago, Illinois: Chicago Linguistic Society. Pp 32—40.
— (1973) Dialect variation and abstract syntax. In: R. W. Shuy (ed.) *Some new directions in linguistics*. Washington, D. C.: Georgetown University Press. Pp 1—35.
Carnap, R. 1937. *The logical syntax of language*. London: Routledge & Kegan, Paul.
Cedergren, H. C. J. & Sankoff, D. 1974. Variable rules: performance as a statistical reflection of competence. *Language* 50. 333—355.
Chomsky, N. A. 1957. *Syntactic structures*. The Hague: Mouton.
— 1965. *Aspects of the theory of syntax*. Cambridge, Massachusetts: M. I. T. Press.
— 1966. *Topics in the theory of generative grammar*. The Hague: Mouton.
— 1969. Some empirical assumptions in modern philosophy of language. In: S. Morgenbesser, P. Suppes & M. White (eds.) *Philosophy, science, and method; essays in honor of Ernest Nagel*. New York: St. Marin's Press. Pp 260—285.
— 1972. Some empirical issues in the theory of transformational grammar. In: P. S. Peters (ed.) *Goals of linguistic theory*. Pp 63—130.
— 1975. Questions of form and interpretation. *Linguistic Analysis* 1. 75—109.
DeCamp, D. 1970. Is a sociolinguistic theory possible? In: J. E. Alatis (ed.) *Report of the twentieth annual Round Table Meeting on Linguistics and Language Studies*. Washington, D. C.: Georgetown University Press. Pp 157—173.
Elliott, D., Legum, S. E., & Thompson, S. A. 1969. Syntactic variation as linguistic data. In: R. Binnick et al. (eds.) *Papers from the fifth regional meeting of the Chicago Linguistic society*. Chicago, Illinois: University of Chicago, Department of Linguistics, Pp 52—59.
Hempel, C. 1965. *Aspects of scientific explanation*. New York: Free Press.
Katz, J. J. 1966. *The philosophy of language*. New York: Harper & Row.
Katz, J. J. & Bever, T. G. 1976. The fall and rise of empiricism. In: T. G. Bever, J. J. Katz & D. T. Langendoen (eds.) *An integrated theory of linguistic ability*. New York: Crowell. Pp 11—64.
Labov, W. 1970. The study of language in its social context. *Studium Generale* 23. 30—87.
Legum, S. E., Elliott, D. & Thompson, S. A. 1973. Considerations in the analysis of syntactic variation. Paper read at the LSA Meeting, San Diego.
Lopreato, J. & Alston, L. 1970. Ideal types and the idealization strategy. *American Sociological Review* 35. 88—96.
Maher, J. P. 1971. Etymology and generative phonology in traditional lexicon. *General Linguistics* 11. 71—98.
Peters, P. S. (ed.) 1972 a. *Goals of linguistic theory*. Englewood Cliffs: Prentice Hall.
— 1972 b. The projection problem: how is a grammar to be selected? In: P. S. Peters (ed.) *Goals of linguistic theory*. Pp 171—188.
Ringen, J. D. This volume. Linguistic facts: a study of the empirical scientific status of transformational grammars.
Rudner, R. 1966. *Philosophy of social science*. Englewood Cliffs, New Jersey: Prentice Hall.
Stolz, W. & Bills, G. 1968. An investigation of the standard-nonstandard dimension of Central Texan English. Final Report to O.E.O. Austin: The University of Texas.

Suppes, P. 1970. Probabilistic grammars for natural languages. *Synthese* 22. 95—116.
— 1971. Semantics of context-free fragments of natural languages. Technical Report No. 171. Stanford: Institute for Mathematical Studies in the Social Sciences.
Weber, M. 1947. *The theory of social and economic organization.* New York: Oxford Universitay Press. Translated by M. A. Henderson & Talcott Parsons.
— 1949. *On the methodology of social sciences.* New York: Free Press. Edited and translated by E. A. Shils and H. A. Finch.
Wolfram, W. & Christian, D. 1975. Sociolinguistic variables in Appalachian English. Final Report to the NIE, NIE-G-74-0026. Arlington, Virginia: Center for Applied Linguistics.

# II. The Methodological Status of Linguistic Theories

# Linguistic Facts*
## A Study of the Empirical Scientific Status of Transformational Generative Grammars

Jon D. Ringen

## Introduction

0. Transformational generative linguists generally assert that transformational generative grammars are empirical scientific theories. This doctrine is most forcefully stated by Noam Chomsky (1957, 1961, 1962 a, 1962 b, 1966, 1970) who claims that the structure, function, and methods for the evaluation of transformational grammars are analogous to the structure, function, and methods for evaluating explanatory theories in disciplines like physics and chemistry. Chomsky (1957, 49) asserts:

> A grammar of the language L is essentially a theory of L. Any scientific theory is based on a finite number of observations, and it seeks to relate the observed phenomena by constructing general laws in terms of hypothetical constructs such as (in physics, for example) "mass" and "electron." Similarly, a grammar of English is based on a finite corpus of utterance (observations), and it will contain certain grammatical rules (laws) stated in terms of the particular phonemes, phrases, etc., of English (hypothetical constructs). These rules express structural relations among the sentences of the corpus and the indefinite number of sentences generated by the grammar beyond the corpus (predictions). Our problem is to develop and clarify the criteria for selecting the correct grammar for each language, that is, the correct theory of this language.[1]

In this paper, I will challenge the adequacy of this defense of the empirical scientific status of explanatory theories in transformational generative linguistics (TGL).[2] I will show that, given the so-called

---

* I am indebted to C. Ringen and G. Sanders for many hours of enlightening discussion of both substantive and philosophical issues in contemporary linguistics and for reading and making extensive comments on earlier versions of this paper. A. Koutsoudas, J. Wesley Robbins and H. Stephen Straight have also read and made helpful comments on an earlier draft. I also thank the members of the Linguistics Department at the University of Minnesota for providing the stimulating and congenial atmosphere which prevailed throughout the year during which this paper was written (1973—74).

[1] For an almost identical statement see Chomsky (1962 a, 223).
[2] The discussion in this paper focuses exclusively on transformational generative linguistics only because existing fragments of transformational generative grammars are the most precise and explicit theories formulated by contemporary linguists. My critical remarks about the foundations of transformational generative linguistics should not be

"standard view" of empirical science, the Chomskyan defense of the empirical scientific status of TGL is successful only if it is shown that the facts explained by transformational generative grammars (TGGs) are empirical facts. I will then argue that, when considered in the light of current linguistic practice and the standard view of empirical science, linguistic facts seem to be no more (and no less) empirical facts than are certain logical, mathematical, and philosophical facts. These conclusions undermine the Chomskyan defense of the empirical scientific status of TGL and call into question the empirical scientific status of contemporary linguistic theories. In particular, I will argue, if one accepts the standard view of scientific theories, there is stronger reason to believe that TGL as currently practiced, is a non-empirical discipline like logic, pure mathematics, or formal analytic philosophy than there is to believe that it is like any of the empirical sciences.[3]

## The "Standard" View of Science

1. While the assumption is not always explicit, linguists apparently take for granted the standard view of the structure, function, and method for evaluation of explanatory theories in empirical science.[4] It is against the model provided by this view that the empirical scientific status of TGGs is either explicitly or implicitly measured (Bach, 1964, 1974; Botha, 1968; Sanders, 1972).

On the standard view, the *structure* of an ideally explicit empirical theory is that of a set of abstract principles relating the hypothetical constructs of the theory to each other and to descriptions of observable

considered as comments on the relative merits of transformational generative grammars and grammars constructed by linguists who are not of the transformational generative persuasion.

[3] The thesis that TGL is like pure mathematics or formal logic has been suggested elsewhere (Black, 1970, 452, 455; Fodor and Garrett, 1966, 152—154; Hutchinson, 1974; Katz and Postal, 1964, 166; Miller, 1962, 756). To my knowledge, the thesis has never been systematically defended nor have its implications been systematically explored. Whatever novelty this paper exhibits must rest with my defense and examination of this thesis.

Aside from their relevance to the foundations of TGL, my arguments have some wider philosophical interest. In arguing that the methodology of theory evaluation in TGL exhibits no significant differences from that employed in certain of the allegedly non-empirical sciences, I am opening the way for claiming that whatever reasons there are for concluding that TGGs are empirical theories are reasons for concluding that theories in logic, mathematics and formal analytic philosophy are also empirical theories.

[4] For elaborations and defenses of the standard view of scientific theories see Braithwaite (1953), Hempel (1952, 1965, 1966), Nagel (1961), Popper (1959).

phenomena. It is suggested that such a system can be construed as an axiomatic system.[5] The basic general principles (the axioms) of such a system and their logical consequences (the theorems of the system) constitute the general laws alleged to be true of the entities constituting the domain of the theory. In a correct scientific theory, the general laws must be true.

The standard account of theory *evaluation* requires that a scientific theory must be empirically testable in a particular way. It is required that (sets of) empirical laws in conjunction with descriptions of appropriate initial conditions must logically imply descriptions of empirical phenomena. Descriptions of such empirical phenomena constitute the test implications of explanatory laws and theories. In evaluating an empirical theory, test implications are checked against the results of experiments or observations. The deductive chains between empirical laws and their test implications may be of varying lengths and degrees of complexity, and the fit between test implications and results of experiment or observation may not be perfect. It is, however, universally agreed that the deductive chain should be tight, that the test implications themselves should be as precisely stated as possible, and that the closer the fit between test implications and empirical data (results of actually performed experiments and observations) the better confirmed (corroborated) the law or theory being tested. These requirements are intended to insure that even though they can never be established with logical certainty, the explanatory laws and theories of empirical science can be subjected to sharp test against directly observable phenomena. These requirements constitute the basic features of the hypothetico-deductive method of evaluating empirical scientific theories.

Although it is universally agreed that empirical theories must be testable against observable phenomena, what is not so clear and what has only recently received close philosophical scrutiny (see Dretske, 1964, 1969; Hanson, 1961, 1969), is the precise range of entities which count as observable. However, proponents of the standard view of empirical theories at least agree that the kind of phenomena against which empirical theories are ultimately to be tested are states of affairs or events which obtain or take place *at a specified time at a specifiable place.* Karl Popper (1959, 103) asserts that descriptions of observable phenomena (i.e., the observation reports of science) are "statements asserting that an observable event is occurring [occurred] in a certain individual region of space and time." I think it fair to claim that any

---

[5] Sometimes (see Braithwaite, 1953; Carnap, 1956; Hempel, 1952, 1958), but not always (see Hempel, 1970) the structure of an ideally explicit empirical theory is represented as that of a partially interpreted formal system.

proponent of the standard view of empirical theories would accept Popper's restriction on the observation reports of empirical science.[6]

Transformational generative linguists have adopted the standard view that the basic *function* of the empirical laws in a scientific theory is to explain and predict phenomena within the domain of the science to which the theory belongs.[7] In the standard view of scientific explanation, a distinction is usually struck between explanations which involve some statistical or probabilistic laws and those explanations which employ only non-statistical or completely general laws (Hempel, 1962). The latter kind of explanations are customarily called deductive-nomological explanations (D-N explanations). It is D-N explanations which transformational generative linguists intend their theories to provide (Botha, 1968; Sanders, 1974).[8]

The requirements for a correct D-N explanation are usually summarized in the following way: (Hempel and Oppenheim, 1948, 247—249)

$$\underbrace{\phantom{xx}}_{\substack{\text{Logical} \\ \text{deduction}}}\left.\begin{cases} C_1, C_2, \ldots C_n \text{ Statements of initial conditions} \\ L_1, L_2, \ldots L_n \text{ Statements of general laws} \end{cases}\right\} \text{Explanans}$$

$$\longrightarrow E \qquad \begin{array}{l}\text{Description of empirical} \\ \text{phenomenon to be explained}\end{array} \left.\right\} \begin{array}{l}\text{Expla-} \\ \text{nandum}\end{array}$$

Thus, it is required of a correct D-N explanation that:

(1) There be a deductive relation between the sentences constituting the explanans and those constituting the explanandum.
(2) The explanans must contain at least one general law and this must be required for the explanatory deduction.
(3) The sentences in the explanans must be empirically testable.
(4) The sentences in the explanans must be true.
(5) If taken account of in time, the explanans can serve as a basis for scientific prediction.

---

[6]  It should be noted that Popper's restriction is intended to permit a construal of observational data which is neutral between "physicalistic" and "phenomenalistic" views. Thus, it is consistent with Braithwaite's (1953, 8) decision to use "... experience, observation and cognate terms ... in the widest sense to cover observed facts about material objects or events in them as well as directly known facts about the contents or objects of immediate experience." On this broad construal, both pointer readings and private sensations qualify as data against which empirical theories can be tested. Popper explicitly accepts this broad construal (1959, 103).

[7]  Nagel (1961, 4), Hempel and Oppenheim (1948, 245, 249), Hempel (1958, 173; 1965, 333; 1966, 1—2) adopt this view of the function of empirical laws.

[8]  Transformational generative linguists have argued very forcefully for the inappropriateness of statistical laws in linguistics. See for example Chomsky and Miller (1963), Chomsky (1956, 1957, 1964, 1965), Lees (1957), Katz and Fodor (1964).

It needs to be stressed that these conditions are presented as conditions which must be met by *correct* scientific explanations which are completely and explicitly formulated. It is not claimed that meeting these conditions guarantees explanatory significance, nor is it claimed that any putative explanations actually put forward by empirical scientists can be shown to meet all of these conditions. In practice, putative explanations are usually less than completely explicitly formulated, and invariably the sentences in the explanans cannot be known to be true with logical certainty. At best, their truth can only be supported by more or less adequate and extremely limited empirical evidence.

In addition to endorsing the preceding view of "ideal" scientific theories and of correct ideally explicit deductive nomological explanations, many defenders of the standard view of empirical scientific theories defend the following four-way distinction.[9]

|  | EMPIRICAL | NON-EMPIRICAL |
|---|---|---|
| SCIENCE | physics<br>chemistry | formal logic<br>pure mathematics<br>formal analytic philosophy |
| NON-SCIENCE | technology | speculative and rational<br>metaphysics |

If one accepts these distinctions, then defending the empirical scientific status of TGGs requires showing not only (a) that TGGs are *like* theories in the empirical sciences, but also (b) that they are *unlike* theories in the non-empirical sciences and non-sciences. To see the problems this raises, consider the following.

Let $T_1$ be an axiomatic version of some theory in physics, say an axiomatization of Newtonian mechanics. Let $T_2$ be an axiomatic theory of one of the non-empirical sciences, say a set-theoretic axiomatization of

---

9   Among philosophers, Ayer (1946), Braithwaite (1953), Carnap (1934, 1939), Hempel (1945, 1966), Kemeny (1959), Popper (1959) endorse the indicated classification of physics, chemistry, logic, mathematics, and metaphysics. Explicit discussions of the status of formal analytic philosophy are difficult to find, but if one considers the enterprise of "rational reconstruction" (exemplified in the work of Braithwaite (1953), Carnap (1956), Hempel (1962, 1965), Kyburg (1968), Pap (1959), Suppes (1970)) to be a kind of "applied logic" (as Carnap seems to consider it) then Carnap (1934) explicitly characterizes formal analytic philosophy as a non-empirical science. Others implicitly adopt such a characterization of formal analytic philosophy.

The four way classification is challenged in a variety of ways by: Boole (1854), Lakatos (1967), Kalmar (1967), Mill (1843), Putnam (1971, 1974), Quine (1935, 1951, 1954), Weyl (1949).

My discussion does not require that the boundaries between the four types of disciplines be sharply drawn. All that is required is that the disciplines I have mentioned actually are clear cases of the indicated type.

elementary arithmetic. Now suppose that from both of these theories we can logically deduce theorems which (if the theories are adequate) are statements (or descriptions) of facts about objects and phenomena which constitute the domain of the theory. In the first case we should be able to deduce descriptions of facts about physical objects, e.g., $s = 1/2\,g\,t^2$ (Galileo's Law). In the second case, we should be able to deduce statements of facts about numbers, e.g., $2 + 2 = 4$, $3 + 4 = 4 + 3$. Let us call facts described by theorems of correct physical theories *physical facts*, and facts described by theorems of adequate theories of arithmetic *arithmetical facts*.

Claims about physical facts and claims about arithmetical facts play a crucial role in the evaluation of axiomatic theories of physics and axiomatic theories in arithmetic, respectively. In particular, an axiomatic theory in either discipline is adequate only if it can generate as theorems descriptions of the well-attested facts in the domain of the theory. A set-theoretic axiomatization of arithmetic is adequate only if it can generate a statement of the fact that $2 + 2 = 4$. An axiomatization of Newtonian Mechanics is adequate only if it can generate a description of the fact that Galileo's Law obtains for bodies in free fall near the surface of the earth. Either theory would be *inadequate* to the extent that it had as theorems false assertions about (incorrect descriptions of) facts in the domain of the theory. It is also true that axiomatic theories of physics or arithmetic can, at least *in principle*, provide explanations and predictions which conform to conditions 1, 2, 4, and 5 of the requirements on D-N explanations. Thus, there is a substantial analogy between axiomatic theories in physics and axiomatic theories in arithmetic:

> The *structure* of both kinds of theories (at least if formulated with ideal explicitness) is that of an axiomatic system (i.e., an interpreted formal system). (Braithwaite, 1953)
> The theories *function* to explain and predict phenomena in a way which can, *in principle*, satisfy conditions 1, 2, 4, 5, of the requirements on deductive-nomological explanations.
> The *method for evaluating* such theories follows the logic of the hypothetico-deductive method for evaluating scientific theories. (Russell and Whitehead, 1925, 59)

There is, on the standard view, a crucial point at which the analogy between physical theories and arithmetical theories breaks down. Claims about physical facts are crucially different from claims about arithmetical facts. Claims about physical facts are verified or refuted by experiment and observation and hence are empirical claims. Claims about arithmetical facts are not empirical claims; they are not verified or refuted by experiment or observation. To determine whether Galileo's Law obtains, one does some relevant experiments with, and observations of, falling bodies. To determine whether $2 + 2 = 4$, one investigates whether the putative fact is, or is not, a consequence of the relevant rules (or conventions) for using numerals and arithmetical operators (for addition, substraction, etc.). A statement of Galileo's Law describes an *empirical fact*. Statements of arithmetical facts (such as 2 + 2 = 4) are *not* statements of empirical fact. [10]

Many defenses of the empirical scientific status of TGGs fail to establish a distinction between the type of facts predicted and explained by TGGs and arithmetical facts (such as 2 + 2 = 4), facts of logic (such as, any sentence of the form p v — p is true; modus ponens is a valid argument form) or facts of formal analytic philosophy (e.g., facts of inductive logic such as, a contingent statement of the form "All P are Q" is confirmed (to a greater or lesser degree) by an observation of a P that is also a Q, or facts of ethics, such as, one has a duty to help another person when that person is in need or jeopardy, provided that one can do so without excessive risk or loss to oneself). In comparing TGGs to theories in physics, linguists usually emphasize only those points of analogy between empirical and non-empirical theories noted above (see for example Bach, 1974, 15—18). It should be clear that, on the standard view of empirical theories, such comparisons could, at best, only establish that linguistics is a *science* like physics, chemistry, formal logic, pure mathematics, and formal analytic philosophy. [11] Nothing in these comparisons shows that TGGs are more like theories in *empirical* sciences like physics than like theories in *non-empirical* sciences like logic, pure mathematics, and formal analytic philosophy. To establish this latter claim within the framework provided by the standard view of empirical theories, one would need to show that the facts predicted and explained by adequate TGGs are empirical facts and that claims about such facts (i.e., claims about *linguistic facts*) are empirical claims. Usually it is *assumed* that linguistic facts are empirical facts, and that claims about linguistic facts are empirical claims. In what follows, I will be primarily concerned to examine these assumptions, but since there is considerable unclarity in the literature as to what constitutes the subject matter of linguistic theory, I begin my examination by considering what linguistic theories are about.

---

[10] One consequence of the distinction between physical facts and arithmetical facts is that explanations in physics are very different from explanations in arithmetic. Sentences in the explanans of arithmetical explanations are not empirically testable, but sentences in the explanans of explanations in physics are empirically testable. Sometimes this difference is explained by saying that general principles in physical explanations are empirical laws, while the general principles in arithmetical explanations are rules (see for example, Dretske, 1974).

[11] Occasionally, linguists suggest that use of rigorous hypothetico — deductive methods is sufficient to establish that linguistics is an *empirical* science (see Botha, 1971, 40; Bach, 1964, 11; Sanders, 1974).

*The Subject Matter of Linguistics: Four Possible Views*

2. Botha (1971) distinguishes two views on the subject matter of linguistics — *mentalism* and *non-mentalism*. According to the mentalist view, a TGG describes a "mental reality" underlying the speech behavior of a speaker of a natural language, and permits the prediction and explanation of facts about a competent speaker's (tacit) knowledge of his language. On the non-mentalist view, a TGG is a general characterization of a natural language which permits the prediction and explanation of facts about (sets of) sentences in a given natural language.

Proponents of the mentalist view maintain that linguistic theories aim to explain (and predict) a speaker's knowledge of a language (Chomsky, 1965, 19, 24; Katz, 1964, 130—31). Many proponents of this view maintain that explanation in linguistics proceeds by construing TGGs as hypotheses about a competent speaker's internalized representation of the rules of his language (Chomsky and Halle, 1968, 4; Chomsky, 1965, 8, 25; Katz, 1964, 133). On this mentalistic view, the subject matter of a TGG is *a competent speaker's tacit knowledge of his language* (i.e., his linguistic *competence*). Thus, on this view, linguistic competence is, and hence linguistic theories are about, a mental reality underlying actual linguistic behavior (Chomsky, 1965, 4; 1972, 28; Katz, 1964, 130).[12]

Mentalists have different views about the interpretation which should be assigned to their mentalistic claims. In particular, they differ over the degree of "psychological reality" which should be attributed to the hypothetical constructs in linguistic theories. Here we find a spectrum of views, ranging from the (strong) claim that there is an isomorphism between a correct TGG and human mental/neurophysiological processes (Katz, 1964, 129, 130), to the (weak) claim that a correct TGG represents the "substance" but not necessarily the "form" of a speaker's knowledge of his language.[13] Within the spectrum of views that lie between these two extremes, it is useful to strike a single distinction between the *strong mentalist view* and the *weak mentalist view*. According to the strong mentalist view, attributing to a speaker tacit knowledge of the sort characterized by a transformational generative grammar is" . . . empirically justified by the role it plays in explaining the facts of *use* and *understanding* and *acquisition* of language." (Chomsky,

---

[12] On the mentalistic view it is customary to distinguish two separate functions of linguistic theory. A grammar of a particular language represents the language specific knowledge of a competent speaker of a given language. A theory of language (universal grammar) is taken to represent the innate intellectual capacities of a child capable of learning a natural language (Chomsky, 1964, 61—62; 1965, 4, 25, 29). In this paper I am restricting my attention to the discussion of TGGs of particular languages.

[13] This distinction is made in Kiparsky (1968, 171). Kiparsky does not endorse the weak psychological reality claim.

1969, 155) [my emphasis, JDR]. According to the weak mentalist view, knowledge of the sort characterized by a TGG can be attributed to a speaker if the grammar correctly enumerates the sentences of his language and assigns them the correct structural descriptions.[14] It is unclear to me whether any single linguist can be identified as being exclusively committed both in principle and in practice to one rather than the other of these two views.[15] This is not my concern.[16] Both views have been influential.

On the non-mentalistic view, grammars (and theories of language) are characterized as being about *language* and not about mental states or mechanisms underlying the speech behavior of individual speakers (Botha, 1971, 172). Many non-mentalists explicitly construe language as a cultural or social object or institution (Bach, 1964, 3, 97, 182; Katz and Postal, 1964, ix; Sanders, 1970, 67; 1974).[17] It is claimed that (tacit) knowledge of the cultural object in question (i.e., the language or langue) is the linguistic knowledge necessarily shared by all competent speakers of the language (Saussure, 1959; Sanders, 1974). Thus, to characterize *langue* is to characterize an object of which all competent speakers of a given language have knowledge. This view, which is most explicitly endorsed by Sanders (1974), maintains (1) that languages and their constituents (qua cultural objects) are as "real" as any other entities posited by scientific theories, and (2) that such cultural objects exist in a way that is in some sense independent of the mental states or behavior of individual human beings. In saying that language (qua cultural object or social institution) is the subject matter of linguistic theory, non-mentalists like Sanders (1974) are denying that the subject matter of linguistics is some mental reality underlying the linguistic behavior of individual speakers of natural languages.

We can distinguish at least two possible non-mentalist views: *strong non-mentalism* and *weak non-mentalism*. These views differ with respect to the nature and degree of "cultural (or social) reality" attributed to the constructs employed in linguistic theories. Let us distinguish a strong cultural reality claim (made by strong non-mentalists) from a weak

---

[14] Kiparsky (1968, 171) characterizes but does not endorse this view.
[15] Indeed, there is substantial evidence that many writers defend whichever view the occasion demands. In this regard compare Katz (1964, 130—131) with Katz (1966, 116—117), and Chomsky (1965, 49) with Chomsky (1964, 52).
[16] But it does concern psycholinguists. Thus, Judith Green (1972, 99) notes: "a distinct tendency among transformational linguists to protect their theories from psychological evidence ... while at the same time ... making extensive claims about the psychology of cognitive functioning."
[17] The view is apparently inspired by Saussure's (1959, 18) striking comparison between language and a symphony. Sanders and Katz and Postal make this comparison. In addition, Sanders adopts something like Saussure's view that "language is purely social and independent of the individual." (Saussure, 1959, 18).

cultural reality claim (made by weak non-mentalists). A linguist makes a strong cultural reality claim just in case he holds that attributing cultural reality to constructs in a grammar is justified only to the extent that the grammar plays a role in explaining the facts of use, understanding and acquisition of a language by the members of the language communities of the world. On the weak non-mentalist view, a grammar is a theory of *langue* which need only be useful in predicting and explaining facts about a language. It need not be useful in predicting and explaining linguistic behavior. I suspect that no transformational generative linguist holds the strong non-mentalist view.[18] Nevertheless, I have tried to formulate the distinction in such a way that no consistent non-mentalist can hold both the weak and strong views without equivocation. Thus, as described above, the mentalist and the non-mentalist views represent four apparently distinct views about the ontology (or subject matter) of linguistic theories. The views also require four rather different types of research strategies.

Those, like Chomsky and Katz, who endorse the strong mentalist view are committed to claiming that grammars are or at least must be, *in principle*, useful in explaining linguistic performance. Those strong mentalists who adopt the standard view on the evaluation of explanatory theories in empirical science, are committed to developing theories which allow prediction of the empirical phenomena they are attempting to explain. *Thus, psychological reality claims of the strong mentalist are justified only to the extent that the theories he endorses can be shown to yield predictions about, and to be confirmed or corroborated by, observation of actual speech behavior.* A grammar itself need not yield such predictions or explanations. It may be an idealization which represents only one of a variety of factors which interact in the complex phenomena of speech behavior (Chomsky, 1965, 4). As such, a grammar would represent only one component of a performance theory. But if the study of language as conceived by the strong mentalist is to be "no different from the empirical investigation of other complex phenomena" (Chomsky, 1965, 4), then a theory of competence is worth taking seriously as an explanatory theory *only if* it can be used in explaining and making predictions about linguistic behavior. Indeed, the ability to do just that is the ultimate measure of whether the constructs in the linguistic theory are psychologically real.[19] Often those who make this point are charged with misunderstanding the goals of mentalistic linguis-

---

[18] However, it is tempting to attribute the strong non-mentalist view to Labov (see for example Labov, 1971, 494).

[19] This point has been defended in detail by Botha (1968), Derwing (1973), Fromkin (1968), Hutchinson (1974), Schlesinger (1971), Schwartz (1968). Botha (1968, 96—101; 1971, 131—132) describes the kind of data necessary for evaluating strong psychological reality claims as results of "ontological experiments".

tics.[20] I plead not guilty to this charge. My defense rests with my discussion of the weak mentalist view.

That transformational generative grammars can contribute to the empirical scientific explanation of linguistic behavior has yet to be shown. On the strong mentalist view, showing that transformational grammars can make such a contribution requires a psychological theory of performance which, in some sense, incorporates a transformational grammar and which is formulated with sufficient precision to have significant test implications about actual linguistic behavior. In light of the fact that no such theories exist,[21] one might have serious qualms about whether there is currently any reason to expect TGGs to play a significant role as sub-components of psychological theories designed to explain linguistic behavior, but determining whether they can play such a role is undoubtedly an empirical scientific problem and a psychological theory which predicts and explains linguistic behavior would undoubtedly be an empirical scientific theory. Linguists committed to strong mentalist views can legitimately claim to be engaged in an empirical scientific endeavor, but commitment to strong mentalist views carries with it some rather heavy responsibilities.

Adopting a strong mentalist view would require a serious alliance with psychology and a serious concern with the construction and evaluation of theories of linguistic performance.[22] It would require considerable humility about the explanatory significance of current linguistic theories. There are indications that some linguists find these consequences a small price to pay for the potential benefits of a serious theory

---

[20]  The charge of misunderstanding, particularly as made by Chomsky, is perhaps best explained by an apparent tendency (noted by Green, 1972, 99) among linguists to vacillate between strong mentalist claims whose evaluation requires behavioral predictions, and weak mentalist claims whose evaluation may not require such predictions.

[21]  As Fodor (1971, 121) describes the current situation:

> What is at issue is the problem of characterizing the relationship between the "performance" devices psychologists investigate and the "competence models" that grammarians study. In particular, at present there exists no satisfactory account of the relationship between a grammar capable of recursively enumerating the sentences and their structural descriptions, and a device (a performance model) capable of simulating the speaker/hearer by recognizing and integrating utterances of sentences.

Notice that this is not simply the claim that no existing performance theory can account for all relevant data, it is the much stronger claim that there is not even consensus about what role a grammar should *in principle* be expected to play in explanations of linguistic behavior.

[22]  Linguists frequently appear to be insensitive to the nature of such a concern. Indeed, in light of procedures actually *used* in evaluating transformational grammars, strong mentalistic claims made by contemporary linguists have the appearance of arm-chair psychologizing. I shall suggest below that the psychological significance of transformational generative grammars is exactly the same as that of a set-theoretic axiomatization of arithmetic or an axiomatization of some branch of logic.

of linguistic performance (see Derwing, 1973; Hutchinson, 1974). Some mentalists resist going that route. They choose to study competence rather than performance, and they are content to characterize the substance of a competent speaker's knowledge of his language. On this more conservative view, characterizing the *form* of linguistic knowledge is the psychologist's task. In whatever sense the substance of a speaker's knowledge is independent of its form, in that sense mentalistic linguistics is independent of psychology. This is the weak mentalist view. After characterizing the strong non-mentalistic research program, we will return to assess weak mentalist and weak non-mentalist claims that transformational grammars are empirical scientific theories.

Clearly, anyone who accepts the essential correctness of the standard view of the testing of explanatory theories in empirical science will be even less impressed by strong cultural reality claims about TGGs than by strong psychological reality claims about them. Testing cultural reality claims requires a theory of social or cultural behavior (e.g., a sociological, anthropological or social psychological theory) formulated with sufficient precision to permit predictions of the actual linguistic behavior observed in the language communities in question, and no such theory exists. Indeed, to my knowledge, the possible contributions of transformational linguistics in developing such a theory has never been seriously discussed. Consequently, there is little, if any warrant either for strong cultural reality claims about existing TGGs or for strong non-mentalists to conclude that existing TGGs can contribute to the development of empirical scientific theories in sociology, anthropology or social psychology.

In the absence of any seriously tested performance theories, it remains to be shown that TGGs *can* contribute to the empirical scientific explanation of linguistic behavior. Until that is shown, the strong mentalist and the strong non-mentalist have no basis for claiming that TGGs are components of empirical scientific theories and only a weak basis for claiming that they *can* be. They must rest content with claiming that (a) it is *in principle* possible that grammars will be components of such theories, and hence that (b) there is no reason *in principle* why TGL cannot be a sub-branch of psychology, sociology, anthropology or social psychology. In this sense, on either the strong mentalist or the strong non-mentalist view, linguistics could be construed as (potentially) an empirical science. Yet, at present, there is simply no hard evidence that TGGs (or theories of language) will ever support either strong psychological reality claims or strong cultural reality claims.

I suspect that most transformational grammarians will find the preceding methodological discussion exceedingly strange. The idea that usefulness in predicting and explaining actual linguistic behavior should be a condition of adequacy on grammars is an idea which many contemporary linguists resist. To accept such a condition of adequacy would require radical revision of linguistic practice.[23] Linguistic theory has not usually been concerned with linguistic behavior. The strong mentalistic and strong non-mentalistic views are simply *not* descriptive of the goals reflected in the research practice of most transformational grammarians. If current practice is described by any of the four views we have mentioned, it must be described by either the weak mentalist or the weak non-mentalist view. I will return to consider which of these two views best describes current linguistic practice in sections 4 and 5. First, however, it will be useful to consider an example of the kind of explanation linguistic theories provide.


*Explanation in TGL*


3. One frequently cited example of a linguistic explanation involves reflexive pronouns and imperative sentences.[24] Note the following:

(6)  a.  I kicked myself.                    c.  Harry kicked himself.
     b.  You kicked yourself.

(7)  a.  *I kicked me.                        c.  *I kicked yourself.
     b.  *You kicked myself.                  d.  *Harry kicked themselves.

(8)  a.  Leave the room.                      c.  Sweep the floor.
     b.  Go home.                             d.  Buy me a quart of beer.

(9)  a.  Shoot me.                            h.  Shoot us.
     b.  *Shoot myself.                       i.  *Shoot ourselves.
     c.  *Shoot you.                          j.  *Shoot you.
     d.  Shoot yourself.                      k.  Shoot yourselves.
     e.  Shoot Harry.                         l.  Shoot Harry and Tom.
     f.  Shoot him.                           m.  Shoot them.
     g.  *Shoot himself.                      n.  *Shoot themselves.

The *facts* to be explained are the following:

Fact I          A competent speaker of English judges/knows that
                (6 a)—(6 c) and (8 a)—(8 d) and the unstarred strings
                in (9) are sentences in his language, while he knows
                that (7 a)—(7 d) and the starred strings in (9) are not
                in his language.

Fact II         Ordinary pronouns can occur as the objects of
                sentences like those in (9) only if they are first or third

---

[23] Some writers seem to be suggesting that this revision is a crucial part of the Chomskyan revolution (see Katz, 1964). For references to apparent inconsistencies on this point, see footnote 15 above.

[24] Succinct informal presentations of this example are found in Postal (1966), and Lakoff (1968, 1971).

person pronouns, i.e., in such sentences, ordinary second person pronouns cannot occur as objects.

Fact III      Only second person reflexive pronouns can occur as objects in sentences like those in (9); first and third person reflexive pronouns cannot occur as objects.

Fact IV      Structures in which the subject pronoun and the reflexive object pronoun could not have the same referent do not occur as sentences in English. (e.g., there are no sentences in which the subject is a first person pronoun and the object is a second person reflexive pronoun.)

Facts V—VII A competent speaker of English (tacitly) knows that Facts II—IV obtain.

In order to explain these facts, Lakoff (1968) makes the following standard assumptions:

A.    Sentences are analyzed on at least two different levels of structure — deep and surface structure — and there are rules relating these structures.

B.    The structures underlying (6 a), (6 b), and (6 c) are respectively
  (6 a′)   I kicked I.
  (6 b′)   You kicked you.
  (6 c′)   Harry kicked Harry.

C.    The structures underlying imperatives like (8 a)—(8 d) are respectively
  (8 a′)   You leave the room.
  (8 b′)   You go home.
  (8 c′)   You sweep the floor.
  (8 d′)   You buy me a quart of beer.

Given the postulated deep structures (which in a fuller account would be represented as phrase markers formulated in some abstract technical notation) it is argued that Facts I—VII can be explained by a transformational grammar which provides appropriate rules which operate on these deep structures to yield all of the sentences and none of the non-sentences which are exhibited above. Thus Lakoff assumes two transformational rules:

D.    Reflexive Transformation: replaces the objects in structures like those underlying (6 a)—(6 c) with the appropriate reflexive pronouns.

E.    Imperative Formation Transformation: deletes second person subjects of the deep structures of imperative sentences.

Lakoff's explanation for Fact I consists of (i) the assumptions that

F.    The grammar of English is a transformational grammar that contains the components mentioned above.

G.  The grammar describes part of the tacit knowledge of competent
    speakers of English.

and (ii) the fact that (6 a)—(6 c), (8 a)—(8 c), and the unstarred strings
in (9) are generated by such a grammar while (7 a)—(7 d) and the
starred strings in (9) are not.

The suggested explanation for Facts II—IV is that the general facts
about English imperative sentences containing reflexives which are
described by Facts II—IV are also general facts about the set of strings
generated by the grammar. For example, it can be shown that all the
sentences (grammatical strings) which occur in (9) and none of the
ungrammatical strings, are generated by the grammar. In this sense, it is
claimed that Facts II—IV are explained (and may even have been
predicted) by the grammar of English in question. The explanation of
Facts V—VII requires, in addition, the assumption G above.

If the preceding sketch of the sort of explanation provided by transformational linguists is representative, then several things are clear. First,
linguistic explanation are explanations provided by grammars of specific
languages, or more precisely, they are explanations provided by fragments of such grammars.[25] Second, what can be *deduced* from such
grammars are strings which constitute *sentences* in the language. The
constraints on the derivations, as codified in the rules of the grammar,
are said to *explain* such facts as Facts II—IV above; these facts are facts
about (set of) *sentences.* Third, when conjoined with the assumption that
the grammar describes the tacit knowledge of a competent speaker, the
grammar is alleged to *explain* facts about a speaker's knowledge of his
language. Facts of this sort are exemplified by Facts I, and V—VII
above. Without the assumption that grammars represent the tacit knowledge of a competent speaker (assumption G above), no descriptions of
facts about a speaker's knowledge of his language can be deduced from
the explanans in a grammatical explanation. Fourth, nowhere in this
discussion has anything been said about the prediction or explanation of
the *actual utterances* or *actual judgments* about utterances of individual
speakers at particular times and particular places.

Transformational generative linguists (e.g., Chomsky, 1964; 1965;
Lees, 1957, 391; Postal, 1966, 170) frequently claim that linguistic
theories *are* designed to predict and explain *facts about sets of sentences* or

---

[25]  In what follows, I will focus primarily on the empirical scientific status of the theories
      which are alleged to provide such explanations. This is a significant task, since such
      putative explanations are exactly what transformational linguists characteristically give
      as examples of the kinds of explanations which they aim to construct.
      In the cited examples, I concentrate primarily on the explanation of syntactic facts, but
      transformational grammars are, of course, also intended to be used to provide explana-
      tions for semantic and phonological features of language.

*facts about a competent speaker's (tacit) knowledge of his language* and *are not* designed to predict and explain *actual utterances* or *actual judgments about utterances* of individual speakers at particular times and particular places. However, some distinctions implicit in this view are frequently overlooked and their implications are seldom explored. Thus, it has been claimed that TGGs can explain and predict (a) speaker judgments/intuitions about utterances (Chomsky, 1962 a, 158, 167—168), (b) speaker knowledge about *sentences* (Chomsky, 1962 b, 531), (c) the occurrence of (certain kinds of) utterances (Chomsky, 1961, 223), (d) facts about (sets of) sentences (Postal, 1966, 158), (e) facts about a competent speaker's knowledge of his language (or facts about sets of sentences in his language) (Postal, 1966, 160). Frequently, the context in which such facts are mentioned suggests that facts about sentences, facts about speaker's knowledge of such facts, and facts about selected utterances or selected introspective judgments/intuitions about utterances, are all the same kind of fact (see for example, Chomsky, 1964, 79; 1972, 27). There are, however, important differences among these sorts of facts, and noting these differences is a first step in clarifying the methodological status of TGGs.

Putative linguistic facts like:

(10) "Flying planes can be dangerous." is an ambiguous sentence in English.
(11) "John is eager to please." and "John is easy to please." are sentences of two different sorts.
(12) English reflexive sentences have underlying objects which are identical to their underlying subjects.

may be predicted and explained by linguistic theories, but descriptions of such facts are not descriptions of events or states of affairs which are observable in Popper's sense.[26] In contrast, occurrences of spoken utterances, sentence tokens in written texts, and the introspective judgments of individual native speakers about expression tokens can qualify as

---

[26] Defenders of the standard view of empirical scientific theories (e.g., Carnap, 1956; Hempel, 1952) customarily strike a distinction between observational terms and theoretical terms, and argue that theoretical terms (or theoretical constructs) cannot be explicitly defined by reference to observation terms and that statements containing theoretical terms are never equivalent to any finite set of statements about observable phenomena. It is claimed that theoretical terms are implicitly defined by those general principles which constitute the basic postulates of the theory and are related via "correspondence rules" to descriptions of possible observable phenomena. Bar-Hillel (1957, 324 ff) argues that terms used in describing linguistic facts (e.g., sentence, grammatical, verb phrase, etc.) are theoretical terms in the preceding sense. Chomsky (1957, 49) and Fromkin (1968, 53) seem to be endorsing a similar view. Chomsky (1965, 18) asserts that facts predicted and explained by linguistic theories "Like most facts of interest and importance . . .[are not] . . . presented for direct observation . . ."

observable events of the sort identifies by Popper. Reports of such events or states of affairs could count as observation reports against which empirical theories could be evaluated.

In recognition of the differences between the putative facts which could be predicted by a grammar and reports of the occurrence of utterances or speaker judgments about utterances, let us strike a distinction between *facts about utterances* and *facts about sentences* (or *facts about language*).[27] Thus, facts about utterances constitute facts about the actual linguistic behavior of individual speaker-hearers, including their expressed intuitions and introspective judgments about utterances. At least some assertions of fact about utterances are reports of observable events occurring in specific regions of space and/or time. Assertions of fact about sentences or facts about language include assertions about sentence structure and meaning. Assertions of fact about sentences or about languages are not descriptions of events or states of affairs which can be observed occurring in specific regions of space and time. Nor are assertions such as:

(13) A competent speaker of English (tacitly) knows or understands that (12) obtains.

Assertion (13) is an example of what we will call *facts about a competent speaker's (tacit) knowledge* of his language. Attributing tacit knowledge or understanding of (10) or (11) to a speaker would provide further examples of such putative facts. I will use the term *linguistic facts* to refer to both facts about language (or facts about sentences) and facts about a competent speaker's tacit knowledge of his language. Distinguishing linguistic facts from facts about utterances is of utmost importance in assessing the empirical scientific status of linguistic theories, because it indicates how the relation between theoretical constructs and empirical verifications in TGL can initially be conceived and profitably discussed.

From TGGs one can derive predictions of putative facts about sentences and putative facts about a competent speaker's tacit knowledge of his language. If grammars are empirical theories, these predictions need to be tested by experiment or observation. It is claimed by many transformational generative linguists that observations of actual utterances and actual speaker judgments constitute the empirical data in terms of which predictions of linguistic theories are tested.[28] So far, this picture is at least consistent with the standard description of hypothesis testing in empirical science. But, if one adopts the standard view of

---

[27] Here I am following a suggestion of Dretske (1974). This distinction is also explicit in Bach (1964, 4, 182—183), Bar-Hillel (1966, 394), Chomsky (1962 b, 531), and Lees (1957, 391).

[28] Bach (1964, 3—4, 182—183), Botha (1968, 64), Chomsky (1961, 223—225; 1962 a, 158, 167, 168; 1964, 79; 1966, 10), Lees (1957, 391), Sanders (1972, 36, 38, 41—43).

empirical theories, a serious defense of the empirical scientific status of linguistic theories must establish that reports of actual speech behavior and reports of actual speaker judgments about utterances are appropriately used in testing predictions derivable from linguistic theories (i.e., descriptions of putative linguistic facts). That is, the relation between linguistic facts and facts about utterances needs to be carefully specified. Difficulties involved in specifying this relation are exactly the difficulties involved in specifying how predictions from linguistic theories should be tested. In what follows, we will examine how contemporary linguists address the testing problem both in principle and in practice.

### Testing linguistic hypotheses: two principles of data selection

4. On the classical Saussurian view, linguistics is not concerned with predicting and explaining linguistic behavior. Linguists inspired by this view frequently reject the suggestion that explanatory success in linguistics depends on alliances with collateral disciplines whose concern is primarily with the explanation of human behavior.[29] Both weak mentalists and weak non-mentalists approvingly cite Saussure's (1959, 9—13) distinction between *langue* and *parole* and agree that the subject matter of linguistic theories is not linguistic behavior *(parole)*. They apparently agree that "linguistic description can be no more concerned with the speech performance of members of a language community than a physicist is concerned *per se* with meter readings" ... (Katz, 1966, 116—117). As Sanders (1974) notes, the claims made by linguistic theories "are tested through observations of human behavior, but they are not *about* human behavior."

It is usually maintained that the kinds of observations of human behavior used as linguistic data are observations of the actual utterances of competent speaker-hearers and reports of speaker judgments. In describing this data, Chomsky (1961, 223) asserts:

> ... I have been concerned with such data as
>
> (1) (a) phonetic transcriptions
>     (b) judgments of conformity of utterance tokens [i.e., intuitive sameness-difference judgments that are fundamental to descriptive phonology, p 224]
>     (c) judgments of well-formedness
>     (d) ambiguity that can be traced to structural origins
>     (e) judgments of sameness or difference of sentence type
>     (f) judgments concerning the propriety of particular classifications or segmentations

Appended to Chomsky's list is a short description of each item that makes it clear that phonetic transcriptions are taken to be reports of

---

[29]  Such as psychology, neurophysiology, sociology, or anthropology.

actual utterances produced by speakers of a given language, and that the kinds of data listed as (1) (b) to (1) (f) can all be described as reports of speaker judgments about actual speech events. Descriptions of this sort are, of course, descriptions of facts about utterances; they do not constitute the class of facts which TGGs can predict and explain. Yet both weak mentalists and weak non-mentalists would certainly accept descriptions of such facts as the kinds of linguistic data against which their theories are tested. *They claim that these data constitute the evidence used in evaluating predictions about linguistic facts derived from TGGs.* To determine whether linguistic facts are empirical facts, we need to consider how putative linguistic facts and linguistic data are *related.*

It is frequently implied that data such as that listed above is useful only if it reflects the *actual* linguistic intuitions of native speakers. This presents some problems. Notorious methodological difficulties accompany the search for the *actual* linguistic intuitions of native speakers. At very least, speaker judgments used as data should be judgments of a *reliable* informant.[30] Even if we assume that linguists select and use reliable informants, we can still ask: Which judgments of reliable informants should be selected for use as linguistic data? Chomsky has frequently addressed essentially this question; he suggests that:

> ... in order to set the aims of grammar significantly it is sufficient to assume a partial knowledge of sentences and non-sentences. That is, we may assume for this discussion

---

[30]  This requirement is not carefully observed in current linguistic practice. In particular, it is frequently suggested that the transformational grammarian qua theorist can act as his own informant (Chomsky, 1965, 18). And linguists frequently do act as their own informants (Labov, 1971, 442). In an empirical science this state of affairs should be viewed with suspicion. Theoreticians frequently have a stake in preserving thier theories. When theoreticians act as their own experimenters, a strong possibility of experimenter bias is introduced. When the number of "experiments" or observations is extremely small, the problem becomes particularly acute. These considerations underpin the stipulation that objective theory testing requires explicit safeguards against bias. When a grammar writer acts as his own informant (particularly if he acts as his only informant) explicit safeguards against bias are simply ignored. But even among unbiased informants, reliability is not assured.

Informant reliability is not simply absence of bias. Informant reliability requires consistency of judgments. Chomsky (1964, 79) has suggested that a possible check on informant reliability would be to sample the judgments reported by the informant on the same items on several occasions under different circumstances. As far as I know, such a longitudinal study of an informant has never been done by a transformationalist. Reliability, of course, is not all that is desired of an ideal informant. By hypothesis, linguistic intuitions "exist independently" of informant reports. The competence-performance distinction stands or falls with this hypothesis. An informant's reports of his own intuitions can be wrong. Hence, it must be required of an ideal informant that what he reports strongly correlates with his *true* linguistic intuitions. Not surprisingly, Labov (1971, 430) reports that the problem of identifying ideal informants remains unsolved. This problem is the problem of assessing the reliability and *validity* of introspective judgments (see footnote 34 below).

that certain sequences of phonemes are definitely sentences, and that certain other sequences are definitely non-sentences. In many intermediate cases we shall be prepared to let the grammar itself decide, when the grammar is set up in the simplest way so that it includes the clear sentences and excludes the clear non-sentences ... A certain number of *clear cases*, then, will provide us with a criterion of adequacy for any particular grammar. (Chomsky, 1957, 14; my emphasis, JDR)

Transformationalists, of course, are not only interested in sentence grammaticality, but also in other properties of expressions including various relationships among sentences. We need to broaden Chomsky's initially simplified description of the grammarian's task to include the construction of theories which account for cases of ambiguity, synonymy, sameness and difference of sentence type, etc. Given this broader conception, which Chomsky (1957, 85—91) explicitly endorses, the initial point is essentially the same. A TGG should be tested against "clear cases" of such properies and relations. Presumably, clear cases will be taken seriously only if reported by reliable informants.

This characterization of the transformational grammarian's task, which weak mentalists and weak non-mentalists would unite in accepting, suggests the following principle of data selection for transformational generative linguistics:

P(1) Reports of judgments of the sort represented on Chomsky's list (see 1 (b) — 1 (f) on p. 114 above) can be taken to represent native speaker intuitions (and hence evidence for evaluating claims about linguistic facts) when and only when they are the reports of reliable informants about clear cases.

Following well established tradition, let us call P(1) "the clear case principle." The clear case principle provides a useful principle of data selection only if we know what constitutes a clear case, and for whom the case must be clear. Let me discuss each of these questions in turn.

Clear cases can be of two kinds. A given informant will judge that some utterances clearly *are* tokens of expressions having certain properties (e.g., grammaticality) or standing in certain relations (e.g., the synonymy relation), and that other utterances clearly *are not* tokens of expressions having these properties or standing in the specified relations. Between these two extremes there are various degrees of clarity. A given utterance may seem more a sentence than a non-sentence, or more a non-sentence than a sentence. In some cases a judgment either way may seem arbitrary. Chomsky recognizes that clear cases define a continuum and not a simple three-way partition,[31] and introduces the notions of "degrees of grammaticality" and "degrees of acceptability" to accommodate the apparent continuum of cases.[32] The initial trichotomy is a

---

[31] Among tokens of expressions which are (1) clearly grammatical, ambiguous, etc., (2) clearly not grammatical, ambiguous, etc., and (3) not clear cases at all.
[32] See Chomsky (1957; 1961, 231—239; 1965, 11—12, 148—153).

simplification, but it provides a place to start. While the concept of a clear case still may not be completely clear, in what follows I will assume that it is intuitively clear and that Chomsky's initial simplifying assumption is methodologically legitimate and strategically sound. Evaluation of these assumptions is not crucial for our purposes. A more crucial question is this: For whom must the cases be clear? I can conceive of two very different answers to this question. The two answers constitute two distinct principles for the selection of lingustic data:

P(2) Reports on clear cases to be used as linguistic data must be of judgments shared by all (or a significant sample of) reliable informants.

P(3) Reports on clear cases to be used as linguistic data must be of judgments reported by at least one reliable informant.

I will call the first of these (i.e., P(2)) the weak non-mentalist principle of data selection and the second (i.e., P(3)) the weak mentalist principle of data selection.[33] In what follows I will argue that there are strong reasons for believing that the weak non-mentalist principle does not describe current linguistic practice and that the weak mentalist principle does. The fact that linguistic data need only satisfy the weak mentalist criterion strengthens the analogy between the methodology of hypothesis (theory) evaluation in TGL and that employed in certain branches of the putatively non-empirical sciences.

## Testing linguistic hypotheses: principles and practice

5. What linguists frequently say (as opposed to what they actually do) suggests that the weak non-mentalist principle of data selection is the principle of data selection that they endorse. Such an endorsement is implicit in a number of Chomskys remarks. Chomsky suggests:

> Linguistic theory is concerned primarily with an ideal speaker-listener, in a *completely homogeneous speech-community,* who knows its language perfectly and is unaffected by such grammatically irrelevant conditions as memory limitations, distractions, shifts of attention and interest, and errors (random or characteristic) in applying his knowledge of the language in actual performance. This seems to me to have been the position of the founders of modern general linguistics, and no cogent reason for modifying it has been offered. (1965, 3—4; emphasis mine, JDR)

---

[33] I would argue that the terminology that I have adopted is appropriate. It reflects my original distinction between mentalism as an attempt to characterize *competence* (which might be construed as a mental reality underlying the speech behavior of *individual* speakers of a language) and non-mentalism as an attempt to characterize *langue* (construed as a cultural object which *all* competent speakers have knowledge of). Insofar as informant judgments reflect shared linguistic knowledge, they must be judgments on which reliable informants agree.

In the passage quoted above, Chomsky suggests an idealization. According to the idealization, linguistic theory is concerned with the linguistic competence of "an ideal speaker-listener in a completely homogeneous speech-community". The ideal speaker-listener is, of course, the theoretical counterpart of a reliable informant. The linguistic intuitions of the ideal speaker-listener are assumed to be approximated in the judgments reported by the most reliable informants which linguists can find. That a given informant is reliable is a crucial empirical assumption. Justifying this assumption raises some serious and interesting problems for linguistic practice.[34] Linguists have barely begun to consider these problems.[35] Nevertheless, we will assume that this portion of Chomsky's idealization is, *in principle*, no more problematic in linguistics than are similar idealizations in other clearly empirical sciences that employ human judges in gathering data.[36] However, the reference to a homogeneous speech community cannot be so lightly passed over.

Presumably, in a homogeneous speech community, the intuitions of all native speakers are identical. In such a community, there might be difficulties in determinig what a given informant's intuitions are, but (performance factors and investigator errors aside): The judgments reported by a single reliable informant will be reports of judgments with which all other reliable informants will agree. But there is evidence that actual speech communities are not homogeneous. Whether a given informant is reporting intuitions shared by members of his actual speech community is an empirical question. It is this kind of empirical question which the weak non-mentalist principle of data selection, P(2), is designed to answer. Chomsky (1964, 79) seems to be entertaining something like P(2) when he says of speaker judgments that "their correctness can be challenged and supported in many ways ... Consistency among speakers of similar backgrounds, and consistency for a particular speaker an different occasions is relevant information." There is

---

[34] It is the problem of checking the reliability and validity of a given person's reports of his introspective observations. For an illuminating and readable survey of these problems, see Boring (1953). Conceptual issues raised by concern with the validity and reliability of intuitive linguistic judgments are discussed in Ringen (1977a, b).

[35] For some illuminating discussions of these problems see Botha (1973, 173—220); Labov (1971; 1972).

[36] There are, however, some interesting differences. Compare linguistics and psychophysics (as Chomsky, 1961, 225, does). Both use reports of introspective judgments as data, but the assumptions required for selecting the reports to be used as data are interestingly different. In linguistics, it must be assumed that the informant is a competent speaker-hearer who is a party to certain conventions of language use. Reports of the informant's intuitions are useful as data only if they reflect those conventions. The reports of introspective judgments used as data in psychophysics are not taken as evidence about what conventions are in force.

substantial evidence, however, that the weak non-mentalist principle of data selection is *not* reflected in what transformational linguists actually do in evaluating transformational grammars.

For the weak non-mentalist, determining which judgments are shared by reliable informants is a necessary part of determining which judgments should be taken to confirm, to disconfirm, or to be irrelevant to the evaluation of any grammars currently existing or yet to be proposed.[37] This is, of course, a kind of problem in which any empirical scientist should be interested. Empirical scientists are not concerned to devise theories to explain putative facts based on observation reports (data) that are either unreliable or known to be false, they have sufficient theoretical problems in accounting for facts based on data that are known to be correct.

The suggestion that transformational generative linguists do serious studies of the patterns of uniformity (and variation) in the informant judgments used as linguistic data (Elliott, Legum, and Thompson, 1968) has been essentially ignored.[38] Occasionally, it is implied that such a study (which I will call an informant survey) would be trivial and of absolutely no interest to transformational linguists. (Lees, 1966, 36—37)

Since transformational generative linguists claim to be empirical scientists and yet apparently have no interest in informant surveys to evaluate their data, I conclude that either the weak non-mentalist principles of data selection are not endorsed in linguistic practice, or if they are endorsed, there is some obvious reason that linguists think that informant surveys are unnecessary. For the moment let me proceed under the assumption that the weak non-mentalist principle is widely accepted by contemporary linguists. Under that assumption, what reason could there be for thinking that it is not necessary to conduct surveys to determine what constitute the clear cases on which reliable informants agree?

One reason might be this: Language is what competent members of a given language community share. Thus, any competent speaker neces-

---

[37] To say this is not to recommend the "majority vote" method (which is clearly far too crude a device for isolating informant agreement) to weak non-mentalists, nor is it to suggest that a weak non-mentalist should have no interest in deviant or even idiosyncratic judgments. Deviant judgments may provide significant evidence about patterns of linguistic variation. Linguists committed to developing theories of *langue* that are useful in the economical characterization of dialectal and idiolectal differences may well find evidence of linguistic variation useful in determining how a grammar for a natural language should be constructed. For discussions of the use of data on linguistic variation in the evaluation of TGGs see: Carden (1970) and Elliott, Legum, and Thompson (1969).

[38] In a more recent article Legum, Elliott,, and Thompson (1974) present an interesting and useful discussion of some evidence of informant agreement and disagreement that might be useful in the evaluation of TGGs.

sarily knows the language of his particular linguistic community. If he did not know the language, he would not be a member of the community in question. Since any reliable informant knows his language, then (everything else being equal), the judgments of one reliable informant are as good as those of another. Indeed, the judgment of one reliable informant is almost as good as the collective judgments of one thousand such informants. Asking for the judgments of many informants is like repeating the same experiment many times. Not only is such repetition dull, it is frequently assumed to be unnecessary in empirical science. In repeating scientific experiments and observations, one rapidly reaches the point of diminishing returns on confirmatorily or disconfirmatorily useful information (see Hempel, 1966, 33—37). In many testing situations the variety of observations is a much more crucial factor than mere quantity. In transformational generative linguistics this implies that a wide variety of judgments from few informants is more valuable than a very narrow range of different judgments from a large number of informants. Data costs time and money, and decisions must be made at least partly in terms of cost effectiveness.[39]

In referring to what he calls "the logic of Saussure", Labov (1971, 443) implies that a variant of the preceding argument is used by transformational generative linguists to justify the use of judgments made by a single native speaker.[40] Although the argument which I have presented is not a faithful reconstruction of Saussure's views, following Labov's suggestive comments, I will call the argument the Saussurian argument.[41]

Without further premises, the Saussurian argument is invalid. Even if linguists were dealing with *perfectly* reliable informants, the fact that the

---

[39] Cost effectiveness considerations don't make the case air tight. A wide variety of judgments by an extremely small number of informants and an extremely small range of judgments by a very large number of informants, constitute a false set of alternatives. They represent the poles on a continuum, and hence inbetween lies considerable variation in the fixed cost ratio of number of informants to number of different kinds of judgments. The cost of data does not explain the traditional reliance on small numbers of informants since many linguistic research projects are extremely well-funded. One suspects that even if time and funds were unlimited, surveying large numbers of informants would be judged an unnecessary and indeed trivial endeavor (as it is in analytic philosophy; for comment see Quine, 1970 and Searle, 1969).

[40] For Labov, the crucial assumption of "the logic of Saussure" is the following proposition: "If *langue* is conceived as the social part of language, and in the possession of every speaker, it should the be possible to obtain data from any one speaker." Labov is, of course, critical of linguists' use of this assumption to justify use of small numbers of informants.

[41] I owe parts of this argument, although not its complete formulation, to Gerald A. Sanders. Some of the assumptions which constitute premises in the argument are also made explicit by Labov (1971). Parts of the argument are familiar to analytic philosophers (see Searle, 1969).

members of a set of reliable informants are native speakers who share knowledge of a given language does not entail that the *introspective judgments* that such informants report will always agree. Native speakers of a given language frequently speak different dialects, and the idiolects of speakers of the same dialect may differ. We need some basis for concluding that intuitions actually reported *are* intuitions shared by all native speakers of the language and *are not* intuitions reflecting only features of the particular idiolect or dialect spoken by the informant. If reports of intuitions are empirical data, then the preceding problem poses an empirical question. One cannot know *a priori* or simply assume that there is a perfect match among the intuitions of native speakers of a given natural language. The Saussurian argument for the unimportance of informant surveys is invalid unless we make assumption which render the distinction between shared and idiosyncratic intuitions simply unnecessary. Hence the Saussurian argument is either invalid or circular.

I know of one other argument that would show that informant surveys are unnecessary. It could be argued that linguists interview their informants in such a way that either the judgments elicited or the judgments selected as data are judgments on which other reliable informants are likely to agree. I will call this the argument from interviewer selectivity.[42]

It may be *possible* to conduct informant interviews so as to achieve the desired end of reliably selecting as data those judgments on which reliable informants would agree. Furthermore, some such interviewing procedures might render informant surveys of only secondary importance.[43] However, the argument serves to establish only that informant surveys are *in principle* of secondary importance. Showing that informant surveys are unnecessary *in practice* requires showing that appropriate interviewing techniques are actually being employed in current linguistic practice. I rather suspect that such practices are not in current use.

I know of no discussions of such interviewing techniques that have appeared in print, and there is little evidence that linguists recognize any obligation to employ interviewing techniques which reliably elicit reports of intuitions which competent speakers share. Indeed, there is considerable evidence that linguists do not feel bound by any such interviewing constraints. Aside from a rather serious lack of concern with

---

[42] This argument was suggested to me by Gerald A. Sanders.

[43] I find it difficult to imagine how the reliability of a given interviewer's selections could be evaluated without evidence that at some time the selections he made were selections of judgments that for the most part were shared by reliable informants other than the informant who made the original judgments. This, of course, would not require that informant surveys were the only way or even the usual way in which evidence about shared intuitions should be gathered.

insuring that informants are reliable, linguists frequently and publicly acknowledge that the reports of intuitions they are using provide data only about the dialect of a single speaker (Botha, 1973, 217—219; Labov, 1971, 441—444). Such acknowledgements characteristically come as responses to evidence of differences between informant intuitions.

Both of the arguments we have considered fail to establish that informant surveys are unnecessary in current linguistic practice. The Saussurian argument is either invalid or circular. The argument from interviewer selectivity requires the use of interviewing techniques not represented in usual linguistic practice. I know of no other arguments which show that informant surveys are unnecessary or of less than fundamental importance for selecting linguistic data. Furthermore, there is substantial evidence that grammars of idiolects are what transformational linguists are primarily concerned to construct (Chomsky and Halle, 1968, 384). Where conflicting informant judgments indicate sifferences of idiolect or dialect, linguists do not conclude that the judgments are not judgments on which a TGG should be based. Rather they conclude that the judgments must be taken into account by different grammars. (Chomsky and Halle, 1968, 249)

I think that we can safely conclude that in contemporary transformational generative linguistics, constructing grammars for informant idiolects is a theoretically significant linguistic task. Transformational generative linguists who accept this conclusion have no responsibility for conducting informant surveys. I believe that this is the only way that responsibility for conducting informant surveys can legitimately be avoided.[44]

Weak mentalists, then, can avoid responsibility for doing informant surveys. They accept the weak mentalist principle of data selection, and they maintain that constructing a TGG for a single idiolect is a theoretically significant task. I think that the weak mentalist assumptions are routinely made in current linguistic practice. I conclude that what constitutes a clear case of the sort required in current practice for the evaluation of a TGG is not determined (even *in principle*) by weak nonmentalist principles of data selection. If this judgment is correct, it explains the current lack of interest in informant surveys, but it is a judg-

---

[44] Linguists who aim to construct grammars for idiolects need not conclude that informant surveys (or their functional equivalents) are of no interest at all. They can agree that informant surveys might be a useful way of determining the boundaries of background or geography within which the homogeneity assumption can legitimately be made. They can also agree that the best test of sameness of dialect or sameness of language is evidence of correlations among judgments reported by reliable informants. What cannot be allowed is that knowledge of the actual linguistic boundaries is a prerequisite for evaluating transformational grammars.

ment which those linguists concerned to defend the empirical scientific status of TGGs should hesitate to accept. Adopting the weak mentalist principles of data selection and rejecting principles of data selection which require informant surveys strengthens the analogy between TGGs and axiomatic theories in logic, pure mathematics, and formal analytic philosophy and weakens the analogy with theories in empirical sciences like physics and chemistry.[45]

### The empirical scientific status of TGGs

6. Those linguists and philosophers who accept the standard view of empirical scientific theories and wish to defend the empirical scientific status of TGGs must establish that claims about linguistic facts are empirical claims. On the standard view, showing that claims about linguistic facts are empirical claims requires showing that they are *evaluated* in ways that are (a) significantly different from the way in which paradigm cases of claims about non-empirical facts are evaluated and (b) very much like the ways in which paradigm cases of claims about empirical facts are evaluated. This is an issue which linguists and philosophers have failed to seriously consider. I will now argue that, as reflected in weak mentalist practice, the evaluation of claims about linguistic facts is exactly *like* the evaluation of certain paradigm cases of claims about non-empirical facts.

The main points I want to make are suggested by the following allegory. Suppose you notice that very young children develop a remarkable facility for a kind of behavior known as counting and doing arithmetic. Since you know how to count and do arithmetic too, and have since you were a very young child, you reflect on that ability. You notice that although there are only a finite number of integers and arithmetic operations, there are an infinite number of well-formed arithmetical expressions. Furthermore you are astounded by the fact that arithmetic is creative. An arithmetically competent person is able to produce, add, subtract, multiply, and divide numbers he has never seen before. You conclude that the arithmetical knowledge of arithmetically competent people can only be characterized by a set of recursive rules and you set out in search of these rules. In your preliminary investigations you notice that the prescriptive rules that you learned in grade school to

---

[45] Here and in what follows I do not intend to imply that if linguists did conduct informant surveys it would necessarily make TGGs like theories in physics and chemistry or even that it would make TGGs empirical theories at all. But, if informant surveys were used in evaluating TGGs, their use would serve to distinguish the methodology of hypothesis testing in TGL from that in paradigm cases of the putatively non-empirical sciences where their use is thought to be completely irrelevant.

facilitate your counting and computing are fragmentary, inexplicit, and sometimes positively misleading and you set out to discover a more explicit, complete, and less misleading set of rules. Since, aside from the rules learned in grade school, a person's knowledge of arithmetic is largely tacit knowledge, you decide that in your investigations you can rely only on fragmentary intuitions of someone whose arithmetic competence is unquestioned (namely yourself), and you consider tokens of arithmetic expressions and make intuitive judgments like 363, 364 is a sequence of consecutive numbers, the sequence of numbers is unending, $2 + 2 = 4$, $275 + 363 \neq 544$, $3 + 4 = 4 + 3$. Judgments such as these provide the basic evidence as to what facts must be accounted for by any adequate axiomatic theory of elementary arithmetic.

The allegory suggests that in constructing and evaluating theories about the underlying rules which describe (or are constitutive of) elementary arithmetic, one does essentially what transformational grammarians do in constructing and evaluating TGGs.[46] Alternatively, in constructing and evaluating TGGs, weak mentalists are doing essentially what people concerned with number theory initially had to do in developing set-theoretic axiomatizations of arithmetic.[47] The points of analogy illustrated by my allegory apply to the construction and evaluation of axiomatic theories in developing branches of other putatively non-empirical sciences as well.

In developing branches of formal logic and formal analytic philosophy, criteria of adequacy for axiomatic theories are characteristically set by the intuitions of some "informant" (usually the investigator himself) plus considerations of simplicity and consistency of the axiom systems developed. *Informant intuitions about clear cases initially determine which claims about facts must appear as theorems in any adequate theory.* Some of the clearest examples of this procedure are provided by investigations in ethics, scientific reasoning, and modal logic.[48] Investiga-

---

[46] For a discussion of the notion of "constitutive rule", see Searle (1969, 33 ff).

[47] The allegory I have presented is suggested by some remarks by Chomsky (1963) and Kiparsky (1968). A similar allegory could be developed with respect to the construction and evaluation of axiomatizations of various branches of logic. One such allegory is presented by Fodor and Garrett (1966).

[48] For a clear discussion of this procedure in modal logic, see Hughes and Cresswell (1968, 25—30). Rescher (1968) discusses the use of intuitions in the hypothetico-deductive procedures employed in evaluating hypotheses in formal analytic philosophy. That intuitions are relied on in determining the facts to be characterized by theories in formal logic and the foundations of mathematics is made explicit by Russell and Whitehead (1929, 59). Goodman (1965, 62—72) emphasizes this point in discussing the justification of principles of deductive and inductive logic. Rawls (1971, 46—53) makes explicit the parallel between the use of intuitive judgments in evaluating ethical theories and their use in evaluating grammars for natural languages. Gert (1970, 60) draws a parallel between the justification of axiomatic theories of logic and the justifi-

tors in these disciplines characteristically reject the suggestion that verification of their factual claims requires anything like informant surveys.[49] Thus, there is a very close parallel between current methods used in evaluating TGGs and methods used in evaluating axiomatic theories in developing branches of logic and formal analytic philosophy. My allegory suggests that the parallel extends to the foundations of mathematics as well. Theses parallels are at least implicitly recognized by Chomsky in *Syntactic Structures* when he describes the task of constructing a TGG as "... the familiar task of explicating some intuitive concept." This is a task in which formal logicians, mathematicians, and analytic philosophers frequently engage.[50]

The point of noting these parallels is simply this: On the standard view of empirical scientific theories, the search for a consistent, complete, sound, and simple axiomatic theory of arithmetic (or for an axiomatic theory of propositional logic, modal logic, inductive logic, utilitarian ethics) is not considered to be an empirical scientific endeavor. Yet the parallel with weak mentalists' attempts to construct TGGs of natural languages seems to be exact. The fact that claims about non-empirical facts (e.g., arithmetical facts) are evaluated by appeal to human intuitions is not thought to establish that such claims are empirical claims or that such facts are empirical facts. Indeed, the fact that the truth of certain claims (e.g., $7 + 5 = 12$) can apparently be established on the basis of intuitive judgments without appeal to experiment and observation and the truth of claims about empirical facts apparently cannot, is one important reason why philosophers originally distinguished arithmetical, logical, and philosophical facts from the sort of facts (e.g., physical, chemical, biological, and psychological facts) which are subject to empirical investigation. Thus, aside from the strong *similarities*

---

cation of moral rules. He also emphasizes the use of intuitive judgments in identifying the facts to be accounted for by both theories in logic and theories in ethics. Scheffler (1963, 7—14) compares the construction and evaluation of philosophical theories about the structure, function, and methods for evaluating scientific theories with the construction and evaluation of TGGs.

[49] Some evidence of this rejection is found in the reaction of philosophers to the investigations reported in Naess (1938, 1953). For a probing and illuminating set of discussions of the nature and evaluation of factual claims in linguistics and analytic philosophy see the articles in Lyas (1971).

[50] I am not claiming that all mathematicians, logicians, and philosophers are engaged in the task of explicating concepts in use. To make that claim would be to overlook the role of pure invention in the construction of some mathematical, logical, and metaphysical theories. Certain self-consistent and sometimes very useful mathematical theories (e.g., the non-Euclidean geometries) cannot be described as the result of explicating some intuitive concepts. The methodology employed in evaluating such systems may be significantly different from that employed in evaluating TGGs and those theories in logic, mathematics and formal analytic philosophy which are clearly meant as explications (or "rational reconstructions") of intuitively understood concepts.

between theory evaluation in TGL and theory evaluation in the putatively non-empirical sciences, there seem to be significant *differences*
between theory evaluation in TGL and theory evaluation in paradigm
cases of empirical sciences.[51]

Of course, it could be that the standard distinction between empirical
and non-empirical sciences is unfounded.[52] But I think the parallel
between methods for evaluating claims about linguistic facts and
methods for evaluating paradigm examples of claims about non-empirical facts is sufficiently strong to raise the following question: If arguments for the non-empirical status of theories in the foundations of
mathematics, formal logic, and formal analytic philosophy are sound,
how can one escape concluding that transformatiional generative grammars are non-empirical theories? To my knowledge no one has shown
how this conclusion can be avoided. I suggest that one *cannot* escape this
conclusion. Transformational generative grammars march together with
the paradigm cases of non-empirical theories. Put another way, if transformational generative grammars are empirical theories (perhaps
psychological or sociological theories) then so are set-theoretic axioma-
tizatins of arithmetic, theories in formal logic, and theories in formal
analytic philosophy.

It seems to me that linguists and philosophers who are concerned to
establish that TGGs are empirical scientific theories have only three
possible responses to that conclusion:

---

[51] One influential explanation of why certain statements of putative facts of arithmetic,
logic, and philosophy can be verified without appeal to experiment and observation is
that the truth or falsity of such statements (in contrast to the truth or falsity of empirical claims) depends *only* on the relevant rules (or conventions) governing the use of
certain symbols (e.g., arithmetical operators, numerals, logical connectives, words and
phrases in a natural language) and not on any states of affairs in the world. If this
explanation is correct, then the analogy between linguistic facts and paradigm cases of
non-empirical facts is strengthened. Both kinds of facts are facts of convention.
Defenses of the conventional status of facts of arithmetic, logic, and formal analytic
philosophy can be found in the writings cited in the first part of footnote 9.

[52] For arguments that it is unfounded see Lambert and Brittan (1970) and Quine (1935;
1951;1954). Several logical empiricist defenses of this distinction can be found in the
references cited in footnote 9 above. Some contemporary writers who are not logical
empiricists suggest a distinction between disciplines like physics, chemistry and
psychology and discipline like logic, ethics, and linguistics on the grounds that the
subject matter of the former diciplines consists primarily on "brute facts" and the
subject matter of the latter disciplines consists primarily of "institutional facts" (i.e.,
facts which obtain simply because certain conventions are force). For a discussion of
the distinction between brute facts and institutional see Searle (1969). For a discussion
of the bearing of this distinction on TGL see Dretske (1974). For its bearing on ethics
see Toulmin (1950). Certain philosophers have considered the relevance of rules and
conventions to explanations in psychology, sociology and anthropology, see Louch
(1966), Peters (1958), Winch (1958). For a detailed discussion of rules see Ganz
(1971).

1.  Change the current conception of the subject matter and methods for evaluating TGGs.
2.  Reject the standard distinction between theories in the empirical sciences and theories in the non-empirical sciences.
3.  Show that I have overlooked some crucial difference between TGGs and axiomatic theories in those non-empirical sciences mentioned above.[53]

So long as none of these things is done, there remains a serious gap in the foundations of transformational generative linguistics.

## Summary

7. I have argued that in light of the standard view of empirical theories, any defense of the empirical scientific status of TGGs must establish that claims about linguistic facts are empirical claims. This requires that test implications of linguistic theories be evaluated in ways essentially similar to the ways in which test implications of theories in physics and chemistry are evaluated. I have examined a number of accounts of how transformational grammars might be tested, and conclude that the test procedures actually sanctioned in current transformational generative practice, are best characterized as the weak mentalistic test procedures. These procedures are exactly parallel to those sanctioned and employed

---

[53]  In response to arguments by Fodor and Katz (1963) that analytic philosophy is clearly an empirical science, Vendler (1967) argues that linguists investigate and codify the rules or conventions which govern the speech of speakers of a given natural language while analytic philosophers investigate and clarify constraints which linguistic rules and conventions place on philosophical discourse carried on in that language. Vendler claims that the former investigations are clearly empirical investigations, while the latter are investigations of *a priori* truths and hence concludes that linguistics is an empirical science while analytic philosophy is not. While I find Vendler's discussion of the relation between linguistics and analytic philosophy insightful, I do not see that Vendler establishes that linguistic investigations are empirical *and* that philosophical investigations are not empirical. Vendler's arguments, if sound, could be used to establish that a set-theoretic axiomatization of arithmetic, qua codification of rules governing symbols in use, is an empirical theory. Also, insofar as philosophers are merely investigating the consequences of linguistic rules and conventions, on Vendler's view it would seem that the justification of philosophical claims depends on empirical investigations aimed at showing what the rules and conventions are. Thus, the reasons for considering linguistics empirical would also show that branches of logic and mathematics as well as formal analytic philosophy are empirical sciences. Even though Vendler claims that linguistics is an empirical science, he distinguishes linguistic theories from theories in physics and chemistry on the grounds that the latter consist of sets of law statements while the former consist of sets of rule statements. Vendler does not discuss the appropriateness of relying on the intuitions of small numbers of informants in either linguistics or philosophical investigations.

by those engaged in explicating intuitive concepts of logic, mathematics, and formal analytic philosophy and are quite unlike those employed in physics and chemistry.

I conclude (i) that the standard defense of the empirical scientific status of transformational generative linguistics does not provide a basis for distinguishing TGGs from axiomatic theories in logic, the foundations of mathematics, and formal analytic philosophy, and (ii) given the current practice for evaluating TGGs, if grammars are to be compared with scientific theories at all, they should be compared with axiomatic theories in the non-empirical sciences like logic and mathematics and not with theories of physics and chemistry.

# References

Ayer, A. J. (1946) *Language, Truth and Logic,* 2nd ed. (revised), New York: Dover Publications, Inc. (third impression, 1948).
Bach, E. (1964) *An Introduction to Transformational Grammars,* New York: Holt, Rinehart, and Winston.
— (1974) *Syntactic Theory,* New York: Holt, Rinehart, and Winston.
Bar-Hillel, Y. (1957) "Three remarks on linguistic fundamentals," *Word* 13, 323—335.
— (1966) "On a misapprehension of the status of theories in linguistics," *Foundations of Language* 2, 394—399.
Black, M. (1970) Comment on N. Chomsky's "Problems of explanation in linguistics," in Borger and Cioffi (1970), 452—461.
Boole, G. (1854) *The Laws of Thought,* New York: Dover (reprint).
Borger, R., and F. Cioffi (1970) *Explanation in the Behavioral Sciences,* Cambridge: Cambridge University Press.
Boring, E. (1953) "A history of introspection," *Psychological Bulletin* 50, 169—189.
Botha, R. (1968) *The Function of the Lexicon in Transformational Generative Grammar,* The Hague: Mouton and Co.
— (1971) *Methodological Aspects of Transformational Generative Phonology,* the Hague: Mouton and Co.
— (1973) *The Justification of Linguistic Hypotheses,* The Hague: Mouton.
Braithwaite, R. (1953) *Scientific Explanation,* New York: Harper and Brothers (1960 Harper Torchbook edition).
Carden, G. (1970) "A note on conflicting idiolects," *Linguistic Inquiry* I, 280—290.
Carnap, R. (1934) "Formal and factual science," *Erkenntnis* 5, translated and reprinted in H. Feigl and M. Brodbeck (1953), 123—128.
— (1939) *Foundations of Logic and Mathematics,* Vol. 1, No. 3 of *The International Encyclopedia of Unified Science,* Chicago: University of Chicago Press.
— (1956) "The methodological character of theoretical concepts," in H. Feigl and M. Scriven (eds.), *The Foundations of Science and the Concepts of Psychology and Psychoanalysis,* Minnesota Studies in the Philosophy of Science, Minneapolis: University of Minnesota Press, Vol. I, 38—76.
Chomsky, N. (1956) "Three models for the description of language," IRE Trans. on Information Theory, II-2, 113—124.
— (1957) *Syntactic Structures,* The Hague: Mouton.

— (1961) "Some methodological remarks on generative grammar," *Word* 17, 219—239.
— (1962 a) "A transformational approach to syntax," in A. A. Hill (ed.), *Third Texas Conference on Problems of Linguistic Analysis in English,* Austin: University of Texas, 125—158 (with dicussion following, 158—169). Reprinted in Fodor and Katz (1964), 211—245; page numbers refer to latter (except for discussion).
— (1962 b) "Explanatory models in linguistics," in E. Nagel, P. Suppes, A. Tarski (eds.), *Logic, Methodology, and Philosophy of Science,* Stanford: Stanford University Press, 528—550.
— (1963) "Formal properties of grammars," in R. D. Luce, R. R. Bush, and E. Galanter (eds.), *Handbook of Mathematical Psychology,* Vol. II, New York: John Wiley and Sons, 419—493.
— (1964) "Current issues in linguistic theory," in Fodor and Katz (1964), 50—118.
— (1965) *Aspects of the Theory of Syntax,* Cambridge: The M.I.T. Press.
— (1966) *Topics in the Theory of Generative Grammar,* The Hague: Mouton and Co.
— (1969) "Comments on Harman's reply" in Hook (1969), 152—159.
— (1970) "Problems of explanation in linguistics," in Borger and Cioffi (1970).
— (1972) *Language and Mind,* enlarged edition, New York: Harcourt, Brace, and Jovanovich.
— and M. Halle (1968) *The Sound Pattern of English,* New York: Harper and Row.
— and G. Miller (1963) "Finitary models of language users," in R. D. Luce, R. R. Bush, and E. Galanter (eds.), *Handbook of Mathematical Psychology, Vol. II, New York: John Wiley and Sons, 323—418.*
Cohen, D. *(ed.) (1974) Explaining Linguistic Phenomena,* Washington, D. C.: Hemisphere Publishing Corporation.
Derwing, B. (1973) *Transformational Grammar as a Theory of Language Acquisition,* Cambridge: Cambridge University Press.
Dretske, F. (1964) "Observational terms," *The Philosophical Review* 73, 25—42.
— (1969) *Seeing and Knowing,* London: Routledge and Kegan Paul.
— (1974) "Explanation in linguistics," in Cohen (1974), 21—42.
Elliott, D., S. Legum, and S. A. Thompson (1969) "Syntactic variation as linguistic data," Papers from the Fifth Regional Meeting, Chicago Linguistic Society, 52—59.
Feigl, H., and M. Brodbeck (eds.) (1953) *Readings in the Philosophy of Science,* New York: Appleton-Century-Crofts.
Fodor, J. (1971) "Current approaches to syntax recognition," in D. L. Horton and J. J. Jenkins (eds.), *Perception and Language,* Columbus, Ohio: Merrill, 120—139.
— and M. Garrett (1966) "some reflections on competence and performance," in J. Lyons and R. J. Wales (eds.), *Psycholinguistics Papers, Edinburgh: Edinburgh University Press, 135—182.*
— and J. J. Katz (1963) "The availability of what we say," *in Philosophical Review,* Vol. LXXII, reprinted in Lyas (1971), 190—203.
— and J. J. Katz (1964) *The Structure of Language,* Englewood Cliffs: Prentice Hall.
Fromkin, V. (1968) "Speculations on performance models," *Journal of Linguistics* 4, 47—69.
Ganz, J. S. (1971) *Rules: a systematic study,* The Hague: Mouton.
Gert, B. (1970) *The Moral Rules,* New York: Harper and Row.
Goodman, N. (1965) *Fact, Fiction, and Forecast,* Indianapolis: The Bobbs-Merrill Company, Inc.
Greene, J. (1972) *Psycholinguistics,* Baltimore: Penguin books, Inc.
Hanson, N. (1961) *Patterns of Discovery,* Cambridge: Cambridge University Press.
— (1969) *Perception and Discovery,* edited by W. C. Humphries, San Francisco: Freeman, Cooper, and Co.
Hempel, C. G. (1945) "On the nature of mathematical truth," *The American Mathematical Monthly,* Vol. 52, 543—556. Reprinted in Paul Benacerraf and Hilary Putnam (eds.),

*Philosophy of Mathematics,* Englewood Cliffs: Prentice-Hall, Inc., 1964, 366—381. Also reprinted in Feigl and Brodbeck (1953), 148—164.

— (1952) *Fundamentals of Concept Formation in Empirical Science,* Chicago: The University of Chicago Press.

— (1958) "The theoretician's dilemma," in H. Feigl, M. Scriven, G. Maxwell (eds.), *Concepts, Theories, and the Mind-Body Problem* in Minnesota Studies in the Philosophy of Science, Minneapolis: University of Minnesota Press, Vol. II, 37—98. reprinted in Hempel (1965), 173—226. Page numbers refer to latter.

— (1962) "Deductive-nomological vs. statistical explanation," in H. Feigl and G. Maxwell (eds.), *Scientific Explanation, Space, and Time* in Minnesota Studies in the Philosophy of Science, Vol. III, Minneapolis: University of Minnesota Press, 98—169.

— (1965) *Aspects of Scientific Explanation,* New York: The Free Press.

— (1966) *Philosophy of Natural Science,* Englewood Cliffs: Prentice Hall, Inc.

— (1970) "On the 'standard conception' of scientific theories," in M. Radner and S. Winokur (eds.), *Analysis of Theories and Methods of Physics and Psychology* in H. Feigl and G. Maxwell (eds.), Minnesota Studies in the Philosophy of Science, Minneapolis: University of Minnesota Press, Vol. IV, 142—163.

— and P. Oppenheim (1948) "Studies in the logic of explanation," *Philosophy of Science* 15, 135—175. Reprinted in Hempel (1965), 245—296. Page numbers refer to latter.

Hook, S. (ed.) (1969) *Language and Philosophy,* New York: New York University Press.

Hughes, G., and M. Cresswell (1968) *An Introduction to Modal Logic,* London: Methuen and Co.

Hutchinson, L. (1974) "Grammar as theory," in Cohen (1974), 43—74.

Kalmar, L. (1967) "Foundations of mathematics — whither now?" in I. Lakatos (ed.), (1967), 187—194.

Katz, J. (1964) "Mentalism in linguistics," *Language* 40, 124—137.

— (1966) *The Philosophy of Language,* New York: Harper and Row.

— and J. Fodor (1964) "A reply to Dixon's 'A trend in semantics,'" *Linguistics* 3, 19—29.

— and P. Postal (1964) *An Integrated Theory of Linguistic Descriptions,* Cambridge: The M.I.T. Press Research Monograph no. 26.

Kemeny, J. (1959) *A Philosopher Looks at Science,* New York: Van Nostrand Reinhold Company.

Kiparsky, P. (1968) "Linguistic universals and linguistic change," in E. Bach and R. Harms (eds.), *Universals in Linguistic Theory,* New York: Holt, Rinehart, and Winston, Inc., 171—204.

Kyburg, H. (1968) *Philosophy of Science,* New York: Macmillan.

Labov, W. (1971) "Methodology," in W. O. Dingwall (ed.), *A Survey of Linguistic Science,* Maryland: University of Maryland, 412—497.

— (1972) "Some principles of linguistic methodology," *Language in Society,* I, 97—120.

Lakatos, I. (1967) "A renaissance of empiricism in the recent philosophy of mathematics?" in Lakatos (1967), 199—203.

— (1967) *Problems in the Philosophy of Mathematics,* Amsterdam: North Holland Publishing Co.

Lakoff, G. (1968) "Deep and surface grammar," Indiana University Linguistics Club Mimeograph.

— (1971) "On Generative Semantics," in D. D. Steinberg and L. Jakobovits (eds.), *Semantics,* Cambridge: Cambridge University Press, 232—296.

Lambert, K., and G. Brittan, Jr. (1970) "The nature of mathematics," in *An Introduction to the Philosophy of Science,* Englewood Cliffs: Prentice Hall, 4—24.

Lees, R. (1957) "Review of Chomsky's *Syntactic Structures,*" *Language* 33, 375—408.

— (1966) "On the interpretation of a Turkish vowel alternation." *Anthropological Linguistics* 8: 32—39.

Legum, S., D. Elliot, and S. A. Thompson. (1974) "Considerations in the analysis of syntactic variation," SWRL Educational Research and Development (unpublished manuscript).

Louch, A. R. (1966) *Explanation and Human Action*, Berkeley: University of California Press.

Lyas, C. (ed.) (1971) *Linguistics and Philosophy*, London: Macmillan and Co., Ltd.

Mill, J. S. (1843) *A System of Logic* abridged in E. Nagel, ed., *John Stuart Mill's Philosophy of Scientific Method*, New York: Hafner Publishing Co., 1950.

Miller, G. A. (1962) "Some psychological studies of grammar," *American Psychologist* 17, 748—762.

Naess, A. (1938) "'Truth' as conceived by those who are not professional philosophers." Skrifter utgitt av Det Norske Videnskaps — Akadem: Oslo, II. Hist. — Filos. Klasse, Vol. IV, Oslo.

— (1953) *Interpretation and Preciseness: A Contribution to the Theory of Communication*. Skrifter Norske Vid. Akademi, Oslo, II. Hist. — Filos. Klasse.

Nagel, E. (1961) *The Structure of Science*, New York: Harcourt, Brace, and World, Inc.

Pap. A. (1959) *An Introduction to the Philosophy of Science*, New York: The Free Press of Glencoe.

Peters, R. S. (1958) *The Concept of Motivation*, London: Kegan Paul.

Popper, K. (1959) *The Logic of Scientific Discovery*, New York: Harper Torchbooks (1968 edition).

Postal, P. (1966) "Underlying and superficial linguistic structure," in J. Emig, J. Fleming, and Helen Popp (eds.), *Language and Learning*, New York: Harcourt, Brace, and World, Inc., 153—174.

Putnam, H. (1971) *Philosophy of Logic*, New York: Harper Torchbooks.

— (1974) "The refutation of conventionalism," *Nous* 8, Pp 25—40.

Quine, W. (1935) "Truth by convention," in Quine (1966), 70—99.

— (1951) "Two dogmas of empiricism," in Quine (1961), 20—47.

— (1953) "The problem of meaning in linguistics," in Quine (1961), 47—64.

— (1954) "Carnap and logical truth," in Quine (1966), 100—126.

— (1961) *From a Logical Point of View*, New York: Harper and Row (second edition, revised).

— (1966) *The Ways of Paradox*, New York: Random House.

— (1970) "Methodological reflections on current linguistic theory," *Synthese*, XXI, 386—398.

Rawls, J. (1971) *A Theory of Justice*, Cambridge, Mass.: Harvard University Press.

Rescher, N. (1968) "Discourse on a method," in *Philosophical Logic*, Dordrecht, Holland: D. Reidel Publishing Co., 332—342.

Ringen, J. (1977a) "On evaluating data concerning linguistic intuition," In Fred Eckman, ed., *Current Themes in Linguistics*, New York: John Wiley, 145—160.

— (1977b) "Linguistic data: Intuition and grammar testing," invited paper, Roundtable Session on Linguistics as an Empirical Science, XIIth International Congress of Linguists, Vienna, Austria.

Russell, B.. and A. Whitehead (1925) *Principia Mathematica*, 2nd edition, Vol. I, New York: Cambridge University Press.

Sanders, G. (1970) "On the natural domain of grammar," *Linguistics* 63, 51—124.

— (1972) *Equational Grammar*, The Hague: Mouton and Co.

— (1974) "Issues of explanation in linguistics," in Cohen (1974), 1—20.

Saussure, F. de (1959) *Course in General Linguistics*, W. Baskin (trans.), New York: Philosophical Library, McGraw Hill Paperback, 1966.

Scheffler, I. (1963) *The Anatomy of Inquiry*, New York: Alfred Knopf.

Schlesinger, I. (1967) "A note on the relationship between psychological and linguistic theories," *Foundations of Language* 3, 397—402.

Schwartz, R. (1969) "On knowing a grammar," in Hook (1969), 183—190.

Searle, J. (1969) *Speech Acts,* Cambridge: Cambridge University Press.
Suppes, P. (1970) *A Probabilistic Theory of Causality,* Amsterdam: North Holland Publishing Co.
Toulmin, S. E. (1950) *The Place of Reason in Ethics, Cambridge: At the University Press (paperback edition, 1964).*
Vendler, Z. (1967) "Linguistics and the *A Priori,*" in *Linguistics in Philosophy,* Ithaca: Cornell University Press, 1—32. Reprinted in Lyas (1971), 245—268.
Weyl, H. (1949) *Philosophy of Mathematics and Natural Science,* Princeton: Princeton University press.
Winch, P. (1958) *The Idea of a Social Science, London: Kegan Paul.*

# Is linguistics empirical? A critique of Esa Itkonen's *Linguistics and Metascience*[*]

Östen Dahl

This paper is a critique of Esa Itkonen's monograph, *Linguistics and Metascience* (1974).[**]
I will concentrate on his view that linguistics is not an empirical science,[1] which I think is mistaken. The critique will thus be almost entirely negative, and it should be emphasized that this negative evalua-

---

[*] *[Editor's note: The following exchange of views is intended to reflect some of the debate provoked by the publications of Esa Itkonen, especially his 1974 monograph,* Linguistics and Metascience *(available in a revised version as* Grammatical Theory and Metascience, *Amsterdam 1978). The material here is organized in debate fashion, with an initial critique of Itkonen 1974 by Östen Dahl, followed by a detailed reply by Itkonen. Thereafter, each discussant provides a short rebuttal addressed to the reply to his initial statement. The discussion could have gone on, of course, but all debates must stop at some point.*

*There have been a number of reactions to Itkonen's work (see the references in Dahl's and Itkonen's contributions below, and the replies circulated as Itkonen 1976). Dahl's critique has been chosen here because it raises the interesting rule vs. regularity issue, and because it has previously only been available as a working paper (dated 1975). Itkonen's reply has likewise been circulated as part of a longer working paper referred to here as Itkonen 1976, wherever the reference comes from outside the scope of the part reproduced here. The rebuttals were written to round out the discussion, but scarcely settle the issues raised once and for all.]*

[**] I am indebted to Jens Allwood for valuable comments on an earlier version of this paper and to Pierre Javanaud for typing the manuscript.

Footnotes marked* have been added in 1977.

[1*] Itkonen (1976, 4) comments on 'what has been taken as the claim that "linguistics is an empirical science"' that 'This is an inexact formulation which I have never used myself. The term "linguistics" must be subdivided into "grammar" and "sociolinguistics and psycholinguistics".'
Although it may be true that this very combination of words does not occur in Itkonen's writings, it must be pointed out that he often uses 'linguistics' as equivalent to 'grammar'.
Itkonen further complains that most of his critics 'do not give any explicit definitions of "empirical"' (1976, 12). For my part, I have nothing to object to the Popperian definition of 'empirical' as 'falsifiable on the basis of observation' and Itkonen's modification of this as 'falsifiable by what happens in space and time', except that I think that 'on the basis of' is preferable to 'by', since the latter can be interpreted as meaning that observation alone can falsify a hypothesis (whereas in fact, any falsification must involve also interpretation of what is observed in terms of 'background knowledge' (Lakatos 1970)).

tion on my part does not extend to the parts of the book that are not treated in this paper. For example, I find Itkonen's treatment of the role of pragmatics in linguistics very valuable and I agree with most of the things he has to say on this topic.

Itkonen formulates the aim of his book as follows:

> "In this book I undertake to examine the meta-scientific status of linguistics, understood primarily as a study of the native speaker's linguistic intuition. I have chosen transformational grammar ( = TG) as a representative case of this kind of linguistics."[2] (p. 7).

To the "average working grammarian"[3] who is used to having his ideas and hypotheses daily refuted by experience, Itkonen's claim about the status of linguistics is of course truly astonishing. He is also slightly offended by the allegation that he is not engaged in an empirical study. He has been told that non-empirical sciences are such as mathematics and logic and most linguists prefer to think that they are closer to the real world than mathematicians and logicians are. So it is natural that our "average working grammarian" should want to look a bit closer at Itkonen's claims.

Itkonen's argument builds on a number of distinctions, and it is necessary to clarify these first. First there is the distinction between *rule* and *regularity*, a rather straightforward and common one.[4] A regularity is something which can be referred to by a general statement like "All pieces of metal expand when heated", i.e., a statement which expresses a

---

2   Itkonen does not criticize at any length the linguistic claims of transformational grammar, only its adherents' view of its metascientific status. It is therefore rather strange to read in Anttila's very positive review of Itkonen (Anttila 1975) that Itkonen's work relegates Chomsky from linguistics ('Nähdäkseni Itkosen työ vetää pohjan pois Chomskyn kielitieteeltä').

3   This concept is due to Charles Fillmore (Fillmore 1970).

4*  Actually, it may not be as straightforward as I make it here. The problem is that Itkonen's concept of 'regularity' is not very clear. Cf. the following quotation from Itkonen 1976, 50, where he comments on Renate Bartsch's paper in Wunderlich 1976: 'I fully agree with Bartsch when she says that rules of language are not reducible to observable regularities. But I strongly disagree when she adds that the same is true of the laws of natural science, i.e., that both rules and scientific laws are "assumed" on the basis of observable regularities. (I take it that "scientific laws" stands here for a high-level regularity in nature, and not for a sentence or theory referring to such a regularity.) 'Here, it seems that regularities are — or at least can be — observable entities. But surely a 'universal hypothesis' — which is the normal case of a 'scientific law' — about an infinite domain, e.g., 'Metals expand when heated', cannot be *observed*, or *reduced* to anything observable. This, however, seems to be what Itkonen presupposes in the quotation. But maybe I have misunderstood him. (I say in the paper (cf. fn. 7 below) that one gets the impression from Itkonen that there is no relation at all between linguistic rules and observed linguistic data. Itkonen retorts (see below, p.149) that he gets the impression that I make no distinction at all between rules and observed data. I can now return the ball to him, saying that I wonder whether he makes any distinction at all between regularities and observed data.)

generalization about some phenomenon in nature. A rule, on the other hand, is something which governs the behavior of intelligent beings. According to Itkonen, rules and regularities are fundamentally different as to how they can be refuted: "It is an axiom of the philosophy of natural sciences that a universal hypothesis referring to a presumed regularity is falsified, if there occur counter-instances to it: e.g., the hypothesis "All pieces of metal expand when heated" is falsified, if we find a piece of metal that does not expand when heated. On the other hand, a sentence referring to a rule is not falsified simply because there occurs (what looks like) counterinstances to it. Thus our rule-sentence "In English the definite article precedes the noun" is not falsified even if we should come across an utterance like *"Girl the came in": such an utterance is *incorrect* whereas rule-sentences are about *correct* utterances (and sentences) only. Now since counter-instances are simply irrelevant, we cannot even specify the circumstances under which our rule-sentence could be taken to be falsified." (p. 83).

This again is something which causes astonishment in the "ordinary working grammarian", who is used to having his theories blown up by counter-examples found by unkind colleagues. He is also confused to find that Itkonen in other places in his book acknowledges the role of counter-instances, e.g., when discussing Chomsky's "A over A princ-iple": "however, the A-over-A principle is "disconfirmed" by showing that it conflicts with, or excludes some perfectly correct constructions, like "Who would you approve of my seeing?" or "The book which I lost the cover of is on the table." (p. 255). Should not these sentences be incorrect according to the argumentation in the preceding quotation?

Actually, the comparison btween the deviant piece of metal and the incorrect sentence is not quite accurate. We could show this by arranging the two examples in parallel ways. We could represent the case of the metal which does not expand as follows:

*Hypothesis*: All pieces of metal expand when heated.
*Test situation*: Object A is a piece of metal.
*Outcome of test*: A does not expand when heated.
Hypothesis refuted.

The general schema will now be:

*Hypothesis*: All S have property P.
*Test situation*: A is an S.
*Outcome of test*: A does not have property P.

If we try to apply this schema to the case with the ungrammatical sentence, we get the following:

*Hypothesis*: All English sentences have the property that if they contain a definite article, it precedes its noun.

*Test situation:* \*Girl the came in is an English sentence.
*Outcome of test:* In \*Girl the came in, the definite article does not precede the noun.

This, however, does not represent what we actually have. The statement that the string \*Girl the came in is an English sentence is, as we know, false, and thus the test situation does not obtain. The only thing we know is that \*Girl the came in is an utterance, but from this we cannot draw the conclusion that the hypothesis is false, only that either it is false or the string in question is not an English sentence. But exactly the same would hold in the case of the "regularity", if we assume that we do not know that A is a piece of metal. In that case, the outcome of the test would not allow us to refute the general hypothesis: it might be false, but it might also be the case that A is a piece of ice. Thus the difference between the two situations that Itkonen points to does not depend on the difference between rules and regularities but rather on the fact that in one case, we do not know whether the entity to be tested belongs to the domain of the general statement. If we look at the case of the counterexamples to the A-over-A principle, we see that it is more like the case of the non-expanding piece of metal. Here it is assumed from the start that the counter-instances belong to the domain of the rule, namely correct English sentences.[5]

Let us now look at his distinctions between different types of rules. According to Itkonen, three concepts should be kept apart:

(a) rule-sentences
(b) atheoretical rules
(c) theoretical rules

---

[5] I am going to make a point here which is not particularly well formulated, which makes Itkonen (see below, pp.147—148) contend that I have only managed to show exactly what he himself wants to show. What I want to say is that Itkonen's assumption — that the two situations are different in that in the physics case we know that A belongs to the domain of the universal statement — is not true as a general statement about hypotheses in linguistics and physics. Very often, situations obtain in natural sciences where two explanations of an apparent counter-example are possible: (a) that the hypothesis is false, (b) that the object which appears to be a counter-example does not belong to the domain of the hypothesis. Similarly in linguistics, we may encounter an utterance — a spatiotemporal event — which we have independent reasons to assume to be 'correct' in the language under investigation (for instance, by observing listener reactions) and which contradicts our hypotheses. But this of course is related to the question of the relations between the existence of rules and the existence of regularities in behavior, which is discussed in more detail in my rebuttal (see pp. 153—156 below). I now see more clearly than I did when I wrote the paper that the argument is not intended to distinguish between what is falsifiable and what is not, but rather between what is 'known with absolute certainty' and what is not. This is evident, since as is acknowledged by Itkonen, counterinstances are relevant for 'theoretical rules', although these are non-empirical. So, the crucial thing in the argument is Itkonen's claim that 'atheoretical rules' are known with absolute certainty.

The distinction between (a) on the one hand and (b) and (c) on the other builds on the rather obvious distinction between the linguistic formulation of a rule and what this linguistic formulation expresses, i.e., the content of the rule. Thus a rule-sentence is a sentence which is used to express a rule, whereas "rule" as used by Itkonen generally refers to the content ot the rule as abstracted from how it is possibly formulated. I do not see any difficulties here: more problematic is the distinction between (b) and (c). Itkonen wants here to distinguish rules as existing so to speak in the minds of their users and rules as parts of a theory about e.g., language. It is the first kind that constitute the "competence" of a speaker, but it is the second kind that the linguist postulates in his grammar. We shall return to the problems with this distinction but shall first look at the relations between the different kinds of rules and the "empirical status" of linguistics. Only in the case of atheoretical rules do we need to pay attention to the distinction between rules and rule-sentences since only in that case is it possible that some rule has not got a linguistic formulation, according to Itkonen. The claim that linguistic statements are necessarily true or false builds on the claim that a rule-sentence is necessarily true or false. This, in its turn, is based on the following argument. A rule-sentence is said to have the following general form: "In X, p" where X is the name of a language (or e.g., a game) and p is a general statement, e.g., "In English the definite article precedes the noun" or "In poker a full house beats a flush". Now, Itkonen says, a language (or a game), being a system of rules, "is constituted or defined by its rules." (p. 104). If we change one of the rules, we do not have the same game any longer. Thus if we omit the rule "a full house beats a flush" from the set of rules that constitute our game, it is not poker any longer but another game. Ergo, it is necessarily true that a full house beats a flush in poker. The argument presupposes that it is the same thing to define a language (i.e., to specify the rules that constitute it) as to define the term which is used to refer to that language. That is, the definition of "English" is the conjunction of all rules that hold in English. But one could equally well argue that since an individual is "constituted" by its properties, any statement to the effect that the individual has such-and-such properties is necessarily true or false.

Itkonen actually mentions a similar objection (p. 109): "It could be argued that defining a language by its rules is comparable to defining the concept "nature" by all the natural regularities known today. This stipulation would turn the corresponding universal hypotheses into necessary truths, because all evidence which could otherwise falsify the hypotheses is decreed to be "unnatural". But this objection overlooks the elementary distinction between rules and regularities, namely that the former can, and must, be known whereas the latter cannot."

To this one can object that at least the term "English" can well be understood without knowing all the rules of English. In any case, one could obtain a clearly contingent statement by substituting a definite description for "English" in the rule-sentence, e.g., "In the native language of William Shakespeare, the definite article precedes the noun". The question is then which of these two statements best exemplifies the statements which are made in linguistics. If we assume that the rules that constitute the linguistic competence of a speaker by definition are at least subconsciously known by him, he need only become aware of his knowledge in order to be able to describe his language. For Itkonen, it follows that the evaluation of the truth of rule-sentences is only a question of becoming aware of what you already know, and further, that linguistic knowledge is not obtained from experience but from introspection. This a priori character of linguistic knowledge is also, according to him, the base for the necessary truth or falsity of rule-sentences (p. 108). He admits, however, that "true rule-sentences are necessarily true only from the view point of one who (intuitively) knows the game." (ibid.). It follows from this that what he says about linguistic knowledge holds only for knowledge about languages that one knows. "It is crucial to my argument that in my opinion the paradigmatic case of language description is the one where the linguist is describing his *native* language." (p. 86). The fact that lots of linguists spend most of their time describing languages that are foreign to them would seem to be a problem for this view, but "native speakers have no uniquely priviledged (sic) status. New languages can be learnt, and when one speaks a foreign language reasonably well, one is entitled to describe it with roughly the same competence as a relatively bad chess-player is entitled to describe chess. Notice that one can be a good chess-theoretician without being a good chess-player, and vice-versa." (p. 87). The comparison with good and bad chess-players is not very adequate, since a bad chess-player is usually understood as one who knows the rules of chess but who frequently loses his games. One could also object that an adult cannot normally attain native competence in a language that he does not know from childhood. The important thing, though, is that Itkonen assumes that the activities of a "field linguist" of the classical type can be divided into two parts: learning the language and describing it. But it is clear that he has his future grammar in mind from the first day in the field. And if we look at the whole process of constructing a grammar for an unknown language, it is clear that it must involve the construction of hypotheses that are tested by experience, i.e., by questioning native speakers and observing their behavior. In fact, Itkonen acknowledges this when saying (p. 108) that "when one is learning a new game — for instance, when a child is learning his first language — his tentative rule-sentences are genuine hypotheses in so far as new evidence (which has to be understood and not only observed) may prove them false. It may be difficult to decide precisely when one has stopped learning the rules of a game and has come to master it, but we cannot avoid making this distinction. Once we see that someone plays (or, more cautiously, seems to play) correctly, it would be absurd to keep on doubting indefinitely whether he has come to master the game ..." This, however, is from the viewpoint of one who is a native speaker and who observes the one who is learning the game, but it does not tell us how the field linguist knows he has now got to the rules that are necessarily true.[6]

It seems that at the bottom of this is a failure on the part of Itkonen to understand the relations between rules and observed data. At least when reading the book, one gets the impression that because the rules of grammar do not correspond to any one hundred per cent regulariries in actual linguistic behavior, there are no relations at all between linguistic rules and observed linguistic data.[7] However, the observed data are in fact the basis in a sense for postulating rules, since we would not want to acknowledge something as a rule if it were not actually followed in at least a sizeable proportion of the possible instances. This takes us back to the question of what kinds of statements are the interesting ones in linguistics, and the discussion of whether "English" as a term is defined by the rules that constitute English. I may postulate a set of rules which generate a certain language which I choose to call $L_1$. But the statement "In $L_1$, so-and-so holds" is not interesting for linguistics if it is not complemented with the statement "$L_1$ is spoken by such-and-such people."[8] Therefore the claim that linguistics concerns itself with neces-

---

[6*] It is also clear that one can describe a rule without having 'mastered' it in the sense that one can apply it correctly in one's behavior. For instance, I may be able to formulated the rule 'The first segment of *zinc* is voiced' and also fully understand what that means in articulatory terms without being able to pronounce a voiced z. This points to a difficulty for the claim that grammatical knowledge is 'agent's knowledge', i. e., knowledge 'about something that we ourselves do, or ought to do'. (Itkonen 1976, 18). Consider, however, the following statement by Itkonen (1974: 139): 'To understand a rule is to be able to follow it oneself under suitable circumstances: e.g., a man with paralyzed legs is fully in a position to understand the rules of football, although he is permanently prevented from actually following them.' Presumably, such a person, would still, according to Itkonen, have 'agent's knowledge' of football. But the vagueness of the phrase 'under suitable circumstances' of course makes the definition of 'understanding a rule' very hard to apply: for instance, have I understood the rule about the pronunciation of *zinc* in the situation described above?

[7*] This formulation is somewhat unfair, in view of the fact that Itkonen does discuss the relations between rules and observed behavior, although he does it in an unsatisfactory way, in my opinion. What I should have said here is that he sometimes argues in a way that gives the impression that he thinks that rules and observed behavior are quite independent of each other (cf. the discussion below).

[8*] To sharpen the formulation a little, and to show how rules are related to what happens in space and time, one should perhaps say '$L_1$ is spoken by such-and-such people at such-and-such occasions', or alternatively, 'Such-and-such discourses are in $L_1$'.

sary truths is misleading. There may be statements in linguistics which can be regarded as necessarily true, but they do not by themselves constitute linguistic hypotheses.[9] Linguistics is not interested in languages as formal systems per se, but as formal systems which underlie actual human behavior.[10] Itkonen is aware of the objection but refuses to admit its consequences: "the existence of a game is contingent and not necessary, and therefore it is informative to see or to hear that such-and-such a game is played. But when one has learned the game, the rules within it hold necessarily, and the sentences referring to them could not be falsified by experience." So let us now have a look at the question whether the last claim holds.

It is crucial for Itkonen's view of linguistics that one assumes that the linguist as a speaker of his native language has in some way direct access to his linguistic competence, i.e., that he can become conscious of the (atheoretical) rules that it consists of. In transformational grammar, it is normally assumed that speakers have direct intuitions about the grammaticality (or acceptability) of individual sentences, but that it is the linguist's job to construct the general rules on the basis of these intuitions about particular cases. Itkonen cannot agree with such a view, because he wants linguistic knowledge — i.e., knowledge of rule-sentences — to be a priori and "known to be true with absolute certainty" (p. 84), which would be impossible if one would have to test a rule against a possibly infinite number of occurrences of it. He labels the claim that "*even when examining our own intuitive knowledge of English,* we can only 'observe' particular 'occurrences' . . . confirming the 'hypot-

---

9* Itkonen's comment on this passage (below, p. 149) is strange. Quoting the two sentences immediately preceding this footnote in the main text, he says: 'I agree. I capture these two aspects (i.e., indubitable normative data vs. falsifiable theoretical descriptions) with my "rule-sentence — grammatical hypothesis" distinction.' He thus manages to give the impression that I have not understood this distinction. But anyone who reads the whole paragraph sees that I am talking about something else. The property of being necessarily true is not something which distinguishes atheoretical and theoretical rules in Itkonen's theory (cf. Itkonen 1974: 202).

10 Of course, one can talk of 'formal linguistics' as the study of possible grammars abstracted from the question whether these grammars are used or not. This would be a branch of mathematics (but with obvious implications for empirical linguistics).
To be fair to Itkonen, one should concede that transformational grammarians including Chomsky himself have sometimes expressed themselves in a way that suggests that they have not been sure if they are doing formal or empirical linguistics. Itkonen quotes some such statements, not without satisfaction. (Most of them derive from the early years of transformational grammar. A great deal of the work Chomsky was doing at that time actually belonged to the field of formal linguistics.)
In this connection, one could also point out that Richard Montague seems to have regarded linguistics as a non-empirical science (see Richmond Thomason's introduction to Montague (1974)).

hesis' (i.e., that a certain rule-sentence is true) as 'surely absurd' (p. 85)."[11] He gives no reasons why it should be considered absurd, though, and I think it can be shown that even transformational grammarians postulate too abstract a level for "direct intuitions". It is by now a well-known phenomenon that informants who reject a sentence as unacceptable when it is presented in isolation often accept it if they get a suitable situation in which it could have been uttered. In other words, it appears that people do not even have direct intuitions about the acceptability of linguistic expressions as types but only as occurring in definite situations. Furthermore, very often, people do not have any clear feelings as to why a sentence is unacceptable (if it is because it violates a syntactic rule or because the situation it describes is absurd or because the sentence is difficult to understand). Itkonen, who mostly uses the terms "correct" and "incorrect", avoids the problem of how to distinguish between acceptability and grammaticality. Further still, it is well-known among linguists that intuitions about the acceptability of utterances tend to be vague and inconsistent, depending on what you had for breakfast and which judgment would best suit your own pet theory. (See e.g., Labov (1971)).[12] Thus, in most cases, we are far from having direct intuitions about rules which concern the grammaticality (not acceptability) of whole sets of expression types (not just individual occurrences of expression types).

In simple cases such as Itkonen's favorite rule sentence "In English, the definite article precedes the noun" it may still seem plausible to assume that people can "see" directly that the rule is true, but in most

---

[11]* I seem to have misrepresented what Itkonen says here, as is pointed out by Itkonen below (p. 150). The full quotation is: 'But it is clear that our rule-sentence is known to be true with absolute certainty. To deny this is to claim that even *when examining our own intuitive knowledge of English*, we can only "observe" particular "occurrences" — e.g., "the man", "the woman", "the boy" — "confirming" the "hypothesis" "In English the definite article precedes the noun" but that we can never know for sure whether the "hypothesis" is true. But such a claim is surely absurd.' I still do not feel, however, that the claim is as absurd as Itkonen thinks it is.

[12]* Itkonen (1976, 32) argues that the unreliability of linguistic intuitions concerns only 'cases which are uncharacteristic of ordinary use of language'. 'These are sentences like "John reminds me of himself" or "The man the girl I used to go with married just got drafted," which no one ever utters, but which are dreamed up by generativists to prove some intratheoretical, purely technical points.' Accordingly, these are cases when 'Wittgenstein would say that . . . "language goes on holiday"'. However, Labov 1975 quotes sentences which seem perfectly normal in everyday conversation and where intuitions are still unreliable (at least concerning their meaning), such as *All the boys didn't leave.* Even if we neglect these cases, the general point is that one may very well have a subjective feeling of certainty about one's intuitions, yet it may turn out that this feeling is unfounded, due e.g. to one's having overlooked some special situation in which a sentence could be used. It is thus not a question of having vague intuitions but rather of having misleading ones. (See my rebuttal below for further discussion).

cases the rules are much more complicated. This, though, is denied by Itkonen who seems to think that most rule sentences are of the same character as the one mentioned: "It is clear that in every language there are hundreds or more probably thousands of equally simple rules that are known or knowable by the speaker." (p. 194).[13] A page later, however, he gives the following formulation of the rule governing *do*-periphrasis in English: "In English, when a whole sentence is questioned, the sentence begins with some form of the verb 'do' and the main verb follows the subject, except when the sentence begins with one of the following verbs: 'be', 'must', etc." The simplicity of this rule-sentence is not impressive. It should be pointed out, too, that it is too vague as it stands to be of any use to anyone who wants to know how to form questions in English. Thus, one would have to indicate which form of the verb 'do' is to be chosen and also that the main verb should be in the infinitive. In other words, the real rule-sentence must be even more complicated.[14]

If we return to the question of the nature of intuitions, one could claim that what we have is not a direct and certain knowledge of rules but rather vague, "visceral" reactions about the oddity or normality of speech acts. One could question whether these reactions about the oddity or normality of speech acts are so terribly different from many other things that happen when we perceive the world, such as when a person who is driving a car "feels" that there is something wrong with it, although he cannot tell what.

The point is there is no clear distinction between "intuitions" of the kind we have about language and "sense-data" or whatever we would like to call the elements of what we "directly perceive", and thus, there is no clear reason why one should not include linguistic intuitions in experience. It is interesting in this connection that some mathematicians, such as Gödel, regard even mathematical intuitions as part of experi-

---

[13]* It is actually a rather uninteresting fact that there are *many* simple rules in the grammar of English; what is crucial is of course whether all of them are. Itkonen (1976, 24) also says: 'The decisive question is whether or not the rule₁ about the place of the definite article is *characteristic* of English in general.' He then adds in support of this assumption that 'there are thousands and thousands of similar rules₁ of English'. This does not prove, though, that the number of rules that are less simple is not also considerable.

[14]* Itkonen comments on this passage (p. 150 below): 'Dahl notes that the simplicity of one of my rule-sentences "is not impressive" (p.11). But there is no reason why it should be. If Dahl's oversights were less impressive, he would have noticed that I define rule-sentences as unscientific, ad hoc formulations. Simplicity is a matter of *scientific* description, in my terminology, of grammatical hypotheses.' But in the quotation in the main text 'simple' in 'equally simple rules' clearly refers to a property of atheoretical rules. Besides, my point here is that the *do*-rule must be even more complicated that Itkonen has it, which makes it even less probable as an object for direct intuitions.

ence, which would make mathematics an empirical science. (I am grateful to Jens Allwood for pointing this out to me.)

One might think that given the assumption that one has direct access to the rules in one's linguistic competence, the construction of a grammar would be a trivial matter. But this is not so, says Itkonen. It is not sufficient to know the atheoretical rules that constitute one's language. These rules are "known to be true and it is precisely for this reason that they are theoretically uninteresting . . . Therefore, if we want to give a *systematic* and *interesting* description of a language, we must resort to (grammatical) rules of a more theoretical kind. Such rules attempt to give a coherent account of all the data involved by discovering (or inventing) "generalizations" which have not been known before. In order to make generalizations and to find out whether they hold or not, one has to be able to reflect in a creative way upon one's linguistic intuition . . . and to master certain formal techniques with which to express the results of one's (immanent) reflections." (p. 198). In other words, what the linguist does is to "generalize" the atheoretical rules to theoretical ones. About this, several things may be said. First, one may doubt that there can be any atheoretical rule-sentences in the proper sense, since any such sentence must contain terms which refer to concepts that cannot be understood except within a theory of grammar. For instance, in the rule "The definite article precedes the noun", the term "noun" presupposes a theory of parts of speech to be understood.[15] (In fact, this is not a trivial case. The term "noun" *(nomen)* originally covered both nouns and adjectives, and if we interpret it that way, the rule might change its truth-value. In Swedish, for instance, the definite article precedes adjectives but follows nouns.) Itkonen acknowledges that the term "definite article" is certainly not directly comprehensible to every native speaker of English, but nevertheless our rule-sentence . . . clearly refers to an atheoretical rule of English, i.e., a rule which can be made comprehensible to anyone, if only suitable, more down-to-earth

---

[15]* Itkonen comments: 'This sentence has been criticized e.g., by Dahl and Lieb because it contains such theoretical terms as "definite article" and "noun". First, this criticism does not affect the issue of empiricalness vs. non-empiricalness. Second, the following sentence serves my purposes just as well: "In English *the man* is correct and *man the* is incorrect" . . . and this sentence does *not* contain theoretical terms.' The question is not unrelated to the issue of empiricalness, as Itkonen claims. If the distinction between atheoretical and theoretical rules cannot be upheld, Itkonen's claims about the possibility to formulate (atheoretical) rule-sentences which are immediately known to be true become less attractive, too. It should also be pointed out that Itkonen's strategy here — that of substituting instances of a category for the theoretical term referring to that category — is not generally possible (perhaps not even possible in this case), due to the fact that some linguistic categories have an infinite number of members, which would render the set of rule-sentences infinite, a possibility which Itkonen seems to want to exclude (1974, 109).

circumlocutions are employed." It remains to be shown, however, how one is to find such down-to-earth circumlocutions for all the terms needed in rule-sentences. People who teach grammar and foreign languages at school would certainly be glad to hear about them.

Sometimes it is not very clear where the great difference lies between the two types of rules. On p. 223, Itkonen quotes as an (atheoretical) rule-sentence describing a certain constructed language $L_1$, the following:

"The correct sentences of $L_1$ consist of any number of $a$'s followed by an equal number of $b$'s."

He also gives the following "theoretical" grammar for $L_1$:

$S \rightarrow aSb$
$S \rightarrow ab$

Now, the only difference between the two "grammars" is that the first one is expressed in ordinary English words and that the second one uses a certain kind of formalism. Otherwise, they contain exactly the same information. So "theory" here seems equal to "formalization", which is not a very interesting use of the term. Actually, Itkonen admits that "the recognition that linguists may have to guide the native speaker's intuition in order to ascertain the extent of what he really knows, points to a certain relativity of the distinction between atheoretical and theoretical knowledge." (p. 200).[16]

One can also doubt the claim that all theoretical rules are in fact generalizations of atheoretical ones, which would imply that for any theoretical rule R, there is always a finite set of atheoretical rule-sentences, the conjunction of which is logically equivalent to R. (The set must be finite since the set of all atheoretical rules is finite in a language (or else it would be unlearnable).) For instance, Itkonen mentions as possible theoretical rules Chomsky's A-over-A principle and Ross' Complex Noun Phrase Constraint. He claims that they are generalizations of "a set of more or less obviously interrelated syntactic data". An example of the data from which the generalizations are made would be that "an NP which is exhaustively dominated by a determiner cannot be questioned or relativized out of the NP which immediately dominates that determiner." It is generally hard to see how rules which refer to technical syntactic relations such as "dominate", "command" etc. can be

---

[16*] In addition, the admission of such 'guidance' (without any criteria for what is permissible 'guidance' and what is not) makes it difficult to distinguish between what the speaker has known all the time and what the linguist tells him. In such a way, the claim that all atheoretical linguistic knowledge is potentially conscious risks becoming vacuous.

reduced to a set of statements which are "immediately understood to be true".

I have not been able in this paper to go into a detailed critique of all parts of Itkonen's book. I do not think either that I have shown conclusively the empirical status of linguistics, but I have pointed to a number of weak points and unwarranted assumptions in Itkonen's argumentation against regarding linguistics as an empirical science. Clearly, the methodology of a science the data of which largely consists of people's intuitions must differ in many respects from a science like physics. I think, however, that Itkonen has greatly overrated these differences and that he has not succeeded in characterizing the metascientific status of linguistic research. [17]

[For the bibliographical references to this contribution, see pp. 156—157 below — Ed.]

---

[17] One reason for this is the following: Itkonen's main object of attack is what he calls 'the positivist view of linguistics'. According to Itkonen, positivist methods 'in their purest form appear within the natural sciences, and particularly in mechanical physics.' Itkonen notes more en passant that positivism as a philosophy of science is not adequate even for the natural sciences. However, in the discussion, he assumes a positivist view of these sciences, which has as a consequence that they seem to be more different from linguistics than they need to be.

# Reply to Dahl

Esa Itkonen

Dahl's critique contains one argument which, if true, would refute my position. It is meant to show that my distinction between rule-sentences like "In English the definite article precedes the noun" and empirical hypotheses like "All pieces of metal expand when heated" does not hold. I claim that the former sentence is nonempirical because it can be falsified neither by correct utterances like "The girl came in" nor by incorrect utterances like "Girl the came in." By contrast, the latter sentence is clearly empirical because it would be falsified by a piece of metal which does *not* expand when heated. Furthermore I claim that grammatical hypotheses like the A-over-A principle are different from rule-sentences in that they *can* be (nonempirically) falsified.

Dahl claims that I am making a mistake here. Let us see which one of us is right. I quote the relevant passage in its entirety, so I cannot be accused of misrepresenting Dahl's position. (For ease of exposition I have numbered the different steps in the two relevant arguments.)

"Actually, the comparison between the deviant piece of metal and the incorrect sentence is not quite accurate. We could show this by arranging the two examples in parallel ways. We could represent the case of the metal which does not expand as follows:

A  1  Hypothesis: All pieces of metal expand when heated.
    2  Test situation: Object A is a piece of metal.
    3  Outcome of test: A does not expand when heated.
    Hypothesis refuted.

The general schema will now be:
Hypothesis: All S have property P.
Test situation: A is an S.
Outcome of test: A does not have property P.
If we try to apply this schema to the case with the ungrammatical sentence, we get the following:

B  1  Hypothesis: All English sentences have the property that if they contain a definite article, it precedes its noun.
    2  Test situation: *Girl the came in* is an English sentence.
    3  Outcome of test: In *Girl the came in* the definite article does not precede the noun.

This, however, does not represent what we actually have. The statement that the string *Girl the came in* is an English sentence is, as we know, false, and thus the test situation does not obtain. The only thing we know is that *Girl the came in* is an utterance, but from this we cannot draw the conclusion that the hypothesis is false, only that either it is false or the string in question is not an English sentence. But exactly the same would hold in the case of the "regularity," if we assume that we do not know that A is a piece of metal. In that case, the outcome of the test would not allow us to refute the general hypothesis: it might be false, but it might also be the case that A is a piece of ice. Thus the difference between the two situations that Itkonen points to does not depend on the difference between rules and regularities but rather on the fact that in one case, we do not know whether the entity to be tested belongs to the domain of the general statement. If we look at the case of the counterexamples to the A-over-A principle, we see that it is more like the case of the non-expanding piece of metal. Here it is assumed from the start that counter-instances belong to the domain of the rule, namely correct English sentences."

First of all, I note that rather than saying with Dahl that "Girl the came in" is not an English sentence, I would say that it is an *incorrect* English sentence, as opposed to the correct sentence "The girl came in." Moreover, since we are discussing spatiotemporal falsifiability, it would be more accurate to formulate B 2 as *"Girl the came in* is an utterance of an English sentence." However, since this would complicate the comparison of B with A, I shall again retain Dahl's terminology.

Dahl notes, quite correctly, that in the case of A a genuine test situation *can* obtain: It is possible that A 2 is true while A 3, i.e., the negation of the conclusion logically entailed by the truth of A 1 and A 2, is also true. If this is the case, then the hypothesis A 1 is falsified by modus tollens.

We are discussing falsifiability, and we just saw that the hypothesis A 1 is (spatiotemporally) falsifiable. Now, there are only two types of sentences (or utterances) which could possibly be relevant to the truth or falsity of the linguistic "hypothesis" B 1, namely correct sentences (or utterances) like "The girl came in" and incorrect sentences (or utterances) like "Girl the came in." Without discussing the matter explicitly, Dahl realizes that a correct sentence cannot falsify a "hypothesis" like B 1 (i.e., a true rule-sentence). Therefore he concentrates on the case where an *incorrect* sentence constitutes "the outcome of the test." He notes, quite correctly, that in such a case the test situation *cannot* obtain because if B 3 is true, which is a precondition for falsifying B 1, then B 2 is necessarily false: but this means that B 1 *cannot* be falsified. (In the terminology of deductive-nomological (D-N) explanation, which I have used in several of my writings, the relation between the antecedent conditions and the explanandum fact is not contingent, as it should be, but conceptual or necessary.)

Now, what has Dahl managed to show? He has shown that while A 1 *can* be spatiotemporally falsified and hence is empirical, B 1 *cannot* be falsified (spatiotemporally or non-spatiotemporally) and hence is nonempirical. *But this is precisely my point* (cf. Itkonen 1974, Ch. IV, Sect. 1). Therefore, insofar as grammatical hypotheses like the A-over-A principle ultimately rest upon, or describe referents of sentences like B 1, they cannot possibly be *empirical* hypotheses.

Dahl points out that if A 2 is false, then the truth of A 3 has no effect on the truth-value of A 1. This is of course correct, but irrelevant. The important thing is that it is possible that both A 2 and A 3 are true, in which case A 1 is falsified (cf. above). But, as Dahl himself so aptly demonstrates, it is *not* possible that both B 2 and B 3 are true, which means that B 1 is unfalsifiable.

In the end of the quoted passage Dahl aptly formulates my distinction between rule-sentence and grammatical hypothesis (which he elsewhere in his critique is quite unable to grasp): Rule-sentences differ from empirical hypotheses in that they are unfalsifiable (and hence nonempirical); grammatical hypotheses like the A-over-A principle are similar to empirical hypotheses in that they are falsifiable (albeit non-spatiotemporally or nonempirically).

The point of the above passage is to show the difference between *rules* and *regularities,* as this difference is generally conceived of in social science (cf. the Ryan-quotation below). In view of this fact and of what Dahl manages to make of it, his following off-hand remark acquires a special poignancy: "Itkonen's argument builds on a number of distinctions, and it is necessary to clarify these first. First there is the distinction between rule and regularity, *a rather straightforward and common one*" (italics mine).

Dahl's other critical comments mostly turn on his "general impressions," which he does not care to develop into exact counter-arguments. I shall mention those which seem the most important to me.

It is not true that, as one might gather from Dahl's discussion, I offer the argument for the *necessary* character of rule-sentences in Ch. IV, Sect. 3 of Itkonen 1974. This argument was offered in Sect. 1 in demonstrating that rule-sentences differ from empirical hypotheses because of their unfalsifiability (cf. above). In that section (i.e., Sect. 3) which Dahl is discussing I try to answer the following question: *If* analytical philosophy is right in claiming that nonempirical truth is "truth by virtue of meaning" (which still leaves open the choice between analytic truth and synthetic a priori truth), how can we then make sense of the nonempirical truth of (true) rule-sentences (which *N. B.* is already a definitively established fact)? The answer which I tried to outline did not seem to me very convincing, as I explicitly noted when stressing the *sui generis* character of rule-sentences:

> "... there is no reason to assume that rule-sentences are neatly classifiable as belonging to one or another of the above-mentioned traditional types of necessary sentence [i.e., analytic and synthetic a priori], because these were established in complete disregard of rules and their peculiarities" (op. cit.: 100). "... there is no need to classify rule-sentences in accordance with those distinctions which have traditionally been thought to be philosophically relevant; it is sufficient to describe rule-sentences in their own right ..." (op. cit.: 112).

Today I think that Dahl is correct in pointing out the unnaturalness of the idea that the nonempirical or necessary character of rule-sentences would depend on the fact that a language is defined (in the sense of "constituted") by its rules. (This I still take to be a fact: The *only* difference between English and Finnish is that they have different rules. If they had precisely identical rules, they would not be two different languages.) The upshot is that, just as I surmised in Itkonen 1974, analytical philosophy does not seem to possess adequate conceptual tools to account for the nonempiricalness of rule-sentences.

According to Dahl, "one gets the impression that because the rules of grammar do not correspond to any one hundred percent regularities, there are no relations at all between linguistic rules and observed linguistic data." Getting such impressions results from not reading my book carefully enough; cf. e.g., the following passage: "It is a remarkable fact that behavior violating a rule does not falsify the corresponding rule-sentence; the reason is simple, of course: what one *does* has no direct relation (although it certainly has *some* relation) to what one ought to do" (Itkonen 1974: 83). For my part, I get the impression that Dahl makes no distinction at all between rules and observed data. He mentions the "straightforward and common" distinction between rule and regularity (cf. above), but he nowhere says what he thinks this distinction consists in, or whether it has any methodological consequences.

According to Dahl, "the claim that linguistics concerns itself with necessary truths, is misleading," and although there may be necessary statements in linguistics, "they do not by themselves constitute linguistic hypotheses." I agree. I capture these these two aspects (i.e., indubitable normative data vs. falsifiable theoretical descriptions) with my "rule-sentence — grammatical hypothesis" distinction.

Dahl argues that I make a much too definite distinction between learning a language and knowing it. He refers in particular to the fact that linguists often have to describe languages which they know only imperfectly. Although he does not seem to intend this as a very serious criticism, I take the issue up here because it is related to a distinction which, in spite of its importance, is practically unknown in contemporary linguistics, namely the distinction between *ontology* and *methodology.*

Natural languages are *native* languages of different communities. One knows one's native language; a community knows its own language. Therefore it belongs to the nature, or to the *ontology,* of natural language that it be known, i.e., that it be the object of "common knowledge," in the technical sense defined, e.g., by Lewis. On the other hand, it does *not* belong to the ontology of natural language that it is described for scientific purposes by people who know it only imperfectly. The difficulties ensuing from the latter situation are of purely *methodological* nature. Now, if we wish to describe language as it *is* (ontologically), then we must *know* it, that is, in the ideal research situation ontology and methodology must coincide; and very often they do in fact. This is my general answer to the question concerning the metascientific status of research on exotic or extinct languages.

My slogan "rules of language and knowledge of rules of language coincide" has occasionally given rise to the charge of "incorrigibilism" or "transcendental idealism." But surely there can be no rules where there is no knowledge (cf. Lessnoff 1974: 44—45). For instance, there were no rules (of language) on the earth before the emergence of life. It is only this quite innocuous truth that I want to express with the above-mentioned slogan. By contrast, it does *not* belong to the ontology of (e.g., physical) regularities that they be known. The laws of mechanics existed before the emergence of life on the earth.

[As for Dahl's criticism of my notion of "rule," cf. my reply to his rebuttal below.]

Dahl portrays me as saying that it is "surely absurd" to claim that when examining our own language we can only observe particular occurrences confirming (or falsifying) our linguistic hypothesis. Dahl adds that I offer no reason for my position. Considering that the view which I am apparently attacking here is nearly universally accepted today, it would be very rash if I really called it "surely absurd." In fact, I do not do so. Although I think that this view is mistaken, it is certainly a rational one, as can be seen from the fact that it is not quite easy to refute it in a convincing way. What I do claim is absurd, is the idea that we could never know for sure whether in our own dialect of English the definite article precedes or follows the noun, but could only observe particular occurrences confirming the hypothesis that the article precedes the noun. This *is* absurd. It is more than odd for Dahl to say that I "give no reason for my claim." The example I use is reason enough.

Dahl notes that the simplicity of one of my rule-sentences "is not impressive." But there is no reason why it should be. If Dahl's oversights were less impressive, he would have noticed that I define rule-sentences as unscientific, *ad hoc* formulations. Simplicity is a matter of *scientific* descriptions, in my terminology, of grammatical hypotheses.

Dahl correctly points out that my simple grammar $G_1$ is a bad example of a "theoretical grammar" (Itkonen 1974: 223—227). The point I try to make with $G_1$ does not concern the distinction between atheoretical and theoretical, or falsifiable and unfalsifiable, which I make elsewhere, but the uniformly *normative* subject matter of all grammatical descriptions, whether atheoretical or theoretical.

In summary, Dahl offers no justification for, but does offer some counter-evidence against, his conclusion that "Itkonen has not succeeded in characterizing the metascientific status of linguistic research."

[For bibliographical references to this contribution, see pp.161—162 below. — Ed.]


## First Rebuttal: Östen Dahl[*]

Itkonen (1976: 2) states that 'I have seen no reason for modifying my position in the least, in particular since most criticisms (at least those I am aware of) are based on quite trivial misunderstandings'. Some shifts in emphasis may be discerned, however. In particular, Itkonen now emphasizes the distinction between 'grammar' — in the sense of 'a science that provides synchronic-grammatical descriptions of (parts of) natural languages' (1976: 62) — and 'sociolinguistics and psycholinguistics.' 'My claim is that grammar is non-empirical whereas sociolinguistics and psycholinguistics are empirical' (1976: 4).

Itkonen devotes a section of his paper to refute my criticisms. Some of his more specific comments I have already tried to answer in footnotes at the appropriate places above; here I shall concentrate on discussing what can be referred to as 'the ontology of rules,' since it seems to be at the heart of the matter and also an area which I may not have treated in sufficient detail above.

Let us say that a rule is any kind of principle which divides possible actions or courses of action into two classes: 'allowed' and 'not allowed.'

What does it mean to say that such a rule or principle 'exists?' We can distinguish at least two kinds of existence that may be attributed to rules: 'possible' and 'actual' existence, and accordingly we may distinguish between two kinds of rules: possible rules and actual rules. The class of possible rules is of course much larger than the class of actual ones. The only requirement we can place on a possible rule is that it be internally consistent. Usually, it is more interesting to talk about specific subclasses of possible rules: for instance, the set of all possible phrase structure rules. The properties of such classes of rules are studied by clearly non-empirical branches of science, such as 'formal linguistics' in the sense defined in fn. 10. For a rule to be actual, on the other hand, we demand that it be in some way reflected in (human or animal) behavior. There are several ways in which this may be the case. First, it may be the case

---

[*] Quite a few linguists have now reacted to Itkonen's work (see for instance Linell 1976, Sampson 1976 and the papers in Wunderlich 1976). Itkonen has now in his turn reacted to these criticisms and comments in Itkonen 1976. When I was offered to publish my paper in this volume, I decided that the best thing to do was to present it in its original form (with a few editorial changes), adding a number of footnotes (see p. 133) and this rebuttal. This will preserve the chronology of the discussion, although some of the things I said in the original paper will now have become obsolete.

that some individual or group of individuals actually conforms to or tries to conform to the rule: in this case, we may refer to the rule as a behavior-guiding rule (or principle). Second, a rule may be accepted or acknowledged in various ways by individuals or groups of individuals, independently of whether they actually conform to it. This may be reflected in various ways: for instance, by explicit acts of accepting the rule, by reactions to other individuals' behavior, e.g., in the form of sanctions against those who violate it, and so on. We shall refer to rules of this kind as 'acknowledged rules.' It is important to see that a rule may be behavior-guiding without being acknowledged and acknowledged without being behavior-guiding. The concept of 'double standards' applies to these very situations where there is a gap between behavior-guiding and acknowledged rules. Accordingly, there is an important difference between behavior-guiding rules and acknowledged rules as to their relations to regularities in behavior. A behavior-guiding rule always corresponds to some kind of regularity in behavior; else it would not be behavior-guiding. An acknowledged rule need not have any relation at all to the behavior which is actually exhibited. However, although there is, as we said, some kind of regularity corresponding to each behavior-guiding rule, it does not follow that a statement of the form 'X's behavior is guided by the rule "Do Y in situations Z" ' entails 'In all situations Z, X does Y.' There are several reasons for this. First, X's behavior may be guided by the rule in the sense that he tries to conform to it, although he does not succeed. Second — as is generally the case with regularities — we must allow for a general *ceteris paribus* clause or assumption that 'normal conditions hold.' In particular, the rule may be overridden by some other, stronger rule.[1]

Notice, however, the fundamental difference between behavior-guiding rules and acknowledged rules with respect to 'violations': Behavior-guiding rules can only be 'violated' if there is 'good excuse' for doing so, otherwise the agent in question cannot be said to follow the rule and there is no reason for assuming the existence of a behavior-guiding rule, which by definition must be followed.[2] An acknowledged

---

[1]   The simpler and more trivial a rule is, the less frequent will the 'violations' of it be. Thus, Itkonen's favorite rule 'In English, the article precedes the noun' is very unlikely to be violated in actual behavior: I doubt that a single instance of the noun preceding the article can be found in actual speech, except for starred examples in linguistic discussions.

[2]   When the rule is part of a 'game' — as in the case of linguistic rules — we obtain another kind of apparent violations, due to the fact that we may not be able to tell with certainty whether the individuals we are observing are actually playing the game (in our case, speaking the language). It seems to me that aberrant uses of languages are often best analyzed as 'secondary games' i.e., games which exploit in some way the rules of the normal (primary) game. This would cover e.g., various kinds of linguistic jobs, poetic language etc.

rule, on the other hand, does not lose its character of being acknowledged even by wholesale neglect of it in actual behavior.

What we have said here does not mean that we have reduced rules to regularities (as Sampson 1976 seems to want to do, at least for linguistic rules): We have only argued that a behavior-guiding rule must at least correspond to a regularity to the effect that the individuals in questions try to conform to the rule, if they have no 'good excuse' not to do so. In fact, this seems quite compatible with Itkonen's statement (1976, 22): '... where a rule₁ obtains, human behavior tries to conform to it but does not always do so in fact.'

In spite of this, Itkonen ignores the distinction we have made here between the two kinds of rules and how they can be 'violated.' Arguing against Sampson 1976, Itkonen (1976, 58) says that 'Sometimes we may (intuitively) understand that people are using incorrect forms because they are joking, teasing, insulting, etc. but in such situations there are mostly no observable correlates which would invariably accompany those situations, and therefore the requirements of empirical explanation are not satisfied. And sometimes we do not even understand why people are saying something incorrect; they just do so.' This, however, does not distinguish linguistics from the natural sciences. A scientist may obtain data that seem to contradict his hypothesis: he may not be able to explain why these data obtain, but that does not necessarily oblige him to discard his hypothesis. He just has to assume that there is *some* explanation for the deviant data. Suppose for instance that we observe a dog with three legs. We may have no possibility of finding out why he has not got a fourth, still we would not like to regard the hypothesis 'Dogs have four legs' as refuted. It is first when there are too many contradicting data to be reasonably assumed to be explainable that the hypothesis is discarded.

It should also be pointed out that in spite of Itkonen's claims to the contrary, the necessity for 'editing' the data does not distinguish linguistics from the natural sciences. Any scientist must be able to exclude 'nonsense data.' If my thermometer shows that my body temperature is 43 °C, I do not conclude that earlier theories about possible variations in body temperature are wrong but that I should buy a new thermometer.

Let us now ask the question: What are the criteria that must be met for us to accept as true a statement of the form 'Rule X holds in the language of Y,' where Y is an individual or a group of individuals?

The crucial situation is when someone has a subjectively clear intuition about some rule in language, e.g., thinks that some construction is clearly ungrammatical or unacceptable but at the same time violates this rule systematically in his speech, e.g., uses the construction over and over again. Would we say that rule X — i.e., in this case, the rule that excludes the construction — holds in his language or not? I think that most linguists would agree on the following: If the violations of the purported rule are so frequent and systematic that unintentional mistakes are excluded, we would say that the speaker's intuitive judgements do not represent his actual grammar. In other words, linguistic rules must guide behavior. (This does not imply, of course, that linguistic rules are not also normally acknowledged in the sense that there is normative social pressure to conform with them.)

In order to show that the situation described in the preceding paragraph is not just a theoretical possibility, I shall quote Labov 1975. Referring to an investigation of the use of *anymore* in non-negated sentences (e.g., in a sentence like *John is smoking a lot anymore*) in the Philadelphia speech community, Labov says that 'since 1972, we have collected 12 cases of speakers who used positive *anymore* quite freely though their introspective judgements were entirely negative' and that 'we are forced to the following conclusion about the introspective judgements of those 20 % of our Philadelphia subjects whose introspections fail to recognize *anymore*: these judgements have no direct relation to the grammar that governs their speech. This puts us in the somewhat embarrassing position of knowing more about a speaker's grammar than he does himself.' In a footnote, he adds: 'In one sense, this is a normal situation, since we know more about the grammatical rules of someone's dialect. But we can say that we know more about his intuitions than he does, if we consider that these represent the knowledge that he actually uses to speak and interpret speech; it is an odd claim to say that we have better access to these intuitions than he does, but the evidence points in this direction.' (1975: 107).

I do not know how Itkonen would treat a case like this, but to me it seems to be a nice example of empirical falsiability of linguistic claims. Itkonen says about Labov and other sociolinguists that they 'investigate the actual behavior of different groups of speakers and therefore their descriptions are definitely empirical' (1976, 35). However, they are not doing grammar, since grammar is not empirical, and the collection of a corpus of factual utterances with grammatical description is 'an idle ceremony' (1976, 8 ff.). Thus, Itkonen would have to say that the description of Philadelphia English that we arrive at on the basis of Labov's data is not 'grammar' but something else.

Itkonen's claim about the relevance of corpus vis-à-vis grammar is contradicted not only by the practice of 'empirical' sociolinguists such as Labov, but also by what has been done within transformational-generative grammar and traditional grammar, about which, according to Itkonen, 'there is no doubt' that they 'are subsumable under grammar.' (1976, 5). Itkonen claims that synchronic-grammatical descriptions of natural languages 'do not investigate a *corpus,* i.e., a limited number (e.g., 1000) factual utterances made by a clearly definable group of persons in clearly definable spatiotemporal surroundings.' As support of his claim, he points out that those of his critics who have reacted adversely to his earlier statements to the same effect themselves make exclusive use of invented examples, if they use examples at all. However, it is of course irrelevant whether 'such champions of "empirical" linguistics as Dahl, Lieb, Sampson, Schnelle and Wunderlich' (1976, 34) investigate corpora of actual utterances or not. What is interesting is whether it is possible to construct grammars exclusively on the basis of a corpus of the kind Itkonen describes. Indeed, this is not only possible but also necessary in the cases when one has no access at all to grammaticality judgements of native speakers, as in the case of extinct languages or in the study of the language of very small children. As a concrete example, I may quote Berman 1972, a paper on relative clauses in Hittite. According to Berman, our knowledge of Hittite is 'with a few insignificant exceptions based on about 27,000 fragments of clay tablets inscribed in cuneiform which have been excavated at Boghazköy.' Berman postulates 9 phrase structure and transformational rules rules which he claims are relevant for Hittite relative clause formation. Again, I do not know how Itkonen would treat such a case of grammatical investigation.

I shall here indicate a few additional features of Itkonen's arguments that tend to confuse the issue.

First, in speaking of falsification, Itkonen concentrates on single counter-examples. It is of course true that a single counter-instance in actual speech will rarely lead anyone to discard a linguistic hypothesis, but things are different if we consider wholesale incompatibility between a linguistic claim and actual behavior.

Second, Itkonen sees no problem in the assumption that 'atheoretical knowledge' of linguistic rules is conscious or at least potentially conscious. But this is certainly not uncontroversial. As Itkonen points out, linguistic knowledge is 'agent's knowledge' in the sense that it concerns knowledge about one's actual or possible actions. Clearly, such knowledge is often unconscious: for example, I know how to maintain my balance when riding a bicycle, but I cannot tell you how I do it, and there is no obvious 'introspective' way by which I could attain understanding of this process. The same goes for much linguistic knowledge, in particular on the phonetic but also on other levels. I may e.g., be able to pronounce a certain vowel 'correctly' and even be able to judge whether other speakers pronounce it 'correctly' or not; still, I may have to use phonetic instrumental techniques in order to 'become conscious' of what actually constitutes the difference between correct and incorrect pronunciations. This is important, since it has bearing on the question whether a rule must be known, as Itkonen claims is 'ontologically' necessary, a claim which needs to be discussed in some detail.

We must first return to the distinction between behavior-guiding and acknowledged rules. An acknowledged rule may very well hold without being known in any sense by any individual. For instance, suppose that a group of persons have signed a contract which contain rules with binding force for them all. It is quite irrelevant for the force of the document that the details of it may be forgotten by everyone, as long as the document is still there to be checked, if needed. A behavior-guiding rule, on the other hand, must of course be known as 'agent's knowledge' insofar as it actually guides behavior. However, it may very well be known only unconsciously and, as we have said, the knowledge may not be accessible to introspection.

My last comment concerns Itkonen's claim that linguistic knowledge is acquired through understanding, not through observation (see e.g., Itkonen 1975, 4). I must admit that I cannot always follow Itkonen's line of reasoning in this area: this may well be due to my limited knowledge of hermeneutics, but it seems to me that Itkonen's comparisons between 'understanding' and 'observation' fail for the simple reason that these two concepts are not parallel in their relation to the process of acquisition of knowledge. Observation is a means used in this process; understanding, on the other hand, is the successful end of the process. Understanding entails acquiring knowledge: this is not the case for observation. And, it seems to me, however we define 'understanding human actions,' this understanding will normally depend on previous observation of behavior. In the same way, one cannot learn a language without observing other people's behavior. Of course, once we have learnt the language, we can stop observing. But that holds for all acquisition of knowledge: when the knowledge is acquired, no further observation is needed, and this fact is of course irrelevant for the empirical character of the knowledge.

## References

Anttila, R. (1975): 'Kielitiede palaa kotiin.' *Virittäjä* 1975: 1, 98—102.
Fillmore, C. (1970): 'On Generativity.' In *Working Papers in Linguistics No. 6,* Ohio State University, Columbus, Ohio.
Itkonen, E. (1974): 'Linguistics and Metascience.' *Studia Philosophica Turkuensia Fasc. II.* Kokemäki 1974.
Itkonen, E. (1975): 'Concerning the relationship between linguistics and logic', Indiana University Linguistics Club.
Itkonen, E. (1976): 'Linguistics and Empiricalness: Answers to criticisms.' Dept. of General Linguistics, University of Helsinki.
Koerner, E. F. K. ed. (1975): *The transformational-generative paradigm and modern linguistic theory.* Amsterdam: Benjamins.

Labov, W. (1971): 'Methodology.' In Dingwall, W. O., ed., *A Survey of Linguistic Science*. University of Maryland, College Park.
Labov, W. (1975): 'Empirical Foundations of Linguistic Theory' in R. Austerlitz (ed.): *The Scope of American Linguistics*. Lisse: Peter de Ridder.
Lakatos, I. (1972): 'Falsification and the methodology of scientific research programmes' in Lakatos and Musgrave (1970).
Lakatos, I., and Musgrave, A. eds. (1970): *Criticism and the Growth of Knowledge*. Cambridge: Cambridge University Press.
Linell, P. 1974: 'Is linguistics an empirical science? Some notes on Esa Itkonen's Linguistics and Metascience,' *Studia Linguistica*.
Montague, R. (1974): *'Formal Philosophy.' Selected papers of Richard Montague*. Edited with an introduction by Richmond H. Thomason. New York and London: Yale University Press.
Sampson, G. (1976): Review of Koerner (ed.) 1975, *Language*.
Wunderlich, D. (ed.) (1976): *Die Wissenschaftstheorie der Linguistik, Frankfurt/M: Atheneum*.

## Second Rebuttal: Esa Itkonen

Grammarians do not even try to empirically explain why somebody at a given moment says something incorrect; and psycholinguists have not yet been able to do so. This fact is due to the largely unpredictable nature of human behavior, one aspect of which is the "free will." By contrast, biologists routinely provide (plausible) empirical explanations. Therefore Dahl's example of a dog with three legs is irrelevant to grammar and only programmatically relevant, so to say, to psycholinguistics. The old debate about determinism vs. indeterminism is lurking here. Dahl is a determinist, I am an indeterminist. (Moreover, there is indeterminism in physics and indeterminism in human science; only the latter, of course, is connected to free will.) It is universally agreed that even if (absolute) determinism in the explanation of human behavior were a logical possibility (which it is not, at least not in relation to any given state of human knowledge), it is today and in the foreseeable future a *practical impossibility*. This implies, *inter alia*, that we are perfectly justified in taking rules, i.e., (possible) correct or incorrect behavior, for granted and in describing them in their own right. In fact, this is what Dahl *qua* grammarian has always been doing.

Dahl, as well as my other critics, chooses to ignore the role of *normativity* in linguistics, i.e., in linguistic data. This is regrettable because all issues discussed here are directly related to it. When we observe linguistic occurrences, we do not simply observe what happens in space and time. Rather, we do it, as it were, through the spectacles of normativity which enable us to divide the spatiotemporal linguistic phenomena into three classes: correct, incorrect, and doubtful. In natural science the situation is different: everything that happens in the natural course of events is "correct." Therefore *the notion of correctness does not apply here at all.* In natural science only researchers can behave incorrectly. In grammar, and in human science in general, both research objects and researchers can behave incorrectly. This is why the editing of data in (socio)linguistics is entirely different from excluding "nonsense data" in natural science. — Grammar investigates the above-mentioned "spectacles of normativity." In a very natural sense they are the "transcendental" precondition to being able to speak and understand any given language; they are, of course, identical with rules of language.

In discussing the relevance vs. irrelevance of corpus to grammar, there are two interesting questions to be asked. First: Is it possible to construct a grammatical description, i.e., a description of "correct sentence in L," without recourse to a corpus? — The answer is *Yes,* and it is justified by a reference to contemporary grammarians' *actual* descriptive practice. (Contrary to what Dahl says, this question *is* interesting because, in criticizing my position, Wunderlich, Lieb, and Sampson vehemently answer *No;* cf. Itkonen 1976.)

Second: Is it possible to construct a grammatical description exclusively on the basis of a corpus? — The answer is *No,* and the reason is that "correct sentence" and "sentence exemplified by, utterances in a corpus" are two different concepts. This is confirmed by, e.g., Labov's actual descriptive practice: First, he has to edit his data (in a sense quite different from excluding "nonsense data" in natural science). Second, a small but still significant part of the edited data is clearly incorrect and must therefore be discarded.

Suppose, however, that someone writes a grammar (of Hittite) exclusively on the basis of a (written) corpus. Then there are two possibilities: Either — by a curious accident — there happen to be no incorrect utterances in the corpus; if so, the grammatical description is acceptable. Or there are incorrect utterances in the corpus, and the grammarian (because of his — and everybody's — insufficient knowledge of Hittite) describes them too; if so, the grammatical description is unacceptable. (In the case of Hittite we may have no way of knowing which alternative is the true one; but this does not mean the alternatives do not exist).

My notions of "rule" and "rule-sentence" have troubled Dahl the most. First of all, I would like to point out that I am not introducing here any new and suspect entities, but merely reinterpreting old ones. On the other hand, this apparently modest reinterpretation suffices to show that the metascientific status of linguistic (i.e., grammatical) research has been almost universally misunderstood.

What I just said, can be clarified in the following way. Each science must have its own set of basic statements, i.e., statements dealing with the simplest aspect of that region of reality with which the science in question is concerned. The basic statements of natural science are about particular spatiotemporal occurrences. What do the basic statements of grammar look like? Bach (1974: 61—63) and Leech (1974: 84—90) give examples of, respectively, morpho-syntactic and semantic basic statements. For instance: "The past tense of *play* is *played;* the past tense of *sing* is not *singed* but *sang.*" "*Sing* can occur in contexts like '\_\_\_\_ me a song.' and 'To \_\_\_\_ is fun,' but not in contexts like 'John is \_\_\_\_ er than Mary' and 'The extremely \_\_\_\_ man told me a long story'." "*This orphan has a father* is a contradiction."

Unlike the basic statements of natural science, the basic statements of grammar do not describe particular spatiotemporal occurrences, but *rules.* For instance, it is a rule of English that the past tense of *sing* is *sang.* Any utterances of *sang* (with the past tense meaning) are cases of conforming to the rule, i.e., they are *correct,* just as any utterances of *singed,* mostly made by children or foreigners, are cases of violating it, i.e., they are *incorrect.* The rule has an intimate connection with utterances conforming or failing to conform to it, but it cannot be *reduced* to them; and the basic statement, or rule-sentence, "The past tense of *sing* is *sang*" clearly describes not utterances, but the rule, i.e., the criterion which enables us to know that (actual or possible) utterances of *sang* and *singed* are, respectively, correct and incorrect.

It is undisputable that rules of the type here discussed can be, and are, known without a possibility of doubt: they simply constitute the basis of any grammatical description, which means that they too, and not just (relations between) particular sentences, are objects of linguistic intuition. (Once rules have been learned — self-evidently on the basis of observation —, they are not *assumed,* as Bartsch (1976) would have it, but *known,* which distinguishes them from regularities *assumed* on the basis of observable data; so the ball re-returns to Dahl.) It is quite obvious that the rules, as here defined, are tied together by some more abstract mechanisms which lie under the level of linguistic intuition. It is the task of experimental psycholinguistics to uncover such mechanisms. In this task it may be guided, to some extent, by grammatical descriptions, which are constructed solely on the basis of (linguistic intuition about) rules. I think it is definitely a mistake to call such unconscious psychological mechanisms "rules," given that there is nothing normative about them. A perpetually unconscious "rule" is identical with a regularity. Stones are perpetually unconscious of obeying the "rule" of gravitation. So Dahl still owes me an account of how he draws the "straightforward" distinction between rule and regularity. — Notice also that the rules here discussed, and a large number of similar rules, exhibit no variability (at the moment). So it is simply not true that all rules of natural language are variable. (As for the relation between invariant and variable rules, cf. my contribution to the present volume.)

We have already seen that rule-sentences (i.e., "basic statements of grammar") are nonempirical. Their actual formulation may be awkward or complex, but their referents, i.e., rules, are by definition maximally simple. This is why both rules and rule-sentences are called *atheoretical.* The distinction between atheoretical and theoretical, just like that between rich and poor, is of course gradual, but this does not mean that it is non-existent. Our rule-sentences already contained such (semi-) theoretical terms as "past tense" and "contradiction." Contrary to what Dahl says, the question of atheoretical vs. theoretical terms is unrelated to the question of empiricalness vs. nonempiricalness. Physics and logic use both kinds of terms, and one is empirical and the other, nonempirical.

Linguists are largely unacquainted with questions of normativity. In neighbouring sciences, by contrast, it is well known that the study of rules and norms requires its own methodology. The following statement represents the standpoint of the theory of social science:

> "A causal generalization has only one task to fulfil, namely telling us what will and will not happen under particular conditions; irregularities are thus falsifying counter-examples to the causal law. But rules are not falsifiable in any simple way — except of course that it may be false to say that there is a rule — and breaches of a rule are errors on the part of those whose behavior is governed by it" (Ryan 1970: 141).

Stegmüller (1973: 13) rules out the possibility of empirical falsification in philosophical analysis as follows:

> „Was durch die wissenschaftstheoretischen Analysen erstrebt wird, sind jedoch keine empirischen Gesetzmäßigkeiten, unter die das Verhalten aller ... als rational bezeichneten Leute zu subsumieren wäre. ... Ein faktischer Verstoß gegen die wahrscheinlichkeitstheoretischen Grundaxiome ist kein Anzeichen dafür, daß diese Axiome empirisch falsifiziert sind, sondern ein Symptom dafür, daß diese Menschen ein irrationales Verhalten an den Tag legen.“

We have precisely the same principle in linguistics: If your actions are in conflict with a (true) rule-sentence, they do not falsify it; your are merely acting incorrectly.

The situation is the same also within logic. Consider one of the axioms of von Wright's (1971) "monadic" system of deontic logic "-(Op & O-p)," which says that it is not the case that one ought to do *p* and one ought to do not-*p*. It is self-evident that if your actions are in conflict with this formula, they do not (empirically) falsify it; rather, you are acting "incorrectly" from the logical point of view, i.e., in a self-contradictory fashion.

Dahl and others have many other objections against my notion of rule. They raise issues related to ontology, variability, learning, certainty, different types of agent's knowledge, etc. I refer the reader to Itkonen 1978, where these questions have already been answered extensively enough.

Although Dahl does discuss the relation of grammar to empirical sciences like physics, he *never* discusses the relation of grammar to nonempirical sciences like logic or philosophy. This is a ruinous asymmetry in his argumentation. I really do not see how he can hope to contest my claim that grammar is nonempirical, if he refuses even to consider the notion of nonempirical science.

My general argument consists of two complementary and interdependent parts: A) Grammar is different from empirical sciences like physics or Durkheimian sociology. B) Grammar is similar to nonempirical sciences like logic and philosophy. Since these two claims are complementary, they are of course equally important, and I have devoted an equal amount of time to proving both of them. I repeat that my critics, including Dahl, have never even touched upon the latter claim. This fact would in itself suffice to render all their criticisms inconclusive.

I would call Dahl a positivist: He claims that the methodology of natural science is valid in all sciences worthy of this name. His positivism suffers from a deep ambivalence which on closer inspection turns out to be an ordinary self-contradiction. He maintains, on one hand, that the methodology of natural science is adequate to describing human language and, on the other, that human language is qualitatively different from the data of natural science; cf. his claim that "the methodology of a science the data of which largely consists of people's intuitions must differ in many respects from a science like physics." Unfortunately, these "many respects" are never specified. Dahl represents that standard conception about the nature of grammatical data according to which it consists *both* of intuitive knowledge *and* of observable events. Moreover, both types of data are supposedly to be described by one and the same method of description. This is a hopeless confusion (cf. Itkonen 1974: 157—163). For my part, I have showed, or have at least tried to show, how, precisely, intuitional (= nonempirical) and observational (= empirical) components of linguistics are to be fitted together so as to obtain a coherent total conception of linguistics.


References

Bach, Emmon, 1974: *Syntactic theory*, New York: Holt.
Bartsch, Renate, 1976: „Kommentar zu Itkonen", in D. Wunderlich (ed.): *Wissenschaftstheorie der Linguistik*, Frankfurt a/M: Athenäum.
Itkonen, Esa, 1974: *Linguistics and metascience*, Studia philosophica Turkuensia II.
—, 1976: *Linguistics and empiricalness: answers to criticisms*, Publications of the General Linguistics Department of the University of Helsinki, 4.
—, 1978: *Grammatical theory and metascience*, Amsterdam: Benjamins.
Leech, Geoffrey, 1974: *Semantics*, Penguin Books.

Lessnoff, Michael, 1974: *The structure of social science,* London: Allen.

Ryan, Alan, 1970: *The philosophy of the social sciences,* London: Macmillan.

Stegmüller, Wolfgang, 1973: *Probleme und Resultate der Wissenschaftstheorie und Analytischen Philosophie IV: Personelle und Statistische Wahrscheinlichkeit, Personelle Wahrscheinlichkeit und Rationale Entscheidung,* Berlin: Springer.

von Wright, Georg Henrik, 1971: "A new system of deontic logic," in R. Hilpinen (ed.): *Deontic logic: introductory and systematic readings,* Dordrecht: Reidel.

# Against Autonomous Linguistics

Bruce L. Derwing

## 1. Introduction

The past few years have witnessed a veritable outpouring of critical attacks against the foundations of that school of linguistics which has come to be known as transformational-generative grammar, or TGG (e.g., Hockett, 1968; Botha, 1971 & 1973; Derwing, 1973; several papers in both Cohen, 1974, and Cohen & Wirth, 1975; etc.). In view of a general lack of satisfactory response to this deluge of criticism, it is becoming increasingly evident that modern linguistic theory is in the throes of a theoretical crisis of major proportions. Though the present paper may seem redundant to the extent that it serves to add even further fuel to an already roaring fire, its main aim is to attempt to put this situation into proper perspective. Specifically, I shall attempt to show that the bulk of the foundational difficulties which now plague linguistic theory all stem from a stubborn adherence to a longstanding historical tradition in the field and are thus chronic rather than acute in character, endemic rather than just newly imposed. Further, although I shall once again focus my main attack on the generative transformational school, it will be clear from the outset that I see the main shortcomings of that school as fundamentally no different from those same ones which virtually all of "descriptive" or "structural" linguistics has long endured. Finally, just as these problems all seem to have a common cause, they seem to me also to be subject to a common cure, the basic outline of which I shall also attempt to indicate, though necessarily in a very limited way.

## 2. On the Origin and Nature of "Autonomous Linguistics."

Though few academic pursuits have had a longer tradition than the study of language and language-related phenomena (see, e.g., Lyons, 1968; Robins, 1969; Hymes, 1974), the discipline called "linguistics" is itself a relative newcomer on the scene, the Bloomfieldian generation being the first to be employed under the label (Hymes & Fought, 1975, p. 1019). There were thus no linguists (in the technical sense of the term) when experimental psychology began in the last half of the nineteenth century, with the investigation of language behavior as an integral part of its early development and with Wundt himself taking a leading role in the effort.[1] There was, of course, a co-existent discipline, known as "philology," which also concerned itself with language phenomena at that time, but the range of this interest was so restrictive as to yield no real conflict of interest between the two disciplines. Specifically, while the psychologists were concerned "to trace the mental processes that precede, accompany and follow utterances" (in the words of one of Wundt's commentators [Blumenthal, 1970, p. 16]), the philologists were mainly concerned with the (regular) ways in which language forms changed through time, as evidenced by similarities and differences among contemporary dialects and "related" languages, as well as between these languages and extant samples of their historical predecessors.

The emergence of linguistics as an identifiable academic (and presumably scientific) discipline was more-or-less concurrent with the rise to dominance of the strict behaviorist tradition in psychology, that anomalous era when psychologists generally lost interest in the psyche. This concurrence of events was hardly coincidental, for when psychology (for a time) abandoned interest in cognitive processes generally, they naturally lost interest, as well, in the special case of *language processes* (cf. Boring's [1950] history, which fails even to mention the term "language" in its index.[2]) This, it seems to me, is precisely the point where the trouble all started (to the detriment of *both* disciplines), for one result of this abrogation of responsibility was to let virtually the whole of language study fall into the hands of the philologists, who, because of their very restricted background and perspective, were bound to view and to treat it in a correspondingly narrow way. One particularly strange and pernicious idea which the philologists had developed was the view that words and other language forms were "things or natural objects with an existence of their own" (Jespersen, 1924, p. 17), and even that languages were "organisms with a mysterious life of their own" (Bierwisch, 1971, p. 13; see also Robins, 1969, p. 181).[3] Responsibility for the perpetuation of this idea no doubt belongs chiefly to Saussure (whom Lyons calls, with much justice, the "founder of modern linguistics" [1968, p. 38]), whose posthumous but very influential book

---

[1]   For a readable, though somewhat biased, account of this early "psycholinguistic" work in psychology, see Blumenthal (1970).
[2]   Kling & Riggs (1971) mention it once, but even that reference turns out to apply to a section on "speech" (pp. 250—259).
[3]   Notice the lingering animism in Bloomfield (1910): "A striking characteristic of the Germanic family of languages is *its feeling for* vowel grades and vowel variations" (Hockett, 1970, p. 1). See also Haugen (1972, pp. 325—326).

(1916) propagated the view of a language as a kind of supraindividual-istic "sociological reality," which supposedly maintained a kind of abstract "existence" all its own, independent of its speakers.[4] It was also Saussure who laid the groundwork for the new discipline of linguistics, by proposing the amalgamation of the old concerns of comparative philology ("diachronic linguistics") with correspondingly detailed inves-tigation and analysis of contemporary speech forms ("synchronic linguistics"). As a result, the main concepts, goals and methods which this new discipline came to adopt were, quite naturally, those of the phil-ological tradition which Saussure represented, rather than the psycho-logical one of Wundtian origin, a point which is often overlooked.[5]

A particularly important and interesting transitional figure in North America was Leonard Bloomfield, who wrote two major books on language in his career. The first of these, now almost forgotten, was a pre-Saussurian 1914 treatise whose orientation was strongly and unabashedly psychological and based "entirely on Wundt" (p. vi). At that time, Bloomfield, too, was concerned primarily "with those mental processes which most immediately underlie the use of language" (1914, p. 56), a phrase which has a surprisingly familiar ring to it in linguistics today. But when Bloomfield saw virtually the whole of psychology take on a strongly anti-mentalist orientation, he had little real choice but to fall in line with the Saussurian scheme, which literally provided the only remaining outlet for serious language study. By the time that his best-known book, *Language*, appeared in 1933, therefore, Bloomfield had radically changed his tune and now championed the autonomy of linguistics as one defense against the kind of "upheavals" in psycholog-ical doctrine which he had witnessed first-hand (p. vii). His proclama-tion has had a profound influence on the development of linguistic theory ever since: "In the division of scientific labor," he wrote, "the linguist deals only with the speech signal . . .; he is not competent to deal with problems of physiology or psychology" (p. 32). Ever since that time, linguistics has been characterized (one might even say plagued) by the following two unique features: (1) the acceptance of the *language product* (i.e., language forms, or the "output" of language processes) as the primary, if not exclusive, object of investigation, taken in isolation from its context of use; and (2) the adoption of a similarly "autono-

---

[4]  Like his modern-day imitators (cf. the discussion of Sanders, 1974, on p. 173 here), Saussure was inconsistent and/or unclear in his characterization of the nature of language, wavering between his best-known "sociological" interpretation and a mani-festly "psychological" one (1959, pp. 6—23).
[5]  One exception is Hymes & Fought (1975), who see this continuity of the compara-tive-historical or philological tradition in the "new descriptive approach" which followed to be "one of the most striking and neglected aspects of the history of modern linguistics" (p. 953).

mous" view of the language "system" (as revealed, say, by analysis of the
language product) as a "thing unto itself," which existed "out there"
somewhere, isolated from real speakers and hearers. Although there
were certainly significant numbers of prominent figures of resistance
along the way (Sapir and Jespersen come to mind as perhaps the two
most outstanding examples), we find that both of these ideas eventually
won out, particularly in North America, and carried right over into the
work of Chomsky and his followers. This double-barreled tradition of
autonomy (from context as well as from psychology generally) thus not
only continues to dominate the contemporary linguistic scene, but has
found in TGG what is perhaps its most extreme form of development
(cf. Hymes, 1975, p. 371).[6]

There is good evidence that Chomsky was himself a Bloomfieldian in
his early years, and Lakoff realizes that "early TG was a natural
outgrowth of American structural linguistics" (1971, pp. 267—8; see
Steinberg, 1975, for a detailed commentary).[7] Numerous accounts since,
however, have sought to inculcate the view that Chomsky eventually
changed all this by bringing about a veritable "scientific revolution" of
Kuhnian (1962) proportions, initiated by even so early a work as
*Syntactic Structures* in 1957 (cf. Lyons, 1970, P 9; Thorne, 1965; etc.).
For reasons which are developed more fully elsewhere (Derwing, 1973),
such a view must be regarded as a considerable overstatement, at best,
and very misleading, in any event.

There was, to be sure, a *terminological* revolution. For example,
language "descriptions" which were "convenient fictions" in the
parlance of a Bloomfield, Harris or Hockett were redubbed "theories"
of languages by Chomsky (1957b) — and (in time) came even to be
called models of "the competence of the ideal speaker-hearer"
(Chomsky, 1965). And linguistics, too, under Bloomfield an admittedly
"independent" discipline, is sometimes referred to these days as "a
branch of cognitive psychology" (Chomsky, 1968).[8] Yet while much

---

6   McCawley (1974, p. 178) seems to be the only reviewer of Derwing (1973) to have
    recognized it as a critique not merely of TGG *per se*, but also of the entire tradition of
    autonomous linguistics, of which TGG is merely the most recent and most influential
    representative.
7   Despite other examples of what Bruck (1977) describes as "generous applications of
    hindsight," Chomsky's introduction to his 1975 reprint of *The Logical Structure of
    Linguistic Theory* does not attempt to deny, at least, these early Bloomfieldian influ-
    ences.
8   It should perhaps be pointed out that even this terminological revolution came about
    rather slowly, as a matter of fact. See Lyons (1970), Derwing (1973) and Steinberg
    (1975) for documented evidence that Chomsky's philosophy showed no bent towards
    psychologizing in his early years (say to around 1956, when Roger Brown may have
    been the first to put the psychological bee in Chomsky's bonnet [cf. Brown, 1970,
    p. 17]) — by which time, of course, the development of the formal apparatus of trans-
    formational-generative grammar was already well under way.

exaggerated emphasis has been placed on all that supposedly changed in
the "new" linguistics (see Derwing, 1973, pp. 25—43 for discussion), it
is more interesting and cogent for our present purposes to take a look at
some of the important things which did *not* change. In his 1926 "Postulates," for example, Bloomfield defined the term "language" as follows:
"The totality of utterances that can be made in a speech-community is
the *language* of that speech-community" (p. 155). In 1957 (and on many
occasions since) Chomsky has defined a language as a "set of sentences"
(1957b, p. 13). Once we understand that "utterances" in the structuralist
tradition were always taken to be "acts of speech" (Bloomfield's Definition 1) as represented in some standardized "phonetic" transcription —
and the notion "can be made" taken to exclude various non-communica-
tive vocal noises (coughs, sneezes, etc.), as well as obviously "defective"
utterances (such as false starts, lapses, utterances which were "non-
native" or which "didn't sound right" to the native speaker, etc.) — it is
hard to see that Chomsky's "new" orientation amounts to anything
more than a (laudable) tightening-up of an old set of definitions. The
fundamental AUTONOMY PRINCIPLE implicit in the original Saussurian concept of *la langue* is still maintained, according to which a
"language" is viewed as *a set of formal objects,* namely, the set of "good"
or "grammatical" utterances, represented in some "generally accepted"
or "universal" mode of transcription. By the same token, I can see no
fundamental difference in kind between the notion of a "simplicity
metric" in generative grammar and any of the various principles of
"economy" proposed by the earlier structuralists: by one device or
another, the implicit goal of either a structuralist "linguistic description"
or a transformationalist "generative grammar" seems still to be to
attempt to describe a "language," as characterized above, in some
optimal, parsimonious form.[9]

One obviously new twist of the Chomskyan era, however, was the
explicit adoption of a supplementary GENERATIVE PRINCIPLE as
part of the attempt to achieve the goal of an economical characterization of sentences. But all this really amounted to was to take those
"things" called "natural languages" to be just special cases of the kind of
formal languages which are the proper concern of that branch of mathematics called automata theory (cf. Rosenbloom, 1950; Davis, 1958;

---

[9] Chomsky's own claim has long been, of course, that his simplicity criteria *are* motivated by empirical considerations, and, indeed, at least some (but by no means all) of
the general conventions proposed in Chomsky & Halle (1968), for example, are justified on the basis of certain quasi-empirical appeals to what might be called the "analytical intuitions" of the professional linguist (on such matters as rule "naturalness,"
various typological expectations, etc.). Such appeals, however, provide scant evidence
for "psychological reality," particularly insofar as the ordinary, linguistically unsophis-
ticated language learner is concerned (see Derwing, 1977, and Section 3 here).

Minsky, 1967; etc.). The form of a linguistic description thus shifted from one in which the analyst simply *listed* various recurring syntactic or morphological patterns to one in which these patterns (or others much like them) were instead "recursively defined" from an algorithmic or generative source.[10] This procedure had a number of descriptive advantages, as its advocates have not failed to point out: it forced linguists to be *explicit* about their statements (i.e., the grammar had to "work"), it allowed for some new kinds of *economies* of description not previously conceived (such as deriving a number of "surface" syntactic patterns from the same "deep" or "base" structure — a natural development of Harris' idea to "equate" various surface syntactic patterns [1957]), and, above all, perhaps, it provided one means for accounting for the *open-ended* character of languages (i.e., it provided one possible descriptive analog for the notion of linguistic "creativity"). But I construe all of these changes as attempts to incorporate various improvements in the formal apparatus of grammatical description, without changing the fundamental notions either of a language as a "thing" (a "subset of sentences") or grammar as a concise and precise "specification" of that thing (cf. Wall, 1972, p. 166). As suggested by the title of Lepschy's historical account *(A Survey of Structural Linguistics,* 1970), it is the *structure* thought to be "immanent" in (Lyons, 1968), "internal" to (Gleason, 1961) or "underlying" (Chomsky, 1965) sentences which has constituted all along the object of analysis, description and formalization in modern linguistics (Hymes & Fought, pp. 1024ff.).[11] Apart from the later terminological "psychologizing" already alluded to, therefore, the only "fundamentally new" element which I have been able to find in the Chomskyan reorientation (cf. Jenkins, 1968, p. 540) has been the degree to which it has allowed its practitioners to take full advantage of the *freedom from psychological constraints* (which the Bloomfieldian declaration already made possible in principle) and to allow their analytic imaginations to run completely wild.[12] The drive for autonomy

---

10  Or, in Postal's terms (1969, p. 413), while the one tradition was concerned primarily with "discovering" the (presumed) structural properties of sentences, the other extended this interest to the development of systems of rules which would formally and rigorously "assign" these properties.

11  "We do in fact think," Hymes & Fought add (p. 922), "that if the fundamental premise of structuralism is seen as the study of language as an autonomous system, a system central to the understanding of the history and use of language, but to be analyzed independently of history and use first, then the ways in which Chomsky's work continues preceding structuralism and completes it seem more decisive than the ways in which it does not."

12  Though the popular view seems to be that Chomsky has broken from the tradition of autonomy for linguistics (cf. Lepschy, 1972, p. 126), the fact of the matter is that he has instead fixed it more firmly than ever before. Sanders is thus quite correct in saying that, despite their verbalized commitment to a psychological perspective, Chomsky and his followers have actually "continued to practice linguistics as it has always been stan-

itself is thus the "dominant focus" of all of structural linguistics, TGG included, transcending the comparatively minor shifts of emphasis and orientation within it (Hymes & Fought, 1975, p. 1023).[13]

Now the transformationalists' position, of course, is a very different one. Their contention is that TGG transcends its structuralist predecessors in many fundamental respects, one of the most important of which is that while the latter merely attempted to "describe" language forms, the former seeks to "explain" them. To be sure, this is a laudable and ambitious new goal, but we may legitimately question the extent to which it has been achieved — or to which such achievement is even possible using the methods at hand (Derwing, 1973 & in press). One point, at least, seems hardly beyond dispute: since language forms (and any associated "linguistic intuitions") do not spontaneously generate in nature but are rather produced by human beings, any valid explanation of these forms (and intuitions) must necessarily make reference to something which resides *within the human organism.*[14] This implies that linguistic models, grammars, formal constraints, etc. can be explanatory in principle only to the extent that they are (i.e., can be shown to be) "psychologically real."[15]

---

dardly practiced" (1977, p. 165), and Hymes & Fought (1975, p. 1144) explain why this is so:

> [F]or Chomsky, what language is to its users, and how it performs its role in human life, are held to depend, so far as linguistic theory is concerned, exactly on what linguists are concerned with in any case: linguistic structure. Enlarged terms, such as 'competence', and appeal to the image of language-acquiring children, do not in fact represent any enlargment of linguistics itself. Linguistics may be defined as a branch of cognitive psychology, but cognitive psychology is not allowed to affect it. Linguistics may stimulate new developments in psycholinguistics, but linguistic theory is not to be changed as a result of psychological experiment. Linguistics remains entirely autonomous, a challenge to psychology, but able to pursue its theoretical goals on the basis of logic and introspection, independent of research of other kinds.

[13] It could even be argued with some justice at this point that relatively little progress was actually achieved during the pre-transformationalist era as far as the description of sentence-sized linguistic units was concerned. But this again just makes TGG look more and more like a perfectly natural extension of structural grammar. Moreover, as Prideaux has pointed out, the filling of this "syntax vacuum" had more than a little to do with the popularity which TGG very rapidly achieved among linguists (cf. Harris, 1970, pp. 69—70). Syntax was, indeed, "the weak link in the Bloomfieldian chain" (Hymes & Fought, 1975, p. 1137), and it was no mere coincidence that "Chomsky's views succeeded first in syntax . . . at a time when the general development of the field had reached syntax" (p. 937).

[14] So Hutchinson argues on the basis of a persuasive computer analogy: "If [the linguist's] descriptions are not imputed to human organisms, are not hypothesized to be part of the system of rules guiding those organisms, then they simply cannot figure into an explanation of human linguistic abilities" (1974, pp. 69—70).

[15] Cowan (1968, p 46), like many others has suggested the even stronger claim that all linguistic explanations must ultimately be physiological in character (i.e., "isomorphic

Since both the strength and significance of this point still seems to have escaped perhaps a majority of the population of professional linguists, even today, I shall risk inserting here an allegory, inspired by Householder (1971, p. 27), which I have found helpful in making clear to my students the distinction between the "autonomous" or "purely linguistic" perspective towards language and a broader, more ambitious one of the kind I am advocating.

Let us envision a fairly complex pattern of bird-tracks on some otherwise unsullied stretch of isolated beach. Let us further imagine what might happen if a spacecraft were to deliver to this beach (from the planet Mars, say) both a linguist and a naturalist who, coincidentally, shared the same "mental sets" as their professional counterparts down here on earth, but who, because of the total absence of flying creatures in their own culture, were totally unfamiliar with the effects which birds' feet would have on smooth sand.

Suppose next, just for the sake of argument, that the alien *linguist* made the natural mistake of construing these strange marks in the sand as manifestations of some sort of novel "linguistic code." Given his well-ingrained "formalistic" outlook, this linguist would undoubtedly set to the task of examining these marks for various kinds of regularities and patterns. If he were a more traditional "structural" linguist he would, perhaps, be satisfied in describing whatever obvious patterns he found, and he would describe them within whatever particular general framework happened to be in vogue at the time; if he were a "generativist" he might, of course, be more more inclined to look for a rather more "exclusive" or "restrictive" set of patterns, but, having found at least some of those (any remainder could easily be dismissed as "mere performance phenomena"), he would then attempt to construct an elaborate and self-contained system of rules in order to "recursively enumerate" these regularities.

The alien *naturalist,* on the other hand, would do neither of these things. (I say "neither," though, in fact, as already stated, I see no *fundamental* difference between the one brand of linguist and the other.) Given his own set of ingrained biases, the naturalist would surely be much less concerned with the patterns to be found than with certain other, more basic questions: "Where did these strange marks come from?," "Why is it that they head generally parallel to the shoreline [let us say], rather than perpendicular to it?," and "Why is do they appear only in this one particular section of the beach and not elsewhere?," etc.

---

to actual neural structures," in Cowan's terms). It is not at all obvious, however, that one must do neurophysiology in order to find out what a person knows (Hutchinson, 1974, p. 48), or whether psychology generally can be reduced to brute physiological terms (cf. Fodor, 1975).

It is clear at the outset, I should think, that of these two types of alien scholars, it is the latter who would be the more likely to come up with the eventual, correct hypothesis: "some sort of flying creature feeding at a favorite spot." Be that as it may, the main point of the story is to provide a background for considering the question of the ontological or empirical status of any *other* theory of the bird-tracks except this correct one — including, for example, the "language model" invented by the linguist. Since we know in this particular instance what the true state of affairs really is (at least insofar as it was a flock of birds who were responsible for the marks, allowing for some measure of doubt as to the birds' motivations), we can say with absolute assurance that any other theory, linguistic or otherwise, which fails to take these birds into account will simply be wrong. In other words, no matter how formally rigorous or elegant any alternative theory may be — and no matter how well it may "predict" those regularities and patterns identified as somehow "most significant" — no such alternative theory can "explain" *anything* — for the simple reason that the theories in question are all empirically false (cf. Hospers, 1946). In fact, it is clear that the alternative theories (bird-track "generator" included) do not even represent an empirical *reality* of any kind, but are mere "fictitious taxonomies," having no empirical status beyond the meagre bird-tracks which they were originally intended to describe.

Now the point of this little story was not, of course, to demonstrate that all linguistic theories are false, for there is obviously no basis here for drawing so sweeping and dramatic a conclusion. In fact, as is evident in virtually all of my own experimental work to date, I see a natural place in the psychological perspective for many of the basic concepts of modern formal linguistics.[16] Nor do I intend to suggest that most linguists are knuckleheads, blinkered though they may be by their own special way of looking at things. I seek merely to illustrate some of the dangers which attach to the now-traditional linguistic view of a language as a "thing" and a grammar as a "characterization" of that thing. For what is *possible* for the bird-tracks is also *possible* for the language product, that is, in a situation where the analog of the tracks is *utterance forms* (say transcribed "phonetically"), produced by some *speaker* (the analog of the birds) for the purpose of *communicating a message* to some hearer (the analog of the birds' motivations). It seems

---

[16] As suggested in Derwing (1973), this is especially true in the case of some of the more concrete (and hence psychologically plausible) Bloomfieldian notions (see Derwing & Baker, 1977 & in press, for some evidence of this). It should not be overlooked, however, that the Bloomfieldian era, too, produced its own share of recklessly imaginative analyses and psychological claims (see, for example, Trager & Bloch, 1941, contrasted with the level-headed review of Haugen & Twaddell, 1942).

obvious that any theory of these natural language "marks" will at least
be grossly inadequate and misleading which fails to take their source
(i.e., the speaker and his knowledge, motivations, etc.) into account.
What assurance do we really have, in fact, that the ontological status of
the earthling linguists' "grammars for utterance forms" is any different
at all from that of the Martian linguist's "grammar for bird-tracks?"
Perhaps they are both (as many structuralists would readily have
admitted) mere "analytic fictions," having no empirical status whatso-
ever.[17]


3.  Are Generative Grammars "Psychologically Real?"

It is uncharacteristic of the autonomous linguist to admit, as Chomsky
does, that language "has no existence apart from its mental representation" (1968, p. 81). Sanders is quite correct in his claim that the mind has
not been the "traditional domain" of linguistics (1974, p.11), but rather
something else much more vague, abstract and empirically inaccessible.
In this domain, apparently, linguistic structure, meaning, and virtually
everything else of interest to the synchronic descriptive linguist does not
represent knowledge in speakers' minds, but is rather "an objective part
of the objectively existing language" (Antal, 1964, p. 10; cf. Hockett,
1968, p. 151). It is strange, though, isn't it, that if the analyst tries to
ascertain what the meaning "is" for a particular sentence, he cannot
appeal to "the language" (where would he look?), but must always go to
one or more individual native speakers (perhaps himself) for the answer
— and this answer may differ drastically from speaker to speaker and
situation to situation. The same is true when judgments about constituent structure are sought (if such judgments can be reliably elicited
from ordinary speakers at all), or "same-different" judgments for
morphemic or phonemic distinctiveness — or even judgments of phonetic identification. It is precisely this characteristic which distinguishes
these 'linguistic' entities from, say, the chemical elements (cf. Sanders,
1977, p. 166): the latter exist independently of human beings and their
judgments, while the former manifestly do not.
　　We can agree that modern linguistics has been preoccupied with the

---

[17]  The issue at stake is thus not the simplistic one of whether or not linguistic theories
have any empirical consequences at all (cf. St. Clair, 1975, p. 444), but whether they
have consequences which go beyond those of any other *arbitrary taxonomic system*. And
surely only from the standpoint of such a purely taxonomic perspective would it be
possible to say that what "is inherent in the structure of language" and what "can most
profitably be imposed upon the linguistic code" are "just two ways of describing the
same thing" (Chomsky, 1957 a, p. 240).

discovery and description of the "system" or "structure" of language (see section 2 above), but what is the ontological and empirical status of that "thing" so described? Where do we find that structure which is "external" to the human language user (Eliasson, 1976, p. 405), and how do we validate it? Just what does it mean to say that a language is a "cultural reality" akin to "the Ten Commandments" or "the United States Senate" (Sanders, 1974, p. 12)? If this indeed represents "knowledge that is shared in common by all competent speakers" (p. 13), is not a psychological test still the appropriate one to apply? Or is "knowledge" not a psychological concept either? Without a commitment to the relevance of psychological evidence, the concept of "sociological reality" must surely degenerate into just another intangible, inaccessible netherworld in which to hide away claims, wishes, or guesses which are of more ideological than scientific interest.[18] It is hard to escape the fact that psychological reality is the *sine qua non* for any linguistic theory which aspires to achieve explanatory power.

It is absolutely necessary, then, to get the grammar inside of the speaker if grammatical theory is to play any possible role in scientific explanation. It is at this point that Chomsky's imaginativeness and ingenuity comes to the rescue: he invented the "ideal speaker-hearer" (1965). This is the fellow whose "intrinsic competence" matches that described in the form of generative grammars and constrained by the "universals" of TGG theory. Fair enough so far. But a totally unpardonable sleight-of-hand occurs in the step which Chomsky takes next: he *assumes* that this make-believe "ideal speaker-hearer" shares fundamental characteristics in common with *real* speakers and hearers, thus making grammatical theory an inherent part of "cognitive" or "psychological" theory (1968).[19]

---

[18] It is perhaps also worth while pointing out here that Sampson (1976) is rather generous in his assessment that the issue of psychological vs. sociological views of language "has ... been rather decisively settled in de Saussure's favor, at least with respect to the semantic aspect of language, by Hilary Putnam (1973)." What Putnam actually does is to adopt an assumption that is tantamount to his own conclusion, viz., that words "have" a fixed meaning. It is absurd to argue that *water* "meant" $H_2O$ before its chemical formula was discovered, and people totally unfamiliar with chemistry can, even today, use the word perfectly well (cf. Swadesh, 1948, p. 256). Words "mean" different things to different people — and apart from people there is simply no "meaning" to be found.

[19] The most straightforward account of the true state of affairs with regard to this assumption can be found in the introduction to the 1975 version of Chomsky's *The Logical Structure of Linguistic Theory* (p. 5): "It is appropriate, *in my opinion*, to regard the grammar of L as a representation of fundamental aspects of the knowledge of L possessed by the speaker-hearer who has mastered L" (italics added). Two pages later, however, this supposition becomes "natural" and "undoubtedly" valid, and by p.9 has become a statement of fact: "This grammar *is* an account of knowledge of L that has been attained by the speaker-hearer who has mastered L" (italics again added)!

However unmotivated and presumptuous this grand leap in logic may be, we can now at least see why this step is absolutely vital to Chomsky's program: since (1) psychological reality is *necessary* in order for linguistics to transcend mere "descriptivism" and become an explanatory science, and since (2) this can *only* be achieved by getting the grammar inside of the *real* language user, then (3) Chomsky finds the formula "ideal speaker-hearer equals real language user" (except for "minor" discrepancies which are ignored in the "idealization") to be the only means at his ready disposal for achieving this end. Valian is right: psychological reality is achieved "by definition" (1976, p. 66). Otherwise, of course, claims of psychological reality would have to be justified empirically, a much more difficult undertaking which would have profound theoretical and methodological implications on the discipline — far more than Chomsky is evidently willing to bargain for (cf. Derwing, 1973 & in press; Derwing & Baker, 1977; and more below). The obvious danger exists, however, that Chomsky's "ideal speaker-hearer" may be itself an artifact, a mere woolen outergarment worn in the attempt to achieve respectability by slipping the wolf of an arbitrary and artifactual grammar into an unsuspecting flock of linguistically naive psychologists (cf. Deese, 1970; Hormann, 1971; etc.). This kind of "ideal speaker-hearer" is no more or less credible than the kind of grammatical theory whose banner it carries.

A study of the relevant linguistic literature reveals in fact that there is but a single, lonely argument offered in support of the claim that some form of a modern TGG may represent any kind of a psychologically valid entity.[20] The classical statement of this argument can be summarized as follows: since TGG's go beyond previous structuralist accounts in that psychological data related to certain kinds of "linguistic intuitions" are taken explicitly into consideration in their construction and evaluation, such grammars become *ipso facto* psychological theories (Bever, 1968, p. 483). There are, however, at least four critical defects to be found in this argument, and these are summarized below in what I regard as an increasing order of cogency:

(1) The first argument is that the kinds of "psychological data" in question here (namely, native speaker "intuitions" about such things as the wellformedness, ambiguity or anomaly of particular sentences — and about the synonymy of and the so — called "syntactic relatedness"

---

[20] I am using the term TGG to refer to any brand of grammatical description which has had its ultimate origins in the particular neo-Bloomfieldian (i.e., autonomous) tradition espoused by Chomsky. This includes everything from the original semantics-free formalisms of *Syntactic Structures* (Chomsky, 1957 b) through the "standard" theory of *Aspects* (Chomsky, 1965), the so-called "generative semantics" of the Lakoff-McCawley-Ross axis (e.g., Lakoff, 1971), Jackendoff's theory of "interpretive semantics" (1972), the "case grammar" of Fillmore (1968), and the more recent "relational grammar" of Perlmutter & Postal (ms.) and "trace theory" of Chomsky (1975 b), etc.

between different sentences) are among what might be called the secondary, derived or even peripheral aspects of normal language use.[21] Linell (1974) makes a distinction between these kinds of marginal phenomena and the other truly central, primary or "first-order" linguistic skills, which involve not merely knowledge of how utterances "sound" or what they "mean", or even how words may be combined into sentences, but also knowledge of the *appropriateness* of utterances to various types of communicative situations (p. 28). This last key skill of producing sentences which are not merely well-formed but also appropriate to the situation of their use — not to mention the corresponding hearer's skill of taking situational (and other) variables into account in his interpretation of utterances — is not (and cannot be) provided for in any kind of "autonomous" grammatical model, transformational-generative or otherwise (see R. Lakoff, 1972, especially n. 12).

Further, it is quite misleading to describe generative grammars as descriptions "of" linguistic knowledge or intuitions (cf. Chomsky, 1975 a, p. 7 for one of the more recent of many such characterizations). As far as we know, ordinary speakers of a language have no reliable intuitions concerning the kinds of things which actually appear in generative grammars (category symbols, rules, etc.) or which determine, for the linguist, the ways in which grammars are constructed (i.e., the formal or substantive "universals" of grammatical theory).[22] The kinds of "linguistic intuitions" that linguists have heavily relied upon in recent years are instead related merely to various interpretations which such subjects may place on some of the kinds of sentences which grammars describe (e.g., estimates of possible intended meanings, construed syntactic and phonological structure, etc.). At best, then, grammars do not "model" intuitions, but merely attempt to "account for" some of them, a requirement which any adequate performance model would also be expected to meet (see Clark & Haviland, 1974, for some plausible suggestions as to how this might be accomplished).

(2) Since "autonomous" grammatical models relate, at best, only to presumed facts concerning sentences and their intuited "structure" and "meaning," they do not (and, not being performance models, cannot in principle) make any further predictions related to *any other* aspects of normal language behavior.[23] Although knowledge is admittedly not the

---

[21] See Derwing (1973, pp. 55—67) and Derwing, Prideaux & Baker (in press) for general treatments of this issue, and see Fletcher (1973) and Patel (1974) for extensive treatments of the notions of "paraphrase" and "structural ambiguity," respectively.

[22] This implies, incidentally, that a thoroughgoing "hermeneutical" approach to the construction and evaluation of grammars (Itkonen, 1974) is also doomed to failure (see Dahl, this volume).

[23] "Unfortunately," as Bever puts it (1968, p. 483), "the points of contact between modern linguistic theory and natural speech phenomena have not been much richer than the basic intuitions of linguists."

same thing as performance, it is also true (as far as we know) that knowledge is always an *inference* from performance, and linguistic knowledge is no exception (cf. Cofer, 1968, p. 534). That is to say, there is no known way to assess knowledge directly, but only by means of assigning some particular performative task. As part and parcel of his quest for "autonomy," however, the linguist has been forced "to make the strong assumption that one's knowledge of language can be separated from the role that knowledge plays in the actual comprehension and production of utterances" (Clark & Haviland, 1974, p. 93). Thus the only support any new grammar receives "is only for its adequacy as a corpus description" (Hutchinson, 1974, p. 56). Though numerous investigators have thus seen the value of expanding the data base of linguistics well beyond the range of the meagre few intuition categories already embraced, the inherent limitations of the grammatical theory itself have given rise to what I (after Harris, 1970) called a *crippling inferential gap* between the linguist's grammar and all these other desirable data sources (Derwing, 1973, pp. 271—275; see also Wirth, 1975, and Vennemann, 1974, p. 211, for a telling analogy).This, in turn, has raised the spectre of a formidable "nonuniqueness" problem for grammars which purport to describe linguistic knowledge (cf. Derwing, in press). Without access or responsibility to such potentially valuable data sources as productivity, processing time, processing complexity, systematic errors, and ease or order of acquisition (to name but some), linguistic theory is restricted to a data base so narrow that insufficient tests are available even to sort out the "best" grammar as formulated within some particular theoretical framework, much less to resolve questions related to alternative grammatical theories (some examples of which are listed in n. 20).[24] Thus, while the acceptance of various "intuitions" as valid data for linguistics imposed some limitations on the "kinds of languages" which generative models might be required to describe (namely, "strongly equivalent" vs. "weakly equivalent" ones, in the parlance of Chomsky & Miller, 1963), the constraints thereby imposed were far from sufficient to eliminate any really serious competitors, as recent developments in

---

[24] Cf. Stich's observation (1975, p. 103) that "since all the contemplated grammars are descriptively adequate, no data about intuitions will suffice to arbitrate among them." This situation well explains why appeals to "simplicity" (Derwing, 1973, pp. 243—247), "esthetic judgments" (Schane, 1976, p. 184) and other, similar arbitrary evaluation criteria have by no means disappeared from linguistics during the Chomskyan era (see n. 9). T. M. Nearey (personal communication) has suggested the analogy that the contemporary linguist is essentially in the same position with regards to theory evaluation as were those early astronomers whose data sources were restricted to the patterns of movement of lights in the sky. On this basis alone, it is by no means clear that the Ptolemaic system would have to be regarded as in any way inferior to its Copernican and Keplerian successors (see Price, 1959).

linguistics have dramatically illustrated.[25] Nelson sums up the situation very nicely in this way:

> Chomsky, by drawing the specific distinction that he did between competence and performance, and by relying on linguistic intuitions as his sole source of 'data,' cut off linguistic theory from its proper concern with empirical language phenomena, as well as from any reasonable criteria for evaluating the resulting competitive formal descriptions and thus destroyed any pretense to its psychological validity (1975, p. 48).

(3) Beyond this already appalling state of affairs, we also find that the data-collection methods which linguists have characteristically employed in their study of these "native-speaker intuitions" have been so blatantly "informal" (to use Chomsky's own term, 1969, p. 56) as to leave room for considerable doubt as to the very trustworthiness or *reliability* of the facts involved (cf. Ringen, 1975, p. 29). This is my warrant for the use of the pejorative phrase "presumed facts" in (2) above, for the alleged "empirical basis" for any claim related to a "psychological status" for grammars proves upon inspection to be as much an act of blind faith as anything else (see Derwing, 1973, and Botha, 1973, for detailed discussion). It is otherwise hard to understand the oddly unbalanced nature of that type of thinking which manifests a serious concern (quite proper in itself) over the possible invalidity of relatively hard experimental data which might threaten TGG, yet which evidently can, at the same time, remain quite comfortably content with all the sloppy, soft and ill-gotten data (itself of very suspicious validity, as argued in (4) below) which provide the only empirical "support" the theory ever had in the first place (cf. Fromkin, 1975).

(4) Finally, and perhaps most disturbing of all, the grammarian is faced with the unfortunate situation that virtually all of the "introspective data" garnered in support of particular grammatical formulations have had as their source native speakers who were themselves professional linguists — and almost always linguists with an ideological stake in the particular formulation at issue. If there was ever any recognition that the motivations and thought patterns of typical language learners and users might differ rather radically from those exhibited by the average professional linguist-analyst, surely Spencer's (1973) study ought to have stirred the realization that linguists may not, after all, constitute a representative sample of the population of interest (see also Derwing, 1977). Here is a validity issue that gnaws at the very bowels of TGG theory, since now we have both empirical and rational grounds for

---

[25] Some attempts have been made, of course, to extend the range of empirical accountability of linguistic theories by supplementing grammars with various "heuristic procedures" (cf. Derwing, 1973, pp. 273—276), but when the experimental results go awry, the tendency has been to blame the heuristics and to preserve the grammar intact (cf. Fodor & Garrett, 1966, p. 152). This is the main line of argument carried throughout Fodor, Bever & Garrett, 1974.

thinking that such factors as the professional expertise and theoretical biases of the typical subjects in most of the "informal experiments" on linguistic intuition reported in the literature might have rendered the results completely *invalid* for purposes of the evaluation of claims related to the general human language faculty. It is clear, of course, that the availability of valid and reliable data concerning the linguistic intuitions of ordinary language users imposes a potential challenge which any fully satisfactory psychological theory must eventually meet. It is not so clear, however, that the mere imposition of formal constraints on grammars, few, if any, of which have any independent claim to psychological validity (cf. Prideaux, 1971; Derwing, 1973 & 1977), must necessarily change the essentially "descriptive", "taxonomic" or "self-confirming" character of these grammars (cf. Schank & Wilks, 1974, p. 315).

Actually, if we take just a moment to reflect just a bit on our own linguistic performance, how *implausible* this whole "underlying generative grammar" concept seems in the first place. (Surely nobody but a linguist would ever have dreamed of such a thing!) What reason have any of us to think that we, in any sense, either "generate" sentences randomly or "derive" one syntactic structure from another, when we use language?[26] The appearance of a certain "dynamic" quality in generative grammars which some psychologists have found to be one of its more appealing characteristics (cf. Hormann, 1971, p. 45—46) proves to be merely illusory upon closer inspection, for, as even the staunchest apologists for TGG readily admit, "understanding and producing a sentence is not a matter of running through grammatical derivations" and "grammatical operations are not, in this sense, psychologically real" (Fodor, Bever & Garrett, 1974, p. 511). In what sense, then, *are* they real?

In the absence of any satisfactory answer to this last question, and in the face of the host of difficulties just catalogued above, it becomes clear that the only thing separating generative grammars from the kind of empty, artifactual interpretation envisioned earlier on in this discussion is the speed — or the wave — of Chomsky's hand. Talk about either the "psychological reality" or "explanatory power" of modern grammatical theories is just that — talk (see n. 19). Moreover, to sum up, there are three main stumbling blocks which attach to the modern grammarians' purely "formal" or "autonomous" approach to linguistic inquiry and detract significantly from its potential usefulness for psychology:

(1) The first difficulty, of course, is with the basic AUTONOMY PRINCIPLE itself, which suggests not only that syntax can be fruitfully

---

[26]  Nor is it intuitively obvious that we operate off of any kind of "invisible" (i.e., silent) syntactic "traces", either, as in one of the more up-to-date versions of autonomous-generative theory (Chomsky, 1975).

studied independently of meaning (an idea which must also be rejected, but for reasons which we may not go into here), but, even more fundamentally, which embodies the suggestion that a "language" is something which is "out there" somewhere and which can be scientifically investigated independently of the human language *user*. We must learn to reject the interpretation of such tyrannical English phrases as "the learning of a language" or the "knowledge of linguistic structure" which implies that either "a language" or its "structure" can have any sort of entitative, empirical existence *outside* of the mind of the user or *apart from* his knowledge of them.[27] What is needed is not a mystical model of some self-supporting "language" or "language system," but rather a psychological model of the real-life language *user*, i.e., a model of the knowledge and behavior[28] of speakers who produce language forms and of hearers who interpret them — all in the context of a great deal of information provided not only by a particular sociocultural *setting*, but also in the context of all the other things which speakers and hearers know about one another and about the world in general. This is indeed a large task and one that must be approached piecemeal. But the particular *kind* of piecemeal approach which is exemplified in modern linguistics does not seem to me to be one which clarifies the phenomenon, but rather distorts and even further complicates it through conceptual confusion at a fundamental level.

(2) A second handicap is the supplementary GENERATIVE PRINCIPLE which implies not only that a language is a "thing," but also that it is the kind of thing which has the formal structure of a fully integrated, well-defined (cf. Hockett, 1968) and "closed" (cf. Linell, 1974, p. 118) mathematical system.[29] As I have already argued, the so-called "Chomskyan revolution" did not really involve any fundamental

---

[27] As Baker has noted (1977, p. 6), all we are really saying when we say that someone "knows a language" is that his linguistic behavior is indistinguishable from that of any other "normal" or "average" speaker in the relevant speech community.

[28] The word "behavior" may require some clarification here, since many linguists, in particular, seem to insist on viewing the term (pejoratively, of course) only in a long-outdated, radical "Watsonian" context. I accept the broad definition given by Henneman (1973, p. 4), which incorporates not merely objectively observable acts of behavior, but also mental activities and neurophysiological processes. The same applies, of course, to the notion of linguistic "performance" (cf. Hymes & Fought, 1975, p. 280).

[29] One particularly unfortunate corollary which attaches to the notion of language as a "closed" formal system is what might be called the STRICT SET-INCLUSION PRINCIPLE. This involves the assumption that all linguistic units must represent clearly-defined categories having sharp and unambiguous boundaries, an idea which is clearly untenable either for the syntax or semantics of natural languages (cf. Ross, 1972). What seems to be required instead is a *normative* notion of "prototype" categories, only vaguely defined, whose boundaries are typically "fuzzy" but whose areas overlap sufficiently from speaker to speaker and situation to situation that adequate communication can ordinarily be achieved.

conceptual or methodological re-orientation at all, but merely supplemented the old autonomy principle with a new generative one — and
what reason have we to think that the latter is on any more solid a
ground than the former? We might more fruitfully replace this idea of a
language as a self-contained "system of generative rules" with the view
of language as a *psychological process*, in which a speaker actively
employs a wide variety of largely non-exceptionless "rules of thumb" for
mapping various (possibly universal) kinds of "semantic" information
into language-specific lexical and "surface" syntactic categories and
eventually into a physical signal — and in which a hearer actively
performs an appropriately modified set of "inverse" operations. And this
seems to call more for a "heuristic" than an "algorithmic" approach to
the concept of linguistic rule, just the opposite of the most recent historical trend (cf. Hymes & Fought, 1975, p. 975).[30]

(3) Finally, the more recent versions of generative grammatical
theory, in particular, suffer from what might be called a formal SELF-
SUFFICIENCY PRINCIPLE, which implies that all information which
is required to interpret the meaning of a sentence must, at some level, be
part of the linguistic structure of that sentence (cf. the treatment of
presuppositions by the "generative semanticists" for a particularly
blatant illustration of this trend). As numerous observers have noted,
especially in Europe (e.g., Uhlenbeck, 1972), but also in America (e.g.,
Hymes, 1972 & 1975), real speakers and hearers manifestly exploit in
communication not only a vast store of background knowledge about
their world (cf. Bolinger, 1965), but also innumerable extra-linguistic,
social or "situational" criteria, and any grammatical theory which
attempts to build such information sources into a model of *linguistic*
structure must automatically be rendered suspect as grossly unrealistic
and likely artifactual in character (cf. Clark & Haviland, 1975, p. 98).[31]

---

[30] All this need not, however, imply any loss of concern with either comprehensive accuracy or explicitness, but merely a recognition that the psychologically valid grammars
may be a lot "fuzzier" than the kind which most linguists are used to dealing with (see
Gleitman & Gleitman, 1970, and n. 29 here). The equation of "explicit" with "generative" (as in Chomsky, 1966, p. 12, for example) is surely one of the most gratuitous and
noxious features of the Chomskyan era.

[31] I have not mentioned here the PRINCIPLE OF MAXIMUM REGULARITY, a
notion which lies at the very heart of the methodological and evaluative practice of
TGG, because I have already dealt with it at length elsewhere (Derwing, 1973, Chap.
5). Suffice it to say here that the psychological implausibility of such a principle should
be readily evident at the outset: why should the ordinary child be just as skillful in
formulating precise and abstract generalizations as the trained linguist, especially
considering the vast differences in both background and orientation which distinguish
them (see Derwing, 1977, and Derwing & Baker, 1977). It is not "fact," but just
another blatant example of unsupported linguistic supposition, to say that "human
beings are constituted so as to acquire a body of knowledge that is optimally represented in a certain abstract form" (Langendoen, 1976, p. 695).

On the evidence, then, "autonomous grammars" (especially of the "generative" or "derivational" variety) do not appear to represent valid psychological constructs at all, but are rather mere descriptive artifacts which have arisen from the linguists' myopic view of the language product as an isolated phenomenon and hence a "natural domain" (Sanders, 1970 & 1974) for a scientific theory. In truth, so-called "natural languages" are really "human languages," and the burden of proof must therefore rest on those theorists who make the empirical claims, namely, on those who insist that anything even remotely resembling a "formal grammar of a language" plays any role whatever in the mental or social life of the *source* of the language product, who is the human language user himself.

## 4. A Summary: Where Linguistics Went Wrong

Until very recently, psycholinguists have tended to take the products of linguistic research for granted and to construe their own discipline as one whose goal was either to establish the "psychological reality" of the proposed grammatical constructs (cf. Greene, 1972; Fodor, *et al.*, 1974) or else to show how the proposed grammars might conceivably fit into a model of the language process (cf. Bever, 1968, p. 482). But what reason have we to believe that grammars must — or even can — function in this way (cf. Osgood, 1968, p. 506; Bartsch & Vennemann, 1972, p. 10; Clark & Haviland, 1975, p. 115; etc.), or, indeed, that the way in which language knowledge is organized in the mind bears any relation to the way in which it is organized in grammars? Language is neither *learned* nor *used* in isolation, so why should it be *described* that way?

If language is not appropriately described in any of the ways prescribed by traditional linguistic precepts, how, then, *should* it be described? It is important to recognize that there is no *a priori* correct answer to that question; one can "describe" in endless ways. Consequently, one does not simply "describe" in science, but rather describes *for some reson.* The *form* of a description is determined by the particular *use* to which that description is going to be put. A biological organ (such as the heart) is described in the way it is (in terms of chambers, valves, etc.) because of the particular *function* which that organ is construed to perform within the body. Likewise, a grammar for some language which was constructed for pedagogical purposes might be very different in form and content from a grammar which was written, say, best to reflect the history of that language. Other goals which have been proposed for grammars include those to "generate all and only the grammatical sentences of a language" (Chomsky, 1957 b), to capture various "linguistically significant generalizations" (Chomsky, 1965), and even to characterize the syntactic basis for various kinds of linguistic "intuitions" regarding sentence relations, paraphrase, ambiguity, and the like. But each of these assumed goals begs one or more important questions: (1) Do native speakers agree as to which sentences "belong to" their language and which do not? Can even the individual speaker decide on a clear-answer (or is this set, too, of the "fuzzy" variety; see n. 29)? How important a consideration is "sentencehood" in ordinary language processing?[32] (2) Does professional linguistic training really impart the skill of divining "psychological reality" and determining which generalizations are "linguistically significant" and which are not (see Derwing, 1973, and n. 9 here)? To what extent is the ordinary language learner even interested in such formal issues as "systematic regularization" (see Derwing, 1977)? (3) Why need we necessarily assume that the basis for linguistic intuitions is *syntactic* in origin, and hence must be characterized by rules which serve to "derive" one syntactic structure from another, and by a general grammatical model in which meaning is a derivative of syntax (cf. Johnson-Laird, 1975, and Bruck, 1977, p. 35)?

The legacy of "autonomy" is thus a very painful one indeed. The linguist is stuck with the kind of models that he has because he was motivated initially to achieve, above all, a parsimonious description of the language product, plus assorted other, often misguided goals, such as the ones just listed. But if the chief goal he chose had been rather Wundt's goal, i.e., to describe language *processes,* his grammars would have been quite different in both form and character.[33] His first question would have been, "What are languages used for?", and his second, "How are these goals accomplished?" The kind of knowledge he would have sought to describe would have been largely *process* knowledge, not *product* knowledge, since language competence is evidently more a matter of knowing *how to* than knowing *what* or *that* (cf. Derwing, 1973, pp. 251—270). The linguist's fundamental error was that he started at the wrong place, and everything else went naturally downhill

---

[32]  Cf. Clark & Haviland (1975, p. 116): "We do not speak in order to be grammatical; we speak in order to convey meaning. We do not attempt to comprehend speech in order to detect violations of grammaticality; we comprehend in order to detect meaning." Further, we do not even *require* fully grammatical sentences in order either to convey or comprehend this meaning, but can ordinarily get along quite famously, in context, with grammatical "inaccuracies," sentence "fragments," anacoluthons, even the occasional mere grunt or smile. It is difficult to see how the TGG-based sentence perception strategies outlined in Fodor, Bever & Garrett (1974) can possibly account for this skill.

[33]  Recall that so-called "item-and-process" or ""generative" *grammatical* models were never intended as models of *psychological* processes (cf. Chomsky, 1965, p. 9). Thus Blumenthal is quite mistaken when he says that "Chomsky did what Wundt would have wanted to do" (1970, p. 198).

from there. He started by examining the tool, rather than by asking
questions about the use to which that tool was put (cf. Anttila, 1975,
p. 292). If we take as our goal the economical description of sentences in
isolation from their use, we come up with all kinds of alternative
descriptive "grammars", some of which may contain quite a variety of
complex and abstract "syntactic structures" and "grammatical operations" — and with this the view that the role of psycholinguistic research
is to "find some use" for these grammars. If, on the other hand, we take
as our initial goal the description and understanding of the language
process, we come to see man as a *semantic* processor at base, and we
tend to view syntax as just one type of vehicle for delivering information
which is required for this processor to work. Our task in this view, then,
is to try to ascertain (1) what *kinds of information* are conveyed by
grammar (as opposed to other means), (2) what specific *linguistic devices*
are employed in languages for this purpose, and (3) what *interpretations*
are placed on the use of these devices by particular speakers in particular
communicative situations (see Baker, 1976, and Derwing & Baker,
1978). Our conception of the form of grammar follows from our understanding of the purpose which grammars are intended to serve: "Rather
than viewing language as an object with independent existence, a thing
to be described for its own sake, it is evident that it must be seen as a
tool, a means to an end outside itself" (Baker, 1976, p. 2). Surely our
chance of success will be much greater if we model the tool to fit the
task, rather than to insist on force-fitting a model which was originally
constructed for an entirely different purpose.

   To be sure, the task of developing a fully explicit, detailed and accurate "information-communication" model of the kind envisioned will be
a long and difficult one, and progress to date has been frustratingly
slow, hampered in no small measure by the dearth of concerned syntac-
ticians (to my knowledge, Prideaux, 1975, represents the only attempt at
formalization to date within this framework). But the results so far
suggest a tentative set of rules for English which don't "move" constituents or "hop" affixes, for example, but rather which *put* constituents in
certain positions for some purposes (e.g., an auxiliary verb is placed in
the first or "most highlighted" position to ask a Yes/No question, or the
WH constituent to ask a content-question, etc.) or which *mark* certain
elements for others (e.g., tense is marked on the leftmost verb of a
sentence).[34] And now Prideaux (1976) has also shown that such rules
may not only serve in descriptions of language use, but may also be

---

[34] Although both "movement rules" (transformations) and "deep structures" now appear
to be gradually disappearing from at least Chomsky's most recent reformulation of
TGG (1975 a), he still seems to maintain the unsupported claim that both are psychologically real (pp. 30—35 and 83—92).

helpful in explaining the kinds of errors which children make in language acquisition.

Call them whatever you like, autonomous grammars are still descriptions of the language *product* which say nothing at all about the language *process*. Yet it is the language process — the language user's *competence to perform* — which is the object of ultimate interest in language study, and the value of product descriptions is only as good as the use to which such descriptions can be put in this larger frame of reference. Individual linguists have nurtured certain formal skills, a patient penchant for detail, and a familiarity with a wide diversity of language types, and these are commodities which language study can scarcely afford to do without.[35] But, for all its accomplishments, linguistics has failed in the sense that it has shown itself incapable of achieving its goals as a scientific discipline. The reason it has failed is because it has consistently held too narrow a view of the problem of language, and because it has reversed its priorities. It has tried to describe "language" without prior consideration of what a language is good for. Sooner or later language study must be restored to its proper place within psychology. The idea that there can be an "autonomous science of language" is ultimately doomed — for the simple reason that language does not exist in a vacuum (Rommetveit, 1974, p. 22), and linguists will only continue to delude and mislead themselves so long as they fail to take due cognizance of this simple fact. In the meantime, the transition from autonomous linguistics to a true psycholinguistics (or, better, linguistic psychology) will involve much more severe and painful a readjustment than the tacit acceptance of a new set of goals and claims. What is required is nothing less than a fundamental re-orientation to the nature of the problem. We must put an end to the reification of *language* as a "thing apart" and begin to see the situation from the perspective of the language *user*. For language is only a means to an end — and that end is achieved by putting linguistic devices at the service of all the other cognitive mechanisms which constitute the general mental make-up of man.

---

[35] If nothing else remained of the structuralist or autonomous era than the field notes of a Boas, Sapir, or Bloomfield, the "linguistics experiment" would have to be regarded as at least a partial success. It is ironic, though, that the more recent "appeal to rationalism" has by now largely removed this one kind of proven contribution: in the new "lazy man's linguistics" (Hymes & Fought, 1975, p. 1139), original field work has been broadly supplanted by the activity of armchair re-analysis of data collected and collated by a previous generation of investigators. Theory construction receives almost all of the attention today, careful data collection almost none.

# References

Antal, L. *Content, meaning, and understanding.* The Hague: Mouton, 1964.

Anttila, R. Generalization, abduction, evolution, and language. In E. F. K. Koerner (Ed.), *The transformational-generative paradigm and modern linguistic theory. Amsterdam studies in the theory and history of linguistic science IV.* Amsterdam: John Benjamins B. V., 1975.

Baker, W. J. An "information structure" view of language. *The Canadian Journal of Linguistics,* 1976, *21,* 1—16.

Baker, W. J. Methodological issues in psycholinguistics. Paper presented at the 4th Salzburg International Tagung for Linguistics, August, 1977.

Bartsch, R., & Vennemann, T. *Semantic Structures.* Frankfurt/Main: Athenaum Verlag, 1972.

Bever, T. G. Associations to stimulus-response theories of language. In T. R. Dixon & D. L. Horton (Eds.), *Verbal behavior and general behavior theory.* Englewood Cliffs, N. J.: Prentice-Hall, 1968.

Bierwisch, M. *Modern linguistics.* The Hague & Paris: Mouton, 1971.

Bloomfield, L. *An introduction to the study of language.* New York: Holt, 1914.

Bloomfield, L. A set of postulates for the science of language. *Language,* 1926, *2,* 153—164.

Bloomfield, L. *Language.* New York: Holt, Rinehart & Winston, 1933.

Blumenthal, A. L. *Language and psychology: historical aspects of psycholinguistics.* New York: Wiley, 1970.

Bolinger, D. L. The atomization of meaning. *Language,* 1965, *41,* 555—573.

Boring, E. G. *A history of experimental psychology* (2nd ed.). New York: Appleton-Century-Crofts, 1950.

Botha, R. P. *Methodological aspects of transformational generative phonology.* The Hague & Paris: Mouton, 1971.

Botha, R. P. *The justification of linguistic hypotheses.* The Hague: Mouton, 1973.

Brown, R. *Psycholinguistics.* New York: The Free Press, 1970.

Bruck, A. Review of N. Chomsky, *The logical structure of linguistic theory. Language Sciences,* 1977, No. 45 (April), 35—40.

Chomsky, N. Review of R. Jakobson & M. Halle, *Fundamentals of language. International Journal of American Linguistics,* 1957 a, *23,* 234—242.

Chomsky, N. *Syntactic structures.* The Hague: Mouton, 1957 b.

Chomsky, N. *Aspects of the theory of syntax.* Cambridge, Mass.: MIT Press, 1965.

Chomsky, N. *Topics in the theory of generative grammar.* The Hague & Paris: Mouton, 1966.

Chomsky, N. *Language and mind.* New York: Harcourt, Brace & World, 1968.

Chomsky, N. Linguistics and philosophy. In S. Hook (Ed.), *Language and philosophy.* New York: New York University Press, 1969.

Chomsky, N. *The logical structure of linguistic theory.* New York: Plenum Press, 1975 a.

Chomsky, N. *Reflections on language.* New York: Pantheon Books, 1975 b.

Chomsky, N., & Halle, M. *The sound pattern of English.* New York: Harper & Row, 1968.

Chomsky, N., & Miller, G. A., Introduction to the formal analysis of natural languages. In R. Luce, R. Bush & R. Galanter (Eds.), *Handbook of mathematical psychology,* Vol. II. New York: Wiley, 1963.

Clark, H. H., & Haviland, S. E. Psychological processes as linguistic explanation. In D. Cohen (Ed.), *Explaining linguistic phenomena.* New York: Wiley, 1974.

Cofer, C. N. Problems, issues and implications. In Dixon, T. R., & Horton, D. L. (Eds.), *Verbal behavior and general behavior theory.* Englewood Cliffs, N. J.: Prentice-Hall, 1968.

Cohen, D. (Ed.) *Explaining linguistic phenomena.* New York: Wiley, 1974.

Cohen, D. & Wirth, J. R. (Eds.), *Testing linguistic hypotheses.* New York: Wiley, 1975.

Cowan, J. L. *The myth of mentalism in linguistics.* Tucson: University of Arizona, 1968.

Davis, M. *Computability and unsolvability.* New York: McGraw-Hill, 1958.

Deese, J. *Psycholinguistics.* Boston: Allyn & Bacon, 1970.

Derwing, B. L. *Transformational grammar as a theory of language acquisition: a study in the empirical, conceptual and methodological foundations of contemporary linguistics.* London: Cambridge University Press, 1973.

Derwing, B. L. Is the child really a 'little linguist'? In J. Macnamara (Ed.), *Language learning and thought.* New York: Academic Press, 1977.

Derwing, B. L. English pluralization: a testing ground for rule evaluation. In G. D. Prideaux, B. L. Derwing & W. J. Baker (Eds.), *Experimental linguistics: integration of theories and applications.* Ghent: Story-Scientia, in press.

Derwing, B. L., & Baker, W. J. On the re-integration of linguistics and psychology. In R. N. Campbell & P. T. Smith (Eds.), *Recent advances in the psychology of language: Formal and experimental approaches.* New York & London: Plenum Press, 1978.

Derwing, B. L., & Baker, W. J. The psychological basis for morphological rules. In J. Macnamara (Ed.), *Language learning and thought.* New York: Academic Press, 1977.

Derwing, B. L., & Baker, W. J. Recent research on the acquisition of English morphology. In P. J. Fletcher & M. Garman (Eds.), *Studies in language acquisition.* London: Cambridge University Press, in press.

Derwing, B. L., Prideaux, G. D., & Baker, W. J. Experimental linguistics in historical perspective. In G. D. Prideaux, B. L. Derwing & W. J. Baker (Eds.), *Experimental linguistics: integration of theories and applications.* Ghent: Story-Scientia, in press.

Eliasson, S. Review of B. L. Derwing, *Transformational grammar as a theory of language acquisition. International Review of Applied Linguistics,* 1976, *14,* 402–406.

Fillmore, C. J. The case for case. In E. Bach & R. T. Harms (Eds.), *Universals in linguistic theory.* New York: Holt, Rinehart & Winston, 1968.

Fletcher, P. J. An experimental approach to syntactic paraphrase. Unpublished Ph. D. dissertation, University of Alberta, 1973.

Fodor, J. A. *The language of thought.* New York: Crowell, 1975.

Fodor, J. A., Bever, T. G., & Garrett, M. F. *The psychology of language: an introduction to psycholinguistics and generative grammar.* New York: McGraw-Hill, 1974.

Fodor, J. A., & Garrett, M. Some reflections on competence and performance. In J. Lyons & R.J. Wales (Eds.), *Psycholinguistics papers.* Edinburgh: Edinburgh University Press, 1966.

Fromkin, V. A. When does a test test a hypothesis? In D. Cohen & J. R. Wirth (Eds.), *Testing linguistic hypotheses.* New York: Wiley, 1975.

Gleason, H. A., Jr. *An introduction to descriptive linguistics.* New York: Holt, Rinehart & Winston, 1961.

Gleitman, L. R., & Gleitman, H. *Phrase and paraphrase: some innovative uses of language.* New York: W. W. Norton, 1970.

Greene, J. *Psycholinguistics: Chomsky and psychology.* Baltimore: Penguin Books, 1972.

Haugen, E. The ecology of language. In A. S. Dil (Ed.), *The ecology of language: Essays by Einar Haugen.* Stanford: Stanford University Press, 1972.

Haugen, E., & Twaddell, W. F. Facts and phonemics. *Language,* 1942, *18,* 228–237.

Harris, P. R. On the interpretation of generative grammars. Unpublished M. Sc. thesis, University of Alberta, 1970.

Harris, Z. Co-occurrence and transformation in linguistic structure. *Language,* 1957, *33,* 283–340.

Hennemann, R. H. *The nature and scope of psychology.* (2nd ed.) Dubuque, Ia.: Wm C. Brown, 1973.

Hockett, C. F. Review of S. M. Lamb, *Outline of stratificational grammar. IJAL,* 1968, *34,* 145—153.

Hockett, C. F. (Ed.) *A Leonard Bloomfield anthology.* Bloomington & London: Indiana University Press, 1970.

Hockett, C. J. *The state of the art.* The Hague: Mouton, 1968.

Hörmann, H. *Psycholinguistics: an introduction to research and theory.* New York: Springer-Verlag, 1971.

Hospers, J. On explanation. *Journal of Philosophy,* 1946, *58,* 337—356.

Householder, F. W. *Linguistic speculations.* London: Cambridge University Press, 1971.

Hutchinson, L. G. Grammar as theory. In D. Cohen (Ed.), *Explaining linguistic phenomena.* New York: Wiley, 1974.

Hymes, D. H. On communicative competence. In J. B. Pride & J. Holmes (Eds.), *Sociolinguistics.* Harmondsworth: Penguin Books, 1972.

Hymes, D. (Ed.) *Studies in the history of linguistics: traditions and paradigms.* Bloomington & London: Indiana Universtiy Press, 1974.

Hymes, D. Pre-war Prague school and post-war linguistics. In E. F. K. Koerner (Ed.), *The transformational-generative paradigm and modern linguistic theory. Amsterdam studies in the theory and history of linguistic science IV.* Amsterdam: John Benjamins B. V., 1975.

Hymes, D., & Fought, J. American structuralism. In T. A. Sebeok (Ed.), *Current trends in linguistics,* Vol. 13, *Historiography of linguistics.* The Hague & Paris, Mouton, 1975.

Itkonen, E. *Linguistics and metascience. Studia Philosophica Turkuensia,* Fasc. II. Kokemaki, 1974.

Jackendoff, R. S. *Semantic interpretation in generative grammar.* Cambridge, Mass.: MIT Press, 1972.

Jenkins, J. J. The challenge to psychological theorists. In R. R. Dixon & D. L. Horton (Eds.), *Verbal behavior and general behavior theory.* Englewood Cliffs, N. J.: Prentice-Hall, 1968.

Jespersen, O. *The philosophy of grammar.* London: George Allen & Unwin, 1924. Reprinted by W. W. Norton, 1965.

Johnson-Laird, P. N. Is all that is not verse just prose? Review of J. A. Fodor, T. G. Bever & M. F. Garrett, *The psychology of language. Nature,* 1975, *255,* 263—264.

Kling, J. W., & Riggs, L. A. (Eds.), *Woodworth & Schlosberg's experimental psychology.* (3rd ed.) New York: Holt, Rinehart & Winston, 1971.

Kuhn, T. S. *The structure of scientific revolutions.* Chicago & London: University of Chicago Press, 1962.

Lakoff, G. On generative semantics. In D. D. Steinberg & L. A. Jakobovits (Eds.), *Semantics: an interdisciplinary reader in philosophy, linguistics and psychology.* London: Cambridge University Press, 1971.

Lakoff, R. Language in context. *Language,* 1972, *48,* 907—927.

Langendoen, D. T. Review of D. Cohen, *Explaining linguistic phenomena. Language,* 1976, *52,* 690—695.

Lepschy, G. C. *A survey of structural linguistics.* London: Faber & Faber, 1970.

Linell, P. *Problems of psychological reality in generative phonology: a critical assessment. Reports from Uppsala University Department of Linguistics,* 1974, No. 4.

Lyons, J. *Theoretical linguistics.* London: Cambridge University Press, 1968.

Lyons, J. *Chomsky.* London: Fontana/Collins, 1970.

McCawley, J. R. Review of B. L. Derwing, *Transformational grammar as a theory of language acquisition. The Canadian Journal of Linguistics,* 1974, *19,* 177—188.

Minsky, M. *Computation: finite and infinite machines.* Englewood Cliffs, N. J.: Prentice-Hall, 1967.

Nelson, K. Review of B. L. Derwing, *Transformational grammar as a theory of language acquisition. Contemporary Psychology,* 1975, *20,* 47—49.

Osgood, C. E. Toward a wedding of insufficiencies. In T. R. Dixon & D. L. Horton, (Eds.), *Verbal behavior and general behavior theory.* Englewood Cliffs, N. J.: Prentice-Hall, 1968.

Patel, P. G. An analysis of the notion 'structural ambiguity'. Unpublished Ph. D. dissertation, University of Alberta, 1974.

Permutter, D., & Postal, P. Some general laws of grammar. Unpublished ms.

Postal, P. M. Review of A. McIntosh & M. A. K. Halliday, *Patterns of language. Foundations of Language,* 1969, *5,* 409—426.

Price, D. J. de S. Contra-Copernicus: a critical reestimation of the mathematical planetary theory of Ptolemy, Copernicus, and Kepler. In M. Clagett (Ed.), *Critical problems in the history of science.* Madison: University of Wisconsin Press, 1959.

Prideaux, G. D. On the notion 'linguistically significant generalization'. *Lingua,* 1971, *26,* 337—347.

Prideaux, G. D. An information-structure approach to syntax. Paper presented at the University of Ottawa, March, 1975.

Prideaux, G. D. A functional analysis of English question acquisition: a response to Hurford. *Journal of Child Language,* 1976, *3,* 417—422.

Putnam, H. Meaning and reference. *Journal of Philosophy,* 1973, *70,* 699—711.

Ringen, J. D. Linguistic facts: a study of the empirical scientific status of transformational generative grammars. In D. Cohen & J. R. Wirth (Eds.), *Testing linguistic hypotheses.* New York: Wiley, 1975.

Robins, R. H. *A short history of linguistics.* London: Longmans, 1969.

Rommetveit, R. *On message structure: a framework for the study of language and communication.* London: Wiley, 1974.

Rosenbloom, P. *The elements of mathematical logic.* New York: Dover, 1950.

Ross, J. R. The category squish: Endstation Hauptwort. In P. M. Peranteau, J. N. Levi & G. C. Phares (Eds.), *Papers from the eighth regional meeting of the Chicago Linguistic Society.* Chicago: Chicago Linguistic Society, 1972.

Sampson, G. Review of D. Cohen, *Explaining linguistic phenomena. Journal of Linguistics,* 1976, *12,* 177—182.

Sanders, G. A. On the natural domain of grammar. *Linguistics,* 1970, No. 63, 51—123.

Sanders, G. A. Issues of explanation in linguistics. In D. Cohen (Ed.), *Explaining linguistic phenomena.* New York: Wiley, 1974.

Sanders, G. A. Some preliminary remarks on simplicity and evaluation procedures in linguistics. In L. G. Hutchinson (Ed.), *Minnesota Working Papers in Linguistics and Philosophy of Language,* No. 4, 1977.

Saussure, Ferdinand de. *Cours de linguistique generale.* Paris: Payot, 1916. English translation, by W. Baskin, *Course in general linguistics.* New York: Philosophical Library, 1959.

Schane, S. A. The best argument is in the mind of the beholder. In J. R. Wirth (Ed.), *Assessing linguistic arguments.* New York: Wiley, 1976.

Schank, R. C., & Wilks, Y. The goals of linguistic theory revisited. *Lingua,* 1974. *34,* 301—326.

Spencer, N. J. Differences between linguists and nonlinguists in intuitions of grammaticality-acceptability. *Journal of Psycholinguistic Research,* 1973, *2,* 83—98.

St. Clair, R. Review of B. L. Derwing, *Transformational grammar as a theory of language acquisition. Foundations of Language,* 1975, *12,* 441—444.

Steinberg, D. D. Chomsky: from formalism to mentalism and psychological validity. *Glossa,* 1975, *9,* 218—252.

Stich, S. P. Competence and indeterminacy. In D. Cohen & J. R. Wirth (Eds.), *Testing linguistic hypotheses.* New York: Wiley, 1975.

Swadesh, M. On linguistic mechanism. *Science and Society,* 1948, *12,* 254—259.

Thorne, J. P. Review of P. M. Postal, *Constituent structure: a study of contemporary models of syntactic description. Journal of Linguistics,* 1964, *1,* 73—76.

Trager, G. L., & Bloch, B. The syllabic phonemes of English. *Language,* 1941, *17,* 223—246.

Uhlenbeck, E. M. Semantic representation and word meaning. In E. M. Uhlenbeck, *Critical comments on transformational-generative grammar 1962—1972.* The Hague: Smits, Drukkers-Uitgevers B. V., 1972.

Valian, V. The relationship between competence and performance: a theoretical review. *CUNYForum,* 1976 (Fall), No. 1, 64—101.

Vennemann, T. Phonological concreteness in natural generative grammar. In R. W. Shuy & C.-J. N. Bailey (Eds.), *Towards tomorrow's linguistics.* Washington, D. C.: Georgetown University Press, 1974.

Wall, R. *Introduction to mathematical linguistics.* Englewood Cliffs, N. J.: Prentice-Hall, 1972.

Wirth, J. R. Logical considerations in the testing of linguistic hypotheses. In D. Cohen & J. R. Wirth (Eds.), *Testing linguistic hypotheses.* New York: Wiley, 1975.

# On the Similarity Between Skinner and Chomsky

Per Linell

B. F. Skinner and Noam Chomsky are two well-known scholars generally thought to be their respective extreme opposites in their views on
language and linguistic behavior. At least this has been the prevailing
opinion since Chomsky's review (Chomsky 1959) of Skinner's *Verbal
Behavior* (Skinner 1957). The purpose of this tiny paper is to bring some
confusion into this picture. I would like to suggest the following:

(A) In his *Verbal Behavior* Skinner in fact leaves radical behaviorism
    in his attempt to account for some aspects of linguistic behavior,
    thereby incorporating traditional linguistic insights such as the
    need for analysis at several levels of abstraction.
(B) Chomsky's theory, or at least one possible interpretation of it,
    shares important features with behaviorism, such as causal deter-
    minism, mechanism and associationism.

It must be admitted, of course, that Skinner's and Chomsky's theories
cannot be directly compared, since they are concerned with rather
different things. Skinner studies what variables in each specific situation
make people say something specific, i.e., what are the 'controlling' and
'reinforcing' 'stimulus dimensions.' This is not a speech act theory,
dealing with the items of a speaker's behavior repertoire, but rather a
theory of the speaker's momentary verbal responses to different stimuli.
Chomsky, on the other hand, is not concerned with linguistic behavior
and the use of language at all; he makes assertions about speakers'
grammatical competence which is a very abstract knowledge not always
directly reflected in linguistic performance. However, Skinner would
surely not accept a Chomskyan 'competence' as an important variable
controlling verbal behavior, while Chomsky, first, vehemently denies
that Skinner's theory of verbal behavior has any significance at all
(Chomsky 1959), and secondly, he definitely argues that the speaker
possesses a 'Chomskyan competence' (i.e., a generative transformational
grammar) which *does* interact in linguistic performance (in *some* way
never made clear by Chomsky; Chomsky's characterizations of the relationship between competence and performance are very vague and
equivocal, see disc. in Derwing 1973, Steinberg 1975). Thus, the fact
that Skinner and Chomsky do make the above-mentioned assertions

(implicitly or explicitly) means that a discussion of whether they are *really* mutually incompatible in all respects is not meaningless.

Skinner bases his theory of verbal responding on the concept of operant conditioning. Verbal operants are classified as follows, depending on the nature of the controlling or reinforcing stimulus (-i) in the specific situation:

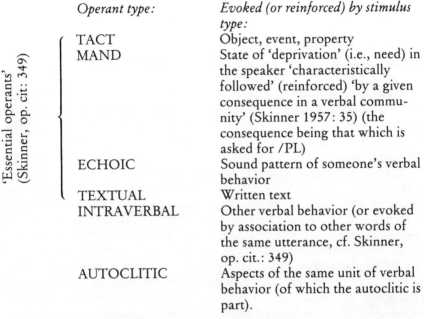

| Operant type: | Evoked (or reinforced) by stimulus type: |
|---|---|
| TACT | Object, event, property |
| MAND | State of 'deprivation' (i.e., need) in the speaker 'characteristically followed' (reinforced) 'by a given consequence in a verbal community' (Skinner 1957: 35) (the consequence being that which is asked for /PL) |
| ECHOIC | Sound pattern of someone's verbal behavior |
| TEXTUAL | Written text |
| INTRAVERBAL | Other verbal behavior (or evoked by association to other words of the same utterance, cf. Skinner, op. cit.: 349) |
| AUTOCLITIC | Aspects of the same unit of verbal behavior (of which the autoclitic is part). |

'Essential operants' (Skinner, op. cit: 349)

An utterance (or even a certain specific aspect of it) may be a function of several different operants at the same time (multiple causality).

Though I cannot go into detail here, two properties of the stimulus-response (S—R) paradigm of behaviorism must be mentioned here, i.e. externalism and associationism. That is, the controlling (or reinforcing) variables of verbal behavior must be observable (or at least: observable in principle) physical entities. Internal mediating variables may exist but need not be referred to (according to Skinner) in the prediction (and explanation) of verbal behavior. (Factors like the individual's genetic endowment, motivational status and history of reinforcements may be treated as constants in the specific situation). The causally efficient mechanisms are explained in terms of (some kind of simple) associations between observable stimuli and responses. In an S—R chain, a behavioral unit which is a response to some stimulus (—i) may itself function as a stimulus thus triggering other responses. A stimulus is causally related to the response and must of course precede (or at least not follow) the response in time.

When a sentence is uttered, the specific words may be controlled by utterance-external stimuli (the cases of 'essential operants') or by inter-verbal associations (e.g., the word(s) emitted so-far may elicit the following word by association). This of course is the view of language which can be formalized in a finite-state grammar. It is well-known (at least since Chomsky, 1957) that this cannot account for even the most common types of utterances, since there are countless cases of properties of words being determined by words which follow (e.g., the choice of the definite article depending on the number and gender of the following noun in German noun phrases; *der* alte Mann vs. *die* alte Frau vs. *das* alte Haus) and cases of various nested dependencies (e.g., examples (5—7) below).

Now, as a matter of fact, Skinner *has* means to deal with these things, and this is what I would like to discuss. Thus, Skinner introduces the class of *autoclitics*. 'The term "autoclitics" is intended to suggest behavior which is based upon or depends upon other verbal behavior' (Skinner, op. cit.: 315). This definition of Skinner's is not quite appropriate, since it does not appear to separate 'autoclitics' from 'intraverbals.' It seems that autoclitics are always verbal responses to other aspects of the same utterance in which they occur. They comprise descriptive autoclitics *(I see, I say, I imagine, I guess* etc), qualifying autoclitics (negation, assertion), quantifying autoclitics *(all, every, some)*, relational autoclitics (predication, inflections, modal verbs, syntactic frames etc) and manipulative autoclitics *(and, but, if . . . then* etc). It is immediately clear that autoclitics is a very powerful category; among other things it covers all of the morphology and syntax of utterances. What is important, however, is that Skinner leaves externalism- with-associationism when he brings in autoclitics. For an autoclitic very often precedes, or is interspersed among, the verbal stimuli to which it is a response. This means that the autoclitic cannot respond to the actual vocalizations in the speech signal but rather to counterparts of these in the speaker's utterance plan. They are not responses to overt behavior, but to 'covert or incipient or potential verbal behavior' (Chomsky 1959: 53). Consider, e.g., (1):

(1)  *Skinner is a genius.*

At most occasions, when (1) is uttered by someone, *Skinner* and *genius* would be 'essential operants.' *Skinner* may, for example, be a tact under the control of an object, namely the person BFS himself, and *genius* may be another tact under the control of a property of BFS, *or* it may be an intraverbal evoked by associations to the word *Skinner.*[1] Now, as

---

[1]  Other possibilities also exist; the whole utterance may, for example, be a textual operant (under the control of a written text).

Skinner observes (cf. op. cit.: 334 ff), the mere pronouncing of *Skinner genius* does not reflect common English practice. 'The responses evoked by a situation are essentially nongrammatical until they have been dealt with autoclitically' (op. cit.: 346). In our case, a 'relational autoclitic of ordering and grouping' plus an 'autoclitic of assertion' are evoked by the two constituent operants, thus together yielding a predication of the form (1). The autoclitic *is* appears before at least one of the stimuli by which it is controlled.[2] In (2) the negation would be an autoclitic under the control of the whole of (1) (or rather some behavioral structure underlying it):

(2)  *Skinner is not a genius.*[3]

In (3), *it is true that* is an autoclitic operating on (2) (or the structure underlying it):

(3)  *It is true that Skinner is not a genius.*

It turns out that Skinner's 'autoclitic under the control of X' very often corresponds to a (token of a) functor of a function applied to X in a function-argument grammar, and sometimes it corresponds to a quantifier binding a variable in X as, e.g., *all* in (4):

(4)  *All swans are white.*

Skinner suggests that *all* is an autoclitic modifying (the structure underlying) *Swans are white* (cf. disc. in Chomsky, 1959: 53). Skinner does not consider any complicated linguistic examples in his book *Verbal Behavior*, but it seems clear that he would need very complex nested stimulus-autoclitic structures in many cases, e.g., (5) and (6):

(5)  *Skinner is not easy to refute.*
(6)  *It is obvious that either Skinner is crazy or our common sense is all wrong.*

Furthermore, he would need at least two different underlying S—R-structures to derive physically identical pieces of overt verbal behavior in countless cases of grammatically ambiguous utterances, e.g., (7):

(7)  *Skinner is ready to eat.*

The utterance of (7) may be either under the control of a situation in which BFS is going to have dinner, *or* under the control of a rather different situation in which (7) is intended as an attempt to trigger the eating of BFS by some cannibals.

---

[2]  I have not accounted for the *a* before *genius*, which would also be some kind of autoclitic.

[3]  Note, however, that *genius* could hardly be a tact under the control of a property of Skinner in this case.

It is commonplace in grammar theory that sentences have to be syntactically analyzed at an abstract level distinct from the actual overt surface level. Skinner in fact recognizes this; his autoclitic structures may provide at least some features of the underlying formal structures of sentences. For example, Skinner's discussion of the sentence *He rented a leaky boat* (op. cit.: 347—8) is slightly reminiscent of a standard generative-transformational derivation.

Thus, Skinner asserts: 'The speaker not only emits verbal responses appropriate to a situation or to his own conditions, he classifies, arranges, and manipulates this behavior. His activity is autoclitic because it depends upon a supply of verbal responses already available.' (op. cit.: 344). This arranging and manipulation must take place before the vocal behavior is executed, i.e., it belongs to the speaker's *planning* of the utterances. Thus, I conclude that Skinner is actually operating with a theory which differentiates (a) a recursive S—R-structure (using plenty of autoclitic functions) which is the speaker's plan for the production of the utterance, and (b) the execution of this behavior plan. His theory is *not* one based on associations of actual external stimuli and responses, though he does not make this important point clear (nor does Chomsky in his review).

One may ask whether autoclitics are the only category which has non-overt controllers. For example, are all 'essential operants' under the control of observable stimuli? Skinner seems to think so. But it is hard to believe him. Take for example the definite article in, e.g., (8), which is both an autoclitic and a tact indicating 'the specificity of the situation:'

(8)   *(I met a man and his son.) The boy cried.*

Presumably, Skinner takes 'the specificity of a situation' to be a property of that physical situation. But anyone familiar with the use of articles knows that there are extreme difficulties in correlating their occurrences with properties of extralinguistic situations (cf. the notion of 'tact'). There are many other types of examples of how Skinner's stimuli are 'driven into the organism' to use a wording of Chomsky's (1959: 32). Chomsky's critique is no doubt justified. Skinner's way of explicating verbal behavior is unilluminative and is mostly just a disguise for mentalistic (I would prefer to say 'phenomenological') terms. A straightforward phenomenological language would serve the purposes much better.[4]

It cannot be true that 'the right way (or even a useful way) of taxonomizing the utterance forms in a language is by grouping together the ones whose production is contingent upon the same (or similar) eliciting

---

[4]   I here leave out of consideration many obvious difficulties in a one-sided behaviorist approach to meaningful behavior, e.g., exclusively extensional semantics, inability or difficulty to cope with intentions, zero expressions, oblique speech acts etc.

stimuli' (Fodor 1976: 100). Utterances are produced as results of complex interactions between the speaker's mental states and processes and the external physical and social environment. This of course is not to deny that people very often do talk about things in the external 'stimulus situation' when they talk, that there are some interesting relations between situations and what people tend to say in these situations, that there are other approaches to the mind-body problem that are much more unsound etc.

It is important to realize that (what I have called) Skinner's 'underlying structures' are behavioral S—R-structures, i.e., entities of the same kind as overt stimuli and responses. These S—R-processes occur 'mechanically;' no recourse to a human agent is necessary. The things involved are 'a train of events no less physical or inevitable than direct mechanical action, but clearly more difficult to describe' (Skinner, op. cit.: 2). But even here, in this respect, Skinner and Chomsky perhaps go together. Chomsky has suggested that theoretical constructs in 'competence' are (psychologically) *real,* and much speculation has been generated as to what kind of reality things like syntactic deep structures and underlying (morpho)phonological forms may actually have. Chomsky is notoriously equivocal on these issues (cf. Derwing 1973, Linell 1974, Steinberg 1975), but at least some interpreters of Chomsky have brought him rather close to Skinnerian mechanism. Chomsky's close colleague J. J. Katz is probably the one who has been most explicit (in his 1964 paper 'Mentalism in Linguistics'). He in fact views 'mentalism' as paramechanism (though he of course does not *say* this quite explicitly).[5]

According to Katz, 'every aspect of the mentalistic theory (e.g., a generative transformational grammar /PL) involves psychological reality' (op. cit.: 133), and a generative grammar 'and all its features have the same ontological status as the utterance itself' (ibid.: 136). The linguist 'invents a theory about the structure of this mechanism (i.e., mechanism underlying linguistic communication) and the causal chain connecting the mechanism to observable events, to explain how these internal causes produce linguistic communication as their effect' (ibid.: 129). 'The events to which the mentalist's constructions refer can stand as links in the causal chain that contains vocalizations and sound waves as other links' (ibid.: 129—130). Clearly this gives us a picture of the mind as a structure of mental entities which are related to each other and causally impinge on each other much like the components of a complicated closed physical system (say, a computer). Speakers are viewed as more or less mechanical input-output systems. This metaphys-

---

[5]    Cf. however Katz (op. cit.: 125): 'Such a version of mentalism (i.e., that Katz advocates /PL) is wholly compatible with the doctrine Bloomfield called 'mechanism'.'

ics does not leave much room for the active creativity and conscious monitoring of a human agent. Instead we are faced with a paramechanistic explanatory paradigm (Ryle 1949) not too different from a multistage S—R psychology. The function of the mental grammatical machinery is to a large extent independent of the speaker's control or conscious monitoring. For example, the creative process in speech production seems to consist solely in the setting up of a semantic-syntactic deep structure and the plugging in of certain lexical items (in morpheme-invariant abstract forms).[6] This input structure to the derivation is some kind of a 'mental thing' (or rather a complex association of such things), the neurological correlate of which must be located somewhere in the brain (since the grammatical model must be 'isomorphic' to a neuro-physiological model [Katz, op. cit.: 129]). For the rest, the derivation will be an automatic process (at least if only 'obligatory' rules apply);[7] the deep structure enters the deterministic rule system of the grammar, where each representation or rule elicits a new rule in a long chain reaction, until the final pronounceable phonetic representation is produced and the articulatory organs can start to work.

Such a model seems very difficult to reconcile with our everyday experience of how meaningful verbal behavior is produced. We would think of verbal behavior as intentional and meaningful. The speaker is normally conscious of his intentions to communicate a certain message in a certain way so as to affect the listener's beliefs, feelings and actions in a specific desired way. In formulating his message he tries to calculate the way in which the listener will presumably react to his message, and these considerations influence his way of communicating the message. The speaker's intentions will influence all aspects (semantic, grammatical and phonological) of his utterance.

Of course, the mechanistic model works no better for listeners. The process of understanding an utterance can hardly be accurately explicated as a mechanical process of transforming a phonetic representation via a syntactic surface representation (or whatever you have) into a semantic representation. Rather, the listener actively uses the utterance (and his knowledge of the rules for its use) to *make sense of it*, i.e., he tries to construct an interpretation which could possibly correspond to what the speaker intended.

Of course, Katz' interpretation of Chomskyan mentalism is by no means universally accepted by generativists. A majority would probably dispute it, particularly since most of Chomsky's characterizations imply a much more indirect relationship between 'competence' and 'perform-

---

[6]  Plus, possibly, some feed-back mechanism which compares the semantic interpretation of the structure thus set up to the message intended. See e.g., Fodor et alii (1974: 391).

[7]  Optional rules may perhaps be assigned some probability measures.

ance' (e.g., 1967: 435—6, 1971: 188). On the other hand, works like
Fodor et al. (1974) and Fodor (1976), which may presumably be said to
be pretty close to Chomsky's own views, are rather akin to Katz' position, and Chomsky (1975) is also quite positive. Moreover, those generativists who really want to explain the role of Chomskyan competence in
linguistic performance, thereby taking Chomsky's claim of psychological reality seriously, seem to come up with some sort of reification of
deep structures, morpheme-invariant phonological forms etc.[8]

The traditional perspective on linguistic behavior is that speakers and
listeners are conscious agents who follow rules which define meaningful
acts and which in themselves may be brought to *some* level of awareness.
Linguistic behavior is conventional, which means that it is the way it is
partly by historical accidence (it could have been otherwise given the
biological constitution of the speaker/listener). That is, it cannot be
exhaustively explained by natural necessity, i.e., by reference to physical
and/or physiological properties of the speaker/listener. In as far as
linguistic behavior is conventional, it is learned through the individual's
experience of what counts as correct according to the social norm. But
this also presupposes that the speaker attends to (or has attended to) the
specific properties of the behavior which are conventionally specified by
the rules. Conventionality thus implies some degree of awareness. Of
course, many linguistic rules have a quite low level of consciousness —
certainly language users are not able to formulate the rules — and in
most instances, people are aware only of violations of the rules.[9]

We thus see that conventionality and awareness are closely tied to
linguistic competence, i.e., the speaker's knowledge of units and rules.
(This is of course not to deny that many aspects of linguistic behavior
can be explained by reference to the possibilities and limitations of the
speech and hearing organs and the central nervous system). Yet,
Chomsky and his associates do not seem to appreciate this point. In fact,
Fodor (1976: 52—3) argues that the distinction between conscious states
and processes of the mind (where the agent has some consciousness of
what he knows, feels or does) and processes that happen to and in the
nervous system and that are often not accessible to consciousness is not
'relevant to the purposes of cognitive psychology.' Chomsky has also
repeatedly pronounced related opinions. 'Any interesting generative
grammar will be dealing, for the most part, with mental processes that
are far beyond the level of actual or even potential consciousness; it is
quite apparent that a speaker's reports and viewpoints about his behavior

---

[8]  Cf. work in 'neurolinguistics' by scholars like Schnitzer and Whitaker. For some
    discussion, see Linell (1974: 144—6).
[9]  For a more detailed argumentation of these points, see Allwood (1976: 13—16,
    25—27).

and his competence may be in error' (Chomsky 1965: 8). 'The greatest defect of classical philosophy of mind ... seems to me to be its unquestioned assumption that the properties and content of the mind are accessible to introspection' (Chomsky 1968: 22).

It may certainly be true that the distinction between conscious and unconscious processes is not very important in a psychological model of the actual physiological processes going on in the nervous system of an individual during thinking, speaking, listening, trying to understand etc. But it *is* important, I would maintain, in a theory of communicative competence. Yet, generativists are, at least sometimes, inclined to give a mechanistic account also of linguistic competence. And obviously, the more inclined one is to argue that conscious vs. unconscious is not a possible distinction, the more one has in common with behaviorism; [10] mental processes are described not as intentional and consciously monitored but rather as something which happens to people. Thus, there are indeed important similarities between Chomskyan generative linguistics and earlier American structuralism (many proponents of which were behaviorists). [11]

Neither Chomsky nor Skinner presents a satisfactory theory of linguistic behavior or its underlying competence. [12] Obviously, they are often wrong in different ways, but they do share some properties. Both give mechanistic or paramechanistic paradigms, which are rather bad adaptations of natural-science type theories to social phenomena. What one would want is a *behavioral* (but not behavioristic) *theory of language* which also provides a proper place for the insight that linguistic behavior is intentional, meaningful and rule-conforming, and that, in all probability, communicative linguistic competence concerns what the individual can perform in terms of such linguistic behavior.

---

[10]  Jens Allwood (pers. comm.) has called my attention to this point.

[11]  Other aspects of this kinship are argued for in Itkonen (1974). See also Steinberg's (1975) excerpts form the works of Chomsky which clearly show his dependence on American structuralism. Consider also Chomsky's explanation of language acquisition which involves the postulation of an innate Language Acquisition Device which, by virtue of an evaluation measure, necessarily selects a unique and most highly valued (i.e., simple and general) grammar given certain linguistic input data. This, Derwing (1973: 53—63) argues, amounts to postulating an innate discovery procedure for grammars. This is remarkable in view of the fact that Chomsky has often argued against discovery procedures in his critique of American structuralist grammar (esp. phonology).

[12]  That Chomsky's theory is loaded with many kinds of other difficulties is shown in, e.g., Derwing (1973) and Linell (1974).

# References

Allwood, J. 1976. *Linguistic Communication as Action and Cooperation.* A Study in Pragmatics. Göteborg: Department of Linguistics.

Chomsky, N. 1957. *Syntactic Structures.* The Hague: Mouton.

Chomsky, N. 1959. Review of Skinner (1957). *Language* 35: 26—58.

Chomsky, N. 1965. *Aspects of the Theory of Syntax.* Cambridge, Mass.: The M. I. T. Press.

Chomsky, N. 1967. The formal nature of language. Appendix A (Pp 397—442) in Lenneberg, E. *Biological Foundations of Language.* New York etc: John Wiley & Sons.

Chomsky, N. 1968. *Language and Mind.* New York etc: Harcourt, Brace & World.

Chomsky, N. 1971. Deep structure, surface structure and semantic interpretation. In Steinberg, D. & Jakobovits, L. (1971) [eds] *Semantics.* An Interdisciplinary Reader in Philosophy, Linguistics and Psychology. Cambridge: Cambridge University Press. 183—216.

Chomsky, N. 1975. *Reflections on Language.* Fontana/Collins.

Derwing, B. 1973. *Transformational Grammar as a Theory of Language Acquisition.* (Cambridge Studies in Linguistics 10). Cambridge: Cambridge University Press.

Fodor, J. A. 1976. *The Language of Thought.* Hassocks: The Harvester Press.

Fodor, J. A., Bever, T. G. & Garrett, M. F. 1974. *The Psychology of Language.* An Introduction to Psycholinguistics and Generative Grammar. New York etc: McGraw-Hill.

Itkonen, E. 1974. *Linguistics and Metascience.* (Studia Philosophica Turkuensia Fasc II). Kokemäki: Societas Philosophica et Phaenomenologica Finlandiae.

Katz, J. J. 1964. Mentalism in linguistics. *Language* 40: 124—137.

Linell, P. 1974. Problems of Psychological Reality in Generative Phonology. A Critical Assessment. *RUUL 4* (Uppsala: Department of Linguistics).

Ryle, G. 1949. *The Concept of Mind.* Penguin Books (latest impr. 1970).

Skinner, B. F. 1957. *Verbal Behavior.* New York: Appleton-Century-Crofts.

Steinberg, D. 1975. Chomsky: From Formalism to Mentalism and Psychological Invalidity. *Glossa* 9: 218—252.

# III. Formal Methods in Linguistic Research

# Axiom, Theorem, and Rule[*]

Larry G. Hutchinson

A transformational grammar consists essentially of a set of formulae[1], and to really understand what kind of thing a transformational grammar is one must have a clear understanding of what these formulae mean. They must have clear and explicit interpretations if rational discussions of transformational grammar are to exist and if individual grammars are to be sensibly evaluated. This paper should be construed as an attempt to clarify some of the issues involved in providing such clear and explicit interpretations.

1.0 One standard interpretation of grammatical formulae is that they are "instructions." They are instructions to do something on the way toward constructing representations of sentences of the object language. More specifically, the type of formula called a phrase structure rule is an instruction to construct a subtree with the symbol on the left of the arrow dominating the symbols on the right, a so-called redundancy rule is an instruction to add feature specifications to a feature complex, a syntactic transformation is an instruction specifying the deformation of one tree into another, and so forth. A transformational grammar is, in fact, interpretable straightforwardly as a computer program, whose instructions, if followed faithfully, permit the construction of sentence representations. Individual grammars are simply programs drawn from a particular programming language. Viewed in this way, Chomsky's "Standard Theory," for example, is a programming language on all fours with some programming language such as SNOBOL I. Standard computer terminology, while not normally encountered in the transformational literature, is perfectly adaptable to such grammars in a natural way. There are in fact some advantages in doing so. One can cite, as an example, the problem of "program control," that is, the problem of which instruction to execute next. This is referred to in the transforma-

---

[*] A preliminary version of this paper was presented at the MMLA meeting in St. Louis, in the fall of 1976.
[1] The bulk of the formulae found in transformational grammars are traditionally called "rules," but since this term is rather suggestive in a number of ways I will suppress it for the most part in what follows in favor of the neutral term "formulae."

tional literature as rule ordering. Real computer programs have, in one form or another,

(a) overt GO TO statements, which specify that some named instruction X is to be executed next (perhaps under some stated conditions), and

(b) covert GO TO statements, wherein the next instruction to be executed is taken to be the next instruction in a list.

Transformational grammars no longer have overt GO TO statements (they once had "traffic rules"), but they do have covert ones in the form of extrinsic ordering in a list format and the principle of the cycle. Some transformational grammars allow for random selection of the next instruction, some allow for simultaneous execution of two or more instructions, and some have "precedence conditions" (procedures for comparing instructions and/or the possible effects of distinct orderings of their executions to select which instruction to execute next). The extension of computer terminology here demythologizes some of the recent rule ordering discussion, it seems to me, and puts that discussion in a profitable new perspective.

Given this instruction interpretation of the formulae of transformational grammar one can ask a number of interesting questions. For example, does such a grammar so interpreted make statements about the sentences of the object language, that is to say, does it "describe" the object language in any ordinary sense? Is it reasonable to say that such a grammar is a theory of the object language? I would contend that if these questions are taken seriously their answers are negative: a set of instructions does not make statements, a set of instructions is not a description, and a set of instructions is most certainly not a theory.

Take as an example the well-known context-free grammar

$$S \rightarrow ab$$
$$S \rightarrow aSb$$

This simple program allows us to derive a set of strings, to make computer runs and actually construct strings. But it does not say that all such strings will have the form $a^n b^n$, where $n \geq 1$. This statement is indeed a true statement about the set of strings generated by the grammar, but it is not stated *in* the grammar. We can prove that it is true, given the set of instructions to reason about, but it must be discovered, stated, and proved outside the grammar by us. For that matter, the grammar does not even say that the string "aaabbb" is in the generated set. We can prove that it is in, either by displaying a derivation of it constructed by following the instructions, or by proving the $a^n b^n$ theorem and showing this particular string to be of the form $a^n b^n$ where $n = 3$.

As grammars in the form of instructions grow more complex it becomes increasingly difficult to formulate truths about the strings generated and to prove these truths. Consider the only slightly more complicated grammar below.

$$S \rightarrow aSBC \qquad bB \rightarrow bb$$
$$S \rightarrow aBC \qquad bC \rightarrow bc$$
$$CB \rightarrow BC \qquad cC \rightarrow cc$$
$$aB \rightarrow ab$$

It should take the average reader of this grammar a while to come to suspect that the language generated contains the string $a^n b^n c^n$ for each $n \geq 1$, for the grammar itself certainly does not state this. It will take even longer to prove it.[2]

A grammar whose formulae are seen as instructions, then, makes no claims at all. It is merely a program which allows the computation of derivations. The linguist can make statements about the derivations and about the strings generated, and he may even be able to prove them by reasoning about the program. It is these statements which would constitute a grammatical description of the language in the ordinary sense, not the instructions themselves.

It is possible, of course, to provide stipulative definitions which allow instructional grammars to make claims. The following would be examples of such definitions:

(i)   We will say that a grammar claims that a particular string $X_1$ is grammatical iff we have proved that $X_1$ can be constructed following this grammar's instructions.

(ii)  We will say that a grammar claims that a particular string $X_2$ is ungrammatical iff we have proved that it is impossible to construct $X_2$ following this grammar's instructions.

(iii) We will say that a grammar claims that a particular string $X_3$ is n-ways ambiguous iff we have proved that $X_3$ can be constructed in $n$ distinct ways following this grammar's instructions.

(iv)  We will say that a grammar claims that two particular strings $X_4$ and $X_5$ are syntactic paraphrases iff we have proved that both $X_4$ and $X_5$ can be derived from the same deep structure.

While it seems excessively metaphorical to me to talk of sets of instructions making claims in this way, this is a matter of personal taste and of no moment. What is important is that it be clear that to talk this way at all requires a set of fully explicit and precise definitions of the sort just outlined. It will not do to have each linguist making up his own interpretations about what another linguist's set of instructions "claims" about

---

[2]   The proof is given on page 12 of Hopcroft and Ullman (1969).

the language generated. It will not do to allow one linguist to point an accusing finger at another's grammar and announce, "This grammar claims it is merely an accident that such-and-such," unless there is an accepted definition of the form

(v)   We will say that a grammar claims that such-and-such is merely an accident iff . . .

2.0   One need not, however, build grammars which tell how to construct strings, leaving it to the grammarian to state truths about the strings. One could simply state truths about the object language sentences directly. This would be a grammar of a quite traditional kind, one consisting entirely of statements about sentences, morphemes, phones, meanings, and so forth. There would be no instructions for constructing anything.

Consider the following syntax example. A grammar might contain the statements

(1)   All tags contain an auxiliary verb which is identical to the first auxiliary, if there is one, of the main clause; otherwise the tag contains a DO auxiliary.
(2)   All passive sentences contain a BE auxiliary.

These statements make truth claims about the object language directly. They do not specify how to construct anything; in particular, tags are not built by copying the first auxiliary verb into the tag, and active structures are not transformed into passive structures. There are no grammatical derivations, no computer runs.

A grammar of the statement type need not consist of a mere jumble of truths of course. One might try organizing the statements in various ways for various purposes, and this is indeed done in actual practice. Reviews of ordinary descriptive grammars often praise or condemn them on the basis of their organization and presentation of descriptive statements. But, to a confirmed formalist perhaps the most obvious mode of organization would be an axiomatization.[3] As an example of such an axiomatization consider the following statement.

(3)   No tag on a passive clause contains a DO auxiliary.

It is reasonably clear that (3) would follow deductively from (1) and (2) above were they but stated a little more precisely. All three statements

---

[3]   Chomsky has interpreted grammars, in *Syntactic Structures* and elsewhere, as a set of rules of "inference," with only one axiom S. In this interpretation the theorems are sentence representations, not statements about sentences. This view should not be confused with the one presently under discussion for there is an important difference between axiomatizing sentences and axiomatizing truths about sentences.

might be true grammatical statements, but if (1) and (2) were designated as axioms, (3) could be deduced as a theorem. In an "axiomatic grammar" all the traditional concerns of axiomatizers come to the fore. What is the minimal number of axioms required? What different axiomatizations are possible for each language? Is a particular system complete? Is it consistent? Are its axioms independent? And so on.

One could also ask of this grammar type in what sense it makes claims about the language under description. The answer might at first seem obvious — such a grammar consists entirely of statements which claim directly that such and such is the case — but there is a question about the term "grammar" that would have to be cleared up here. Is a grammar just the set of axioms, or is it the full thesis set, that is, the axioms and theorems taken together? If it is to be the former, then there are indefinitely many true statements which the grammar does not state directly but only implies. These statements must be found, stated, and proved. Axioms do not state or prove their theorems, the user does. Let this suffice for the moment; the question will be taken up again below.

3.0 Two distinct grammar types have now been outlined; one consists entirely of a set of instructions detailing how to construct sentence representations, and the other consists entirely of true statements about sentences. The former describes nothing, the latter tells how to construct nothing. One might take as an analogy a model airplane kit in which pictures, blueprints, and descriptive statements have been separated from assembly instructions. Anyone given only the description of the completed model will have his hands full trying to figure out how to assemble it, while anyone given only the assembly instructions will have a difficult time constructing a description of what the completed model should look like. These are utterly distinct enterprises, and the force of the analogy should not be lost on those who have worked with even the simpler airplane kits.

However, this paper began by interpreting the formulae of a transformational grammar to be instructions. Suppose we now set out to interpret them as statements in an axiomatic grammar. Suppose, for example, the formula (4)

(4)  $[+ \text{ obstruent}] \rightarrow [- \text{ voice}]/\underline{\qquad} \#$

were to be interpreted as stating (5).

(5)  All word final obstruents are voiceless.

Taken as a statement, (4) does not instruct one to "devoice" word final obstruents, it simply says such obstruents *are* voiceless. The arrow in (4) is being taken as (material) implication rather than as a rewrite instruction, that is to say, (4) is being taken as a notational variant of the ordinary predicate calculus formula (6)

(6)  (x) (Obstruent$_x$ $\wedge$ Word final$_x$ $\supset$ Voiceless$_x$)

Note that (4) is now something that can be true or false; under an instruction interpretation it would not have been. But, rather than abandoning the instruction interpretation of grammatical formulae and considering a transformational grammar to be just an axiomatic grammar, let's provide a *double* interpretation for each grammatical formula. A formula of a given type is to be given an explicit interpretation as an instruction, which is to be followed in the construction of derivations, and an explicit interpretation as a statement, which makes a specific claim about the language. For example, the formula (4) could be interpreted both as

(a) the *instruction* to add[4] the feature [— voice] to any word final obstruent

and as

(b) the *statement* that all obstruents are voiceless in word final position.

The statement may be true or false, since it is a statement, but it wouldn't make sense to say the instruction is true or false. On the other hand, the statement doesn't say what to do in a particular derivation. It is important to observe that (b) cannot be inferred from the presence of (a); it must also be determined if there is some other instruction which partially undoes (a). For instance, an apocope instruction ordered after (a) might produce new voiced word final obstruents. It should also be observed that (a) cannot in any sense be inferred from (b); if a word final voiced obstruent should occur in a derivation we wouldn't know whether to devoice it, delete it, or insert a word final vowel. In other words, (a) and (b) are fundamentally distinct, and their only connection here is that they are both interpretations of the grammatical formula (4). A grammar consisting entirely of instructions doesn't make statements, and a grammar consisting entirely of statements doesn't specify how to construct anything; but a grammar whose formulae are interpreted simultaneously as instructions and statements tells both how to build and what's true.[5]

---

[4]  "add" should generally mean
  1. Change ([+ voice] to [— voice])
  2. Insert ([— voice] if no voicing feature were present)
  3. Do nothing (if [— voice] were already present)

[5]  It is interesting that English passive constructions and predicate adjective constructions are often identical, giving a parallel double interpretation to sentences such as "Initial voiceless stops are aspirated."
That is, one aspirates them in constructing derivations or they just are aspirate.

The double interpretation idea is, I feel, an interesting one, and is worth pursuing a bit. Consider the following piece of grammar.

(i)   $V \rightarrow \tilde{V}/\underline{\hspace{2cm}} \begin{bmatrix} C \\ + \text{ nasal} \end{bmatrix}$

(ii)  $V \rightarrow [+ \text{ long}]/\underline{\hspace{2cm}} \begin{bmatrix} C \\ + \text{ voice} \end{bmatrix}$

(iii) $\tilde{V} \rightarrow [+ \text{ long}]$

When these formulae are interpreted as (ordered) instructions, (iii) turns out to have only vacuous applications, i.e., all nasal vowels will already be [+long] (provided that nasal consonants are voiced in this language). Formula (iii) is totally unnecessary in the grammar, and any work it might have done is handled quite satisfactorily by (i) and (ii) alone. When these three formulae are interpreted as statements, all of them may very well be true of the language under analysis. But (iii) is deducible from (i) and (ii), that is to say, if (i) and (ii) were selected as axioms, (iii) would be a theorem. In this example, reducing the number of statements in the axiom set corresponds to reducing the number of instructions. Note that if (iii) is suppressed, however, the grammar does not directly state that all nasal vowels are long nor does it specify that in building strings one should lengthen nasal vowels. One could ask here just how it is that a grammar consisting only of (i) and (ii) "captures the generalization" that all nasal vowels are long.

There are, however, several difficulties in providing this double interpretation for the formulae of transformational grammar.

The first difficulty is that while fairly explicit interpretation principles have been given for formulae as instructions, very few have been given for formulae as statements. Phrase structure formulae are straight forward enough, with

A → B C

being interpreted as the instruction (7) and the statement (8).

(7)   rewrite any string containing A as that string with B C instead of A (in constructing derivations)
      or
      form subtree $\overset{\displaystyle A}{\overset{\diagup \diagdown}{B \quad C}}$ (in constructing trees)

(8)   B C is an A

Other kinds of formulae are less explicitly specified for statement interpretation. The interpretation is allowed to be done intuitively and on a case by case basis, with the result that it is not always clear exactly what a given formula states. What is needed is a set of clear and explicit interpretation principles of the type

(9) Any grammatical formula of the form x is to be interpreted as stating that y.

One instance of this interpretation type would be

(10) Any grammatical formula of the form $[\alpha F_1] \rightarrow [\beta F_2]$ (/A—B), where $F_1$ and $F_2$ are distinct phonological features, is to be interpreted as stating that all segments containing $[\alpha F_1]$ also contain $[\beta F_2]$ (in environment A—B).

Interpretation principle (10) is designed to be applied to formulae which do not involve feature changing as part of their overt specification. For example, the formula (11)

(11)  [+ back] → [+ round]

is immediately interpreted by (10) as stating that all segments containing [+ back] also contain [+ round]. The formula (4) is immediately interpreted by (10) as stating that all segments containing [+ obstruent] also contain [− voice] in word final position. Observe that although this formula as instruction could involve the replacing of $\begin{bmatrix} + \text{ obstruent} \\ + \text{ voice} \end{bmatrix}$

with $\begin{bmatrix} + \text{ obstruent} \\ - \text{ voice} \end{bmatrix}$, the feature switch is not part of the formula itself and hence the statement interpretation given is not inappropriate. If the formula had been

(12)  $\begin{bmatrix} + \text{ obstruent} \\ + \text{ voice} \end{bmatrix} \rightarrow [- \text{ voice}]/\underline{\hspace{1cm}} \#$

the interpretation would have been that all segments containing $\begin{bmatrix} + \text{ obstruent} \\ + \text{ voice} \end{bmatrix}$ *also* contain [− voice] in word final position. This is simply a contradiction; no segment can be voiced and voiceless at the same time. The same sort of self-contradictory interpretation would be given to alpha-switching formulae.

Deletion and insertion formulae would require their own rules of interpretation. For example

(13)  C → ∅/\underline{\hspace{1cm}} #

might be interpreted as stating that no word ends in a consonant, and

(14)  ∅ → i/CC \underline{\hspace{1cm}} C

might be interpreted as stating that no CCC clusters occur. A single interpretation principle could be given here, perhaps something like the following:

(15) Any formula involving ∅ on the left or right of the arrow is to

be interpreted as stating that the material on the left together with the context does not occur.

This principle interprets the formulae (13) and (14) as stating that C # does not occur and that CC∅C = CCC does not occur.

The "does not occur" interpretation could be extended to metathesis formulae too. The formula

(16)  $S_1 S_2 \rightarrow S_2 S_1$ ,

where $S_1$ and $S_2$ are particular segment types, could be taken to assert that $S_1 S_2$ sequences never occur. Such an interpretation would not be appropriate, however, for the kind of formulae considered above which do not involve feature changing in their formulation. The formula (4) is not to be interpreted as stating that word final obstruents do not occur. On the other hand, the formula (12) could be appropriately taken as asserting that word final voiced obstruents do not occur. This is a nice illustration, incidentally, that two formulae which have identical effects when interpreted as instructions might be interpreted rather distinctly as statements.[6]

It is not being claimed, I hasten to point out, that the statement interpretations given here would be accepted by all generative phonologists.[7] That they would not be is part of the point being made; interpretations of phonological formulae are non-standardized. Until they are it will be unclear exactly what such formulae are claiming about the object language.

In the case of syntactic transformations, the interpretating of grammatical formulae as statements about the object language is in even worse shape. With optional transformations, one might try to claim that a formula

$$\text{(17)  X} \xrightarrow{\text{optional}} \text{Y}$$

states that if X is a well-formed sentence then so is Y, but this won't wash because transformations do not relate sentences to sentences in this direct way. A somewhat more adequate interpretation would be

(18)  If $S_1$ is derived from X and $S_2$ is derived from Y, then if $S_1$ is a grammatical sentence so is $S_2$.

---

[6]  The fact that the statement interpretations of these two formulae are logically equivalent should not obscure the fact that they were arrived at via quite distinct interpretation principles.

[7]  Another possible interpretation of (12) is that any morpheme which ends in a voiced obstruent in other contexts always ends in that obstruent's voiceless counterpart word finally. Yet a third interpretation, involving well-formedness conditions on derivations is given below.

The passive formula, for example, would in effect assert that if $S_1$ is a grammatical sentence derived from the active structure X then $S_2$ (derived from Y) is also a grammatical sentence. With obligatory transformations even this move is blocked. In

(19)  X $\xrightarrow{\text{obligatory}}$ Y

no sentence will be derivable from X which is not also derivable from Y, making the statement interpretation of the formula pointless.

It must be pointed out that a single statement interpretation could be given for every formula of transformational grammar, namely,

(20)  Any formula X → Y asserts that the two line sequence $\alpha X\beta$, $\alpha Y\beta$ is a well-formed subpart of a derivation.

In other words, the set of grammatical formulae could be taken as a description of well-formed derivations. I would contend that this way of interpreting formulae as statements is totally pointless unless derivations have independent existence, that is, unless it is possible to measure these statements against derivations in the real world to determine their truth content. In any event, this mode of interpretation takes the object language to be a set of derivations, and, hence, does not square with the initial characterization of axiomatic grammar given in this paper, wherein the object language is taken to be the set of grammatical sentences (and their subparts) of some natural language.

In point of fact, the difficulty in determining what a TG is supposed to be about constitutes a more serious problem, a more basic difficulty, than that posed by the difficulty in providing general statement interpretations for individual formulae. For example, the formula

(21)  S → NP VP

when interpreted as saying either that any noun phrase followed by a verb phrase is a sentence or that all sentences consist of a noun phrase followed by a verb phrase is magnificently false of English sentences. Similarly, the typical NP phrase structure formula for English is quite false when interpreted as a statement about that language's noun phrases. The only way to retain these formulae as expressing truths is to take them to be not about English sentences and noun phrases but about "deep structure strings," that is to say, that S does not denote sentences and NP does not denote noun phrases.[8]

---

[8]  One may well ask how the truth of the S and NP statements is to be determined. Unless deep structure strings have independent existence and their properties can be compared with phrase structure statements it is not at all clear that these statements have any real significance. If phrase structure formulae as statements are supposed to be true of just the set of derivations sanctioned by the very same formulae as instructions, then their truth is of a tautological and thoroughly uninteresting character.

Phonological formulae, on the other hand, may be intended to be true of the object language. For German the formula (4) is intended to be true of actual German words, that is, it is supposed to be true that no German word ends in a voiced obstruent. This particular formula is not, however, intended to be true of deep structure strings or of surface structure strings (referring to the outputs of the syntactic component), for these strings are intentionally set up to contain voiced obstruents in word final position. It is certainly not the case, however, that all phonological formulae are intended to be true of the object language. In principle, the effect of any phonological instruction may be undone by a phonological instruction executed at a later stage. It would not be considered unusual, for example, for a formula to specify the placement of stress on penultimate syllables, with an apocope formula being executed later; the result would be that stress would in some instances fall on ultimate syllables and the stress formula as statement would be (intentionally) false. Such an analysis is not only commonplace, the possibility of such analyses is often hailed as a major virtue of transformational grammars. What this means, obviously, is that examining one formula alone, even when it has been given a statement interpretation, is not sufficient to determine which claims are intended to be true. In phonology, as in other components of transformational grammar, formulae are intricately ordered, interrelated, and abstract. Segments which are nonexistent in the language are introduced and then deleted, paradigmatic regularities are constructed and then destroyed, constituencies are built up and then dismantled. All of this may or may not be a good way to construct strings and derivations, but it absolutely guarantees that grammatical formulae cannot be interpreted as statements about the object language in any simple, straightforward way.

I have been hoping to illustrate in the last few pages that the construction of general principles to interpret grammatical formulae in transformational grammars as statements is rather complex, and, further, that it is difficult to determine their intended domains of discourse. As a result, determining what claims a transformational grammar actually makes about the object language is a decidedly murky business. Any argument that rests on evaluating the claims made by a specific transformational grammar will therefore be murky too. This is simply a concomitance of imprecision.

4.0 One final issue I'd like to mention concerns the evaluative notions "capturing a generalization" and "missing a generalization." These notions are clearly important to transformationalists in assessing competing grammars, but it seems to me that they are difficult to understand. At least they stand in need of clarification. Perhaps a brief discussion will suffice to illustrate some of the issues involved.

In an axiomatic grammar capturing a generalization would most straightforwardly seem to mean including it in the thesis set, that is to say, guaranteeing that it is an axiom or a theorem. A missed generalization would be one not in the thesis set, and presumably the axiomatic system would be taken to be incomplete. This construal does not appear to be what transformationalists have in mind, however. More likely, capturing a generalization is to mean stating it in the grammar, where "the grammar" denotes the set of axioms. This interpretation seems a little odd, though, given the axiomatizer's commonly noted desire to decrease the number of axioms and increase the deductive cohesion of the system. In this sense, capturing a generalization would be a pejorative phrase, not an honorific. If capturing a generalization meant having to state it as an axiom we would presumably rather not capture it.

Understanding what it means to capture a generalization in a purely instructional grammar is even harder, since such grammars don't express generalizations at all. Generalizations about the strings generated have to be discovered and proved, commonly by long lines of reasoning about the ways in which the various instructions interact. Capturing a generalization about the set of strings might be construed as discovering it and proving it, but then it is the grammarian who does all the capturing, not the grammar. If the notion of capturing were extended to the grammar as well, then any grammar which correctly generated the set would capture all the generalizations about the set. Again it would appear that this is not what transformationalists have in mind.

About the best interpretation I can give these notions goes as follows. Consider the formulae of a transformational grammar to be doubly interpreted as discussed above. A formula which states a true generalization is to be included in the grammar as an axiom if it leads to a simpler and more efficient set of instructions.[9] To argue that a generalization should be captured is to argue that its instruction counterpart is useful. For example, in the vowel nasalization and lengthening illustration given above, the generalization that all nasalized vowels are long is not to be captured, since the instruction to lengthen nasalized vowels is totally redundant. If this interpretation comes at all close to the mark, and I have no confidence that it does, then individual arguments about capturing a generalization should revolve around whether or not a particular generalization is or should be incorporated as an instruction in some way. One might also expect to find many pointless arguments, that is, arguments which hinge on axiom versus theorem status of certain

---

[9]   This is notoriously difficult to spell out. It is well known that a larger number of axioms may shorten proofs (derivations) considerably. The same goes for instructions. "Redundant" instructions may lead to shorter and more elegant derivations. Should such instructions be suppressed anyway?

generalizations with no consideration being given to the utility of the corresponding instructions. Whether a particular item is to be an axiom or a theorem in axiomatic theories is commonly a matter of little moment.

Two examples, chosen somewhat at random, might be helpful. First, consider again the formula

$$[+ \text{ back}] \rightarrow [+ \text{ round}]$$

This, when taken to state that all back vowels are round, might be a true generalization about some language. How is this generalization to be captured? If it is necessary to state it in the grammar, then the formula must be written in the grammar, which means under our current assumptions that it must have a useful instruction interpretation as well. In a lexicon with redundant features unspecified, the instruction would have a point, for it would specify the insertion of the feature [+ round] into all [+ back] segments. Note that the statement would not be true of the lexicon, however. In a lexicon with fully specified matrices, on the other hand, the instruction would be vacuous (at least as far as the lexicon is concerned), although the statement would now be true of this lexicon. In addition, the statement itself is of course provable, for by simple inspection of all back vowels in the lexicon one can demonstrate that they are also round. In other words, the generalization is clearly a theorem and should not be included in the grammar as an axiom.[10] Knowing whether a certain generalization should be captured or not requires, on my tentative interpretation of "capture," knowing whether it can be utilized significantly as an instruction.

The second example, perhaps of some historical interest, concerns Chomsky's argument in *Syntactic Structures* that a generalized conjunction transformation should be formulated which tells how to construct sentences with compound constituents from sentences without such constituents. He first makes an observation about English sentences, reproduced below.

---

[10] It might be argued that the generalization is supposed to be a "constraint" on the lexicon, something not intended to be interpreted also as an instruction. It might be argued too that the constraint is stronger than suggested, that it is not just true of the lexicon (hence provable by inspection of that lexicon) but a real constraint on new lexical items, and even perhaps that without an overt statement of the constraint the grammar would be claiming it is only an accident that all back vowels have been rounded so far. I hope it is obvious that such lines of argumentation require a considerable amount of clarification concerning claims, goals, and interpretations. It means extending the grammar to include statements not designed to have instruction counterparts, it means agreeing in advance on exactly when a grammar "claims" something is an accident, it means being able to distinguish a statement of fact from a subjunctive statement about what would happen, and so forth.

If $S_1$ and $S_2$ are grammatical sentences, and $S_1$ differs from $S_2$ only in that X appears in $S_1$ where Y appears in $S_2$ (i.e., $S_1 = ---X---$ and $S_2 = ---Y---$), and X and Y are constituents of the same type in $S_1$ and $S_2$, respectively, then $S_3$ is a sentence, where $S_3$ is the result of replacing X by X + and + Y in $S_1$ (i.e., $S_3 = ---X + and + Y---$). (p. 36)

This can be taken as a straightforward implicational generalization about triples of English sentences, with the "where" clauses merely specifying the forms of $S_1$, $S_2$, and $S_3$. Sentence $S_3$ is claimed to exist, if $S_1$ and $S_2$ do. The generalization is, as Chomsky was aware, quite false, but we can suppress this fact in the present discussion. Even if it were true, we are not committed to actually constructing $S_3$ via some analysis which first tells how to build $S_1$ and $S_2$, then specifies their dismemberment to obtain the components needed for constructing $S_3$. Sentence $S_3$ could be constructed quite independently of $S_1$ and $S_2$, with the generalization still being true. Consider the following rule schema:

(22)  $X \rightarrow X (and X)^n$,   $n \geq 1$
      where X = S, NP, VP, Adj, etc.

This is to be interpreted as a conflation of the ordinary phrase structure formulae[11] below.

S  → S  and S
S  → S  and S  and S
        .
        .

NP→ NP and NP
NP→ NP and NP and NP
        .
        .

VP→ VP and VP
VP→ VP and VP and VP
        .
        .

It is a trivial matter to prove of such a grammar that if it generated, say,

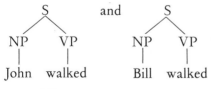

---

[11] Chomsky's view that a schema of this sort is a pernicious, ad hoc extension of phrase structure grammar is quite beside the point here; even so, I should state that I disagree with him totally.

then it would also generate

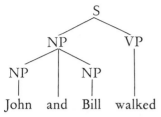

John and Bill walked

It must, for any independent NP generated would also be generated inside a compound NP. The same holds true for any other conjoinable constituent. This in fact forms the nucleus of a proof; in this grammar, Chomsky's putative generalization is a theorem about the generated strings and is not stated in the grammar at all. Has it been captured or has it been missed? Should it be captured? Observe that it would be possible for a grammarian to construct such a grammar and fail to notice the generalization, even though it remains provable.

For Chomsky's argument that the grammar must contain a formula which, when interpreted as an instruction, specifies the actual construction of $S_3$'s from $S_1$'s and $S_2$'s, he must demonstrate the utility of such an instruction. It would not be sufficient to assert that the generalization must be "captured." And Chomsky fails, for he does not demonstrate the utility — he merely asserts it (see pp. 36—38).

This very brief discussion of the notion "capturing a generalization" is designed to show that it is unreasonable to demand that every true generalization, or even every true "linguistically significant" generalization, be captured, if this means being stated in the grammar. But if generalizations are captured merely by virtue of being provable in an axiomatic grammar or provable of the strings generated by an instructional grammar, then most of the steam appears to go out of complaints that a certain grammar misses an important generalization. Of course, this discussion is only preliminary, and the real intent in presenting it has been to demonstrate that this concept, as well as many other basic concepts mentioned in this paper, stands in need of clarification. Until such clarification is provided the very foundations of transformational grammar are suspect. This is not an abstract, philosophical comment, a comment of no direct relevance to day to day "normal" linguistic science, for day to day grammatical argumentation is contaminated by the very same lack of clarification. Until clarification is provided no one, not even those who construct them, can really understand what transformational grammars are, nor sensibly argue that one is better than another.

# References

Chomsky, Noam. 1957. *Syntactic Structures.* Mouton & Co.
Hopcroft, John E. and Jeffrey D. Ullman. 1969. *Formal Languages and Their Relation to Automata.* Addison-Wesley.

# The Relevance of Mathematical Linguistics to Empirical Linguistics*

F. B. D'Agostino

Precisely constructed models for linguistic structure can play an important role, both negative and positive, in the process of discovery itself. By pushing a precise but inadequate formulation to an unacceptable conslusion, we can often expose the exact source of this inadequacy and, consequently, gain a deeper understanding of the linguistic data. (Chomsky, 1957: 5)

## 1. Introduction

A major problem of continuing interest in transformational linguistics is that of strengthening the theory $T$ of possible languages. $T$ implicitly defines the set of possible languages by defining a set of possible grammars in terms of certain properties which each of them must have. Thus, strengthening the theory $T$ consists in discovering *additional* properties of this kind. One familiar way in which such properties are discovered is in the context of the problem of achieving *explanatory adequacy* for $T$. Here, typically, *empirical* considerations suggest that some additional property be incorporated into the definition of possible grammars.

There is, however, another way in which additional defining properties of possible grammars can be discovered; a way that does not rely on (though it can be checked against) empirical considerations. This method involves the investigation of certain *mathematical* properties of grammars. It starts from a certain very abstract (though empirically motivated) condition on the appropriate *generative capacity* of grammars and proceeds, via mathematical proofs and proof-analyses, to the discovery of properties whose incorporation into the definition of possible grammars insures that such grammar *do* satisfy this condition.

My aim in this paper is to explicate this second method of discovery. My main concern will be to show that aprioristic mathematical considerations can and do have an important *heuristic* role to play in linguistic

* My thanks to Geoffrey Sampson, Colin Howson, and Robert Wall for helpful comments on previous drafts of this paper, and to Emmon Bach and Stanley Peters for encouraging my interest in this subject. I also owe a theoretical debt to Elie Zahar, who first drew my attention to the heuristic importance of mathematical considerations in scientific research.

discovery. I will, thus, be anxious to counter the I think rather widespread impression that mathematical linguistics has only a kind of negative *diagnostic* role to play in linguistic research.

I will argue to this effect in five stages. *First,* I discuss the general problem of strengthening the theory *T* and try to indicate why this is important. *Secondly,* I briefly and rather abstractly discuss the first, empirical method of discovering additional defining properties of grammars. *Third,* I outline the second, mathematical method of discovery and say something about the abstract assumptions on which it rests. *Fourth,* I review a series of cases in which mathematical considerations *have* led to the proposal of new defining properties of grammars. Here I pay particular attention to the relation between the mathematically-guided *discovery* of such properties and the empirical *consequences* of incorporating them into a definition of possible grammars. *Fifth,* I conclude with some reflections on the significance of the role of mathematical heuristics in linguistic research.

## 2. The Importance of Strengthening the Theory T

Before saying something about the various *ways* in which linguists have proposed to strengthen the theory *T* of possible grammars, it might be appropriate to indicate *why* it is important to try to do this. There are, it seems, at least four reasons why this kind of exercise is important.

(1) The theory *T* is an implicit definiton of the set of possible human languages. Thus, the weaker the theory *T,* the less it tells us about what makes human languages different from arbitrary symbolic systems. On the other hand, the stronger *T* is, the more clearly it distinguishes the human languages from other kinds of possible communicative systems. This is a particularly important consideration for those linguists, like Chomsky, who argue from the degree to which human languages are unexpectedly different from other possible communicative systems to the conclusion that the ability to use such languages necessarily presupposes some innate predisposition to acquire this ability.

(2) For those who take this kind of view about the relationship between a theory of language *T* and the innate predisposition to acquire linguistic abilities of a certain kind, the strength of *T* is also important for the following reason: On the assumption that the innate predisposition to acquire abilities of a certain type is mediated by a language acquisiton device *(LAD)* that incorporates a 'mental representation' of *T,* then, the weaker the theory *T,* the more empirically adequate grammars of each language L provided by the *LAD.* And thus, the more difficult it is to explain

the acquisition of the unique 'psychologically real' grammar of L. (Peters 1972)

(3)  Related to the problem of explaining language acquisition is the problem of defining some suitable evaluation measure $E$ over the grammars provided by $T$ for some language L. For, when $T$ provides multiple grammars for some language, $E$ is supposed to select from those the psychologically real grammar of that language. Thus, if such a measure can be defined, then language acquisition can be explained — albeit less elegantly — even when $T$ provides many different possible grammars for some language. But, when $T$ is a very weak theory, it may be very difficult to define $E$ in terms of some (relatively) easily defined metric such as 'simplicity.' For the *simplest* $T$-grammar of L may *not* be the psychologically real one. Thus, it seems likely that the possibility of defining the measure $E$ in any natural way will vary inversely with the strength of $T$.[1] (Chomsky 1965: 35)

(4)  Given two different and competing theories of language $T_1$ and $T_2$ the weaker these two theories are, the more difficult it may be to decide *on empirical grounds* which of them is the better theory. This follows from the fact that if these theories are weak enough, they may be able to model almost any linguistically significant phenomenon. And, in this case, no empirical evidence could decide between them and the debate between their proponents would, thus, remain sterile and indecisive. This problem is perhaps most strikingly illustrated by the recent debate between Lakoff and Baker and Brame. Thus, Lakoff proposed (1970) that 'global rules' are necessary in order to model certain linguistically interesting phenomena. But, because the 'standard theory' advocated by Baker and Brame was so weak, they were able to show (1972) that the same phenomena could be accounted for without using such rules. And, although Lakoff replied (1972) that this could be done only in an 'ad hoc' fashion, this *methodological criticism* of the 'standard theory' could not have nearly the force that an *empirical refutation* of a *strong* 'standard theory' would have had. Thus, the strength of competing theories of language seems to be a presupposition for the decisiveness of debates between their proponents.

These are at least four reasons, then, why the problem of strengthening the theory $T$ is an important one.

---

[1]  Kiparsky makes the same point, essentially, when he notes (1968: 171) that while the 'simplest' description of combinatorial arithmetic may involve set theoretic considerations, it is nevertheless highly implausible that a person's underlying competence to perform arithmetic operations involves a tacit knowledge of set theory.

3. The *Empirical* Discovery of Additional Properties of Possible Grammars

In this section I want, *very* briefly, to say something about the kind of situation in which empirical considerations lead to the discovery of additional properties of possible grammars. As I have already indicated, such properties are typically proposed in the context of attempts to achieve explanatory adequacy for some theory $T$. The following scenario seems characteristic: (i) Some theory $T$ of possible grammars is assumed. $T$ defines the set of possible grammars in terms of the properties $P_1, \ldots, P_n$. (ii) For some language L under consideration, a grammar $G_1$, permitted by $T$, is proposed. (iii) $G_1$ is found to be descriptively *ina*dequate — typically, in generating strings *not* in L and/or in permitting 'counterintuitive' derivations of sentences in L. (iv) $G_1$ is thus refuted as a grammar of L and another grammar $G_2$, also permitted by $T$, is proposed in its place. (v) $G_2$ is found to be descriptively adequate as a grammar of L. (vi) But $T$, and its associated evaluation measure $E$, do not distinguish between $G_1$ and $G_2$ as possible grammars of L. Thus, $T$ is an explanatorily *ina*dequate theory of language. (vii) $G_1$ and $G_2$ are compared and it is found that $G_2$, but not $G_1$, has the property $P_{n+1}$, where $P_{n+1}$ is *not* one of the properties in terms of which $T$-grammars are defined. (viii) The theory $T'$, which defines possible grammars in terms of the properties $P_1, \ldots, P_{n+1}$ does not permit the grammar $G_1$ and is, thus, *with respect to the language L,* an explanatorily adequate theory of language. (ix) It is then conjectured that the property $P_{n+1}$ is a criterial property for possible grammars and, thus, that the theory $T'$ is an explanatorily adequate theory with respect to *all* languages. (x) This conjecture is tested by trying to construct descriptively adequate $T'$-grammars for languages other than L. It could be falsified by finding some language for which there was *no* descriptively adequate grammar with the property $P_{n+1}$. In this case, we would review our original conjecture that it was having the property $P_{n+1}$ that distinguished descriptively adequate from descriptively inadequate grammars of L. This conjecture could also be falsified by finding some language for which $T'$ provides both descriptively adequate and descriptively inadequate grammars which its evaluation measure fails to distinguish. In this case, we would have reason to believe that there is some additional property $P_{n+2}$ which needs to be incoporated into the definition of possible grammars.

It is by something like this kind of process, I believe, that many putatively criterial properties of possible grammars have been discovered and incorporated into the theory of language. Among these we might mention, for instance, the A-over-A condition (Chomsky, 1962), Ross' constraints on movement transformations (Ross, 1967), Emonds' structure-preserving condition on transformations (Emonds, 1970). For the purpose of this paper, the important thing to notice about the discovery of these properties is that this was motivated essentially by empirical considerations related to the problem of achieving explanatory adequacy for some theory of grammars.

## 4. The *Mathematically*-Mediated Discovery of Additional Properties of Possible Grammars

In this section I am going to sketch very briefly what I believe is a typical scenario for the mathematically-motivated discovery of additional criterial properties of possible grammars. I will also discuss, at somewhat greater length, the major assumption about languages which lies behind this method.

Typically, mathematically-motivated criterial properties of grammars are discovered under the following conditions: (i) For one reason or another, it is felt that every grammar of a possible human language must satisfy some very abstract requirement D. (ii) Some theory of language $T$ is assumed. (iii) It is found — by means of a mathematical proof, not an empirical investigation — that not every grammar permitted by $T$ does satisfy the requirement D. It might be discovered, for instance, that $T$-grammars $G_1, \ldots, G_n$ do not satisfy the requirement D. (iv) This proof is then anylyzed to see whether there is some property $P_i$ *(not among the criterial properties of $T$-grammars)*, which the grammars $G_1, \ldots, G_n$, but *not* the other $T$-grammars have, and by virtue of which the grammars $G_1, \ldots, G_n$ do not satisfy requirement D. (v) It is then conjectured that the property not-$P_i$ is a criterial property of possible grammars, and that the theory $T'$ formed by adding this property to those already specified by the theory $T$, will be an empirically adequate theory of language. (vi) This conjecture is tested by trying to construct descriptively adequate $T'$-grammars for various natural languages. It could be falsified by finding some language for which there was no descriptively adequate grammar which had the property not-$P_i$. In this case, we would review our original conjecture that it was by virtue of having the property $P_i$ that some $T$-grammars failed to satisfy requirement D. We might then try to formulate some (weaker) property not-$P_j$, which, if added to those already specified by $T$ insured both (a) that grammars with this property satisfy requirement D, and (b) that there is a descriptively adequate grammar with this property for every natural language.

Two things are worth noticing about the kinds of properties discovered in this way: (1) Their discovery is motivated entirely by abstract, non-empirical considerations. The theory $T$ at issue might not, prior to this kind of investigation, have been *known* to be inadequate in any way that might be reflected empirically. This is *not* to say that $T$

might not have *been* inadequate in some way that *could* have been reflected empirically. For Linguists might have *used* only those $T$-grammars which *do* satisfy requirement D, and *those* grammars might have been empirically adequate at every level. Nevertheless, to the extent that those grammars which linguists used were only a (small) subset of those which the theory $T$ made available, linguists would have been working with an insufficiently strong theory, and thus may have encountered problems like that mentioned in (4) of § 2. Thus, the effect of discovering additional criterial properties of grammars in this way may frequently be to bring the possibilities provided by linguistic theory in line, *in some principled way*, with those exploited in linguistic practice. In this case, then, such a discovery serves to explicate and formalize the tacit intuitions about language that may have been guiding linguistic research. And, of course, once explicated in this way, such intuitions are more readily available for providing just such guidance.

(2) A second thing worth noting about properties of grammars discovered in this way is that, although discovered by means of non-empirical considerations, their incorporation into a theory of grammars does, nonetheless, have testable empirical consequences in just the same way that the incorporation of empirically-motivated properties does. This is the point of (vi) above. This is important for two reasons: (a) Because it underlines the fact that some putatively criterial property of grammars discovered in this way can appropriately be incorporated into a theory of grammars under exactly the same circumstances as some property discovered by more conventional empirical means: i.e., *only* if the theory into which it is incorporated proves to be *empirically* adequate. This should dispel the qualms of those who think I have been suggesting, in a rather Idealistic way, that mathematical considerations can provide some kind of *infallible* aprioristic insight into the nature of language. In my view, mathematical considerations of this kind only *propose* possible criterial attributes for grammars. The nature of language, as empirically determined, *disposes.* (b) On the other hand, the fact that, on the basis of purely mathematical considerations, we *can* propose possible criterial attributes of grammars suggests quite strongly, I think, that the mathematical investigation of grammars *can* play more than a merely negative diagnostic role. Given considerations of the kind just developed, such investigations can quite clearly play an important *heuristic* role in the discovery of facts about grammatical structure.

Before trying to increase the plausibility of this last claim (by presenting, in § 5 below, some cases where such considerations have played this kind of role), I must first say something about the so-far mysterious requirement D that motivates investigations of this kind.

Recalling that the theory $T$ constitutes an implicit definition of the 'possible human languages,' requirement D can best be stated as: 'Every possible human language constitutes a *decidable* set of sentences.' Or in other words, D requires that every grammar G permitted by $T$ generate a decidable set of sentences. (By 'decidable' here I mean roughly the following: A language L is decidable if and only if there is a grammar G which generates exactly the grammatical sentences of L *and* a grammar Ḡ which generates exactly the ungrammatical strings of L. Or, in a more formal vocabulary: L is decidable if and only if L is recursively enumerable *and* the complement of L is recursively enumerable.) This is, clearly, a highly abstract requirement to place on possible grammars. What reasons could we have for supposing that every grammar of a possible human language would have to meet it?

In fact, there are at least three such reasons — some perhaps more persuasive than others. Historically, this requirement was first suggested by the philosopher Hilary Putnam. He gave three reasons for suggesting this requirement, which I collapse here to (1) and (2).

(1) Putnam suggested (1961: 39—40) that language users can, under a mild idealization, classify strings of words of their language L as either grammatical or ungrammatical. He thought, in other words, that, from the point of view of users' abilities, L is decidable and, thus, that any model of L must reflect this fact. This argument may seem to have little weight today since we are now aware of a great many strings about which users can reach no uniform and consistent decisions. (Fillmore, 1972). And this may seem to imply that L is *not*, from the users' point of view, decidable. Nevertheless, we can't completely reject the force of Putman's claim, as consideration of the following argument (due to Levelt) will show.

Levelt claims (1974: II, 40—41) that judgements of ungrammaticality are, at least in the clear cases, just as strong and direct as judgements of grammaticality. From this *symmetry* he argues that if, on the basis of the existence of unclear cases, we decide to drop the requirement that the ungrammatical strings of a language be recursively enumerable, then we must, in turn, and to preserve the symmetry of the situation, drop the requirement that the grammatical strings of the language be recursively enumerable. But, he continues, dropping this requirement amounts, in effect, to giving up the idea of writing a grammar for this language at all, since, if its grammatical sentences aren't recursively enumerable, then (by Church's Thesis) there is no formal device of any kind which could serve as a grammar of the language. So, if we accept Levelt's claim about the symmetry of grammaticality and ungrammaticality judgements, it follows that both the language and its complement are recursively enumerable and, thus, that the language itself is decidable. And from this, of course, it follows that every grammar of a possible human language must generate a decidable set of sentences.

(2) The second reason which Putman gave for imposing a decidability

requirement on possible grammars takes the form not so much of an argument as of a suggestion. Thus, he suggested (1961: 40) that the ease of language learning points to the decidability of the language learned. As I said, Putman doesn't argue for this, he merely suggests it. As so vague and informal a suggestion it can carry little real weight. This suggestion can, however, be reformulated in a much precise way that *does* show some strong connection betwen the decidability and learnability of languages. The reformulation at issue is that due to Gold (1967).

Following Gold, an argument to the effect that all natural languages are decidable might run as follows: (i) Recall that the theory $T$ implicitly defines a set of possible human languages. Thus, every language L that has a $T$-grammar is a possible human language. (ii) Under standard assumptions, all possible natural languages are learnable. (iii) But, as Gold establishes, if $T$ includes grammars for undecidable languages, then not every language with a $T$-grammar is learnable. On the other hand, if $T$ includes grammars only for decidable languages, then every language with a $T$-grammar is learnable. (iv) Thus, a theory $T$ which includes grammars for undecidable languages defines as possible human languages some languages which are not learnable and, therefore, not possible (on the standard assumptions). Such a $T$ is, thus, an inadequate theory of the possible human languages. On the other hand, a theory which includes grammars only for decidable languages is *not* inadequate in this way.[2] In other words, learnability and decidability of languages are connected, much as Putnam suspected. The connection is, in fact, quite strong enough to constitute quite a good prima facie argument that every grammar of a possible human language ought to meet requirement D.

(3) The third and final reason for supposing that all natural languages are decidable has its origins partly in a methodological principle and partly in some observations about the weak generative capacity of grammars of various kinds. An argument to this effect might run as follows: (i) Based on the general methodological principle of maximizing the strength of theories, we choose the strongest theory $T$ compatible with the known facts. (ii) Due to a — now known to be mistaken[3] — argument of Chomsky's (1956: 113—124), the class of finite state grammars

---

[2]   This argument does not seem to me to be undermined by the results of Hamburger and Wexler (1973 a, b), which show the learnability of certain trannsformational grammars. For their 'learnable' transformational grammars seem — although it is difficult to be sure of this, given the sketchiness of their presentation — to satisfy requirement D.

[3]   Daly (1974) pointed out the inadequacy of these proofs, though Levelt (1974: II, 25—6, 31—2) presents perhaps more acceptable arguments that finite state and context-free grammars cannot generate all the natural languages.

is not compatible with the facts — in particular, because there are human languages which cannot be weakly generated by *any* finite state grammar. (iii) Due to a similarly mistaken argument of Postal's (1964: 137—154), the class of context-free grammars is not compatible with the facts either. (iv) There are, however, no known languages which cannot be weakly generated by some context-sensitive grammar. (v) Thus, although the *strong* generative capacity of context-sensitive grammars may be inadequate (Chomsky 1956), no empirically adequate theory of language need provide grammars which exceed context-sensitive grammars in weak generative capacity. (vi) But every language weakly generated by a context-sensitive grammar is decidable (Chomsky 1959: 131). (vii) Thus, any acceptable theory of natural languages need provide grammars only for decidable languages. (viii) Finally, the strongest theory compatible with the known facts will provide grammars *only* for decidable languages.[4] (ix) Thus, in terms of this strongest acceptable theory, every grammar of a possible natural language generates a decidable set of sentences.

These, then, are three reasons why linguists have supposed that every grammar of a possible human language must meet requirement D — viz. that such a grammar generate a decidable set of sentences.

These considerations complete my discussion of the way in which mathematical considerations can lead to the discovery of additional criterial properties of possible grammars. The discovery procedure outlined earlier in this section is motivated by the need to insure that possible grammars satisfy the requirement D, and will, thus, seem like a reasonable procedure partly to the extent that requirement D itself is seen to be a reasonable condition on possible grammars. Nevertheless, there is another way of making this procedure seem reasonable, and that is to show how it has, in fact, led to the discovery of additional criterial properties of grammars. This I will try to show in the next section of this paper.

## 5. Cases in Which Mathematical Considerations have Led to the Discovery of Additional Criterial Properties of Possible Grammars

In this section, I want to review a series of cases in which additional criterial properties of possible grammars have been proposed in contexts

---

[4]  Notice that this conclusion is not affected by the fact that Chomsky's and Postal's argument about the weak generative capacity of finite state and context-free grammars may be mistaken. In fact, the possibility that all possible natural language could be generated by finite state grammars, for instance, only strengthens the basic conclusion here — viz. that an empirically adequate theory *T* need not permit grammars for undecidable languages. For all finite state and context-free languages are decidable languages too.

which fit the scenario outlined in § 4 above and for reasons related to the satisfaction of requirement D. I want, especially, to draw attention to the fact that some of these proposals have *not* been adopted, and to the essentially empirical reasons for this.

(1) The first case I want to deal with involves the theory of grammars $T_{SS}$ implicitly embodied in Chomsky's *Syntactic Structures.* In an influential paper, already referred to, Putman claimed (1961: 41), without proof, that not every $T_{SS}$-grammar meets requirement D. Putman then looked for properties which distinguished those $T_{SS}$-grammars which do meet requirement D from those which don't. One such property $P_1$, he thought, was that all the $T_{SS}$-grammars meeting requirement D had only 'cut free' rules — i.e., rules whose output was at least as long as its input. Furthermore, it is easy to show that every grammar having the property $P_1$ does generate a decidable language.[5] This quite naturally suggests that $P_1$ be incorporated into the definition of possible grammars. Nevertheless, Putnam did not feel that this property could appropriately be incorporated into the definition of possible grammars. For he realized (1961: 42), grammars having this property were *empirically* less adequate than grammars which do not have this property. This is so because, for some language L, observationally adequate grammars of L having the property $P_1$ are not likely to be descriptively adequate — in particular, because they will generate sentences of L by means of highly counterintuitive derivations. (This will be particularly the case where descriptively adequate grammars of L, *not* having the property $P_1$, generate sentences by means of deletion transformations.) This is one case, then, where mathematical considerations *suggest* an additional criterial property of grammars but are *overruled* by empirical considerations.

(2) The second case I want to deal with also involves Putnam's reflections on the theory $T_{SS}$. Having rejected $P_1$ as an additional criterial property of possible grammars, Putman looked for another property such that grammars having it would meet requirement D. This, he thought (1961: 42) might be the property $P_2$: (a) that not more than $n$ words are deleted in any transformation, and (b) that not more than $m$ non-cut-free transformations apply in the derivation of any sentence — where $n$ and $m$ are constants which may depend on the language being modelled. Grammars having this property — like those having property

---

[5]    That having the property $P_1$ is sufficient to insure that a grammar satisfy requirement D is easily shown as follows: Given a language L and a grammar G of L, then, if every rule R of G is cut free, and if S is a putative sentence of L, then, if G generates S, there is no line in any derivation of S by G that is longer than S itself. But, there are only a finite number of such lines and, therefore, only a finite number of possible derivations of S by G. Thus, all we need to do to determine whether or not S in L is to inspect this finite number of derivations to see if at least one of them has S as its last line. Thus, there is a 'decision procedure' for grammaticality in L and L is, therefore, decidable.

$P_1$ — can easily be shown to generate only decidable languages.[6] This suggests, then, that $P_2$ perhaps should be incorporated into the definition of possible grammars. Putnam himself did not propose to do this since he felt that this property was 'ad hoc and unattractive.' (1961: 42). Nevertheless, we can (and should) ask what the empirical consequences would be of supposing all possible grammars to have this property. In fact, Peters has argued (1973: 374) that this supposition is refuted by the fact that English has no descriptively adequate grammar which has the property $P_2$. In particular, Peters argues that every descriptively adequate grammar of English must permit unbounded deletion. But, of course, such grammars fail to meet condition (b) of property $P_1$. This, then, seems to be another case where mathematical considerations suggest an additional criterial property of grammars but are overruled by empirical facts about language.

(3) The third case I want to discuss departs a bit from this so far rather gloomy picture. For, in this case, mathematical considerations seem to have led to the discovery of an additional criterial property of grammars which has not (yet) been ruled out by empirical considerations. Furthermore, not only is this property not ruled out by empirical considerations, it actually seems to have had the effect of increasing the empirical (and not just the abstract mathematical) adequacy of grammars which have it. The property in question, $P_3$, is that of satisfying the condition on the recoverability of deletions, where this condition is customarily stated as follows: A transformation can delete an element of a string only if *either* that element is one of a finite number of constant single elements designated by the grammar as so deletible, *or* that element is marked by the structural condition of the transformation as identical to some other element of the string. (Chomsky, 1964: 41).

That possible grammars have property $P_3$ was first proposed by Matthews (1961: 534), who felt that this insured that such grammars would meet requirement D. Katz and Postal (1964: 80, 167) and Chomsky (1965: 208 n. 37) seem to have agreed with Matthews that having this property is a sufficient condition for grammars to meet requirement D. As we shall see in (4) below, they were mistaken about this. But the fact that having the property $P_3$ is *not* a sufficient condition for insuring that grammars meet requirement D does *not* necessarily argue against $P_3$

---

[6]   That having the property $P_2$ is sufficient to insure that a grammar satisfies requirement D is easily shown as follows: Given a language L and a grammar G of L, then, if G has the property $P_2$, and if S is a putative sentence of L, then, if G generates S, there is no line in any derivation of S which is longer than $m \times n \times l$, where $l$ is the length of S. But, there are only a finite number of such lines and, thus, of possible derivations of S by G. Thus, all we need to do to determine whether or not S is in L is to inspect this finite number of derivations to see if at least one of them has S as its last line. Thus, there is a 'decision procedure' for grammaticality in L and L is, therefore, decidable.

being an appropriate criterial attribute of grammars. In fact, there are a number of reasons for supposing that $P_3$ *is* an appropriate criterial property of grammars:

(a) $P_3$, unlike $P_1$ and $P_2$, does seem to have some intuitive linguistic significance. Very roughly, on the standard transformationalist assumptions (i) that language users understand the meaning of an utterance by reconstructing its deep structure, and (ii) that this reconstruction is mediated by the user's 'mental representation' of the grammar of his language, then having the property $P_3$ seems to be a necessary condition for grammars to be able to mediate this process of reconstruction in the required way. (Katz and Postal, 1964: 167) For if some sentence is derived from its deep structure by means of *irrecoverable* deletion transformations, then this sentence might not contain enough of a 'reflex' of its deep structure to permit this to be reconstructed in any efficient way. Thus, on the assumption that users do understand utterances by reconstructing their deep structures by means of some 'mentally represented' grammar, having the property $P_3$ does seem to be a necessary condition for any explanation of the means by which users understand utterances to be satisfactory.

(b) A second reason for supposing that $P_3$ is a criterial attribute of possible grammars is that there is no negative empirical evidence that it is not. Such evidence, if available, would take the form of showing that there is a language L which has no descriptively adequate grammar which has the property $P_3$. But no such evidence has, to my knowledge, been presented.

(c) The third and most compelling reason for supposing that $P_3$ is a criterial property of possible grammars is that a theory of language $T$ which incorporates this property is explanatorily adequate in ways in which a theory $T'$, which does *not* incorporate it, is not. To see this, consider an *Aspects*-like theory $T'$, which does *not* incorporate the property $P_3$. $T'$ provides a grammar $G_1$ of English which , for instance, derives imperatives from any underlying phrase-marker that can be analyzed as NP + tns + VP, by deleting the elements dominated by the nodes tns and NP. Thus, for example, $G_1$ might derive *Go home* from the phrase-marker underlying *He went home*. This is clearly a 'counterintuitive' derivation and $G_1$ is, in this sense, a descriptively inadequate grammar of English. Now $T'$ also permits the grammar $G_2$, which, *as it happens,* does have the property $P_3$. Now $G_2$ will derive *Go home* only from the phrase-marker underlying *You (will) go home.* Thus, $G_2$, at least on these grounds, is a descriptively adequate grammar of English. But $T'$ does not distinguish between $G_1$ and $G_2$ as possible grammars of English and, thus, fails to be an explanatorily adequate theory of language. But the theory $T$, which *does* incorporate the property $P_3$, permits *only* the grammar $G_2$ and, thus, a fortiori, *does* distinguish it from $G_1$, and, finally, is, at least on these grounds, an explanatorily adequate theory of language. Thus, $P_3$ does seem to be a criterial property of possible grammars, in the sense that theories which incorporate it as such are more explanatorily adequate than theories which don't.

For all these reasons, then, we have, in case of $P_3$, a property which was proposed as criterial of possible grammars for essentially mathematical reasons and whose claim to criteriality seems to have been vindicated by empirical considerations. This would seem to be a clear case, then, where mathematical considerations have played 'an important role . . . in the process of discovery itself.'

(4) Next, I would like to discuss the fact that having the property $P_3$ is not, nevertheless, a sufficient condition to insure that a grammar meet requirement D. In my discussion here, I would like to be especially careful to show that this result does *not* undermine a belief that $P_3$ *is* a criterial attribute of possible grammars. That grammars which have the property $P_3$ do not necessarily satisfy requirement D was established by Peters and Ritchie (1973 a) when they showed that there is an *Aspects*-grammar (i.e., one which has the property $P_3$) for every recursively enumerable language. It follows that having $P_3$ is not a sufficient condition to insure the decidability of *Aspects*-languages since some recursively enumerable languages are not decidable. Notice that this result does *not* show that having the property $P_3$ would not be a sufficient condition to insure the decidability of languages generated by grammars of another kind. Notice also that this result does *not* show that having the property $P_3$ is not a *necessary* condition for grammars to satisfy requirement D. Nor does this result undermine the belief that having the property $P_3$ (or something like it) is a necessary condition for an *Aspects*-like theory of grammars to be explanatorily adequate. All that this result shows is that having the property $P_3$ is, alone, not a sufficient condition to insure that grammars satisfy requirement D.

This result may seem to be a classic example of the merely negative diagnostic function of mathematical investigations in linguistic research. For, it may seem that all the Peters-Ritchie result establishes is that the *Aspects* theory is too weak. And this may seem rather like belaboring the obvious. Nevertheless, what happened in the aftermath of this result does provide a good illustration of the heuristic role of mathematical investigations of language. For Peters and Ritchie — in the spirit of the scenario of § 4 above — tried to discover what it is about those *Aspects*-grammars which generate undecidable languages that enables them to do this. That is, Peters and Ritchie took their result as a challenge to discover new potentially criterial properties of grammars that might insure that grammars having them satisfy requirement D. In (5) and (6) below I discuss two of the properties that they proposed and try to evaluate how well their incorporation into a theory of language is justified by empirical considerations.

(5) In investigating those *Aspects*-grammars which generate only *decidable* languages, Peters found (1973: 382) that they all had the property $P_4$, which he called the 'survivor property.' $P_4$ states that for every derivation *d*, the output of every cycle must be at least as long as any subpart of the input on which transformations operated during that cycle. Peters then asked whether having this property was sufficient to insure that *Aspects*-grammars generate only decidable languages. In fact, as he proved (1973: 383), having this property *is* sufficient to insure this. What is interesting about this proof is that it depends on grammars also having the property $P_3$.[7] This is important because it shows that $P_3$ and $P_4$ are two different properties of grammars. In particular, it shows that having $P_4$ does not imply having $P_3$. And, because of this, we can expect to find derivations which have the property $P_4$, but not $P_3$. In fact, such derivations are easily found — as, for instance, that of *John wanted to come to the party* from the phrase marker underlying *John wanted Bill to come to the party*. And these considerations point to the fact that having the property $P_3$ seems to be a separately necessary condition for grammars to be descriptively adequate. This, coupled with the fact that having $P_3$ also seems to be a separately necessary condition for grammars to satisfy requirement D, thus justifies the belief that $P_3$ *is* a criterial property of possible grammars.

But what of the empirical consequences of supposing $P_4$ to be a criterial property of possible grammars? Peters himself mentions (1973: 382) that *almost* all the descriptively adequate grammars actually proposed by linguists have this property, and that the grammars which deviate from it do so only in a certain very limited way. That grammars deviate at all from this property may suggest that it is *not* a criterial property of grammars. Nevertheless, the cases in which grammars do deviate from it seem marginal enough to warrant at least an attempted reanalysis of those cases, to see if they could be brought into line with other *confirming* cases. If we could do this in some non-ad hoc way, then this would offer a particularly striking example of the positive, heuristic role which mathematical considerations can play in grammatical investigation. For, in that case, we would have been led to *correct* an empirically motivated analysis on the basis of non-empirical considerations.[8]

---

[7]    Thus, Peters' proof makes reference to and depends on the proof in Peters and Ritchie (1973 a) of Lemma 6.3. But the proof of this Lemma depends on grammars having the property $P_3$.

[8]    Lest I seem once again to be taking an overly Idealistic tone, in suggesting that mathematical considerations can lead to the *correction* of analyses arrived at empirically, it will be well to recall that Newton frequently corrected the observations of the Astronomer Royal by means of a mathematically articulated theory of atmospheric refraction.

(6) As a result of analyzing their proof that some *Aspects*-grammars generate undecidable languages Peters and Ritchie discovered (1973 b) that this result depends on such grammars making heavy use of 'filtering.' They then proposed that placing a restriction of the filtering function of *Aspects*-grammars might insure that they generate only decidable languages. In this spirit, they proposed that $P_5$ might be a criterial property of possible grammars. $P_5$ states that, for every derivation $d$, if the output of any cycle of $d$ contains a sentence boundary symbol, then the last line of $d$ contains a sentence boundary symbol. (Peters and Ritchie, 1973 b: 183) As it happens, Peters and Ritchie were able to show (1973 b: 185—6) that having the property $P_5$ does *not* insure that a grammar satisfies requirement D. Nevertheless, they showed that the set of grammars having this property is a proper subset of those not having it and, thus, that by incorporating this property into a theory $T$ of possible grammars we *do* strengthen $T$. What of the empirical consequences of supposing $P_5$ to be a criterial property of grammars? Peters and Ritchie don't discuss this issue, but Bach (1974) does. Thus, he points out (1974: 242—3), in effect, that a theory of grammars $T$ which incorporates this property is more explanatorily adequate than a theory $T'$ which does not. Thus, it is a merely *arbitrary* property of $T'$-grammars that EQUI and RAISING transformations are cyclic (rather than last cyclic), whereas this is a *necessary* property of $T$-grammars. But, he points out, there are many empirical considerations which suggest that EQUI and RAISING are cyclic. Thus, $T$ is a better theory of grammars than $T'$ since $T$, but not $T'$, predicts this fact. Of course, the ultimate test of the suitability of $P_5$ as a criterial property of possible grammars is whether there are descriptively adequate grammars with this property for every natural language. To my knowledge, this question has not yet been answered. Nevertheless, Bach's argument does suggest that $P_5$ is a good candidate for being a criterial property of grammars.

Summing up the material presented in this section, I think we can see that mathematical considerations *have had* (and, a fortiori, *can have*) an important role to play in the discovery of criterial attributes of possible grammars. Such considerations must, of course, always be *checked* against empirical ones, but it is by now obvious, I hope, that the discovery of additional criterial properties of grammars needn't always be *motivated* by empirical considerations. In fact, because of the disparity between the possibilities exploited in linguistic *practice* and

---

I am not, in any event, claiming that mathematical considerations take precedence over empirical ones. All I *am* suggesting is that mathematical considerations may lead us to try to rethink empirical analyses in certain ways. The ultimate test is still empirical — i.e., we will reject the claims of such mathematical considerations if our analyses cannot be recast in the way that mathematical considerations suggest that they ought to be.

those made available by linguistic *theory,* it seems not unlikely that some
of the properties discovered by means of mathematical heuristic techniques might never have been discovered otherwise. This establishes, I
think, the relevance of mathematical linguistics to empirical linguistics.

## 6. Conclusion

In this paper I have discussed ways in which mathematical linguistic
investigations of theories of grammars can play a role in strengthening
those — viz. by leading to the discovery of additional criterial properties
of grammars. Since the general problem of strengthening the theory of
grammars is one of the very most important problems of transformational research, any contributions which mathematical investigations
have made or can make to its solutions are correspondingly important.[9]
Implicit in my entire discussion has been a criticism of that point of view
which holds that mathematical linguistics is an arcane subdiscipline with
little real or potential impact on the day-to-day work of empirical
linguists. On this view, mathematical linguistics is credited, at most, with
occasionally showing that some theory of language is inadequate in one
way or another. It is rarely realized, from this perspective, that mathematical linguistics has made some positive contributions to general
linguistic theory as well; that it can occasionally show us not only *that*
our theory of grammars is inadequate, but also, to some extent, how to
repair this inadequacy. Perhaps my paper can best be seen, then, as an
attempt to justify Wall's remark to this effect, when he noted that:

> [Results in mathematical linguistics] not only show *that* the standard theory is
> inadequate but to some degree also *how* it fails. (971: 708)

---

[9]  Since this paper was first written, additional evidence of the fruitfulness of mathematical investigations of transformational grammars has appeared. Thus, Culicover has
noted (1976: Ch 11) that mathematical investigations of learnability of grammars have
shown that, for instance, a 'Freezing Principle' and a 'Binary Principle' are conditions
on learnable transformational grammars, and that imposing these conditions on T then
*explains* what had hitherto been only empirically motivated (i.e., *ad hoc)* conditions on
T — e.g., the A-over-A Principle, Complex NP Constraint, etc. This work only
strengthens the moral of the story drawn here.

# References

Bach, E. (1974) *Syntactic Theory*, New York, Holt, Rinehart and Winston.
Bach, E. and Harms, R. (1968) *Universals in Linguistic Theory*, New York, Holt, Rinehart and Winston.
Baker, C. and Brame, M. (1972) '"Global rules": a rejoinder,' *Language* 48: 51—75.
Chomsky, N. (1956) 'Three models for the description of language,' *I. R. E. Transactions on Information Theory*, 2: 113—24.
Chomsky, N. (1957) *Syntactic Structures*, The Hague, Mouton.
Chomsky, N. (1959) 'On certain formal properties of grammars,' *Information and Control*, 1: 137—67.
Chomsky, N. (1962) 'The logical basis of linguistic theory,' in Lunt (1962).
Chomsky, N. (1964) *Current Issues in Linguistic Theory*, The Hague, Mouton.
Chomsky, N. (1965) *Aspects of the Theory of Syntax*, Cambridge, Mass., M. I. T. Press.
Culicover, P. (1976) *Syntax*, New York, Academic Press.
Daly, R. (1974) *Applications of the Mathematical Theory of Linguistics*, The Hague, Mouton.
Dingwall, W. (1971) *A Survey of Linguistic Science*, College Park, University of Maryland.
Emonds, J. (1970) *Root and Structure-Preserving Transformations*, Unpublished M. I. T. doctoral dissertation.
Fillmore, C. (1972) 'On generativity' in Peters (1972 b).
Fodor, J. and Katz, J. (1964) *The Structure of Language*, Englewood Cliffs, N. J., Prentice-Hall.
Gold, M. (1967) 'Language identification in the limit,' *Information and Control*, 10: 447—74.
Gross, M., Halle, M. and Schützenberger, M. (1973) *The Formal Analysis of Natural Languages*. The Hague, Mouton.
Hamburger, H. and Wexler, K. (1973 a) 'Identifiability of a class of transformational grammars' in Hintikka, et al. (1973).
Hamburger, H. and Wexler, K. (1973 b) 'On the insufficiency of surface data for the learning of transformational languages' in Hintikka, et al. (1973).
Hintikka, J., Moravcsik, J. and Suppes, P. (1973) *Approaches to Natural Languages*, Dordrecht, Reidel.
Jakobson, R. (1961) *Structure of Language and its Mathematical Aspects*, Providence, R. I., American Mathematical Society.
Katz, J. and Postal, P. (1964) *An Integrated Theory of Linguistic Descriptions*, Cambridge, Mass., M. I. T. Press.
Kiparsky, P. (1968) 'Linguistic universals and linguistic change,' in Bach and Harms (1968).
Lakoff, G. (1970) 'Global rules,' *Language* 46: 627—39.
Lakoff, G. (1972) 'The arbitrary basis of transformational grammar,' *Language* 48: 76—87.
Levelt, W. (1974) *Formal Grammars in Linguistics and Psycholinguistics*, The Hague, Mouton.
Lunt, H. (1962) *Proceedings of the Ninth International Congress of Linguists*, The Hague, Mouton.
Matthews, G. (1961) 'Analysis by synthesis of sentences of natural languages,' *First International Conference on Machine Translation*.
Peters, S. (1972 a) 'The projection problem' in Peters (1972 b).
Peters, S. (1972 b) *The Goals of Linguistic Theory*, Englewood Cliffs, N. J., Prentice-Hall.
Peters, S. (1973) 'On restricting deletion transformations' in Gross, et al. (1973).

Peters, S. and Ritchie, R. (1973 a) 'On the generative power of transformational grammars,' *Information Sciences,* 6: 49—83.

Peters, S. and Ritchie, R. (1973 b) 'Nonfiltering and local-filtering transformational grammars' in Hintikka, et al. (1973).

Postal, P. (1964) 'Limitations of phrase structure grammars' in Fodor and Katz (1964).

Putnam, H. (1961) 'Some issues in the theory of grammar' in Jakobson (1961).

Ross, J. (1967) *Constraints on Variables in Syntax,* Unpublished M. I. T. doctoral dissertation.

Wall, R. (1971) 'Mathematical linguistics' in Dingwall (1971).

IV. The Interpretation of Linguistic Arguments

# 'The Theory Comparison Method' vs. 'The Theory Exposition Method' in Linguistic Inquiry*

Rudolf P. Botha

## 1. Introduction

The methodological bases of current approaches to the study of natural language constitute a relatively neglected area of study. Owing to this neglect, fundamental questions about the nature of linguistic explanations, about the ontologic status of linguistic theories, and about the nature and properties of the logic of justification of modern linguistics cannot be answered with any confidence. Consequently, when a scholar — be he linguist or philosopher — addresses himself to questions of this sort, he is thereby taking a step that deserves to be applauded. A linguist who has taken this step is Ray C. Dougherty. In recent years he has produced various papers dealing with methodological aspects of current approaches to the study of language.[1] In these papers he has concentrated on offering criticisms of a methodological sort against generative semantics. In a recent paper of his, "The logic of linguistic research," Dougherty uses a particular distinction for developing his criticisms of generative semanticist work: the distinction between "the theory comparison method" (henceforth: TCM) and "the theory exposition method" (henceforth: TEM).[2] The aim of my present paper is to show that this distinction of Dougherty's should be rejected on account of both its philosophical inadequacy and its empirical inadequacy. Since Dougherty's methodological work exhibits, as a whole, numerous instances of these two sorts of inadequacies, this work, regrettably so, cannot be received with the applause mentioned above.[3]

---

\* I would like to express my gratitude to Walter K. Winckler for making many contributions to the content and form of this paper which was reproduced by the I.U.L.C. in 1976.

[1] Cf., e.g., Dougherty 1972, 1973, 1974, 1975, 1976.

[2] I will denote this paper of Dougherty's as "Dougherty 1975." It has apparently been circulated widely in preprint form. I gather that it has been accepted for publication by *Foundations of Language.*

[3] The present paper presents a part (§ 6.8) of the content of a more extensive study of mine: *On the logic of linguistic research* (= Botha 1977). This study contains a detailed critique of Dougherty's methodological work as this work is presented in Dougherty 1975. Moreover, this study offers a full rebuttal of Dougherty's (1975) criticisms of my

To his distinction between the TCM and the TEM Dougherty assigns the following content:

(1) "Figure 8. Two alternative instruments of research.
The theory comparison method requires a researcher to:
(a) consider all previously proposed or 'natural' alternatives to his proposals,
(b) formulate the descriptive devices of each theory sufficiently to make clear what each theory claims about the data to be considered,
(c) determine where the alternative grammars differ in empirical consequences,
(d) compare the alternative grammars with the data and with each other,
(e) search for crucial examples and arguments to choose one grammar over the others. Crucial examples arise in areas where the competing grammars make different claims about a given range of data. They provide substantive reasons for selecting one grammar over the others.

The theory exposition method requires a researcher to:
(a) consider in depth only the theory he advocates, although alternative theories may be mentioned slightly, perhaps as an aid in clarifying his own theory,
(b) formulate descriptive devices sufficiently to describe a few illustrative examples,
(c) cite selected examples where the theory works to illustrate his meaning and intentions,
(d) consider counterexamples to the theory in any of four ways: (1) Consider counterexamples as exceptions. Devise efficient means to catalog them, perhaps by extracting whatever statistical regularities exist. (2) Consider counterexamples to provide evidence to prefer the theory to which they are counterexamples. (3) Consider counterexamples as discoveries about how the data should be. And (4) Ignore them."
(Dougherty 1975: 66—67)

Dougherty adds to his Figure 8 the following remarks about the TCM and TEM:

(2) "The theory comparison method and the exposition method are two alternative methods of research. Each method reflects a specific attitude about the goals of research, the relation of a theory to the data, the role of exceptions to a theory, and the nature of arguments which motivate and justify a theory. Each method will give rise to a certain range of research activities. It would be clear that, if our goal is to construct an explanatory theory of language, then the theory comparison method is superior to the exposition method.
(Dougherty 1975: 65)

Subsequently Dougherty (1975: 68 ff.) proceeds to "examine the research on coordination and pronouns to see just what type of methods have been used in recent years to justify proposals." The essence of this "examination" consists in Dougherty's comments on the squib by Lakoff and Ross (1970) on coordination, the paper by Postal (1966) on so-called pronouns, and the paper by Postal (1972) on anaphora. The research methodology of these papers is judged to instantiate the TEM. In

book *The justification of linguistic hypotheses: A study of nondemonstrative inference in transformational grammar.* Cf. also Botha 1976 for a critical analysis of an aspect of Dougherty's methodological work: his use of the Rosetta Stone Strategy as a means of concealing a lack of evidence and of camouflaging a nonvalid argument.

a later paper, Dougherty (1976) has renamed the TEM and the TCM "the theory exposition argument form", and "the theory comparison argument form" respectively. In that paper he openly claims that

(3) (a) "It is certainly true that GS [i.e., generative semantics — R.P.B.] researchers use the theory exposition form of argument and not the theory comparison form . . ."
(Dougherty 1976: 136)

(b) "Those researchers working in the SS-Aspects perspective [i.e., "generative grammarians" — R.P.B.] use TC [i.e., "theory comparison"] and not TE [i.e., "theory exposition" — R.P.B.] as their research tool for advancing their insight into language processes."
(Dougherty 1976: 129)

In the present paper I will critically analyze the content which Dougherty assigns to his distinction between the TEM and TCM. Moreover, the manner in which Dougherty projects this distinction on to actual linguistic inquiry will be subjected to close scrutiny. Two general points will be argued below:

P.1. From the point of view of philosophy of science, Dougherty's distinction between the TEM and TCM is untenable.

P.2. From the point of view of data about actual linguistic inquiry, Dougherty's projection of the TEM and TCM on to present-day linguistics is incorrect.

## 2. Philosophical Objections to the Distinction

It is not easy to subject Dougherty's distinction between the TEM and TCM to any sort of analysis. The reason for this is that, in crucial respects, the content of this distinction is obscure. Thus, Dougherty presents this content in terms of such obscure notions as "'natural' alternatives", "formulate . . . sufficiently", "empirical consequences", "compare the alternative grammars with the data", "search for . . . arguments to choose one grammar over the other", and so on. Dougherty makes no attempt to state in clear logical and/or epistemological terms what "'natural' alternatives" are, what it means to "formulate" something "sufficiently", what an "empirical consequence" is, what it entails to "compare a grammar" with "the data", what the nature of the "arguments" would be "to choose one grammar over the others", and what the "search" for such arguments would entail.[4] Observe, in addition, that Dougherty's TCM is outlined in terms of a notion "crucial example." I have shown elsewhere that this notion of Dougherty's is multiply defective.[5] Thus, to proceed with an analysis of Dougherty's TEM and TCM

---

[4]  Cf. Botha 1977: § 6.2. for a discussion of the generally obscure nature of Dougherty's methodological claims.

[5]  Cf. Botha 1977: §§ 6.6. and 6.7.

a particular assumption has to be made: the assumption that the content of the notions "theory exposition" and "theory comparison" is intuitively clear.

As regards the TEM, note that "theory exposition" — in an intuitively clear sense of the expression — entails in essence two things:

1.  explicating the content of a theory, and
2.  showing that there is an initial plausibility or antecedent probability that this theory may be (near) correct.

In this sense of "theory exposition", testing the theory by means of confronting its test implications with statements about empirical data is NOT an aspect of "theory exposition." Thus, at a general metascientific level Dougherty's inclusion of (d) under the TEM is confusing. Considering counter-examples to a theory — what (d) is about — is part of testing a theory; and theory testing, in turn, is not an aspect of "theory exposition" in the intuitively clear sense of "theory exposition."

As regards the TCM: it, too, is assigned by Dougherty a content which has a number of misleading aspects. A first one is represented by Dougherty's (b): "formulate the descriptive devices of each theory sufficiently to make clear what each theory claims about the data to be considered." This aspect (b) of the TCM represents, essentially, an aspect of "theory exposition." Below I will take "theory comparison" not to include this aspect of "theory exposition."

Thus to talk, at a general metascientific level, in a nonconfusing manner about "theory exposition" and "theory comparison" it is necessary to

1.  exclude the consideration of counterexamples from "theory exposition," and
2.  exclude the explication of the content of theories from "theory comparison."

Against this background, let us consider two of the claims that Dougherty makes about the mutual interrelatedness of the TEM and TCM:

(4)  (a)  The TCM and TEM are "two alternative instruments of research." (Dougherty 1975: 66)
     (b)  ". . . if our goal is to construct an explanatory theory of language, *then the theory comparison method is superior to the exposition method.*" (Dougherty 1975: 65)[6]

In the discussion above it has become clear that at the basis of Dougherty's distinction between the TEM and TCM there is a more fundamental metascientific distinction: that between "theory exposition"

---

[6]  The italics are mine.

and "theory comparison." Consequently, Dougherty's claims about the mutual interrelatedness of the TEM and TCM constitute, at a deeper metascientific level, implicit claims about the mutual interrelatedness of "theory exposition" and "theory comparison." Each of Dougherty's claims (4) embodies such an implicit claim about "theory exposition" and "theory comparison":

(5) (a)  "Theory exposition" and "theory comparison" are alternatives, i.e., are mutually exclusive aspects of scientific inquiry.
    (b)  "Theory comparison" is, in some sense, "superior" to "theory exposition."

Now, if "theory exposition" and "theory comparison" are taken to have the intuitively clear content considered above, then both of the implicit claims of (5) must be rejected. And if this is done, then the general metascientific basis for the distinction between the TEM and TCM collapses.

Two theories cannot be compared of course, unless their content has been explicated. Moreover, if scientific inquiry is to be a rational affair, two theories need not be compared unless it has been shown that it is plausible that these theories may be (near) correct. It is senseless to go about the comparison of two theories if it is antecedently known that they have "no chance of turning out" to be (near) correct. But, in an overall view of empirical inquiry, this is what "theory exposition" is all about. To "expose" a theory is, in essence, to do two things: to explicate its content, and to provide reasons from which it is clear that there is a likelihood that this theory may turn out, as a result of testing, to be (near) correct. "Theory exposition" is, therefore, an essential aspect of scientific inquiry — if scientific inquiry is to be a reasonable enterprise. But, Dougherty's presenting the TEM and the TCM as "alternatives" implies the contrary about "theory exposition", if we take the notion "theory exposition" to have the intuitively clear content outlined above.

Dougherty's implicit claim (5) (a) that "theory exposition" and "theory comparison" are alternatives indicates his lack of comprehension of a number of fundamental principles of philosophy of science. Let us briefly consider these. First, Dougherty fails to distinguish between two logically distinct aspects of scientific hypotheses (and theories): the plausibility or probability aspect, and the (dis-)confirmatory aspect. Scientific hypotheses have a plausibility or probability aspect inasmuch as, before having been subjected to testing, they possess initial plausibility or antecedent probability. Scientific hypotheses have a (dis-)confirmatory aspect inasmuch as they have been (dis-)confirmed to a given extent by testing.[7]

---

[7]  The distinction is drawn by Salmon (1967: 114). Salmon provides for a third, distinct, logical aspect of scientific hypotheses: *the heuristic aspect.* The nature of this aspect, however, is immaterial to the present discussion.

Second, Dougherty's failure to draw the logical distinction discussed above is symptomatic of his lack of comprehension of the role of nondemonstrative inference in scientific inquiry. Explanatory arguments represent one form of nondemonstrative arguments. These are arguments — incorporating the logical relation of reduction — in terms of which it is argued that a scientific hypothesis has explanatory power in regard to some set of problematic data. Having such explanatory power is one of the considerations from which a scientific hypothesis derives its initial probability.[8]

In sum: to claim that "theory exposition" and "theory comparison" are alternatives is, from a philosophical point of view, an indefensible thing to do. But precisely this claim is an implication — (5) (a) — of Dougherty's assigning the TEM and TCM the status of "two alternative instruments of research" — (4) (a). The claim that "theory exposition" and "theory comparison" are alternatives can be upheld only under a bizarre interpretation of the content of the concepts "theory exposition" and "theory comparison."

This brings us to Dougherty's second implicit claim: (5) (b). This is the claim about the mutual interrelatedness of "theory exposition" and "theory comparison." If "theory exposition" and "theory comparison" cannot be viewed as "alternatives", then Dougherty's implicit claim (5) (b) that "theory comparison" is "superior" to "theory exposition" must be rejected as well. If scientific inquiry has two complementary logical aspects, then one of these aspects, clearly, cannot be "superior" to the other.

Dougherty's implicit superiority claim of (5) (b) is objectionable for a second reason as well. Thus in the claim (4) (b), he suggests in a vague manner that the measure of the explanatory power of a theory is somehow linked to a researcher's use of the TCM. Unfortunately, however, Dougherty omits to spell out the theory of scientific explanation in which "theory comparison" becomes in a motivated manner a determinant of the explanatory power of scientific theories. This omission of Dougherty's yields the second reason for rejecting his implicit superiority claim of (5) (b).

There is still a further, third, reason for rejecting Dougherty's implicit claim of (5) (b): through "theory comparison" a scientist, in assessing the merit of a theory, may arrive at an appraisal which is

---

[8]   This topic is dealt with at length at various stages, e.g., §§ 2.4., 3.3.1., 3.3.2.1., of the discussion of Botha 1973. Although he has made an attempt at reviewing this book, Dougherty seems to have skipped the sections of it which deal with this topic. The above-mentioned distinction between the plausibility/probability aspect and the (dis-) confirmatory aspect of scientific hypotheses has been discussed in some detail in Botha 1973 (§ 2.4.) as well. It appears as if that part of the book is one which Dougherty has also failed to study.

wholly misleading. By means of "theory comparison" the merit of a given theory $T_1$ is, naturally, established relative to the merit of a second theory $T_2$ alone. This has the following consequence, among others: the worse $T_2$ is, the better $T_1$ appears to be. Thus, by selecting a bad theory $T_2$, as the theory with which his theory $T_1$ is to be compared, a scientist may come to a totally misleading appraisal of the merit of $T_1$. $T_2$ may be selected for the purpose of such comparison because it is the only alternative to $T_1$ that has been proposed. Or the selection of the bad $T_2$ from among the alternatives may be a deliberate act by the scientist. In the latter event, this scientist is using "theory comparison" as the basis of a nonrational strategy of persuasion:

(6) Draw attention to a hypothesis/theory which constitutes an "alternative" to your own hypothesis/theory such that you know beforehand that this alternative hypothesis/theory is not the best conceivable alternative, and, moreover, that it is demonstrably less meritorious than your own hypothesis/theory.[9]

"Theory comparison", therefore, may yield results which are misleading. In § 3.1 below two cases will be presented in which Chomsky uses — what is alleged to be "theory comparison" — in a manner which yields misleading results of this sort. The potentially misleading use that may be made of "theory comparison" constitutes a third reason why it makes poor sense to use an expression such as "superior" — as Dougherty does — to characterize the mutual interrelatedness of "theory exposition" and "theory comparison."

In sum: there are various philosophical reasons why Dougherty's claims (4) (a) and (b) about the mutual relatedness of the TCM and TEM must be rejected. The crux of the matter is that, at a general metascientific level, these claims have unacceptable implications for the mutual interrelatedness of "theory comparison" and "theory exposition", if these concepts are assigned an intuitively clear content.


## 3. Empirical Objections to the Distinction

Recall that Dougherty claims that whereas the TEM is the method of inquiry of generative semantics, the TCM is the method of inquiry of "generative grammar." These two claims have a number of test implications:

(7) (a) All research papers of generative semanticists will show clear signs of the use of the TEM.

---

[9]  For this nonrational strategy of persuasion cf. Botha 1973: appendix 7.1.

> (b) No research papers of generative semanticists will show clear signs of the use of the TCM.
> (c) All research papers of "generative grammarians", i.e., Chomskyans, will show clear signs of the use of the TCM.
> (d) No research papers of "generative grammarians" will show clear signs of the use of the TEM.

Within Dougherty's own conception of the logic of disconfirmation, the incorrectness of any one of these test implications will disconfirm Dougherty's projection of the TEM and TCM on to actual linguistic inquiry.

In the present paper I will concentrate on one of the test implications of (7): test implication (d). I will do so with regard to research carried out by Chomsky. Now, Dougherty (1975: 111) considers *"all of Chomsky's work"* to be in accord with the "TGG perspective." According to Dougherty, that is, none of Chomsky's research papers should show clear signs of the use of Dougherty's TEM. But this is not so. At least one of Chomsky's major research papers does show clear signs of the use of the TEM: "Remarks on nominalization" (= Chomsky 1972 b); henceforth *Remarks*... And this is so, in spite of the fact that this paper appears to compare two alternative theories — the lexicalist one and the transformationalist one — of nominal derivation. Let us consider the manner in which this paper by Chomsky exhibits signs of the use of each of the four aspects that Dougherty assigns to the content of the TEM.

### 3.1. Consideration Given to Alternative Theories

Recall, that the first aspect of the content of the TEM is characterized by Dougherty as follows:

> (8) "The theory exposition method requires a researcher to:
> (a) Consider in depth only the theory he advocates, although alternative theories may be mentioned slightly, perhaps as an aid in clarifying his own theory..." (Dougherty 1975: 66)

In *Remarks*... the major alternative theory is the transformationalist one. The question, then, is this: Has Chomsky given sufficient consideration to the latter theory?

A major criticism by McCawley of *Remarks*... is that Chomsky has failed to give adequate consideration to the transformationalist theory:

> (9) "Chomsky's terms 'lexicalist' and 'transformationalist' set up a false dichotomy, though one which is inherent in his assumption that all syntax is postlexical. The one thing about nominalizations which virtually all generative grammarians are agreed on is that the morphemic makeup and semantic content of nominalizations must be listed in the lexicon of a grammar. That conclusion, however, does not imply that in the relationship between nominalizations and their meanings all hell breaks loose. By rejecting Chomsky's dichotomy, it is possible to avoid treating the relationship of words (including nominalizations) to their meanings as totally idiosyncratic. Each language has certain prelexical transformations, and

rather than all logically conceivable combinations of semantic material being candidates for inclusion in a dictionary, only those which can arise from well-formed semantic structures through the application of those rules would be possible; any combination of semantic material which could so arise would correspond to a 'possible lexical item', and an analysis of nominalizations would be required not merely to provide dictionary entries for all existing nominalizations but to correctly predict which non-occurring ones are accidentally excluded and which ones systematically excluded. One big advantage of such a treatment over any 'lexicalist' treatment is that it would explain the absence of a subject NP in agent nominalizations and of an object NP in object nominalizations: *The inventor of dynamite (\*by Nobel); Newton's writings (\*of treatises) on theology."
(McCawley 1975: 218—219)

These remarks by McCawley boil down to the following: there are several variants of "the" transformationalist theory, e.g., a variant that does use prelexical transformations and a variant that does not. Chomsky under the heading "THE transformationalist hypothesis" considers only one of these variants, and, in fact, erroneously suggests that there is only one. Moreover, the variant considered by Chomsky is not the best alternative to the lexicalist hypothesis. But, in terms of Dougherty's first aspect of the content of the TEM, for Chomsky to do this is for Chomsky to be using the TEM.

McCawley points out, from *Remarks...,* a further case in which Chomsky compares a given theory with what is not the "most obvious" transformationalist alternative available:

(10) "Chomsky's third class of arguments for a lexicalist treatment of nominalizations and against a transformationalist treatment in fact provides only an argument against a transformationalist treatment in which the deep structure of the nominalization consists of nothing but the embedded sentence. Chomsky states that 'It is difficult to see how a transformational approach to derived nominals can account for the fact that the structures in which they appear as well as their internal structure and, often, morphological properties are those of ordinary noun phrases' (p. 21). However, the most obvious recasting of Lees' treatment of nominalizations into the *Aspects* framework implies that nominalizations will have exactly the properties that Chomsky mentions, i.e., the deep structure can have all the material that NP's ordinarily allow, and the nominalization transformation simply adjoins the verb of the embedded sentence to the 'abstract' head noun of the NP, leaving the determiner, etc. of the NP undisturbed and leaving the NP's of the embedded sentence as postadjuncts to the derived head noun."
(McCawley 1975: 221 cf. also McCawley 1975: 215—216)

Thus, in the opinion of McCawley at any rate, *Remarks...* exhibits a second instance of the use of the first aspect of the TEM. It seems to me that, in the light of McCawley's criticisms, one cannot maintain that *Remarks...* shows clear signs of the use of the first aspect of the content of the TCM. This aspect has been characterized by Dougherty as follows:

(11) "The theory comparison method requires a researcher to:
    (a) consider all previously proposed or 'natural' alternatives to his proposals..." (Dougherty 1975: 66)

I, for one, take McCawley's observations of (9) and (10) above to
mean that in *Remarks...* Chomsky has failed to consider "ALL previously or NATURAL proposed alternatives" to his proposals. Yet,
according to Dougherty, such a failure represents generative semanticist
methodology.

### 3.2. Formulation of Descriptive Devices

The second aspect of the content of the TEM Dougherty characterizes as follows:

> (12) "The theory exposition method requires a researcher to:
>
> ...
>
> (b) formulate descriptive devices sufficiently to describe a few illustrative exam-
> ples..." (Dougherty 1975: 66)

The TCM, by contrast, has as the second aspect of its content the
following:

> (13) "The theory comparison method requires a researcher to:
>
> ...
>
> (b) formulate the descriptive devices of each theory sufficiently to make clear
> what each theory claims about the data to be considered..." (Dougherty
> 1975: 66)

As has been noted above in § 2., the content of Dougherty's notion
"formulate... sufficiently" is obscure. In regard to a grammar,
however, it appears to me not unreasonable — it appears, in fact, to be
in the spirit of generative grammar — to read this requirement of (3) (b)
as follows: the descriptive devices of the grammar — the rules, lexical
items, and so on — must be represented explicitly, viz. formalized.

The question now is whether *Remarks...* exhibits the use of the
second aspect of the TEM or the use of the second aspect of the TCM.
In *Remarks...* Chomsky does present a number of formalized base rules
of his lexicalist grammar of English.[10] The content of the overwhelming
majority of the descriptive devices considered for inclusion in this
grammar, however, Chomsky in fact merely indicates in a nonprecise
manner. That is, the content of the majority of these devices is not
presented in a clear formalized manner. Consider, first, the lexical items.
In *Remarks...* Chomsky proposed — as a defining trait of the lexicalist
account of nominalization — a new form for lexical items: a so-called
"neutral" lexical entry.[11] But Chomsky does not explicitly present the
"neutral" lexical entry for even a single lexical item of English.
Consider, second, the rules of Chomsky's proposed lexicalist grammar

---

[10]   Cf. Chomsky 1972 b: 30, 36, 37, 47.
[11]   Cf. Chomsky 1972 b: 21—22.

of English. Here is a list of twenty cases in which Chomsky gives only an indication of the content of rules pertinent to his lexicalist grammar of English. (I list them in the order in which they are presented in *Remarks* . . .):

(14) (a) A transformation of gerundive nominalization: p. 18
   (b) Morphological rules determining the phonological form of *refuse, destroy,* etc.: p. 21
   (c) An "analogical" rule that converts X-ing to the noun X *nom:* p. 27
   (d) A "principle of semantic interpretation" to handle the ambiguity of such expressions as *good dentist:* p. 32
   (e) Redundancy (or "lexical") rules to extract the generality from (nonspecified) lexical entries such as *election, belief, consideration:* p. 39
   (f) The transformation "with roughly the effect of (37) . . . :
      (37) *X-the-Y picture that John has →*
         *X-John's-Y picture":* p. 40
   (g) The transformation "with roughly the effect of (38) . . . :
      (38) *X-John's-Y picture →*
         *X-the-Y picture of John's":* p. 40
   (h) The transformation "with roughly the effect of (39) . . . :
      (39) *X-the-Y picture of John →*
         *X-John's-picture":* p. 40
   (i) (A "lexical property" or) a redundancy rule to indicate the passivizability of verbs: p. 41
   (j) A rule spelling out *destroy* phonologically as *destruction:* p. 41
   (k) A "general rule applying to N-NP constructions" and having the function of inserting prepositions: p. 42
   (l) "A minor transformational rule" that replaces *by* by *of* "under certain conditions": p. 44
   (m) "A rule that applies automatically after (37) and (39) [see (f) and (h) above — R. P. B.] [that] assigns the possessive formative to the final word of the noun phrase in question": p. 47
   (n) "A new substitution transformation [that] replaces the unspecified predicate Δ of (46) by the object of the embedded sentence, *a book about himself,* leaving a 'PRO-FORM' in its place": p. 51
   (o) An "extension" of the rule of *do*-insertion: pp. 51—52
   (p) "Rules of semantic interpretation" to account for meaning equivalence in the case of pairs of the type *read-readable:* p. 56

(q) Redundancy rules/selectional rules to state sub-regularities of selection in pairs of the type *read-readable:*          p. 56

(r) "A lexical rule that assigns the feature [X—] to a lexical item [V-able] where V has the intrinsic selectional feature [—X]          p. 56

(s) Universal redundancy rules specifying that "an intransitive with the feature [+cause] becomes transitive and that its selectional features are systematically revised so that the former subject becomes an object.":          p. 59

(t) "Similar principles of redundancy [similar to the universal redundancy rules of (s) — R. P. B.] apply to the associated rules of semantic interpretation [which are not presented — R. P. B.]":          p. 59

With respect to some of the rules mentioned under (14), critics of Chomsky could charge that he has, moreover, failed to specify the formal properties of these rules. McCawley (1975), in fact, has done just this in regard to Chomsky's redundancy rules, semantic interpretation rules, and analogical rules.

Chomsky's formulation of the descriptive devices of his lexicalist grammar of English in *Remarks...* clearly does not instantiate the second aspect of Dougherty's TCM. Chomsky, in fact, merely formulates these descriptive devices sufficiently clearly to indicate how they would describe a few illustrative examples. Thus, *Remarks...* shows clear signs of the use of the second aspect of the TEM by a linguist ALL of whose work, Dougherty claims, is in accord with "the TGG perspective".

Finally, with reference to the article by Postal (1966) on so-called pronouns, Dougherty has made the following comments about its testability:

> (15) "Postal presents no explicit rules. The fact that his analysis does not exist in an explicit form means that it cannot easily be tested; we cannot easily determine which sentences it will generate and which it will not."
> (Dougherty 1975: 85)

But the essence of these observations holds true for Chomsky's lexicalist grammar which incorporates, at least, the large number of inexplicit rules listed in (14) above. If Chomsky's lexicalist grammar under consideration is within the "perspective of TGG" — as claimed by Dougherty — how could it be claimed that Postal's above-mentioned grammar is not within this "perspective"?

## 3.3. Citation of Selected Examples

The third aspect of the content of Dougherty's TEM is the following:

> (16) The theory exposition method requires a researcher to:
>     . . .

(c)   cite selected examples where the theory works to illustrate his meaning and
      intentions . . ." (Dougherty 1975: 66)

If in (16) "where the theory works" is intended to mean "for which
the theory accounts" or "which may be reduced to the theory", then (16)
is an apt description of the manner in which Chomsky presents the
majority of the rules listed above in (14). It cannot be claimed that
Chomsky follows the practice of (16) for all of these rules. For, in the
case of certain ones of these rules Chomsky does not cite a single
example "to illustrate his meaning and intentions": e.g., in the case of
"the principle of semantic interpretation" of (14) (d), the redundancy
rule of (14) (i), the "lexical rule" of (14) (r), the "principles of redundancy" and the "rules of semantic interpretation of (14) (t). What
Chomsky does not attempt in regard to the rules of (14) is

1.   to establish in a systematic manner what their test implications
     are, and
2.   to check a representative sample of these test implications against
     a comprehensive body of data.

In addition to the rules of (14), "neutral" lexical entries constitute
descriptive devices crucial to Chomsky's lexicalist grammar of English.
But Chomsky (1972 b: 21 ff.) cites no more than a handful of lexical
items to illustrate what he means by "'neutral' lexical entries": *refuse,
destroy, easy, eager, certain, amuse.* And for none of these lexical items
does he present an explicit, i.e., fully specified formalized, "neutral"
lexical entry. Moreover, McCawley has pointed out that Chomsky
refrains from considering such examples of lexical items which may
expose the limitations of the notion "'neutral' lexical entry":

(17)  "The only kinds of nominalizations which Chomsky explicitly discusses are
      action and property nominalizations, which normally take exactly the same NP's
      as do corresponding verbs or adjectives and for which a single dictionary entry
      giving the nominalization and the related verb or adjective, with a single state-
      ment of selectional and strict-subcategorization properties, has at least some
      plausibility. However, it would take great ingenuity in the employment of curly
      or angular brackets (though nothing in the way of linguistic insight) to combine
      action, agent, and object nominalizations and a related verb into a single
      dictionary entry that gives the strict subcategorization properties of all."
      (McCawley 1975: 219)

Thus, Chomsky's comparison of his lexicalist "grammar" with the
data is in accord with the third aspect assigned by Dougherty to the
content of the TEM. [12]

---

[12]  Recently, Lightner (1976: 196) has drawn a similar conclusion about Chomsky's
      (1972 c) paper, "Some empirical issues in the theory of transformational grammar":
      "My greatest disappointment with C (i.e., Chomsky — R. P. B.) is his title. One would
      expect two or three empirical issues to be at least mentioned, but I find none. My ques-

## 3.4. Consideration of Counterexamples

The fourth aspect of the content of the TEM relates to the manner in which "a researcher" views counterexamples to his theory:

(18) "The theory exposition method requires a researcher to:

. . .

(c) Consider counterexamples to the theory in any of four ways: (1) Consider counterexamples as exceptions. Devise efficient means to catalog them, perhaps by extracting whatever statistical regularities exist. (2) Consider counterexamples to provide evidence to prefer the theory to which they are counterexamples. (3) Consider counterexamples as discoveries about how the data should be. And (4) Ignore them."
(Dougherty 1975: 67)

The gist of (18) appears to be the following: the researcher who uses the TEM will consider counterexamples to his theory in any manner except one in terms of which he concedes that these counterexamples disconfirm the theory. There are more "ways" than Dougherty's four of protecting a theory against the impact of counterexamples. A number of theses, as they have been used by Chomsky and Halle in their *Sound Pattern of English*, I have discussed elsewhere under the heading of "Blocking (the disconfirmation of the SPE grammar)." [13]

How does Chomsky react in *Remarks . . .* to apparent counterexamples to his lexicalist grammar of English? There is no doubt that he is willing to consider such "apparent" counterexamples. [14] There are also, however, a number of cases in which Chomsky takes rather remarkable steps to make his lexicalist grammar "work" in the face of apparent counterexamples. These cases involve Chomsky's poorly explicated and motivated extension of the power of, among other things, redundancy rules. McCawley (1975: 225—228) has commented on two such cases. [15]

---

tions in § 6.1. are honest; but because of C's reluctance to discuss empirical data, one doesn't know how his lexicon will handle a word like *salt*, not to mention more complex forms like *calisthenics.*"

[13] Cf. Botha 1971: 205—244.
[14] Cf. Chomsky 1972 b: 27—28, 36, 54, 55, 58.
[15] The second of these cases concerns the properties of nominals such as *John's refusing of the offer:*

(A) "The discussion so far has been restricted to gerundive and derived nominals, and has barely touched on a third category with some peculiar properties, namely, nominals of the sort illustrated in (56):
(56) a. *John's refusing of the offer*
     b. *John's proving of the theorem*
     c. *The growing of tomatoes*
These forms are curious in a number of respects and it is not at all clear whether the lexicalist hypothesis can be extended to cover them. That it should be so extended is suggested by the fact that these forms, like derived nominals, appear to have the internal structure of noun phrases: thus the possessive subject can be replaced by a determiner, as in (56 c). On the other hand adjective insertion

Let us consider a third case, one involving the postulation of, among other things, "analogical rules."

The details of the third case are the following:

(19) "Notice also that although gerundive nominalization applies freely to sentences with verb phrase adjuncts, this is not true of the rules for forming derived nominals. Thus we have (15) but not (16):[17]

(15) *his criticizing the book before he read it (because of its failure to go deeply into the matter, etc.)*

(16)* *his criticism of the book before he read it (because of its failure to go deeply into the matter, etc.)*

This too would follow from the lexicalist assumption, since true verb phrase adjuncts such as *before*-clauses and *because*-clauses will not appear as noun complements in base noun phrases.

The examples (15) and (16) raise interesting questions relating to the matter of acceptability and grammaticalness.[18] If the lexicalist hypothesis is correct, then all dialects of English that share the analysis of adjuncts presupposed above should distinguish the expressions of (15), as directly generated by the grammar, from those of (16), as not directly generated by the grammar. Suppose that we discover, however, that some speakers find the expressions of (16) quite acceptable. On the lexicalist hypothesis, these sentences can only be derivatively generated. Therefore we should have to conclude that their acceptability to these speakers results from a failure to take note of a certain distinction of grammaticalness. We might propose that the expressions of (16) are formed by analogy to the gerundive nominals (15), say by a rule that converts X-*ing* to the noun X *nom* (where *nom* is the element that determines the morphological form of the derived nominal) in certain cases. There is no doubt that such processes of derivative generation exist as part of grammar in the most general sense (for some discussion, see *Aspects*, Chapter IV, Section 1, and references cited there). The question

---

seems quite unnatural in this construction. In fact, there is an artificiality to the whole construction that makes it quite resistant to systematic investigation. Furthermore, the construction is quite limited. Thus we cannot have *the feeling sad, the trying to win, the arguing about money, the leaving*, etc."
(Chomsky 1972 b: 58—59).

Chomsky proceeds to propose an account of the properties of nominals such as those in his (56) in terms of a novel sort of redundancy rules. On the objectionable nature of these rules McCawley has commented. In addition to what McCawley has observed about this case, I would like to make one more point about it. Consider in the quote above the following remark by Chomsky:

(B) "In fact, there is an artificiality to the whole construction that makes it quite resistant to systematic investigation."

This remark by Chomsky instantiates what I have described elsewhere (Botha 1968: 111 ff.) as "the 'fuzzy edge' approach to counter-examples." The essence of this approach has been characterized as follows:

(C) "The 'fuzzy edge' approach to linguistic data which pose difficulties to linguistic theory thus implies that such 'uncertainties' or 'fuzzy edges' are brushed aside by regarding them as being inherent features of 'language' or 'linguistic utterances'."
(Botha 1968: 111—112)

In his remark quoted as (B) above, Chomsky's notions of "artificiality" and "resistant to systematic investigation" appear to have the methodological function similar to that of "uncertainties" and "fuzzy edges" in (C). For my criticisms of the "fuzzy edge" approach to counterexamples cf. Botha 1968: 112.

is whether in this case it is correct to regard (16) as directly generated or as derivatively generated, for the speakers in question. There is empirical evidence
bearing on this matter. Thus if the expressions of (16) are directly generated, we
would expect them to show the full range of use and meaning of such derived
nominals as his *criticism of the book*. If, on the other hand, they are derivatively
generated in the manner just suggested, we would expect them to have only the
more restricted range of use and meaning of the expressions of (15) that underlie
them. Crucial evidence, then, is provided by the contexts (17) in which the
derived nominal *his criticism of the book* can appear, but not the gerundive nominals (15) (with or without the adjunct):

(17)  a.  *... is to be found on page 15.*
     b.  *I studied ... very carefully.*

The fact seems to be that speakers who accept (16) do not accept (18) though
they do accept (19):

(18)  a.  *His criticism of the book before he read it* is to be found on page 15.
     b.  I studied *his criticism of the book before he read it* very carefully.
(19)  a.  *His criticism of the book* is to be found on page 15.
     b.  I studied *his criticism of the book* very carefully.

    If correct, this indicates that speakers who fail to distinguish (16) from (15)
are not aware of a property of their internalized grammar, namely, that it generates (16) only derivatively, by analogy to the gerundive nominal. It would not be
in the least surprising to discover that some speakers fail to notice a distinction of
this sort. As we see, it is an empirical issue, and there is relevant factual evidence."
(Chomsky 1972 b: 27—28)[16]

In regard to the quote (19) the question is whether the fact that some
speakers of English find Chomsky's (16) acceptable is or is not a counterexample to his "lexicalist assumption." Chomsky's answer is in the
negative. To arrive at this answer he has, however, to take a number of
remarkable steps:

1. Chomsky has to provide for a particular ability of speakers: the ability
"to take note of a certain distinction of grammaticalness." This allows
him to claim that the acceptability of (16) to certain speakers "results
from a failure to take note of a certain distinction of grammaticalness."
Chomsky fails, however, to make clear in what sense speakers may or
may not "take note" of distinctions of grammaticalness. This is strange,
since distinctions of grammaticalness are drawn in terms of an internalized grammar. This internalized grammar, it is claimed, represents the
"tacit knowledge" that speakers have about their language. Consequently, it is not clear that speakers are able at all to "take note" of
distinctions drawn within a knowledge or faculty of whose content they

---

[16] In this quote the footnote numbers 17 and 18 have the following values:
    17 = "This was pointed out to me by M. Kayita. Notice that *his criticism of the book for
    *its failure* ... is grammatical. Presumably, *for* phrases of this sort are part of the
    complement system for verbs and nouns.
    18 = "I refer here to the distinction drawn in Chomsky (1965, p. 11 f.). For the distinc-
    tion between direct and derivative generation, see Chomsky (1965: p. 227, n. 2.)."

are supposedly unaware at a level of consciousness. What is more, if speakers did have the above-mentioned ability, it is unclear what the potentialities and limitations of this ability are. For Chomsky to appeal to speakers' "nonawareness of a property of their internalized grammar" in an attempt to show that (16) is not a counterexample to his "lexicalist assumption" is, therefore, for him to be begging a number of questions, to say the least. This appeal is quite ad hoc. Hankamer draws an even stronger conclusion about this sort of appeal: it reduces the empirical content of the lexicalist assumption to nil.

(20)  "Chomsky's suggestion that the acceptability of nominalizations like (1) to some speaker results from their 'failure to take note of certain distinctions of grammaticalness' cannot be taken seriously as a defense of an analysis which predicts grammaticality judgements opposite to those observed. This amounts to saying that in general, if sentences which a given analysis characterizes as ungrammatical are nevertheless judged grammatical by native speakers of the language, such sentences do not necessarily constitute counter-evidence to the analysis. Clearly, in the absence of some substantive constraints on the notion of analogical generation, a disclaimer of this kind reduces the empirical content of the analysis to nil." (Hankamer 1972: 111)[17]

Chomsky (1972 b: 28) does not contribute to the strength of his case by claiming that "It would not be in the least surprising that some speakers fail to notice a distinction of this sort". For, he fails to present the factual or theoretical considerations in terms of which such a discovery would be non-surprising. And, moreover, this claim of his implies that certain speakers do "notice" the distinction in question. But he fails to make clear how a speaker could "notice" a distinction between "direct generation" and "derivative generation" — both of which, presumably, are to be taken as aspects of a mental capacity about whose functioning speakers have no knowledge of a systematic and conscious sort.

In regard to the remarks (21) (a) by Postal on so-called pronouns, Dougherty has made, among other things, the observations of (21) (b):

(21)  (a)   "I am definitely claiming that were it not for this highly restricted and low level rule our so-called pronouns would in fact have the terminal forms *Ione, *usones, *heone, *itone (or perhaps better *itthing analogous to the indefinite something." (Postal 1966: 212—213)

      (b)   "By overgenerating, the [i.e., Postal's — R. P. B.] grammar does not characterize the informant's ability to discriminate wellformed from ill-formed sentences. Postal's argument converts a counterexample which the informant rejects as ill-formed into a discovery about what the informant should have said" [footnote 21 omitted — R. P. B.] (Dougherty 1975: 88)

---

[17]  In this quote Hankamer's (1) denotes the nominal *his criticism of the book before he read it.*

Against the background of the discussion above, why should these observations of Dougherty's not be adapted so as to apply to Chomsky's reaction to the acceptability of his expressions of (16)?

> (22) "By undergenerating, the lexicalist grammar of Chomsky's does not characterize the informant's ability to discriminate well-formed from ill-formed expressions. Chomsky's argument converts a counterexample which the informant accepts as well-formed into a discovery about a distinction in his internalized grammar that the informant should have taken note of."

2. Chomsky, moreover, in attempting to "accommodate" the acceptability of his (16) is willing to postulate a new sort of rules: analogical rules. Within the context of *Remarks...* this step is completely ad hoc. Moreover, Chomsky fails to clarify the formal nature of analogical rules and refrains from specifying any restrictions on them. This has led McCawley to make the following comments:

> (23) "Chomsky's remarkable willingness to accept a significant theoretical innovation ('analogical rules' are really a kind of 'transderivational constraint', in the sense of Lakoff (1973)) in a case where he probably didn't really need it may be the result of his attitude towards the data: he considers (27) to be only 'pseudo-grammatical' and indeed speaks of 'failure [on the part of speakers who accept (27)] to take note of a certain distinction of grammaticalness'. His attitude appears to be that theoretical innovations need no particular justification if they can be relegated to 'performance'. It should be noted, though, that the phenomena that lead Hankamer and Cole to propose analogical rules are by no means matters of 'performance'."
>
> (McCawley 1975: 229)

Even when conceived as "devices of performance", analogical rules are ad hoc within the framework of *Remarks...* This is clear from the fact that in 1974 — several years after Chomsky's completion of *Remarks...* — a scholar such as Bever is still very careful in what he claims about the status of "analogies":

> (24) "The concept of a sequence that is ungrammatical but acceptable because of the predictability in a nongrammatical system may seem strange. But what we have done is merely to make precise the notion of linguistic "analogy", which is often invoked to account for the acceptability of forms that are otherwise predicted to be ungrammatical. This notion has been extended into generative grammar to explain certain phenomena and been attacked because it appears ad hoc.[7] However, given the present considerations we can make precise the limits on possible analogies, *and thus render the concept potentially an explanatory one.*"
>
> (Bever 1974: 184—185)[18]

It is significant that what Bever claimed in 1974 was merely that the concept of analogy is POTENTIALLY an explanatory one. In *Remarks...* this concept cannot even be considered to be POTEN-

---

[18] The italics in the final sentence are mine. The content of note 7 in this quote adds nothing of substance to our discussion.

TIALLY explanatory. For, *Remarks* ... offers no information on "the limits on possible analogies".

3. Chomsky (1972 b: 27 — 28) postulates a special rule for generating the expressions of his (16): "We might propose that the expressions of (16) are formed by analogy to the gerundive nominals of (15), say by a rule that converts X-*ing* to the noun X *nom* (where *nom* is the element that determines the morphological form of the derived nominal) in certain cases." This rule is remarkable for more than one reason. First, notice its nonexplicit nature as this is reflected by Chomsky's use of the expressions *say* and *in certain cases*. Second, observe that Chomsky offers no justification for the adoption of this rule in addition to its "accounting for" potential counterexamples to his lexicalist hypothesis.

In sum: to account for the potential counterexamples of (16) to his "lexicalist assumption" Chomsky uses a strategy that includes the following steps:

(25) (a)  He attributes to speakers, in a non-motivated manner, a special mental ability the nature of which is left quite unclear: the ability to "be aware of", "take note", or "notice" properties of an internalized grammar.

(b)  He claims that those speakers whose acceptability judgements yield potential counterexamples to his "lexicalist assumption" fail to "take note of" or "notice" a particular distinction drawn in their internalized grammar.

(c)  He postulates in an ad hoc manner a new, formally unconstrained, sort of rule to generate the problematic nominals: analogical rules.

(d)  He proposes a particular (analogical) rule which is both nonexplicit and ad hoc.

This strategy of (25) appears to me to be essentially one of protection: protection of a "lexicalist assumption" against disconfirming counterexamples. But to use a strategy such as (25) is to implement the essence of the fourth aspect of the content of Dougherty's TEM.[19]

## 3.5. Conclusion

In the preceding paragraphs we have seen that Chomsky's *Remarks* ... is a research paper which shows clear signs of the use of every aspect of the content of Dougherty's TEM. Thus we have found that:

---

[19]  In Botha (to appear) I discuss a number of devices that function so as to protect claims of the X̄ convention against the impact of counterexamples. It is shown that two of these devices are provided for by Chomsky in *Remarks* ...

(26) In *Remarks* . . . Chomsky

   (a)  does not represent accurately and consider in depth theories
        which are alternatives to his own,
   (b)  only formulates the descriptive devices of his lexicalist
        grammar "sufficiently" to indicate how they could account
        for just a few illustrative examples,
   (c)  cites, not even in the case of all the descriptive devices of this
        lexicalist grammar, selected examples to illustrate his
        meaning and intentions, and
   (d)  is not averse to protecting hypotheses of his in an objection-
        able manner from the impact of disconfirming counterexam-
        ples.

*Remarks* . . . , consequently, shows (7) (d) to be incorrect. This point
(7) (d) was a particular test implication of Dougherty's projection of the
TEM and TCM on to data about linguistic inquiry: the test implication
claiming that no research papers of "generative grammarians" will show
clear signs of the use of the TEM. The incorrectness of this test implication disconfirms, in turn, Dougherty's projection of the TEM and TCM
on to data about linguistic inquiry. Thus, Dougherty's distinction
between the TEM and TCM should be rejected for a second fundamental reason as well: its empirical inadequacy.

What, now, should we make of the finding that Chomsky, all of
whose work is "in the TGG perspective", uses the TEM which represents, to Dougherty, the method of generative semantics? This finding is
problematic in a Doughertian framework within which the TEM and
TCM constitute "alternatives", the latter being "superior" to the former,
alone. The scholar who rejected this framework and who adopted
philosophically clear and non-objectionable notions of "theory exposition" and "theory comparison" would expect to find, in an empirical
field, that in some research papers "theory exposition" was the dominant
mode of presentation. These would be the papers presenting a new
theory about problematic phenomena which had not previously been
subjected to thorough investigation. These papers would be those presenting a new, "first", theory: explicating the content of this new theory
and showing that it possessed some initial plausibility. Such papers may
make contributions to a field in that they open up new perspectives, i.e.,
suggest new lines of inquiry. This scholar, moreover, would expect that
in other research papers "theory comparison" would represent the dominant mode of presentation. These would be the papers dealing with
problematic phenomena which had already been extensively investigated
and about which alternative, not improbable, theories had already been
"exposed." These papers would have as their main aim the making of a
motivated assessment of the relative merit of antecedently proposed

theories which constituted alternatives to one another. This scholar, finally, would expect to find a third class of research papers: research papers in the presentation of which both "theory exposition" and "theory comparison" played a role. These would be research papers proposing a modification of a component of an antecedently "exposed" theory.

The three above-mentioned expectations sound rather "uninteresting", rather "trivial." These expectations represent the rather "uninteresting", rather "trivial", point that the progress that has been made in the investigation of a given set of problematic phenomena will determine what the mode of discussion will be of the research papers dealing with this set of phenomena. The fact that such a rather "uninteresting", rather "trivial", point has to be made is, however, significant. For, the need to make this point in relation to Dougherty's distinction between the TEM and TCM shows just how erroneous this distinction is.

# References

Bever, Thomas G., 1974, "The ascent of the specious or there's a lot we don't know about mirrors," in Cohen (ed.) 1974: 173—200.
Botha, Rudolf P., 1968, *The function of the lexicon in transformational generative grammar* (=*Janua Linguarum, Series Maior,* Nr. 38) The Hague and Paris: Mouton.
— 1971, *Methodological aspects of transformational generative phonology* (=*Janua Linguarum, Series Minor,* Nr. 112) The Hague and Paris: Mouton.
— 1973, *The justification of linguistic hypotheses: A study of non-demonstrative inference in transformational grammar* (=*Janua Linguarum, Series Maior,* Nr. 84) The Hague and Paris: Mouton.
— 1976, On the Rosetta Stone Strategy or How to camouflage nonvalid arguments. I. U. L. C. forthcoming.
— 1977, *On the logic of linguistic research* (= Utrecht Working Papers in Linguistics, No. 2.)
— to appear, On the refutability of the $\bar{X}$ convention.
Cohen, David (ed.), 1974, *Explaining linguistic phenomena,* Washington, D. C.: Hemisphere Publishing Corporation.
Cohen, David, and Wirth, Jessica R. (eds.), 1976, *Assessing linguistic arguments,* Washington, D. C.: Hemisphere Publishing Corporation.
Chomsky, Noam, 1972 a, *Studies on semantics in generative grammar* (=*Janua Linguarum, Series Minor,* No. 107) The Hague and Paris: Mouton.
— 1972 b, "Remarks on nominalization," in Chomsky 1972 a: 11—61.
— 1972 c, "Some empirical issues in the theory of transformational grammar," in Chomsky 1972 a: 120—202.
Chomsky, Noam, and Halle, Morris, 1968, *The sound pattern of English,* New York: Harper and Row.
Dinneen, F. P. S. J. (ed.), 1966, *Monograph series on language and linguistics,* Nr. 19. Washington, D. C.: Georgetown University Press.
Dougherty, Ray C., 1972, Generative semantic methods: A Bloomfieldian counterrevolu-

tion. Formerly reproduced by I. U. L. C. To appear in *Indian Journal of Dravidian Linguistics.*

— 1973, "A survey of linguistic methods and arguments," *Foundations of Language,* Vol. 10: 423—490.

— 1974, "What explanation is and isn't," in Cohen, (ed.) 1974: 125—151.

— 1975, The logic of linguistic research (A review of Botha 1973). Mimeographed.

— 1976, "Argument invention: the linguist's *feel* for science," in Cohen and Wirth (eds.), 1976: 111—165.

Hankamer, Jorge, 1972, "Analogical rules in syntax," CLS, Vol. 8: 111—123.

Kachru, B. et al. (eds.), 1973, *Issues in linguistics: papers in honor of Henry and Renée Kahane,* Urbana and Chicago: University of Illinois Press.

Lakoff, George, 1973, "Some thoughts on transderivational constraints," in Kachru et al. (eds.) 1973: 442—452.

Lakoff, George, and Ross, John Robert, 1970, "Two kinds of *and,*" *Linguistic Inquiry,* Vol. I: 271—272.

Lightner, Theodore M., 1976, Review of Peters (ed.), 1972, *Language,* Vol. 52/1: 179—201.

McCawley, James D., 1975, "Review of Chomsky's *Studies on Semantics in Generative Grammar*" in *Studies in English Linguistics,* Vol. 3, Tokyo, Japan: Tokyo University of Education.

Peters, Stanley S., (ed.), 1972, *Goals of linguistic theory,* Englewood Cliffs, N. J.: Prentice Hall.

Postal, Paul M., 1966, "On so-called 'pronouns' in English," in Dinneen (ed.) 1966: 177—206.

— 1972, "Some further limitations of interpretive theories of anaphora." *Linguistic Inquiry,* Vol. III: 350—371.

Salmon, Wesley C., 1967, *The foundations of scientific inference,* University of Pittsburgh Press.

# On Grammatical Ambiguity*

Michael B. Kac

The phenomenon of ambiguity induced by grammatical structure rather than by the presence in linguistic expressions of ambiguous words has long been a touchstone for the evaluation of linguistic descriptions and theories of grammar, and accordingly is given considerable attention both in the research literature and teaching. A standard argument form is as follows:

(1) a. A sentence $s$ and others like it display an $n$-way ambiguity which cannot be attributed to the presence of ambiguous words.
   b. Grammar G assigns to $s$ and its fellows $n$ distinct syntactic representations, whereas
   c. Grammar G' assigns fewer than $n$ distinct syntactic representations to the sentences in question.
   d. Therefore, G is, ceteris paribus, more highly valued than G'.

In order for arguments in this form to be valid, the following premise must be true:

(2) In an optimal grammar, any sentence which is $n$ ways grammatically ambiguous must be assigned $n$ distinct syntactic representations, and conversely.[1]

It will be useful to restate (2) as an explicit biconditional, thus:

(3) In an optimal grammar,
   a. Any sentence which is $n$ ways grammatically ambiguous must be assigned $n$ distinct syntactic representations; and
   b. Any sentence which is assigned $n$ distinct syntactic representations must be $n$ ways grammatically ambiguous.

---

* This paper reports some recent results of an ongoing inquiry into the foundations of syntactic theory and methods of argumentation. My awareness of the significance of the issue addressed here first developed through my teaching of an introductory course in linguistics; I hope that the moral is clear with regard to the issue of the relationship between teaching and research in contemporary higher education.
[1] Such a premise is called a WARRANT (Botha 1971); the term is originally due to S. Toulmin.

Michael B. Kac

Suppose that (3 a) is false. Then the fact that G' assigns fewer than *n* syntactic representations to *s* and its fellows has no automatic bearing on the adequacy of this grammar with regard to providing an account of the ambiguity in question; and this 'failure' will have no bearing at all on the matter if G' provides a way of accounting for this ambiguity of some other sort. Conversely, if (3 b) is false, then the fact that G DOES assign *n* distinct syntactic representations to *s* and its fellows is of no automatic consequence, since there is no guarantee that any two such representations determine different interpretations.

The falsity of either (3 a) or (3 b) is sufficient to falsify (2); and if (2) is false, then no argument conforming to the schema (1) is valid. The conclusions to be argued for in this paper are as follows:

A. That (2) can be taken as an empirical hypothesis, open to test.
B. That, so construed, (2) is false.
C. That (2) is false by virtue of the falsity of BOTH conditions of the biconditional.
D. That (1) is thus an invalid argument form, and must be replaced by a different form if grammatical ambiguity is to continue to be employed as a basis for evaluating grammars.
E. That the notion 'interpretive rule' must be included in linguistic theory.


1. The Epistemological Status of Proposition (2)

Among the propositions of which a science is constituted, some are EMPIRICAL and some RATIONAL. The empirical canon consists of the hypotheses advanced by the science concerning the nature of the objects with which it is concerned; these hypotheses are, if true, contingently rather than necessarily true, and their truth is determined by evidence consisting itself of contingent facts. The rational canon, by contrast, consists not of hypotheses but rather of assumptions governing what shall be taken by the science as procedurally valid with regard to the evaluation of hypotheses. Such principles are tested not on the basis of contingent facts, but rather, on their plausibility as determined by abstract reasoning and an appeal to common sense. Typically, in fact, the truth of a rational proposition (when the proposition itself is fully explicit, which it need not be in actual practice) is taken as both necessary and self-evident. As an example, consider the 'principle of control' underlying the experimental method: This principle states that in an experimental test of the hypothesis that variable $v$ is a function of variable $v'$, all known relevant parameters other than $v'$ must be held constant throughout the experiment. Otherwise, self-evidently, there would be no way of knowing if $v'$ alone were responsible for variation in $v$, or if it were responsible at all. Another rational proposition underlying experimental sciences is the requirement that experiments be replicable. As a clear example of such a proposition from linguistics, consider the following assumption: that if a single mechnism $m$ is involved in determining some property or set of properties of each member of a set of linguistic objects, then insofar as $m$ is involved, the description of these linguistic objects must employ the same devices in characterizing them. For example, if in the sentences

(4) a.   The men are/*is coming.
    b.   Which men are/*is coming?
    c.   Which men does Harry think are/*is coming?
    d.   The men who are/*is coming are/*is bald.

it is assumed that the same mechanism is responsible throughout for the admissibility of the verb form *are* as opposed to *is,* then whatever principle or principles are posited to account for the choice of the verb form in any one must account for the corresponding choice in all the others. A grammar which meets this condition is said to 'capture a generalization' about the objects in question, and one which fails to meet this condition is said to 'miss a generalization.'[2] The principle in question has all the features associated with a rational proposition: it governs what shall be procedurally valid, it derives its support from common sense, and its truth is taken to be self-evident.[3]

To which of the two canons, empirical or rational, does (2) belong? Actual practice, particularly the prevalence of (1) as an argument form, attests at least to the degree of faith placed in (3 a); that (3 b) is apparently taken as self-evidently true in such influential sources as Chomsky 1957 (p 28) and Lyons 1968 (§ 6.2.7) is also highly suggestive. I think it fair, therefore, to assume that most linguists would take (2) as a part of the rational canon of the science; it seems, in any case, never to have been subjected to any kind of serious question, and appears to have been used as a means of limiting what shall be taken as procedurally valid.

For a principle to form a necessary part of the rational canon of a

---

[2]   This of course does not address the crucial, and sometimes knotty, question of what does and does not constitute a generalization. It should also be noted that linguists sometimes confuse CAPTURING generalizations with INVENTING them; for further discussion, cf. Kac 1976.

[3]   Notice that it does not follow that the principle IS true; that something presents itself to common sense as true guarantees nothing. There are cases where scientific disputes turn principally on whether or not some uncritically accepted methodological principle is valid; as examples, consider the arguments now raging over the interpretation of the notion 'heritability' in Jensen's IQ studies, or of the many instances of misuse of statistical or probabilistic measures.

science, it must be demonstrable in a convincing way that without it, the science would lose procedural rigor. If no such demonstration can be given, then clearly the principle is dispensable. Thus, we must next ask whether (2), taken as a rational proposition, has any compelling motivation. That it does not can easily be shown; that is, it can be shown that a theory of grammar which assumes the truth of (2) has no necessary advantage over one which does not, insofar as procedural rigor is concerned.

I think it would be agreed that any approach to grammatical description that was to be presumed even minimally rigorous would have to assume the following:

(5) In an optimal grammar,
    a.   If a sentence in $n$ ways ambiguous, then it must be assigned $n$ nonequivalent SEMANTIC representations; and
    b.   If a sentence is assigned $n$ nonequivalent semantic representations, then it must be $n$ ways ambiguous.

Now, the crucial point is simply this: It is at least logically possible for a grammar to satisfy (5) WITHOUT SATISFYING (2). Imagine a theory of grammar which assumes that explicit rules of semantic intrepretation exist, where such principles may take at least the following forms:

(6)  a.   Obligatorily assign reading R to expressions of the form F;
     b.   Optionally assign reading R′ to expressions of the form F′.

Suppose now that we have a sentence $s$ having $n$ distinct readings but containing no ambiguous words, and having only one syntactic representation. But suppose that there is more than one way in which $s$ may be taken as satisfying the structural description of some rule of semantic interpretation, and that the outcome of applying the rule is different depending on how its structural description (SD) is presumed to be met. Then for each of the $m$ ways in which the SD can be satisfied with nonequivalent results, $m$ of the $n$ distinct readings of $s$ are accounted for. If $m$ is less than $n$, such an account will not be fully adequate, but further possibilities remain. Suppose that the rule in question is optional: then there will be at least one additional reading assigned to $s$, corresponding to nonapplication of the rule. Or, suppose that several optional rules, singly or in combination, are applicable to $s$ and that each of the various applicational possibilities yields a distinct result. Given just these possibilities (and there are no doubt others), one would expect at least some cases of grammatical ambiguity to be easily accounted for. As a concrete example, consider how in such a framework, we would deal with the three-way ambiguity of

(7) Harry wants Fred to think he's smart.

where *he* may be taken as coreferential with either *Harry* or *Fred,* or as coreferential with neither. Jackendoff (1972) proposes an interpretive coreference determination rule which may be given in part as follows:

(8) Optionally assign to a pronoun PRO the specification [+ COREFERENTIAL WITH NP$_i$] under the following configurational conditions:
   a.   PRO and NP$_i$ are in different clauses; and
   b.   PRO does not both precede and command NP$_i$.

The two possible coreferences in which *he* may be taken as participating are accounted for in this rule since the configurational conditions are satisfied by either *Harry* and *he* or by *Fred* and *he*. But since the rule is optional, the third possibility, no coreference at all, is also accounted for.[4] Although to my knowledge it has never been seriously considered, the possibility of accounting for a wide variety of nonlexical ambiguities in a parallel manner might well exist. Until all such possibilities are ruled out, the position of (3 a) is hardly secure.

As an example of a related kind, consider the two-way ambiguity of a sentence like

(9) The chicken is ready to eat.

for which there is only one well motivated surface P-marker. Suppose that we wish to approach such a sentence via a grammatical model in which grammatical relations are read directly off surface structure (as is proposed in Kac 1978), and no abstract level of underlying syntactic representation is recognized. It is nonetheless possible to explain (as well as to represent) the ambiguity of (9) on the basis of independently motivated principles. Within the framework of such a model, we would need to proceed in something like the following way: Observe first that the ambiguity clearly has something to do with the specific properties of certain lexical items, viz. *ready* and *eat*. The ambiguity can be removed by replacing either with another predicate, as in

(10)  a.   The chicken is ready to go.
      b.   The chicken is eager to eat.
      c.   The chicken is though to eat.

In a transformational framework, these properties are captured in terms of a notion of 'control' of deletion operations; certain elements in superordinate clauses in remote representations are allowed to act as antecedents of NP's subject to deletion whereas others are not. Moreover, to a considerable extent, lexical items are idiosyncratic as to how they influence control, and these idiosyncrasies must be stated in the lexicon. In a

---

[4]   Jackendoff also assumes that there is a Noncoreferentiality Rule which, at the end of derivations, marks as noncoreferential all pairs of NP's to which no coreference relation has previously been assigned.

nontransformational framework such as that under discussion, the
approach is a bit different. We must still recognize the same degree of
lexical idiosyncrasy, but the relevant distinctions are captured in a somewhat different way. Assume that we have a way of knowing, in any
sentence of the form NP—BE—A—*to*—V, that NP is the Subject of A
(or possibly of a whole composite BE—A—*to*—V) and that A is the
main predicate while V is subordinate to it. (If adjectives in such
constructions are treated in the same way as verbs taking Object
complements, this can easily be done; cf. Kac 1978, Ch. 3). Now, we
need to subcategorize adjectives according to the following properties:

(11) a.   ability of Subject thereof to also act as Subject of subordi-
          nate predicate (henceforth designated by the abbreviatory
          feature symbol $[F_1]$);
     b.   ability of Subject thereof to also act as Object of subordi-
          nate predicate ($[F_2]$);
     c.   ability of Subject of subordinate verb to be construed as
          unspecific/indefinite if not overt ($[F_3]$).

In terms of the relevant features, we can have such possibilities as

(12) a.   *eager:*   $[+ F_1, - F_2, - F_3]$
     b.   *tough:*   $[- F_1, + F_2, + F_3]$
     c.   *ready:*   $\left[+ \begin{Bmatrix} F_1 \\ F_2 \end{Bmatrix}, + F_3\right]$

where the braces around $[F_1]$ and $[F_2]$ indicate that in a given construction, *ready* may be positively specified for either but not both. Corresponding lexical specifications would have to be given in a transformational model to indicate the control properties of the items in question.

In addition to the lexical entries (12), one more thing is needed: a
specification associated with *eat* allowing its Object to be construed as
unspecified/indefinite when nonovert. Now: in (9), we have as given
that *the chicken* is the Subject of *ready* and that *eat* is the subordinate
verb. Given further the specifications associated with these two predicates, the following possibilities exist:

(13) a.   Suppose that *ready* is construed in this construction as
          $[+ F_1]$; its Subject is then the Subject of *eat.* But *eat* can
          have an unspecified Object if there is no overt NP to serve
          this function — hence it must be so construed in this case.
          We thus obtain the following result:
          SUBJECT OF *eat:*   *the chicken*
          OBJECT OF *eat:*   unspecified
     b.   Suppose on the other hand that ready is construed as
          $[+ F_2]$; we then obtain

SUBJECT OF *eat:*  unspecified (via specification of *ready*
as $[+ F_3]$);
OBJECT OF *eat:*  *the chicken*

These two results correspond to the two senses in which (9) is grammatically ambiguous. The ambiguity is here treated as being due not to
different configurations of significant material at some level of analysis,
but rather, as being a function of the interaction in a certain type of
construction, of properties of lexical items. Notice moreover that these
properties would have to be recognized anyway, since they are relevant
to the characterization of ambiguous sentences containing the associated
items — just as lexical specifications for control are.[5]

The foregoing two examples are sufficient to show that the fact that a
grammar might assign fewer than *n* syntactic representations to a
sentence that is *n* ways grammatically ambiguous is not in itself sufficient evidence that the grammar cannot account for the ambiguity in
question. The requirement imposed by (5 a) can, even in cases of grammatical ambiguity, be satisfied in more than way. Accordingly, (3 a) is
dispensable to the rational canon of grammatical theory. One might, of
course, wish to argue that there are empirical considerations which
favor a model which assumes (3 a) over one which does not — but (3 a)
is then being treated as an empirical proposition, not a rational one.

Conversely, in a theory which makes use of explicit principles of
semantic interpretation, there is no logical reason why a given structural
difference should affect the outcome of any application of the rules.
That is, the optimal set of interpretive rules might well turn out to be
sensitive to certain structural properties of sentences but insensitive to
others. To deny such a possibility would be to make the claim that literally every feature of syntactic structure must have semantic relevance —
which might turn out to be true, but which would require extensive justification. And in any case, the adjucation of such a claim looks again like
an empirical matter; accordingly, the place of (3 b) in the rational canon
of grammatical theory is not secure either.

In sum: I claim that (2) need not be maintained in grammatical theory
as an essential constraint on procedural rigor. It may, on the other hand,
be treated as an empirical hypothesis and as such might turn out to be
correct, at least in part. This is a matter to be taken up later in the paper.

---

[5]  It remains something of a mystery why a third possibility does not occur, namely that
of construing both the Subject and Object of *eat* as unspecified. But the standard transformational analysis has no more to say on this matter than the nontransformational
one under discussion.

## 2. Syntax, Semantics, and Levels of Representation

In the preceding section, I have, for expository reasons, left out of consideration an important and complicating factor. Within the context of transformational generative grammar (though not necessarily of other theories of grammar), the issue cannot concern the truth or falsity of (2) as stated, but rather must concern the truth or falsity of

(14)  In an optimal grammar.
   a.  Any sentence which is $n$ ways grammatically ambiguous must be assigned $n$ distinct syntactic representations AT APPROPRIATE LEVELS; and
   b.  Any sentence which is assigned $n$ distinct syntactic representations AT APPROPRIATE LEVELS must be $n$ ways grammatically ambiguous.

The capitalized qualification is essential since, in transformational theory, not all derivational levels have the same relevance to semantic interpretation. How the variable 'at appropriate levels' is to be instantiated depends on which of the various versions of transformational grammar is under discussion; in the Standard Theory and Generative Semantics it is the most deeply underlying level, whereas in the Extended Standard Theory, different portions of the semantic representation of a sentence are determined at different stages of the derivation, including surface structure.[6]

I raise this point not only because the discussion would be incomplete without it, but because it invalidates, at least in the context of transformational theory, a commonly used argument form. Arguments of the type in question are typically used to justify incorporating the notion of constituent structure in grammatical theory, and proceed along the following lines:

(15)  a.  Sentence $s$ and others like it display an $n$-way ambiguity not attributable to the presence of ambiguous words.
   b.  Sentence $s$ and its fellows can be assigned $n$ distinct constituent structure analyses.
   c.  Hence, the grammatical ambiguity of the sentences in question can be explained in terms of constituent structure.
   d.  Hence, further, the notion of constituent structure is an essential one in grammatical theory.

---

6   Actually, (14) would be presumed false in any model which, as suggested by McCawley 1968 (p. 167 f.), incorporates explicit principles defining equivalences among syntactically distinct underlying structures.

The reason that (15) is invalid in a transformational framework is that the syntactic structure of SENTENCES has no automatic bearing on semantic interpretation as long as at least some (and possibly all) semantic interpretation is presumed to be determined not by the sentences themselves but by the remote structures that are hypothesized as underlying them. A minimum condition on validity for an argument in the form (15) would be that the component of the semantic interpretation relevant to the ambiguity of $s$ and its fellows be one that is presumed to be determined by surface structure; and, of course, in the Standard Theory and Generative Semantics, there is no such component.

As it happens, failure to make reference to appropriate levels is only part of the reason for the invalidity of (15); arguments in this form are also fallacious in that they are guilty of identifying correlations with cause-effect relationships. It does not follow merely because two properties are correlated that one is the cause of the other. Thus, merely because some $n$-way ambiguous expression can be shown to have $n$ structural analyses of a certain sort does not mean that the ambiguity is due to the possibility of the alternative analyses; additional analysis is required to make the causal connection. The consequences of this fact must now be examined in detail.

## 3. Constituent Structure and Grammatical Ambiguity

At this point, I would like to deal with a specific type of grammatical ambiguity, one which is commonly and correctly accounted for in terms of constituent structure; the underpinnings of this account, however, require some examination. The example in question is the familiar one involving A—N—CONJ—N nominals, e.g., *old men and women*. Before proceeding to the discussion proper, one preliminary remark:
In a standard transformational account, for reasons discussed in § 2, the demonstration that some surface structure configuration has more than one structural analysis is of no consequence with regard to ambiguity. Suppose that semantic interpretation is determined entirely at the most deeply underlying level, that prenominal adjectives originate as predicates of relative clauses (or, more accurately, of full S's which directly underlie relative clauses), and that there is a transformation of Conjunction Reduction of the familiar sort (henceforth 'CR'). Then the ambiguity of a sentence like (16 a) can be attributed to its being derivable from source structures like (16 b) or (16 c):

---

[7]   The role of distributional naturalness in the validation of claims about underlying structure will be discussed in detail in § 4. Cf. also Kac 1977, § 1.4.

(16)  a.   Old men and women are wise.
      b.

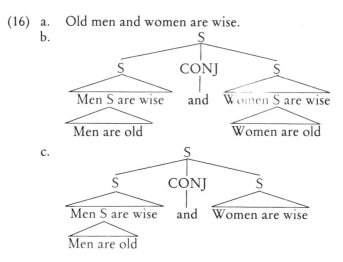

      c.

After Adjective Preposing and VP deletion (via CR), we have

(17)  a.   Old men and old women are wise.
      b.   Old men and women are wise. (= (16 a))

A second application of CR to (17 a), to delete the second occurrence of *old*, likewise yields (16 a). I will not at this point debate the relative merits of a transformational account such as that sketched above vs. one based on alternative bracketings in surface structure; I will, rather, content myself with arguing that if the latter alternative is adopted (and it must be borne in mind that there is noting sacrosanct about the standard transformational account) it must be formulated in a certain way. Then, in § 4, I will argue that the alternative bracketing account will have to be built into even a standard transformational grammar of English.

Let us consider first whether there are any reasons other than the ambiguity of A—N—CONJ—N sequences for setting up a grammar of English so that it will assign alternative bracketings to such structures. I take this to be an essential step since to show that one CAN account for the ambiguity this way is not to show that one MUST. I also am interested in coming up with something that could be considered an EXPLANATION of the phenomenon in question, rather than merely an ad hoc characterization of it for momentary descriptive convenience.

That the grammar of English must in fact be set up so as to assign alternative structures to A—N—CONJ—N sequences can be shown by considering certain properties of expressions of the form A—N and N—CONJ—N. Such consideration will lead to the conclusion that sequences of both types are constituents, and that they are constituents of type N.[8] The most compelling demonstration of this fact that I know of involves *one*-pronominalization, and proceeds as follows: Consider first a sentence like

(18) Harry knows the man who builds harpsichords and Fred knows the one who builds clavichords.

Notice that in such a structure, the anaphor *one* clearly isolates a noun (i.e., an N) as its antecedent in the preceding conjunct: *man.* Now consider the further sentence

(19) Harry knows the man who builds harpsichords and Fred knows one who builds clavichords.

In this case (note the absence of an article before *one*), *one* seems to function as an NP rather than an N, in the sense that the corresponding position in the first conjunct is occupied by an article-noun sequence. But it does not seem correct in this case to say that *one* has an NP as its antecedent, since it is not really correct to say that it has ANY antecedent. In this context, *one* has to be analyzed as having the semantic content of the expression *a man,* and no such expression exists anywhere in the structure to serve as antecedent. Without dwelling on what problems this may or may not cause for anyone's theory of pronominalization, we can make the following observation: That the head N of a definite NP can serve as the antecedent of *one,* whereas the determiner-noun sequence in such an NP cannot — or at least not in the same way. If determiner-noun sequences are themselves analyzed as NP's, then cases like (18, 19) show that *one*-pronominalization provides a clear criterion for distinguishing the two constituent types. An analogous situation holds for the plural *ones.* But now compare

(20) a. Harry knows the old man who builds harpsichords and Fred knows the one who builds clavichords.
b. Harry knows the men and women who build harpsichords and Fred knows the ones who build clavichords.

In (20 a), it is *old man* that serves as a 'clear' antecedent to *one,* just as *man* does in (19); similarly, *men and women* serves as a clear antecedent to *ones* in (20 b). I thus submit that English has the phrase-structure rules

(21) a. N → A—N
b. N → N—CONJ—N

Some additional motivation for these rules can be obtained from considering certain properties of NP's. If there are such things an NP's, and if DET—N sequences are constituents of this type, then it is clear that

---

[8] Many analyses treat such sequences, incorrectly, as NP's rather than N's. Cf. the discussion to follow in this section, and also Kac 1976, fn. 4.

A—N sequences are N's rather than NP's. The reason is that, within NP's, A's may precede N's directly, but not NP's: thus *the good man* but not *\*good the man* or *\*the good the man*. But this fact is an automatic consequence of rule (21 a), thus further motivating it.

I am aware that some readers will object that (21 a) is 'counterintuitive' since it will permit trees with 'too much structure,' like

(22)  a.

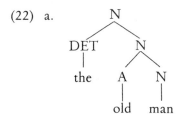

(22)  b.

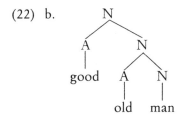

But such objections cannot possibly have any force. The only reliable indicator of what kind or how much structure is needed in a given case is what is required by the best motivated rules for the constructions in question. If the motivation is compelling, then the assigned structures must be correct, regardless of how much this offends someone's possibly fallible intuition.

A different question arises in regard to (22 b). Note that as soon as the number of conjuncts goes beyond two, multiple trees become possible; indeed, there will, for a sequence of *n* conjuncts, always be *n* − 1 distinct trees assignable to the sequence. This is commonly regarded as a failing of such rules since (so the argument goes) ambiguity is thus predicted where none may actually exist. For example, in a sentence like

(23)  Clavichords and spinets and harpsichords are keyboard instruments.

the conjoined Subject seems clearly unambiguous but will be assigned two trees by (22 a). But an automatic prediction of ambiguity, as we have already seen, comes about only if proposition (2) is granted, and the truth of this proposition is now at issue. The overall question here is a very complex one, and will require for its resolution a detailed inquiry into the various uses of conjunctions. For example, it is not at all clear that the *and* used in (23) is the same *and* as that used in (16); for further discussion (though of a still incomplete and fragmentary nature) cf. Kac 1976, fn. 5.[9]

Returning now to A—N—CONJ—N, we can see that (22 a, b), which must obviously be involved in the generation of such sequences, will generate them with either of two structures being assigned:

(24) a.

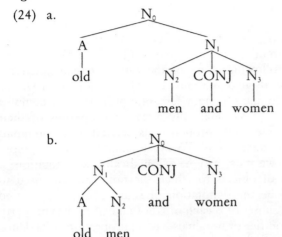

b.

At this point, it might well appear that the case has been made: We have shown not only that certain rules are needed for unambiguous structures of a certain kind, we have shown as well that these rules automatically assign two distinct structures to expressions of a kind that happen to be ambiguous. It might thus seem that we have explained the ambiguity, but this is not so: a crucial step remains to be taken. All we have shown so far is a CORRELATION of properties; but, as has already been pointed out, we are not thereby entitled to assume any sort of causal connection between them. To put the matter another way: At this point we must ask ourselves whether or not this coincidence of

---

[9] Note that the problem — if it is a problem — cannot be resolved by altering (22 b) to
(i)  N → N—(CONJ—N)*
  since this rule will still generate multiple trees under certain conditions. This is so since having, for example, applied the rule so as to generate

[9] (ii)   N
        /  |  \
      N  CONJ  N

one may reapply it so as to expand either the right or the left conjunct N, and thereby generate an N—CONJ—N—CONJ—N sequence with two trees. What (i) DOES provide is an option not available under (22 b), namely generation of sequences of arbitrarily many equipollent conjuncts; but it does this in addition to rather than instead of generating multiple trees for sequences of more than two conjuncts.

semantic and syntactic properties (i.e., ambiguity and multiple bracketing) isn't simply a happy accident. Or, to put things still differently, we must look for some 'bridge' between the syntactic and semantic facts, some valid principle which tell us what, if any, semantic consequences should ensue from such a syntactic indeterminacy.

Fortunately, this extra step is quite an easy one to take. What is principally at issue is a matter of how to determine the scope of a relation within a given type of structure, the relation being 'is modified by.' I propose to approach this problem in a certain way, for reasons which will become fully apparent later in the paper (§ 5); for the moment, suffice it to note the following: One of the things that an adequate semantic theory of natural language must be able to do is to provide a way of allowing us to compute certain semantic properties of complex expressions on the basis of axiomatically assigned properties of their ultimate constituents. One such property, associated with nominals (both N's and NP's), is denotation. To every simple noun (or, more accurately, noun stem) we must assign, axiomatically, a denotation: a specification of the set of objects to which the noun may be used to correctly refer.[10] Let S be the denotation of some arbitrarily selected nominal, and let $S_p$ be a subset of S each of whose members has property $p$; finally, let $M_p$ be a modifier of nominals having property $p$ as its denotation. We now posit the following rule:

(25)  MODIFICATION RULE[11]
      If a nominal $NOM_0$ (be it an N or an NP) directly dominates a
      modifier $M_p$ and a nominal $NOM_1$ having denotation S, then the
      denotation of $NOM_0$ is $S_p$.

This is a 'projection rule' in the sense of Katz and Fodor 1964; applied to a nominal like *old men* (where S for *men* is axiomatically specified as being the set of men and $p$ for *old* is similarly specified as being the property of being old), the rule tells us that the denotation of the entire expression ($S_p$) is the subset of the set of men consisting of those who are also old. Applied to so simple example, this rule does not appear to have particularly exciting consequences — though at this point, all we require of it is that it make the right predictions, however simpleminded they

---

[10]  I here follow Donnellan 1971 in distinguishing between denotation and reference. As he points out, an expression can be used to refer to an object which it does not denote (e.g., if I see a man holding a martini glass full of water and refer to him as 'the man with the martini'). I suspect that there are many hidden pitfalls involved in any attempt to make this distinction absolutely precise, and I will not attempt to do so.

[11]  This rule is actually limited in two ways. First of all, it is appropriate to nominals involving restrictive modifiers but not necessarily nonrestrictive ones; secondly, it will not be appropriate to a special class of expressions such as *mechanical man, false pregnancy* and others of similar ilk.

may seem. Notice now that applied to (24 a), the Modification Rule yields a result different from that which ensues from its application to (24 b). Assume that we have determined via the appropriate rule (which I will not formulate here) that the denotation of $N_1$ in (24 a) is the set of men and women; then, by the Modification Rule, $S_p$ for $N_0$ is the subset of the set of men and women such that each of its members is old. In (24 b), by contrast, the Modification Rule is relevant only to $N_1$, not to the entire nominal $N_0$. $S_p$ for $N_1$ is the subset of the set of men whose members are old, and the denotation of the entire expression $N_0$ is the set consisting of $S_p$ as just specified plus the set of women. Clearly, these two denotations are not equivalent, and the WAY in which they are nonequivalent is consistent with just the semantic distinction that we are trying to capture. Morevoer, it is clear that the Modification Rule would be needed anyway — denotations of simple A—N sequences, for example, must also be computable.

The argument is finally complete. The Modification Rule is the bridge principle required to connect the observed syntactic and semantic facts; it is clear, in addition, that this principle was not adduced ad hoc just to serve this purpose. My main reason in presenting such a detailed discussion of a familiar, almost shopworn example has been to make clear just how far it is necessary to go in order to justify the equally familiar account of its ambiguity. The account is correct, but the route to its validation is not quite as straightforward as comtemporary discussions make it seem. Even ignoring the matter of appropriate levels, as discussed in § 2 above, we can now see clearly why arguments in the form (16) are invalid; and yet it is in just this form that the justification is usually presented for the claim that A—N—CONJ—N sequences are ambiguous by virtue of having multiple constituent structures.

## 4. Interlude: A Defense of the Alternative Bracketing Account

I want at this point to recapitulate a principle alluded to earlier in this paper, which we may give in relatively precise form as follows:

(26) A linguistic description is highly valued to the extent that, for any significant property $p$ associated with the members of a set 0 of linguistic objects, where $p$ is attributed to the operation of mechanism $m$: the assignment of $p$ to every member of 0 via $m$ is accounted for within the grammar by exactly the same formal device or devices.

In (4) above, the sentences (a—d) are members of 0, $p$ is admissibility of the verb *are,* and $m$ is the mechanism of Subject-Verb Agreement. If a grammar is highly valued according to (26) with regard to the case in question, then whatever rules it posits to account for Subject-Verb agreement in any one of the sentences (4) must also account for Subject-Verb agreement in all the others.[12] I will now argue the following:

(a) That a grammar which does not include the PS-rules (21) and some principle comparable to the Modification Rule will be forced, if so formulated as to satisfy certain naturalness conditions, to violate principle (26); and

(b) That the standard transformational account contributes nothing over and above what is provided by the alternative bracketing account, and is, moreover, not particularly well motivated.

Consider first the matter of how we are to treat adjectives like *former* and *erstwhile,* which never occur in post-copula position. So, for example, we do not have sentences like

(27)  a.  *The teacher is former.
      b.  *The teacher who is former addressed the graduating class.

It is, however, possible in principle in a transformational grammar to generate such 'expiratives' (as I shall call them) in post-copula position in underlying structure, but to mark them with a rule feature [+ ADJECTIVE PREPOSING] to guarantee that they will surface only in prenominal position. Alternatively, one could generate expiratives in their surface positions via the base rules, and mark them in the lexicon as [— COPULA ____] so as to guarantee that no sentences like (27) are generated. Of these two alternatives as thus far presented, the following can be said:

(a) The first takes advantage of the existence of an ostensibly independently motivated transformation (Adjective Preposing) to correctly position expiratives; thus, in this account, all prenominal adjectives are derived via the same mechanism. Expiratives, even if generated in post-copula position, get a 'free ride' on the transformation in question.

(b) The second alternative, while seemingly more complex (but see below) has the advantage of not requiring any distributionally unnatural structures. The price paid for this greater degree of naturalness is that it is necessary to provide an additional PS-rule (i.e., (21 a)),[13] which would

---

[12]  Moreover, this condition must be met nonvacuously. For example, it is not valid to posit four distinct and ad hoc rules, one for each case, group them together under a single heading 'Subject-Verb Agreement,' and then claim that a single rule has been given.

[13]  Note that if CR exists, and if deletion from left branches operates forward, then structures of the form

ostensibly not be required if all prenominal adjectives are positioned by a transformation.

In adjudicating these two alternatives, we face a basic conflict. Formal simplicity (exemplified by the free ride analysis) turns out to be inconsistent with naturalness.[14] How is this conflict to be resolved? It is, of course, common to argue for unnatural analyses such as the free ride account of expiratives on the grounds that it is often necessary in science to posit hypothetical entities that are not directly observable (the synonym for 'not directly observable' in linguistics being, for reasons which I do not fully understand, 'abstract').[15] But recourse to such hypothetical (or, more accurately, fictitious) entities like (27 a, b) at the underlying level does not have the same sort of legitimacy as the postulation of electrons or genes. Hypothetical entities of this general sort are validly posited only if (on the basis of the available evidence) they are indispensable to the explanation of facts in the domain of the science. But to assume fictitious underlying structures explains nothing; for example, no property of the adjective *former* in English is explained (in any interesting sense of this term) by assuming that full S's like (27 a, b) exist in deep structure. Indeed, such an assumption by itself fails even to provide an adequate REPRESENTATION, being as it is, at variance with the facts of adjective distribution in English. To achieve just the level of descriptive adequacy, we must at least provide a rule feature making Adjective Preposing obligatory for the item in question.

At this point, the following reply will inevitably be made: Since descriptive adequacy can be more simply achieved with the free ride analysis than with the natural one, the former must be chosen on those

---

are favored over structures of the form

since, under the former, A's hang from left branches whereas under the latter, they hang from 'neutral' branches — neither left nor right.

[14] Although transformationalists do not in general require that underlying representations be distributionally natural, at least some of them are prepared to invoke such a requirement when it can be used as ammunition against a proponent of another approach. Thus Chomsky (1962, p. 88) criticizes 'taxonomic' phonology on the grounds that some of the abstract (i.e., phonemic) representations that would be required under its alleged methodological principles '[run] counter not only to the speaker's intuition, but COUNTER TO OTHERWISE VALID RULES OF CONSONANT DISTRIBUTION' (emphasis supplied). See also the immediately following note.

[15] Chomsky maintains (1971: p. 32) that 'there is nothing strange or occult in [positing 'abstract' underlying stuctures], any more than in the postulation of genes or elctrons' despite the fact that he elsewhere criticizes his opponents for doing the same thing — see the preceding note; cf. also Kac 1976 for discussion of conditions on validation of hypothetical constructs.

grounds alone. In other words, where simplicity and naturalness are in
conflict, simplicity wins. But this is a most unpalatable assumption;
indeed, the most plausible conclusion to draw from such a conflict in a
given case is that the theoretical framework giving rise to it is suspect.[16]
Let us therefore take the natural analysis of expiratives as the preferred
alternative and see what further consequences this choice entails.

Just as we do not want to treat all prenominal adjectives as underlying relative clause predicates, we also (for generally accepted reasons)
do not want to derive all conjoined nominals via CR. The reason
involves sentences like (28 a), for which (28 b) is not a natural source:

(28)  a.     Laurel and Hardy were a funny pair.
      b.     *Laurel was a funny pair and Hardy was a funny pair.

What is wrong, in a standard transformational grammar, with deriving
(28 a) from (28 b) is not just that (28 b) is ill-formed, but that it does not
provide a proper input to the semantic component. Now consider a
sentence like

(29)  The students and teachers from a small department are usually
      a more cohesive unit than the ones from a large one.

Here, *ones* has the coordinate N *students and teachers* as antecedent, thus
suggesting that PS-rule (21 b) will also have to be included in our
grammar (given that, in such a context, we do not want to obtain such a
constituent via reduction of full conjoined S's).

At this point, the matter of bridge principles comes up again. Notice
that *former* is different not only syntactically from an adjective like *old*,
but semantically as well. The denotation of, say, *former teacher*, is not a
subset of the set of teachers, though that of *old teacher* is; hence our

---

[16] Actually, the gain in complexity of the natural analysis is not quite as great as it might
first appear. The reason becomes apparent when we give a full formalization of the
structural change of Adjective Preposing; with a rather roughly sketched SD, we
would have

SD:    ...N ...A ...
        1      2
SC:    a.   move 2 into position directly ahead of 1
       b.   Chomsky-adjoin 2 to 1

Note now that if we were to have rule (21 a) in the base, then the (b) part of the SC of
the transformation, required to account for the correct derived constituent structure,
can be eliminated since the d. c. s will be accounted for by the general principle
(Chomsky 1957, p. 73) 'If X is a Z in the phrase structure grammar, and a string Y formed by a transformation is of the same structural form as X, then Y is also a Z.' In
other words, although addition of (21 a) to the base component produces a complica-
tion there, there is a corresponding simplification in the statement of the SC of Adjective Preposing in that an ad hoc instruction for imposition of the correct d. c. s. is
eliminable. The general principle of Chomsky op. cit. has, of course, independent motivation — e.g., to account for the correct labelling of *by*-phrases in passives.

Modification Rule as given above will be inapplicable. The appropriate analogue of the Modification Rule is

(30)  EXPIRATIVE RULE

If a nominal $NOM_0$ directly dominates an expirative E and a nominal $NOM_1$ having denotation S, then the denotation of $NOM_0$ is the set of individuals who were once members of S but are no longer.

Notice that, despite the necessary differences in content, the Modification and Expirative rules are nonetheless formally very similar. Indeed, they could be partially collapsed into the following:

(31)  EXTENDED MODIFICATION RULE

If a nominal $NOM_0$ directly dominates a modifier and a nominal $NOM_1$ having denotation S, then

a.  If the modifier denotes property $p$, the denotation of $NOM_0$ is $S_p$; and

b.  If the modifier is expirative, then the denotation of $NOM_0$ is the set of individuals who were once members of S but are no longer.

The two rules are similar in that they have the same structural description, and also in that they have an important effect in common: both determine the denotation of $NOM_0$ on the basis of information pertaining to elements directly dominated thereby.

Consider now how *former student and teacher* will be treated by the Expirative Rule. The denotation of a conjunction N—*and*—N of singular terms will be, where $S_1$ and $S_2$ are denotations of the two terms, a set $S_3$ one of whose members is a member of $S_1$ and the other of whose members is a member of $S_2$, with the possibility that there might be only one individual having both properties simultaneously. Thus, given, for example, the conjoined nominal *student and teacher*, $S_3$ could be either a 2-member set, one member being a student and the other a teacher, or a 1-member set whose sole member is both a student and a teacher. Accordingly, the nominal *former student and teacher* will have the following denotations:

(32)  a.  a 2-member set one of whose members used to be a student and is no longer, the other member being a teacher;

b.  a 1-member set whose sole member used to be a student and is no longer, and is a teacher.

---

[17]  Note that such an approach would also violate Jackendoff's principle that predicate-argument relations are determined at the deep structure level; the Subject of *are an interesting pair* cannot be determined until after CR (which creates a conjoined nominal, appropriate to serve this function whereas ordinary singular noncollective terms are not).

    c.   a 2-member set one of whose members used to be a student and is no longer, the other member being one who used to be a teacher and is no longer;

    d.   a 1-member set whose sole member used to be a student and is no longer, and also used to be a teacher and is no longer.

The denotations (32 a, b) correspond to the constituent structure in which *former* and *student* form an N that does not include the remainder of the expression, while (32 b, c) correspond to the structure in which the conjoined nominal *student and teacher* forms an N with the modifier *former.* That there are four readings here rather than just two is due to the property of expressions in which singular terms are conjoined with *and* that allows them to be construed as singular or plural.

Let us now return to the problem at hand. If we generate expiratives (but not 'ordinary' adejctives) in prenominal position via PS-rules, then in the case of a sentence such as

(33)   The former teacher and student were an interesting pair.

the following situation obtains: The sentence could be generated, in this form, directly via PS-rules; its two senses could thus be accounted for by the alternative bracketings provided, given the Expirative Rule or the Extended Modification Rule. On the other hand, the sense in which *former* modifies both *teacher* and *student* could also be accounted for by deriving (33) via CR from

(34)   The former teacher and former student were an interesting pair.

(Despite the existence of a predicate calling for a collective Subject, we are still free to posit a full source such as (34) for (33), since it is only the adjective that is relevant, not the entire Subject nominal.) We thus suffer from an embarrassment of riches, about which more shortly. Now consider an analogous sentence to (33) involving an 'ordinary' adjective like *old,* e.g., (16 a). The ambiguity of THIS sentence would be accounted for (in a standard transformational grammar) via convergent derivations from the structures (16 b, c). But certainly the two sentences are ambiguous for the same reason, and we are now being forced to miss a generalization in that the PS-rules (21) and the Extended Modification Rule play a role in accounting for the ambiguity of (33) but not for that of (16 a).

This difficulty may, however, be resolved if we do the following: Drop the transformation of Adjective Preposing from the grammar, and replace it with the Extended Modification Rule. (This rule will serve to determine denotational values for both A—N and N—WH—*be*—A sequences as long as there is a way to determine what properties are denoted by relative clauses — a requirement that can easily be satisfied. Accordingly, we can account for the semantic similarity between, say, *old men* and *men who are old* without requiring that there be a transformation relating them.) If we adopt this approach, then the semantic properties of the Subject nominal in (16 a) will be determined in a manner exactly parallel to the way in which (33) would be handled. This leaves us, however, with a situation in which one sense of either sentence could be accounted for in two ways: either via the bracketing $[_N A [N-CONJ-N]]$ and the associated effects of applying the Extended Modification Rule, or, via a deriviation via CR from a nominal of the form $A_i-N-CONJ-A_i-N$. Now, I see nothing inherently wrong with such a situation (in which a certain fact can be accounted for in more than one way) providing that all the apparatus involved has adequate independent motivation. But of all the devices introduced so far, CR has the least. For the cases presently under discussion, CR contributes nothing that is not provided by the PS-rules and the Extended Modification Rule. Moreover, the two main arguments usually given for CR are quite weak. The first is that there is a systematic relationship between certain 'full' and certain 'elliptical' coordinations — e.g., *Harry likes Maxine and Fred likes Maxine* and *Harry and Fred like Maxine;* but the existence of such a relationship does not in and of itself justify positing a transformation such as CR — since it could be (logically speaking) just as adequately captured by appropriately formulated interpretive principles which just happen to give similar results when applied to the members of such pairs. (Such a set of principles can be found in Kac 1978.) The second is that without such a transformation, it is impossible to derive all passive VP's (for example) in the same way: thus, in a sentence like *Harry hit Fred and was kissed by Maxine;* the second VP is derivable via the passive transformation only if at some point in the derivation there is a full conjunct *Maxine kissed Harry.* Analogous arguments can be given for VP's arising from other transformations, such as *tough*-Movement. But such motivation suffers from the weakness of being entirely intratheoretic; it derives not from facts, but from the logical consequences of a particular (and not universally accepted) set of assumptions about the specific rules required in a generative grammar of English. Regardless of whether CR is retained or not, however, our new account on balance has significant advantages — specifically:

(a) All facts of adjective distribution are accounted for without recourse to fictitious underlying structures, and without duplication of the apparatus required to generate prenominal adjectives. (Since we have dispensed with Adjective Preposing, we generate all prenominal adjective constructions directly via PS-rule (21 a).)

(b) The semantic relationship between prenominal adjective constructions and corresponding relative constructions is accounted for via the Extended Modification Rule.

(c) All instances of ambiguity of A—N—CONJ—N sequences are accounted for in the same way.

In sum: whether or not CR plays a role in English grammar, the apparatus associated with the alternative bracketing account developed in § 3 appears indispensable.

## 5. Multiple Bracketing Without Ambiguity: Restrictive Relative Constructions

In § 3, we established the important principle that the semantic consequences of the fact that some expression possesses a certain syntactic structure cannot be determined without 'bridge principles' that link the syntactic and semantic facts. We have thus far given two such principles, the Modification Rule and the Expirative Rule, which we collapsed partially into the Extended Modification Rule. We also observed that such principles are equivalent to 'interpretive' or 'projection' rules. The significance of bridge principles will become further apparent as we address the following question: can a sentence or expression which is assigned $n$ distinct syntactic structures have fewer than $n$ semantic interpretations? If so, then (3 b) is false — a demonstration of which is of some importance in the context of present-day linguistic investigation since its truth is not only widely assumed, but taken as a means of evaluating grammars. We noted earlier, for example, that (21 b) will assign more than one structure to some apparently unambiguous conjoined nominals, a fact which is sometimes taken as evidence against having such rules in generative grammars. But, as we also noted, this might not be so if (3 b) does not hold. I will not deal with conjoined nominals in this paper, but will present evidence of a clear kind form examination of English restrictive relative constructions that falsifies (3 b); it thus follows that, while some evidence against (21 b) and similar rules might in fact be found, it cannot consist in the demonstration that such rules generate 'too many' trees for unambiguous expressions.

Under many analyses of English relative constructions, an NP like *the man who is old* would be assigned the structure

(35)

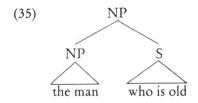

I will argue below that there is also motivation for assigning to this NP the structure

(36)
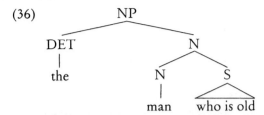

The reasons are formal, and will be detailed momentarily. That such an indeterminacy does not result in ambiguity can be shown on the basis of appropriate bridge principles.

The justification for structure (36) is of the same type as that given previously for our proposed analysis of A—N constructions: the sequence *man who is old* can be an antecedent of *one*, as in

(37)   Harry knows the man who is old from Minneapolis, and Fred knows the one from Duluth.

To show the justification for (35), we must proceed somewhat more indirectly, though *one* pronominalization is also involved in the demonstration. We begin by noting that *one* behaves differently in definite nominals than in indefinite ones: specifically, in definite nominals, such as those found in (37), *one* takes N's as antecedents, whereas in cases of indefiniteness, it takes NP's as antecedents. Thus, compare

(38)   a.   Harry knows a man who is old, and Fred knows one who is young.

       b.   *Harry knows a man who is old, and Fred knows a one who is young.

If we take these facts together, then we must posit the PS-rules

(39)   a.   NP → NP—S
       b.   N  → N—S

More generally, making use of our cover notion 'nominal,' we may posit the single rule

(40)   NOM → NOM—S

This means that for any expression of the form DET—N—S, whether definite or indefinite, there will be two structures, one analogous to (35) and one analogous to (36), except in sentences involving *one*-pronominalization, where the syntactic context of the anaphor will determine which of the two structures must be assigned to the nominal containing the antecedent.

The bridge principles relevant to the structures in question include the Modification Rule and two others. One, the Definiteness Rule, assigns specifications for definiteness to higher-order nominals; the other, the Upward Transmission Principle, has a function which will be described momentarily. The principles themeselves are as follows:

(41) DEFINITENESS RULE
A noncoordinate nominal is [α DEFINITE] according as it directly dominates a determiner marked [α DEFINITE].

(42) UPWARD TRANSMISSION PRINCIPLE
All grammatical and semantic information associated with a given nominal (e.g., person, gender, number, denotation, definiteness) is transmitted to any directly dominating nominal, providing no other principle for assigning such information to the latter is applicable.

The two rules can be illustrated as applied to the structure

(43)

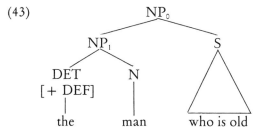

By the Definiteness Rule, $NP_1$ will be marked [+ DEF]; no other principle exists which would assign a definiteness specification to $NP_0$, so the Upward Transmission Principle applies and it too acquires the marking [+ DEF]. Then, by the Modification Rule, $NP_0$ will also acquire the denotational information: $NP_1$ will, by upward transmission, acquire the denotational specification of *man,* the Modification Rule then applying to indicate ultimately that $NP_0$ denotes a set each of whose members is a man having the property of being old.

Suppose now that we operate on the same expression, with the structure

(44)

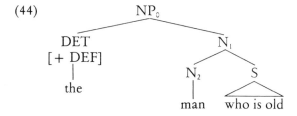

The procedure is slightly different, but the result will be the same as before: $NP_0$ is marked [+ DEF] by the Definiteness Rule; $N_1$, by the

Modification Rule, will be marked as denoting the set of men having the property of being old, and this information, by upward transmission, will then also be associated with $NP_0$. Clearly, then, the structural difference between (43) and (44) is of no consequence sematically.

It is important to stress that there is noting exotic or farfetched about the bridge principles involved here, nor are any questions begged: each principle must be recognized in any case for a variety of reasons quite apart from the need to make this particular argument go through. This being the case, I submit that the falsity of (3 b) has been demonstrated.


## 6. Conclusions

If the foregoing is correct, then arguments in the form (1) cannot be used to evaluate linguistic descriptions or theories of grammar. This does not, however, mean that grammatical ambiguity is irrelevant to such evaluation. Rather, the significance of the above arguments is simply that a more rigorous mode of argumentation must be employed; specifically, we require arguments conforming to the following schema:

(45) a.   A sentence $s$ and others like it display an $n$-way ambiguity.
     b.   Grammar G assigns to $s$ and its fellows, by whatever means are available to it to do so, $n$ nonequivalent semantic representations.
     c.   Grammar G' either fails to do so, or fails to do so in as natural and well-motivated a way as G.
     d.   Hence, grammar G is, ceteris paribus, more highly valued than G'.

Notice that (45 a), unlike (1 a), does not contain the clause 'which cannot be attributed to the presence of ambiguous words.' No such qualification is necessary, since (45) will serve as a basis for evaluating grammars with regard to their ability to account for ANY kind of ambiguity. A second important difference involves (45 b) vs. (1 b): The former contains the clause 'by whatever means are available to it,' meaning: attribution of more than one meaning to individual words, assignment of more than one structure to an expression such that the appropriate bridge principles derive more than one meaning, assignment of a single structure to an expression which is nonetheless subject to alternate interpretations via the bridge principles, and so on. Needless to say, in cases where both lexical and grammatical ambiguity are involved, various combinations of these means will be employed. From our point of view, the principal failing of the usual way of evaluating grammars on the basis of their ability to account for grammatical ambiguity is one of excessive narrowness: it has been widely, but wrongly, assumed that the only way to achieve such an account in a given case is by assigning alternate syntactic structures, and, conversely, that to do so is to make an automatic prediction of ambiguity.

I have repeatedly stressed the importance of bridge principles, and will assert their importance one final time. No linguistic theory can do without them, even if it has recourse to the most highly 'abstract' underlying representations; to ignore them is to surrender not only rigor but coherence as well.

Although it has not been my primary message here, I have also argued (by example) one further point: that considerations of naturalness in grammatical description require that 'syntax' be construed exclusively as 'surface syntax.' There is still a rather considerable amount of sentiment against such a view, but I venture to predict that it will become increasingly short lived as more attention is given to matters of the sort dealt with in these remarks.

## Appendix

It is sometimes argued that an abstract underlying level of syntactic representation is required for the implementation of an explanation of the ambiguity of a sentence like

(46)   Flying planes can be dangerous.

That this is in fact untrue can be very easily shown. Note first that there will have to be devices for generating some adjectives of the form Vs—ing (where Vs means 'verb stem'); and there must also be a rule V → Vs—ing for generating present participles. Note, then, that — given other commonly assumed rules — the Subject nominal of (46) may be assigned the following distinct constituent structures:

(47)   a.

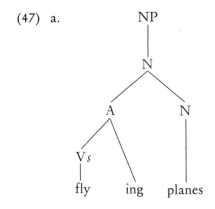

b.

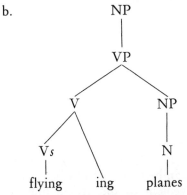

Observe further that (47 a) will, by the Modification Rule, be interpreted as denoting the subset of planes that consists of those which are
flying — corresponding to the relationship between *fly* and *planes* such
that the latter is Subject of the former. In the case of (47 b), *planes* will
have to be the Object of *fly* since it is directly dominated by the VP of
which *fly* is the main verb. The denotation of the entire NP, by an
appropriately formulated principle, will be an activity rather than a
subset of the set of planes, consistent with the fact that NP directly
dominates VP rather than some other nominal constituent. (By this
means we also capture the status of the entire expression as a 'nominal-
ized' VP).

Independent evidence in favor of the structures in (47) comes from the
following facts. Note that the following are unambiguous:

(48)  a.   The flying planes can be dangerous.
      b.   Flying the planes can be dangerous.

In (48 a), *planes* can be construed only as Subject of *fly;* the structure
must be

(49)

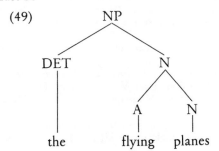

That *flying planes* is an N but not also an NP follows from the fact that
articles can form NP's with N's but not with NP's. The structure of
*flying the planes,* where *the planes* must be Object of *fly* will, by the same
token, have to be

(50)

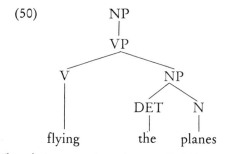

That *flying* must here be a verb follows from the fact that *the planes* is an NP — since, as just noted, A's can be sisters of N's but not of NP's in nominal constituents. Each placement of the article thus forces one structure or the other to be picked, and each individual structure is just the one associated with the correct grammatical relations.

## Acknowledgement

I would like to express my thanks to the Regents of the University of Minnesota for releasing me from teaching duties during the winter of 1976 so that I could pursue the line of inquiry leading to the writing of this paper.

## References

Botha, R. 1971. The Methodological Status of Grammatical Argumentation. The Hague: Mouton and Co.
Chomsky, N. 1957. Syntactic Structures. The Hague: Mouton and Co.
— 1962. Current Issues in Linguistic Theory. The Hague: Mouton and Co.
— 1971. Problems of Knowledge and Freedom. New York: Random House.
— and M. Halle. 1968. The Sound Pattern of English. New York: Harper and Row.
Donnellan, K. 1971. Reference and definite descriptions. In J. Rosenberg and C. Travis, eds., Readings in the Philosophy of Language. Englewood Cliffs, N. J.: Prentice-Hall, Inc. Pp 195—211.
Jackendoff, R. S. 1972. Semantic Interpretation in Generative Grammar, Cambridge, Mass.: MIT Press.
Kac, M. B. 1976. Hypothetical constructs in syntax. In J. R. Wirth, ed., *Assessing Linguistic Arguments.* Washington, D. C.: Hemisphere Press-John Wiley, and Sons. Pp 49—83.
— 1978. Corepresentation of Grammatical Structure. Minneapolis: University of Minnesota Press and London: Croom Helm, Ltd.
Katz, J. J. and J. A. Fodor. 1964. The structure of a semantic theory. In J. A. Fodor and J. J. Katz, eds., The Structure of Language. Englewood Cliffs, N. J.: Prentice-Hall, Inc. Pp 479—518.
McCawley, J. D. 1968. The role of semantics in grammar. In E. Bach and R. T. Harms, eds., Universals in Linguistic Theory. New York: Holt, Rinehart, and Winston. Pp 125—170.

# Generative Semantics: Ethnoscience or Ethnomethodology?*

F. B. D'Agostino

One goal of early transformational linguistic theory, as formulated by Chomsky in *Syntactic Structures* (1957), was the *strictly syntactic* delimination of the corpus of grammatical strings. Chomsky further suggested the use of native intuitive judgements about the grammaticality of strings to provide a 'pre-theoretical' delimitation of a language; a delimitation which it was the linguist's task then to formalize. Thus, the concept of grammaticality is for this theory 'both a topic and resource of inquiry' (to use Garfinkel's felicitous phrase — see Garfinkel, 1972: 321). Notion also, *pace* Katz's claim (1971: 4) that generative grammar opened up an 'underlying linguistic reality' hidden to structuralist linguistics, that, since early transformational grammar assumed 'that grammatical regularities could be completely characterized without recourse to meaning . . . [it] was a natural outgrowth of American structural linguistics, since it was concerned with discovering the regularities governing the distribution of surface forms' (Lakoff, 1971 a: 267—8).

Against this position, which he calls 'autonomous syntax' (1971 a: 267), George Lakoff and other 'generative semanticists' (e.g., McCawley, Postal, Ross) object that 'such a limitation of the discipline is impossible,' that even the strictly syntactic question of the 'distribution of morphemes depends upon various aspects of context, conveyed meaning, and the model-theoretical interpretation of logical structures' (Lakoff, 1974: 175). Their position, in short, is that grammars cannot be written without reference to meaning and to facts about the contexts within which and the purpose for which language is actually used. Both of these factors Chomsky and his followers would undoubtedly dismiss as 'performance' variables.

The claims of generative semantics, while *prima facie* plausible to

---

* The first version of this paper was written for Prof. George Lakoff's class on Generative Semantics at the 1973 Summer Institute of Linguistics. Various versions were presented that fall at Princeton, Leuven, and Brussels. I would like to thank my friend Yvan Putseys for the opportunity to go to Leuven and Brussels and for his encouragement. The present version is a May 1977 revision of a version which has been circulating for some years in Europe. Between fall 1973 and May 1977 I have changed my views on many subjects related to issues discussed in this paper. I have tried, however, to maintain as much of the spirit of my original work as possible.

many social scientists, might be be justified and explicated by means of an example. Thus, for instance, consider the rules which govern the surface distribution of the morpheme *but.* Lakoff claims (1971 b: 66—7) that (1) below is grammatical only relative to the presupposition (2) below.

(1) *John is a Republican, but he is honest (too).*
(2) The speaker expects that the hearer believes that if $x$ is a Republican, then $x$ is *not* honest.

From this, he concludes that 'the general principle for the occurrence of *but* is that when S 1 *[John is a Republican] and* S 2 *[John is honest]* is asserted and there are one or more presuppositions from which Exp (S 1 $\supset \sim$ S 2) can be deduced, then *but* can replace *and* and the sentence will be grammatical only relative to those presuppositions *(ibid.).*

This example also has the virtue of answering, I think, the objection, frequently voiced by those encountering this system for the first time, that once one allows facts about context to enter into judgements about grammaticality, one creates a situation in which (a) any utterance can be made to appear grammatical given a suitably complicated or bizarre context; and (b) the specification of those contexts with respect to which an utterance *is* well-formed would become, practically speaking, impossible, given the infinity of contexts that *could* fit the bill. Both of these objections can be answered by noting that, as in the example above, a sentence *can* be grammatical *only* relative to that class of presuppositions or contexts which have certain deductive relations to a certain *finite* characterization (such as 'Exp (S 1 $\supset \sim$ S 2)').

What this example (and each of many others which could be cited) suggests, then, is that in order to account for surface syntactic regularities, rules of grammar must refer to descriptions of events, attitudes, propositions, etc. outside the derivational sequence from 'deep structure' to phonetic realization. That is, rules of grammar cannot, on this view, be written solely in terms of syntactic considerations (constituent ordering, relations of dominance or coordinance in tree structure, strictly syntactic categories like NP, VP, etc.). Specifically, some derivational rules will depend on the meaning that the sentence conveys (as opposed, that is, to its 'literal' deep structural meaning), and on the context within which a sentence is uttered.

It will be obvious, of course, that these kinds of rules cannot be expressed in terms of the usual transformational formalism, because transformations operate solely on adjacent syntactically defined trees in a single derivational sequence. Lakoff has, however, suggested an expanded framework within which such rules can be stated. These are called, variously and somewhat differently, 'global rules' (Lakoff: 1970) and 'transderivational constraints' (Lakoff: 1973). The rule specifying the surface distribution of *but* could, for instance, be represented in these terms in something like the following way:

I:   Input tree: S 1 *and* S 2.
II:  Output tree: S 1 *but* S 2.
III: Condition: If the speaker expects that the hearer believes that
     S 1 ⊃ ~ S 2.

In any event, formalisms aside, we can see that grammatical rules of this kind go far beyond those characteristic of Chomsky's 'Extended Standard Theory.' For, the kinds of grammatical rules for which Lakoff is arguing would constitute, if anything, nothing less than a proto-grammar of cultural appropriateness and relevance. For the claim is, clearly, that particular sentences are not either absolutely grammatical or absolutely ungrammatical in isolation, but appropriate or well-formed only relative to certain contexts and conveyed meanings — that is, that ONLY CERTAIN KINDS OF CULTURAL TABLEAUX ARE 'WELL-FORMED.' In this sense, then, generative semantics is clearly related to the concerns of anthropological 'ethnoscientists.' Consider, for example, Roger Keesing's claim (1970: 432, 441) that 'What we need apparently is a theory of the cultural definition of situation. . . . Perhaps it will be formally akin to the generative devices of a grammar, whereby an infinite series of unique definitions of situations can be produced by the operation on a finite set of elements of a finite set of rules of combination. . . . A "cultural grammar" would describe . . . the organized knowledge that enables this idealized actor-observer to produce appropriate acts'.

Notice, moreover, that all of the following questions all of obvious sociological interest, are of crucial importance for generative semantics:

> 1. When you use a given sentence to mean a given thing, are you being sincere or not, polite or not, formal or not, joking or not, etc.? 2. Given a sentence and a fixed context, if it [the sentence] can have more than one meaning, is one 'stronger' than another? Or more likely? Or more 'normal?' 3. Are certain sentences with certain readings limited to given types of discourse, e.g., answers to questions, astounded responses, stories, meek inquiries, etc.? 4. What assumptions is a speaker making when he uses a given sentence to convey a given meaning in a situation? 5. What is the literal meaning of a sentence in a given situation, and what is conversationally implied by the sentence? (Lakoff, 1974: 156)

Furthermore, if we accept the claim that the surface forms of sentences depend on cultural, contextual features (i.e., facts and native opinions about the social and natural worlds), then we can see precisely how assumptions about nature and culture are encoded linguistically. And this in a way which goes far beyond Whorf's (undoubtedly clever) intuitions about the lexicon and abstract grammatical form. In other words, generative semantics puts us in the position of seeing quite specifically how, in Gellner's words (1970: 115), our concepts (i.e., our language) 'are correlates of all the institutions of a society.'

According to generative semantics, another important way in which cultural and social facts find expression linguistically involves phenomena related to the so-called 'performative' use of verbs. Rather than attempting to jump right into this complicated subject — which, in many ways, lies at the very heart of Lakoff's position — let me first offer some historical background.

The philosopher, J. L. Austin, speaking at Harvard in 1955, drew attention to a class of utterances which

> can fall into no hitherto recognized grammatical category save that of 'statement,' which are not nonsense, and which contain none of those verbal danger-signs which philosophers have by now detected or think they have detected ... all of which have, as it happens, humdrum verbs in the first person singular present indicative active. Utterances can be found, satisfying these conditions, yet such that A. they do not 'describe' or 'report' or constate anything at all, are not 'true or false;' and B. the uttering of the sentence is, or is part of, the doing of an action, which again would not normally be described as saying something. (Austin, 1962: 4—5)

Austin offered, *inter alia,* the following examples: 'I name this ship the *Queen Elizabeth,*' 'I bet you sixpence it will rain tomorrow,' etc. He further suggested that 'In these examples it seems clear that to utter the sentence (in, of course, the appropriate circumstances) is not to *describe* my doing what I should be said in so uttering to be doing or to state that I am doing it: it is to do it'. (*op. cit.:* 6) One problematic aspect of such utterances is immediately apparent. Thus, as Austin points out, it is not clear at all how we could possibly assign truth values to sentences of this kind. Nevertheless, despite the fact that performative sentences (and this is what Austin called them) seem to lack truth value, they can, as we know, still 'go wrong' or 'misfire.' That is, they can be used improperly, inappropriately, insincerely, etc. For example, there is something very different about the sentence 'I order you to pick up that cigarette butt, soldier' used by a sergeant to a private and that same sentence used by the private to the sergeant. It is this difference and, specifically, our feeling that the latter use is inappropriate, that we would like to be able to capture and, perhaps, to formalize.

A major step in this direction was taken by the philosopher John Searle, in his recent book *Speech Acts* (1969). He simply noted that the kinds of things that can 'go wrong' in the preformative use of sentences with such verbs as 'promise,' 'bet,' 'order,' etc. are just those things which can render false a sentence in which these verbs are used nonperformatively. Consider, for instance, the kinds of things which could render false the sentence 'John promised to give Harry £ 5.' We would want to say that this sentence would be false if, among other things, John did not, in fact, *intend* to give Harry £ 5. And, of course, it is under just these same kinds of circumstances that we would want to say that the sentence 'I promise to give you £ 5' would be used insincerely; that is, if I didn't intend to give you £ 5. Thus, intention to act as stated is a truth-condition on the non-performative use of 'promise' and a 'felicity-condition' on its performative use. In other words, declarative sentences have truth-conditions, performative sentences have felicity-conditions.

But, of course, declarative sentences can both 'go wrong' and be false. That is, I think we would want to differentiate between the insincerity of the utterance 'The moon is made of green cheese' (as spoken by someone who didn't really believe this to be the case) and the falsity of its propositional content. The problem we are faced with, though, is that there is no overt performative verb 'state,' for instance, in this sentence with which to associate a felicity-condition on belief. Recent work by Ross, however, supplies the solution for this problem, for he argues (1970: 223) that 'declarative sentences ... must be analyzed as explicit performatives and must be derived from deep structures containing an explicitly represented performative main verb.' Thus, by his analysis, the deep structure of the sentence 'The moon is made of green cheese' might be represented by something like the following labelled bracketing:

$[_S[_{NP}I]\ [_V STATE]\ [_{NP}you]\ [_{NP}[_S\textit{The moon is made of green cheese}]]]$

This deep structure labelled bracketing would then be related to its surface form by transformations that delete the abstract performative verb and its pronominal arguments. Ross' result, then, allows us to give a uniform performative analysis for all sentences, including those, typically declaratives, which contain no overt performative verb.

Thus, it appears that the facts represented in speech act theory are (like facts about context, converyed meaning, etc.) encoded into the structure of language itself. To be more specific: facts about the very nature of human social interaction (e.g., facts about belief, sincerity, authority, intention, etc. and their interrelations) are, on this account, encoded into and reflected back from linguistic form. This seems to me to be a terribly significant result; one for which Habermas' comment seems apt. Thus, he noted (1970: 140) that 'The dialogue constitutive universals [in the terms used here, the performative analysis] at the same time generate and describe the form of intersubjectivity which makes mutuality of understanding possible.'

To carry this analysis even further, we can see that many facts about 'indirect illocutionary force' (i.e., the indirectly conveyed meanings of sentences) can be accounted for within this framework. Consider, then the following sincerely spoken sentence:

(A)    *Mary betrayed me.*

Given the performative analysis of declaratives, such that (A) has a deep structure something like this:

[$_S$[$_{NP}$*I*] [$_V$STATE] [$_{NP}$*you*] [$_{NP}$[$_S$*Mary betrayed me*]]],

and a conversational postulate (which maps deep structures into conveyed meanings) like this:

STATE (x, y, A) ⊃ BELIEVE (x, A) ,

we can derive the indirect meaning 'I believe that Mary betrayed me,' as well as accounting for the oddity, if not downright unacceptability, of 'Mary betrayed me, but I don't believe that Mary betrayed me.' In this way, then, the performative analysis, in conjunction with empirically justified meaning postulates like the one invoked above, allows us to characterize formally and systematically not only the syntactic and semantic properties of individual sentences, but also the inferences which can be drawn from them. More specifically, it provides the foundations for 'a logic which is capable of accounting for all correct inferences made in natural language' (Lakoff, 1972: 589).

'Natural logic' (as Lakoff calls it) would, then, characterize ordinary, everyday, non-scientific reasoning itself. This is, of course, a remarkably ambitious program, though, as Lakoff points out, not an entirely new one. Thus, he claims (1972: 646) that

> Natural logic is by no means new. The study of logic began and developed as an attempt to understand the rules of human reasoning. . . . The development of logic has followed a pattern common to many fields. As formal techniques developed for dealing with certain aspects of the field's subject matter, the subject matter tends to shrink until it encompasses only those aspects of the original subject matter that the techniques developed can cope with. . . . Unfortunately, the concentration on the development of known techniques has the consequence that most of the original subject matter of logic was ignored, if not forgotten. . . . It seems to me [however] that recent developments in modal logic, together with recent developments in linguistics, make the serious study of natural logic possible.

At this point, we might pose the following problem: Since the notion of 'correct inference' seems to play the same role in 'natural logical' studies as the notion 'grammatical string' plays in 'autonomous syntactic' studies — i.e., as both topic and resource of inquiry — we might suppose that Lakoff, like Chomsky, proposes to delimit the corpus of 'correct inferences' in 'folk logic' in terms of native intuitive judgements (e.g., about whether A 'follows from' B). Against this *prima facie* quite plausible suggestion, however, Lakoff proposes delimiting this corpus in terms of the formal notion of semantic entailment. That is, Lakoff proposes that the set of 'folk logically correct inferences' from premisses P to conclusions C is the set {⟨P, C⟩|P⊦C}. Consequently, in these terms, native judgements about the validity of inferences stand to strict entailment as performance does to competence. Thus, Lakoff argues (1971 c: 330) that:

> The study of the relationship between a sentence and those things it presupposes about the nature of the world by way of systematic rules is part of the study of linguistic competence. Performance is another matter. Suppose that S is well-formed only relative to [the presupposition] PR. Then a speaker will make certain judgements about the well-formedness or ill-formedness of S which will vary with his extralinguistic knowledge. If the presuppositions of PR do not accord with his factual knowledge, cultural background, or beliefs about the world, then he may judge S to be 'odd,' strange,' 'deviant,' 'ungrammatical,' or simply ill-formed relative to his presupposition about the nature of the world. Thus, extra-linguistic factors very often enter into judgements of well-formedness. This is a matter of performance. The linguistic competence underlying this is the ability to pair sentences with the presuppositions relative to which they are well-formed.

Lakoff, then, proposes to identify the native's 'natural logical competence' with his ability to draw inferences in accordance with the relation of semantic entailment. That is, he claims, in effect, that the criterion in terms of which the native recognizes an inference as 'correct in folk logic' is that of entailment.

Let us assume, for the sake of argument, that Lakoff's proposal is correct to the following extent — namely, that it is part of each individual's innate human natural logical potential that, given appropriately facilitating conditions of cultural learning, he is capable of developing a natural logical ability to draw inferences in accordance with a criterion of strict semantic entailment. We can now ask — Are there human social conditions under which the development of such skills might be impaired? Furthermore, if we can identify such conditions, we will be entitled to conclude, I think, that Lakoff's proposal to identify *mature* natural logical competence with the ability to draw inferences in accordance with a criterion of entailment is incorrect. For, under such conditions, native natural logical competence might not be based on such a criterion. And, in this case, then, we *might* propose that native intuitive judgements about inferences provide a more revealing pre-theoretical criterion for delimiting their natural logical competence than the entailment criterion Lakoff proposes. Are there, then, conditions such as I have mentioned? I think there may be and would offer the following scenario in support of this claim:

(1) Certain objectively valid inferences from facts about the world known to the native may be blocked if they contradict or fail to support theoretical notions in which his community (or some part of it) has some substantial pragmatic interest. Think of a ruling class or party which discourages precisely those inferences from facts about society that threaten to undermine its political control. As Mueller has put it (1970: 102), 'Censure and directed

communication are traditional means of manipulating consciousness in order to prevent subversion by counter-symbols.'

(2) Expanding this last notion, we can see that particular pragmatic 'scenes' (racism, sexism, colonialism) tend to be productive of 'pseudo-consensus' — that is, of a situation in which a subordinate group accepts the ideology of a dominant group, not because this ideology is logically consistent with what they know about the world, but, rather, out of perceived pragmatic necessity.

(3) Thus, given suitable political circumstances, the validity of certain and the invalidity of certain other inferences may take on a quality of inevitability (i.e., non-negotiability, naturalness) and thus become independent both of any knowledge natives may have about the world, and of any innate potential they might have had to evaluate such inferences in terms of a criterion of semantic entailment. And this process may proceed in stages from (a) in which C is seen as 'following from' P only given a political situation S in which it is necessary to recognize this inference as correct in order to avoid censure; through (b) in which, because of repetition, propoganda, etc., the inference from P to C no longer appears to depend upon the realities of political life; to (c) in which, by directed communication, censure, etc., the inference from P to C comes to seem to be a tautological inference.

(4) By the time stage (c) has been reached, the native's entailment-based natural logical potential has surely been impaired. For, in particular, the native now *habitually* recognizes as valid inferences which are *not formally valid*. And, in this case surely, it is simply incorrect (or, at best, misleading) to identify the skills which underlie the inferences which the native does draw with any entailment-based ability. Whatever potential the native might have had to this effect has surely at this point been eroded.

But, in this kind of case, what is the point of maintaining that the native's natural logical competence *is* based on a notion of semantic entailment? Wouldn't a theory of natural logic based on such a notion fail to be even 'observationally adequate?' Shouldn't we, then, in this kind of situation be forced, *contra* Lakoff, so fall back on native intuitive judgements about inferences as our pre-theoretical criterion of delimitation between natural logically 'valid' and 'invalid' inferences?

The only way I can see of answering this question is to say, 'It depends.' In short, it depends on what our (political) purposes are in writing a 'grammar of cultural tableaux.' There seem to be two cases: (i) If we are simply interested in describing native natural logical competence (as Lakoff appears to be), then, *pace* Lakoff, native intuitive judgements about the 'validity' of inferences must serve as the criterion in terms of which we carry out our descriptive exercise. The scenario sketched above shows nothing if not that a criterion of strict entailment may be useless in such a case. (ii) If, on the other hand, we are interested in diagnosing the causes of native communicative disability, then, it seems, adopting Lakoff's suggestion (though for rather different purposes) may be a heuristically natural move to make. For, in this case, our objective is not to describe native inferences taken at face value, but rather to try to understand why these diverge so sharply from formally valid inferences. And here the notion of strict entailment may provide a valuable diagnostic tool. For this notion may help us to work backwards from formally invalid but folk logically 'valid' inferences to a description of those pragmatic conditions (awareness of which is suppressed by natives drawing such inferences) whose addition to our (reconstructed) inference schema would render the inference valid. And this kind of reconstruction could lead to a better understanding, perhaps, of the pragmatic political conditions whose effects have been to undermine communicative ability.

How do we choose between these alternatives? The question might also be phrased this way: Is generative semantics to be ethnoscientific or ethnomethodological? Will it choose to rely on the naive acceptance of native intuitive judgements about cultural appropriateness? If so, it cannot serve, as I think it is worthy to, as the foundation for a *critical* science of human interaction. For, as Lukacs has put it:

> As long as man adopts a stance of intuition and contemplation he can only relate to his own thought and to the objects of the empirical world in an immediate way. He accepts both as ready-made — produced by historical reality. As he wishes only to know the world and not to change it he is forced to accept both the empirical material rigidity of existence and the logical rigidity of concepts as unchangeable. His mythological analyses are not concerned with the concrete origins of this rigidity or with the real factors inherent in them that could lead to its elimination. (1971: 202)

## References

Austin, J. L., 1962, How to do things with words. New York: Oxford University Press.
Chomsky, N., 1957, Syntactic structures. The Hague: Mouton.
Davidson, D. & Harman, G. (eds.), 1972, Semantics of natural language. Dordrecht: Reidel.
Dreitzel, H. P. (ed.), 1970, Recent sociology 2. New York: Macmillan.
Fillmore, C. & Langendoen, T. (eds.), 1971, Studies in linguistic semantics. New York: Holt, Rinehart & Winston.
Garfinkel, H., 1972, 'Remarks on ethnomethodology' IN Gumperz & Hymes.

Gellner, E., 1970, 'Concepts and society' in Wilson.

Gumperz, J. & Hymes, D. (eds.), 1972, Directions in sociolinguistics. New York: Holt, Rinehart & Winston.

Habermas, J., 1970, 'On communicative competence' in Dreitzel.

Jacobs, R. & Rosenbaum, P. (eds.), 1970, Readings in English transformational grammar. Waltham, Mass.: Ginn.

Kachru, B. et al. (eds.), 1973, Papers in linguistics in honor of Henry and Renee Kahane. Urbana: University of Illinois Press.

Katz, J., 1971, The underlying reality of language and its philosophical import. New York: Harper & Row.

Keesing, R., 1970, 'Toward a model of role analysis' in Narroll & Cohen.

Lakoff, G., 1970, 'Global rules,' *Language* 46.

— 1971 a, 'On generative semantics' in Steinberg & Jacobovits.

— 1971 b, 'The role of deduction in grammar' in Fillmore & Langendoen.

— 1971 c, 'Presupposition and relative well-formedness' in Steinberg & Jacobovits.

— 1972, 'Linguistics and natural logic' in Davidson & Harman.

— 1973, 'Some thoughts on transderivational rules' in Kachru.

— 1974, 'Interview with Herman Parret' in Parret.

Lukacs, G., 1971, History and class consciousness. Cambridge: M. I. T. Press.

Mueller, C., 1970, 'Notes on the repression of communicative behavior' in Dreitzel.

Narroll, R. & Cohen, R. (eds.), 1970, Handbook of method in cultural anthropology. New York: Natural History Press.

Parret, H. (ed.), 1974, Discussing language. The Hague: Mouton.

Ross, J. R., 1970, 'On declarative sentences' in Jacobs & Rosenbaum.

Searle, J., 1969, Speech Acts. Cambridge: Cambridge University Press.

Steinberg, D. & Jacobovits, L. (eds.), 1971, Semantics: an interdisciplinary reader. Cambridge: Cambridge University Press.

Wilson, B. (ed.), 1971, Rationality. New York: Harper & Row.

# V. Quantitative Methods in Linguistic Research

# Syntactic Frequency and Acceptability

Sidney Greenbaum

Linguists differ as to the status within linguistic theory of the frequency with which items occur in language use. Different opinions among linguistic schools (not always made explicit) reflect differences in what are conceived to be the goals of linguistics, and hence in what should be included in a linguistic description. The basic division is between those who wish linguistics to account for language function — the ways in which language is put to use — and those who wish linguistics to be restricted to an account of the system or of the set of rules in language from which considerations of use have been abstracted. Linguists of the Prague School and those influenced by the British linguist Firth are typical advocates of functional approaches to language description. In general, Bloomfieldian linguists and most transformational linguists — most, at least until recently — have excluded language use from the goals of linguistic description. Thus, the goal of linguistic description has been said to be 'a description of the ideal speaker-hearer's intrinsic competence, rather than a description of linguistic performance' (Chomsky 1965: 4). Competence includes the knowledge of which sentences are in the language, the ability to perceive ambiguities in sentences, and the awareness of semantic relations between sentences; but it excludes social and stylistic factors that influence choices in language, and it therefore excludes the frequency with which choices are made. The clarity, validity, and delimitation of the competence/performance dichotomy have all been questioned, by both linguists and psycholinguists (for example in Reich 1969; Bever 1970: 341—348; Campbell and Wales 1970: 246—249; Schlesinger 1971; Derwing 1973: 259—300; Lakoff 1973: 286—288). The restriction on the goal of linguistics to an account of linguistic competence in this circumscribed sense has led many linguists to disregard frequency of use.

We can nevertheless argue that judgements of frequency — in particular judgements of the frequency of syntactic constructions — have a theoretical importance even within a narrowly-conceived competence theory, and this is so even though frequency of use is considered irrelevant. The primary data for the grammar within a competence theory are provided by the intuitions of native speakers of the language, in particular their judgements of whether sequences are sentences in the language. Competence theory differentiates between grammaticality, which is what the grammar can account for, and acceptability, the judgement made by native speakers (Chomsky 1965: 10—15; 1970: 193—195). The extent to which the results of decisions on grammaticality and acceptability diverge depends on how broad a concept of grammar the linguist has (cf.Fillmore 1973) and on whether general psychological principles are to be excluded from the grammar (Bever 1970: 279—362; Kimball 1973; Langendoen and Bever 1973; Langendoen et al. 1973). At all events, linguists have to take account of acceptability judgement when deciding what to incorporate in their grammar, whether these judgements are drawn from their own introspection or collected from groups of informants. One factor that seems to influence acceptability judgements of syntactic constructions is an opinion on the frequency with which the structures are used. Empirical evidence for the relationship between the two types of judgement is important for any theory of grammar.[1]

We shall later see that there is some experimental evidence for an association between the two types of judgements. But first we should consider other examples of the importance of frequency in linguistics.

A linguistic concept that has some bearing on distinctions in relative frequency is the marked/unmarked contrast. It often happens that when two or more units are in contrast one is taken to be the neutral or unmarked unit while the others are said to be marked. There are various ways in which this contrast has been used in linguistics. They include:

(1) *Morphological marking.* The marked form contains one or more morphemes that are absent in the unmarked form. Thus, in English emphasis on the positiveness of what is said is often marked by the introduction of the auxiliary *do* while the unemphatic is unmarked, as in the contrast between *I saw him* and *I did see him.* Similarly, the plural of nouns is normally marked in English by an additional morpheme.

(2) *Distribution.* The marked form has a more restricted distribution, because it is excluded from certain linguistic or stylistic environ-

---

[1] An interesting use of counts of syntactic frequency as a discovery procedure for grammaticality appears in a work by Halliday. He investigated the frequencies of syntactic classes in a book written in a Chinese dialect, and then predicted frequencies for combinations of the classes on the assumption that proportional frequency is regular throughout. If a combination was absent where a certain number of occurrences was predicted, he claimed that the combination was irregular or did not exist in the language; if only a few instances occurred where a large number was predicted, the combination was said to be rare in the language. The procedure was intended to distinguish whether non-occurrence or low occurrence in the corpus was due to chance or whether it was evidence for the ungrammaticality or rarity of the combination in the language (Halliday 1959: 58).

ments (cf. Halliday 1967 a: 49; and the concept of dominance in Greenberg 1966: 97—101; and Jakobson 1966: 268 f). An example of the former is the zero-*that* clause, which cannot be used as subject. Thus, we have *I know that he likes her* and *I know he likes her*, but only *That he likes her is all too obvious* and not *\*He likes her is all too obvious.* An example of markedness because of stylistic restrictions is the omission of the article in restrictive appositives, as in *Democratic leader Robinson refused to answer questions;* this form is virtually limited to newspapers and magazines (Quirk et al. 1972: 9.153).

(3) *Semantic marking.* The marked form is more restricted in sense, having an additional semantic feature. Thus, the use of the present perfect implies some orientation to the present of the speaker, an implication that is absent if the simple past is used instead. Similarly, imperative and interrogative sentences have been said to be marked in contrast to the unmarked declarative (Lyons 1968: 307).

(4) *Neutralization.* The unmarked form is used where there is an absence of normal contrast. Thus, the upper extreme in contrasting measure adjectives is used to denote the whole scale for *How* questions and with measurements, e.g. *How old is he?, He is three months old.* Compare the marked form in *How young is he?*

(5) *Normal and non-normal.* One form is said to be the norm from which others diverge. Thus, there is assumed to be a normal position for elements in a sentence; informational prominence can be given to an element by placing it in a non-normal position, e.g. *Joe his name is* (Quirk et al. 1972: 14.11). Similarly, if coordinated clauses have identical subject and auxiliaries, it is normal for both to be ellipted in the second and subsequent clauses, e.g. *Alice is washing and dressing* (Quirk et al. 1972: 9.68). 'Normal' can be used interchangeably with 'neutral' in the distributional sense of 'dominance' referred to above. But it can also mean the typical or usual, introducing the notion of relative frequency.

These different uses of the marked/unmarked contrast often coincide. Thus, according to Jakobson (1966: 270), "language tends to avoid any chiasmus between pairs of unmarked/marked categories, on the one hand, and pairs of zero/non-zero affixes (or of simple/compound grammatical forms), on the other hand" (and so also Lyons 1968: 79). That this is not always the case is shown by our two examples of forms marked because of their distributional restrictions. Both Greenberg (1966: 97) and Jakobson (1966: 268) are careful to distinguish the dominant (or unmarked) from the more frequent. However, it is likely that there is a similar tendency for the unmarked to be the more frequent. Thus, Halliday terms a clause consisting of one and only one complete tone group as 'neutral in tonality' in contrast to the two 'marked' possibilities. But the choice of the neutral or unmarked possibility is based on frequency: "There is a tendency for the tone group to correspond in extent with the clause; we may take advantage of this tendency by regarding the selection of one complete tone group for one complete clause as the neutral term in the first of the three systems" (Halliday 1967 b: 18—20). Halliday does not offer any textual evidence to support his choice of the unmarked form; we therefore assume that he is relying on his own judgement of relative frequencies when he refers to *a tendency*. We can have greater confidence in such judgements when they are corroborated by a large group of informants.

Frequency of occurrence and the native speaker's knowledge of frequency of occurrence have an obvious significance for linguistic theories that are concerned with language function.[2] A basic concept of the Prague School (not exclusive to that linguistic school, but more explicitly discussed there) is a distinction between the central and peripheral in all aspects of language, a distinction which draws in part on frequency differences (cf. Daneš 1966). In evaluating componential analysis of vocabulary, the British linguist Lyons cites a semantic example of this distinction (Lyons 1968: 479). He points out that componential analysis "tends to neglect the difference in the frequency of lexical items (and therefore their greater or less 'centrality' in the vocabulary)". As an illustration, he notes that *brother* and *sister* can be replaced with *male sibling* and *female sibling* only in an anthropological or quasi-anthropological context, and that most English speakers probably do not know the word *sibling*. Because there is no *common* superordinate term for *brother* and *sister*, Lyons concludes that the opposition between them is semantically more important in English than what they have in common. In an example from phonology, Lyons claims that "we must allow a place in our theory of language-structure for the undoubted importance, both synchronic and diachronic, of the concept of functional load." Among the factors he mentions as contributing to the functional load of phonological contrasts is the frequency of occurrence of the contrasts (Lyons 1968: 83—84). We can extend the same lines of argument to syntactic frequency. If, for example, the frequency difference in English between actives and passives is far greater than that

---

[2]  Frequency of occurrence in use is to be distinguished from frequency of possibility of occurrence within a system. Quantitative analysis may be based on whether a unit can occur in certain contexts, as in the procedures used by Harris for segmenting into morphemes (Harris 1968: 24—28) or in the phonological analysis of English in Trnka 1968.

between declaratives and interrogatives, or at least is felt to be far greater, we can claim that the declarative/interrogative contrast is more central for English syntax and the functional load of that contrast is greater.[3]

The role of relative frequency of occurrence in the acquisition of a first language has yet to be established, but there are indications that it is likely to be important. Demonstrations that more complex structures are acquired later than less complex structures — as attempted in C. Chomsky 1969 and Brown and Hanlon 1970 — may be vitiated by the intervention of relative frequency as a confounding factor (cf. Brown and Hanlon 1970: 37—40, 50 f). A possible example of the more potent effect of relative frequency is the acquisition of truncated passives *(The boy was hit)* before full passives *(The boy was hit by his father)*, even though the truncated passive is linguistically more complex, given current formulations of passive in transformational grammar (cf. Watt 1970 a: particularly 169 and 183; and for another example of the effect of frequency on the process of acquisition, see Ervin-Tripp 1970: 97). It is possible that relative frequency in actual use may be less significant than what has been called 'felt preponderance' (Watt 1970 b: 62), in which case comparison needs to be made with judgements of relative frequency rather than with the relative frequencies in speech samples. The child presumably acquires a syntactic construction after a period of exposure to hearing it. We do not know the experiential frequency that constitutes the saturation level for passive and then active acquisition of a construction. But it may well be that though two constructions differ in actual frequency such that one occurs twice as frequently as the other (say, declaratives and questions), perhaps most children (and adults, for that matter) perceive them as equally frequent and acquire them at about the same period. For older children, it should be possible to elicit perceptions of relative frequency to ascertain whether there is a felt preponderance for one construction over the other. If, as has been suggested (Watt 1970 a: 215), some children are still acquiring grammatical structures as late as 13 and 14, there is ample

---

[3] Frequency of use has been most commonly studied on the lexical level. Word frequency lists have been compiled for many languages (Kučera and Francis 1967 is a recent English example, and cf. Roceric 1973: 26), principally because they are assumed to be of value for grading vocabulary in language teaching. (But see Corder 1973: 214—218 on problems in applying information from word frequency lists to foreign language teaching.) In Firthian linguistics, a statement of the meaning of a lexical item includes the set of lexical items with which it habitually collocates, i.e., co-occurs (cf. Firth 1957: 194 ff.; Sinclair 1966: 410 ff., Greenbaum 1970: 87). Bolinger has proposed that the lexicon should indicate probabilities for the grammatical behavior of lexical items, for example the tendency of particular nouns to be used as count rather than non-count (Bolinger 1969: 37 f).

scope for investigating the effect of relative frequency in adult language on the order in which structures are acquired. Whereas for the very young child we might wish to restrict the frequency investigation to his parents, for older children we have to take account of a more diverse exposure.

Relative frequency may also be important for historical linguistics. Anttila cites a number of examples of the role of relative frequency in promoting or resisting sound changes and morphological changes (Anttila 1972: 101, 187 f; and cf. Winter 1971). A description of an earlier period cannot, of course, draw on the judgements of relative frequency by native speakers of the language. But a conception of the language system as non-static and unstable requires even a synchronic description to take account of the process of change (cf. Vachek 1966: 31—37). Labov's studies of speech communities in Martha's Vineyard and New York City provide analyses of linguistic changes in progress, based on frequency data drawn from variation due to differences in age-groups and to sociological factors (cf. Labov 1972 a: 160—182).

Comparison of genetically-unrelated languages has been undertaken to establish typological classifications of languages. Characterizations of languages are only valid if they take account of features that are important rather than marginal in the languages. Here too frequency of occurrence may legitimately be considered in deciding what is fundamental in a language (cf. Greenberg 1960; Kučera and Monroe 1968). And here too it may be legitimate to take account of felt preponderance, where feasible.

Linguists who emphasize a functional approach to language description are interested in the differential use of language according to such factors as the medium, the speaker's attitude to what he is speaking about, his attitude to his audience, the purpose of the communication, and the format he uses (cf. Crystal and Davy 1969; Dubský 1972). Categories of use or combinations of these categories are sometimes treated as if they were distinct varieties of the language — for example scientific English, legal English, advertising English, telephone conversation English — and the language of a variety is described in isolation or a comparison is made between varieties. Normally, these differences of style — style being used in a wider sense than in the context of literary criticism or literary stylistics — are marked by differences in the frequencies with which certain linguistic features are exploited rather than by absolute distinctions. At all events, frequencies have been computed to characterize such language varieties (e.g., Leech 1966; Huddleston 1971: Pytelka 1972), and studies of particular aspects of language have incorporated comparisons of frequencies in the varieties (e.g., Svartvik 1966: 152—155; Mistrík 1971). So far these stylistic studies have been based on frequency counts in texts, but it could be

argued that what matters here too is the perception of what is characteristic of particular varieties rather than actual frequencies.

Some variation in language use corresponds to diversity in the region,
socio-economic class, or ethnic community of speakers. Differences
between regional and social dialects may also be manifested in the relative frequencies with which certain linguistic features are used. Within
the last few years, socio-linguists (notably Labov) have produced
evidence for the existence of variable rules in language that account for
differences in language between sociologically-distinguished speech
groups. Furthermore, the rules also apply to stylistic differentiation
within and between the groups (Labov 1972 a: 216—251; 1973:
76—85). The frequency with which a form is used or with which one
variable is used instead of a competing variable depends on the linguistic
environment or on such extralinguistic factors as the relationship
between the participants in the discourse. The variable rule incorporates
an indication of the probability with which the rule will apply for a given
sample under a given configuration of factors. For certain variables that
differ in prestige value in the community, Labov found that there was an
interaction between sociological and stylistic factors such that lower
social groups used more non-prestige variants than higher groups, and
all groups used more non-prestige variants as the context became more
informal. Labov has formulated this new type of rule within the framework of a model of transformational grammar that takes account of the
use of language within a social context. He has claimed that variation
within a speech community is systematic and regular, and based on
quantitative relations (Labov 1972 b: 124—129; but cf. Bickerton 1973:
17—21).

Variable rules have been formulated on the evidence of data obtained
from direct observation of language use. If their psychological reality
can be established it would indicate that the native speaker's knowledge
of relative frequency is an important part of their linguistic competence.
But can native speakers report with confidence on this kind of knowledge in at least clear cases? Labov has asserted, without citing any
evidence, that "no one is aware of this competence [to accept, preserve,
and interpret rules with variable constraints], and there are no intuitive
judgements accessible to reveal it to us. Instead, naive perception of our
own and others' behavior is usually categorical, and only careful study
of languages in use will demonstrate the existence of this capacity to
operate with variable rules" (Labov 1972 a: 226). At the same time, he
notes that certain judgements require "the observer to be (unconsciously) sensitive to frequency." Labov's assertion appears in the
context of a discussion of variables that are strong markers of social
values, markers differing sharply in prestige. For such variables, categorical perception is perhaps common, so that up to a certain frequency

the variable is not noticed at all, while beyond that frequency the variable is perceived as always being used.

But much language variation does not evoke social prejudice. Speakers of English make many grammatical choices that preserve cognitive meaning. A tentative classification of optional rules that state choices is given in Fraser 1973. Examples include the choice between passive and active, between full and reduced conjunction, between the indirect object construction and the *to* phrase, and between full and contracted forms of *be*. Similarly, speakers can choose the positions of adverbials, whether to put the particle of a phrasal verb before or after the noun phrase, and whether to use pro-forms. A number of factors may affect the choice, such as the immediate linguistic environment (e.g., the length or complexity of relevant constituents, or the phonotactic context), the preceding linguistic environment (e.g., the information that has already been conveyed), the speaker's decision on the distribution of prominence to the parts of his communication, and a complex of stylistic factors (e.g., the medium, the purpose of the discourse, or the level of formality). There is evidence that native speakers are aware of relative frequency between such variants. Fraser 1973 (13 f.) gives examples of environments favoring the *to* phrase equivalent over the indirect object construction, basing his predictions on "native intuitions of a few English speakers and a limited amount of observation of the speech of university students."

In an experiment to investigate the relationship between frequency and acceptability judgements, I presented subjects with pairs of sentences that exhibit minimal syntactic variation, for example *Marvin saw Susan/Susan was seen by Marvin; He has spoken to me several times since he came here/He spoke to me several times since he came here; We were waiting for three hours on Monday/We were waiting on Monday for three hours; We're not going/We aren't going; Tom gave the boy a dime/ Tom gave a dime to the boy.* The subjects were 87 linguistically-naive students, mostly freshmen and sophomores, attending an elementary History course at the University of Wisconsin-Milwaukee.[4] They were predominantly from Wisconsin or other Midwest states. Their ages ranged from 18 to 26 and two-thirds were males.

The subjects were asked to judge 50 minimal pairs of sentences (randomized for each subject) for their overall frequency in the English

[4]  I am grateful to Professor John Schroeder of the Department of History at the University of Wisconsin-Milwaukee, who gave me the opportunity to conduct the experiments. I am heavily indebted to Professor Robert Remstad of the Department of Educational Psychology for advice on statistics and to Paul Keuler of the Social Science Research Facility of the College of Letters and Science for the computational work. I am also indebted to a number of students who helped in the administration of the experiments or in the scoring of the results.

Language on a five-place scale, the extremes of which were marked *very rare* and *very frequent*. A week later they were asked to judge the identical pairs of sentences for their acceptability on a five-place scale, with the extremes marked *completely unacceptable* and *perfectly OK*. The subjects were untimed, though they were encouraged to work quickly.

The mean scores for the two types of judgements differed less than the value of one position in the five-place scale for any of the 100 sentences. The greatest difference was 0.94, in 67 sentences it was less than 0.5, and in as many as 22 sentences it was less than 0.1. The difference was predominantly in the direction of the Acceptability mean score being higher than the Frequency mean score: 86 out of 100 sets of judgements. Of the 14 sets where the reverse occurred — Frequency mean score higher than Acceptability mean score — the mean difference was less than 0.1 in all but one set, where it was less than 0.21.

The relationship between the two types of judgements on the 100 sentences was also analyzed for individual subjects. Two measures were devised for intra-subject consistency. A subject can be said to be consistent if he marked the same position on both occasions ('Direct Hits'). A weaker acknowledgement of consistency between the two judgements will allow for adjacent positions as well; that is to say, the subject will be considered consistent not only if he marked identical positions but also if on the second occasion he marked an adjacent position, whether immediately higher or lower ('Direct Hits ±1'). The second measure is a justifiable indication of the extent of agreement, since the subject is after all making judgements on two independent scales. The results for the two measures are given in table 1. The first column gives a percentage range for the number of subjects; the second column shows for how many sentences the given percentage range achieved 'Direct Hits'; the third column shows for how many sentences the given percentage range achieved 'Direct Hits ±1'. The table shows that in 88 of the 100 sentences 65 % or more of the subjects gave either identical or adjacent positions in their two judgements.

Table 1
Intra-subject consistency in frequency and acceptability scores.

| Percentage range | Direct Hits | Direct Hits ±1 |
|---|---|---|
| 95—100 | | 4 |
| 90— 94 | | 5 |
| 85— 89 | | 2 |
| 80— 84 | | 13 |
| 75— 79 | 1 | 19 |
| 70— 74 | | 25 |

| Percentage range | Direct Hits | Direct Hits ± 1 |
|---|---|---|
| 65 — 69 | 3 | 20 |
| 60 — 64 | 2 | 9 |
| 55 — 59 | 1 | 3 |
| 50 — 54 | 2 | |
| 45 — 49 | 8 | |
| 40 — 44 | 12 | |
| 35 — 39 | 23 | |
| 30 — 34 | 24 | |
| 25 — 29 | 20 | |
| 20 — 24 | 4 | |

As general measures for the two sets of data, we can devise an intra-subject consistency index by adding percentages of subjects achieving Hits and dividing the total number by 100, the number of paired judgements. The intra-subject consistency index for 'Direct Hits' is 37.2 %, while for 'Direct Hits ± 1' it is 74.6 %. Thus, if we allow a one-position difference for the two kinds of judgements, there was a good measure of agreement in individual responses.

We can also consider consistency in the directionality of judgements within the minimal pairs. Again, two measures were devised. A subject can be said to be consistent if on both occasions he marked the same sentence as higher than the other in the pair or if he marked both as equal on the scale. The subject is totally inconsistent if he judges the frequency of sentence *a* as higher than sentence *b* but judges the acceptability of a as lower than *b*. A weaker indication of consistency will also allow for the subject to mark the same position for the sentences on one occasion and different positions on the second occasion ('partial consistency'); for example, he judges *a* and *b* as equally frequent, but *a* as more acceptable than *b*. The three columns in table 2 give the percentage range, the number of sentences where there is total consistency in direction of judgements, and the number of sentences where there is either total consistency or partial consistency.

Table 2
Intra-subject consistency in directionality of paired judgements for frequency and acceptability.

| Percentage range | Total consis-tency | Total + partial consistency |
|---|---|---|
| 95 — 100 | | 4 |
| 90 — 94 | | 4 |

| Percentage range | Total consistency | Total + partial consistency |
|---|---|---|
| 85— 89 |    | 8  |
| 80— 84 | 3  | 10 |
| 75— 79 | 3  | 17 |
| 70— 74 | 2  | 7  |
| 65— 69 | 3  |    |
| 60— 64 | 5  |    |
| 55— 59 | 5  |    |
| 50— 54 | 11 |    |
| 45— 49 | 5  |    |
| 40— 44 | 8  |    |
| 35— 39 | 5  |    |

As can be seen from the table, in 32 of the pairs over 50 % of the subjects marked the sentences in the same direction for both judgements, while in all 50 pairs over 70 % of the subjects were either totally or partially consistent. Total inconsistency ranged for individual pairs from 3.6 % of the subjects to 28.6 %. The intra-subject consistency index for total consistency is 55.1 %, while for combined total and partial consistency it is 81.7 %. The index for inconsistency — contrary directions — is therefore just over 18 %.

The analysis of results supports the hypothesis that there is an association between frequency and acceptability judgements, with the latter type of judgement tending to register higher positions on a scale. Moreover, the analysis provides support for the suggestion that frequency and acceptability ratings for a given pair of sentences will tend to go in the same direction.

If further research establishes the sensitivity of frequency judgements to variation in the linguistic environment and to stylistic factors, we shall have a method of investigating an important aspect of the communicative competence of native speakers. If, in addition, the results of frequency experiments are generally in harmony with the evidence of frequency in corpus studies, we shall have an easily-available source for information on relative frequency in use, though stylistic variables must be controlled for valid comparisons to be made. Even if there is a discrepancy between objective and perceived frequencies, perceived frequencies have a psycholigical reality (cf. Carroll 1971 and Galbraith and Underwood 1973 for experiments involving judgements of word frequency).

I have suggested a number of areas in linguistic research where information about judgements of syntactic frequency is relevant. There are also two areas of applied linguistics where such information will be helpful: foreign language teaching and stylistics. It seems reasonable to recommend that learners of a language should generally be taught the more frequent structures at an earlier stage. In particular, where there are alternative forms of a construction (for example, various positions of adverbials or full and elliptical forms) they should be told which is the most common form, with explanations of reasons for the choice of the less common alternatives, e.g., balance or relative informational prominence. Perceived frequency may be a better indication of the norm than studies of frequency of occurrence. Frequency judgements can also provide norms for comparative studies in stylistics. Differences that are perceived in style can be attributed at least in part to differences that are perceived in frequency, including syntactic frequency.

# References

Anttila, R., 1972. An introduction to historical and comparative linguistics. New York: Macmillan.

Bever, T. G., 1970. The cognitive basis for linguistic structures. In: J. R. Hayes (ed.) 1970, 279—362.

Bickerton, D., 1973. The structure of polylectal grammars. In: R. Shuy (ed.) 1973, 17—42.

Bolinger, D., 1969. Categories, features, attributes. Brno Studies in English 8, 38—41.

Brown, R., and C. Hanlon, 1970. Derivational complexity and order of acquisition in child speech. In: J. R. Hayes (ed.) 1970, 11—53.

Campbell, R., and R. Wales, 1970. The study of language acquisition. In: J. Lyons (ed.), New horizons in linguistics, 242—60. Harmondsworth: Penguin.

Carroll, J. B., 1971. Measurement properties of subjective magnitude extimates of word frequency. Journal of Verbal Learning and Verbal Behavior 10, 722—29.

Chomsky, C., 1969. The acquisition of syntax in children from 5 to 10. Cambridge, Mass.: MIT Press.

Chomsky, N., 1965. Aspects of the theory of syntax. Cambridge, Mass.: MIT Press.

Chomsky, N., 1970. Remarks on nominalization. In: R. A. Jacobs and P. S. Rosenbaum (eds.), Readings in English transformational grammar, Waltham, Mass.: Ginn. 184—221.

Corder, S. P., 1973. Introducing applied linguistics. Harmondsworth: Penguin.

Crystal, D., and D. Davy, 1969. Investigating English Style. London: Longman.

Daneš, F., 1966. The relation of centre and periphery as a language universal. Travaux linguistiques de Prague 2, 9—21.

Derwing, B. L., 1973. Transformational grammar as a theory of language acquisition. London: Cambridge Univ. Press.

Dubský, J., 1972. The Prague conception of functional style. In: V. Fried (ed.), 112—27.

Ervin-Tripp, S., 1970. Discourse agreement: How children answer questions. In: J. R. Hayes (ed.) 1970, 79—107.

Fillmore, C. J., 1973. A grammarian looks to sociolinguistics. In: R. W. Shuy (ed.) 1973, 273—87.

Firth, J. R., 1957. Papers in linguistics 1934—1951. London: Oxford Univ. Press.

Fraser, B., 1973. Optional rules in grammar. In: R. Shuy (ed.) 1973, 1—15.

Fried, V. (ed.), 1972. The Prague School of linguistics and language teaching. London: Oxford Univ. Press.

Galbraith, R. C., and B. J. Underwood, 1973. Perceived frequency of concrete and abstract words. Memory and Cognition 1, 56—60.

Greenbaum, S., 1970. Verb-intensifier collocations in English: An experimental approach. The Hague: Mouton.

Greenberg, J. H., 1960. A quantitative approach to the morphological typology of language. IJAL 26, 178—94.

Greenberg, J. H. (ed.), 1966. Universals of language. Cambridge, Mass.: MIT Press.

Greenberg, J. H., 1966. Some Universals of grammar with particular reference to the order of meaningful elements. In: J. H. Greenberg (ed.) 1966, 73—113.

Halliday, M. A. K., 1959. The language of the Chinese 'Secret History of the Mongols'. Oxford: The Philological Society.

Halliday, M. A. K., 1967 a. Notes on transitivity and theme in English: Part I. Journal of Linguistics 3, 37—81.

Halliday, M. A. K., 1967 b. Intonation and grammar in British English. The Hague: Mouton.

Harris, Z., 1968. Mathematical structures of language. New York: Wiley.

Hayes, J. R. (ed.), 1970. Cognition and the development of language. New York: Wiley.

Huddleston, R. D., 1971. The sentence in written English: A syntactic study based on scientific texts. London: Cambridge Univ. Press.

Jakobson, R., 1966. Implications of language universals for linguistics. In: J. H. Greenberg (ed.) 1966, 263—78.

Kimball, J., 1973. Seven principles of surface structure parsing in natural language. Cognition 2, 15—57.

Kučera, H., and W. N. Francis, 1967. Computational analysis of present-day American English. Providence, R. I.: Brown Univ. Press.

Kučera, H., and G. K. Monroe, 1968. A comparative quantitative phonology of Russian, Czech, and German. New York: Elsevier.

Labov, W., 1972 a. Sociolinguistic patterns. Philadelphia, Univ. of Pennsylvania Press.

Labov, W., 1972 b. Language in the inner city. Philadelphia: Univ. of Pennsylvania Press.

Labov, W., 1973. Where do grammars Stop? In: R. W. Shuy (ed.) 1973, 43—88.

Lakoff, G., 1973. Fuzzy grammar and the performance/competence terminology game. In: C. Corum, T. C. Smith-Stark, and A. Weiser (eds.), Papers from the Ninth Regional Meeting of the Chicago Linguistic Society, 271—91. Chicago: Univ. of Chicago Dept. of Linguistics.

Langendoen, D. T., and T. G. Bever, 1973. Can a Not Unhappy Person be called a Not Sad One? In: S. Anderson and P. Kiparsky (eds.), A festschrift for Morris Halle, 392—409. New York: Holt, Rinehart and Winston.

Langendoen, D. T., N. Kalish-Landon and J. Dore, 1973. Dative questions: A study in the relation of acceptability to grammaticality of an English sentence type. Cognition 2, 451—78.

Leech, G. N., 1966. English in advertising: A linguistic study of advertising in Great Britain. London: Longman.

Lyons, J., 1968. Introduction to theoretical linguistics. London, Cambridge Univ. Press.

Mistrík, J., 1971. Frequency of syntactic types in the Slovak language. Prague Studies in Mathematical Linguistics 3, 35—43.

O'Connor, J. D., and J. L. M. Trim, 1953. Vowel, consonant and syllable — A phonological definition. Word 9, 103—23.

Pytelka, J., 1972. The Prague School and studies in the language of commerce. In: V. Fried (ed.) 1972, 211—23.

Quirk, R., S. Greenbaum, G. Leech and J. Svartvik, 1972. A grammar of contemporary English. London: Longman/New York: Academic Press.

Reich, P. A., 1969. The finiteness of natural language. Language 45, 831—43.

Roceric, A., 1973. Statistical linguistics and theoretical linguistics. Language Sciences 26, 25—8.

Schlesinger, I. M., 1971. On linguistic competence. In: Y. Bar-Hillel (ed.), Pragmatics of natural languages, 150—72. Dordrecht (Holland): Reidel.

Shuy, R. W. (ed.), 1973. Georgetown University Monograph Series on Languages and Linguistics, 23. Washington, D. C.: Georgetown Univ. Press.

Sinclair, J. McH., 1966. Beginning the study of lexis. In: C. E. Bazell et al. (eds.), In memory of J. R. Firth, 355—58. London: Longman.

Svartvik, J., 1966. On voice in the English verb. The Hague: Mouton.

Trnka, B., 1968. A phonological analysis of present-day Standard English. Alabama: Univ. of Alabama Press.

Vachek, J., 1966. On the integration of the peripheral elements into the system of language. Travaux Linguistiques de Prague 2, 23—37.

Watt, W. C., 1970 a. On two hypotheses concerning psycholinguistics. In: J. R. Hayes (ed.) 1970, 137—220.

Watt, W. C., 1970 b. Comments on the Brown and Hanlon paper. In: J. R. Hayes (ed.) 1970, 55—78.

Winter, W., 1971. Formal frequency and linguistic change: Some preliminary comments. Folia Linguistica 5, 55—61.

# Syntactic Markedness and Frequency of Occurrence[*]

Linda J. Schwartz

1.0 In Greenberg (1966) a number of criteria are cited which are taken to jointly characterize the notion of relative markedness in syntax and phonology. These are taken mainly from Jakobson (1939), Hjelmslev (1953), Trnka (1958) and Trubetzkoy (1939), and are summarized in (1) below.

(1)   1. *Universal implicational statements:* given a statement of the form 'If a language has A, then it necessarily has B but not *vice versa*', this is to be interpreted as characterizing the *implicans* as marked and the *implicatum* as unmarked.
   2. *Zero expression:* the unmarked term may show a zero inflection in contrast to the marked term, e.g., *prince* (unmarked) vs. *princess* (marked).
   3. *Par excellence expression:* the unmarked category may respresent either the generic category or the specific opposite member of the marked category, e.g., *man* 'human being/male human being' (unmarked) vs. *woman* 'female human being' (marked).
   4. *Facultative expression:* the overt grammatical expression of a category is optional; the form without overt expression (i.e., the unmarked form) may be interpreted as having or lacking the category, e.g., English use of some terms like *author* and *poet* to represent writers of either gender, vs. *authoress* or *poetess* used only with reference to female writers.
   5. *Syncretization:* distinctions existing in the unmarked member of a category are neutralized in the marked member, e.g., in English the masculine-feminine distinction in third person pronouns exists in the singular but is neutralized in the plural.
   6. *Contextual neutralization* (Hjelmslev's 'participation'): the

* I am grateful to J. Ard, F. Householder, A. Raun and A. Valdman for their comments and suggestions on various points raised here, and to Gerald Sanders for his careful reading and criticism of a preliminary draft. An abbreviated version of this paper was given at the 30th University of Kentucky Foreign Language Conference, 29 April 1977, Lexington, Ky.

unmarked member of an opposition appears in certain contexts where the marked member does not, e.g., in Hungarian, only the singular form of nouns may appear with cardinal numbers.

7. *Degree of morphological variation:* more morphological alternation appears in the unmarked member of an opposition, e.g., in Classical Arabic base verb forms show internal vowel changes in the imperfect, while derived forms do not.

8. *Defectivation:* the marked category may lack certain categories present in the unmarked. [1]

9. *Dominance:* when a heterogeneous collection is to be named, (i) one category — the unmarked — is regularly chosen as representative, and (ii) in agreement when words of various categories have a common modifier, the modifier is from the unmarked category. [2] An example of (i) is the Spanish use of the form *padre* 'father' in the plural to mean either 'fathers' or parents,' and of (ii) is the use in Spanish of the masculine plural agreement in adjectives which agree with conjoined noun phrases of both genders.

10. *Text Frequency:* the unmarked member of an opposition will have a higher text frequency than the marked member.

This paper will attempt to examine the various markedness criteria in relation to each other, concentrating particularly on the relation of text frequency to the other criteria. This relation can be stated in the form of the hypothesis given in (2).

(2) *Relative Frequency Hypothesis* [3]

Markedness relations as determined by relative text frequency will (genrally/always) agree with markedness relations as determined by zero expression, dominance, syncretization, etc.

If it is in fact true that text frequency always correlates positively with other factors which determine relative markedness, then the linguist would have an extremely effective tool for automatically determining

---

[1] Greenberg suggests that defectivation is a sub-type of syncretization in that another way of viewing this lack of categories is that the distinction between categories is neutralized in the marked category; we may consider this to be so for our purposes.

[2] Greenberg considers dominance to be a sub-type of *par excellence* expression in that it represents a category which may be either specific and opposed to other categories or general and covering the categories in opposition. While this is true of sense (i), it is not clear how (ii) can be subsumed under *par excellence* expression, and thus for our purposes these will be considered separate predicates.

[3] This hypothesis is stated here in both a weak ("generally") and a strong ("always") form; only the strong form is actually considered in the discussion which follows.

the markedness relationships among a set of linguistic objects of the same category.[4] However, the existence of such a tool would be more than a matter of simple convenience, for it might be the only criterion for determining relative markedness relations which could be applied to all pairs of terms in opposition in all languages, since, e.g., not all languages which have singular and plural nominal inflection will have zero expression, syncretization in the plural, etc., but text frequency will always in principle be available for examination, wherever the singular-plural distinction is expressed syntactically.

Although Greenberg does discuss the logical relations among a few of these criteria — which we will examine in Section 4 — for the most part, it is not clear why these various evidently independent factors should converge to jointly characterize one category of an opposition as marked relative to another, nor is it clear what linguistic significance it has if they do. However, if they do so converge, this is an extremely interesting fact, and worthy of further investigation into the nature of what linguistic significance this convergence may have and into the nature of the relationships among the criteria.

That is, if all of these criteria can be used independently or jointly to determine relative markedness, one way of defining the notion 'relative markedness' would be as a conjunction of these predicates, any one of which is sufficient to apply the definition to an object which conforms with that criterion. As Greenberg suggests (p. 33), we should certainly want to go beyond this type of definition to a level at which the various interrelations among these predicates are established, and the definition of relative markedness concomitantly reduced to just that predicate/those predicates which do not follow logically from any other predicate in the definition or from any other predicate in the definition in conjunction with any universal facts about language or specific facts about a given language.

In the following section I will first examine and evaluate the arguments which have been put forth for the non-independence of the criterion of frequency in characterizing phonological markedness and discuss several specific phoneme frquency counts which bear on the issues raised here. In Section 3, I will return to contrast the role of frequency in relation to markedness in syntax to its role in phonology, addressing specifically the question of the independence or non-indep-

---

[4]   This is, of course, true to the extent that the text is a representative sample, i.e., that factors such as content, style, etc. have been controlled for in the sampling process (see Householder (1960) for a discussion of the problem caused by drawing conclusions concerning the typological classification of languages without first determining the range of stylistic variation within a single language on the parameters used for typological ordering along a continuum).

endence of frequency from facts about the syntactic and semantic structure of natural languages. I will examine a number of sets of frequency statistics currently available on syntactic data and suggest and evaluate a number of testable hypotheses from which these particular frequency statistics may be deduced. It is hoped that this examination will be suggestive of some specific and potentially productive areas of research in the area of syntactic frequency investigations with the goal of providing some elements of explanation for the apparent correlation between frequency and the other criteria given in (1). The final section addresses the question of the relations among these criteria, and concludes that a number of them can be deduced from the notion of relative frequency and general cognitive functions involving memory as well as the basic function of language as a system of communication, while others of the criteria do not seem to be deducible from frequency but rather probably are factors (though not the only factors) in determining relative frequency.

2.0 Greenberg cites several reasons for the assumption that relatively unmarked phonological segments will have a greater text frequency than relatively marked segments. In his initial discussion of phonological markedness and frequency (p. 14), he cites Zipf's Principle of Least Effort (Zipf 1935), and again later in his discussion of the relations of frequency and other markedness criteria, the notion of ease of articulation as a source of explanation for many kinds of phonological change is cited, where he suggests that this correlation is deducible from other factors in phonology but not so in syntax. Specifically, Greenberg states (p. 65) that "while frequency is a mere resultant, though a very important one, of overall diachronic tendencies in phonology, it is tempting to judge its role in grammar-semantics as primary."

If in phonology relative markedness is defined by reference to articulatory and acoustic complexity, and since according to the Principle of Least Effort, the less articulatorily complex alternative will be favored, all other things being equal, it follows that the more articulatorily complex — in other words, the more marked — phonological alternative will be avoided by speakers whenever possible, and therefore the less marked alternative will be more frequent.

However, besides the ease of articulation produced by loss of additional features and resulting in neutralization to the unmarked member ('paradigmatic ease' in Greenberg's terms), Greenberg points out that there is also an ease of articulation which is assimilatory in nature ('syntagmatic ease' in his terms) and which has the effect of producing more marked segments (i.e., segments with more complex articulations), e.g., nasal vowels from a vowel followed by a nasal consonant, palatalized consonants from a consonant followed by a palatal vowel, etc.

Despite these conflicting results regarding markedness and ease of articulation, Greenberg maintains that the relation between frequency and markedness still follows from this principle, because in the case of more complex segments produced due to syntagmatic ease, the environments which produce the new marked phoneme will always be a subset of the environments of the protophoneme. Though Greenberg does not do so, this same argument can be extended to the synchronic level in that the unmarked member of an opposition appears in positions of neutralization. Then, if there are some contexts in which both the marked and unmarked members of an opposition occur, and some contexts in which only the unmarked member of the opposition can occur, the set of contexts in which the marked member can occur will be a proper subset of the set of contexts in which the unmarked member can occur.

It is totally fallacious, however, to move — as Greenberg does (Cf. p. 64) — from this premise to the conclusion that because the relatively unmarked member of an opposition appears in a wider range of contexts, it will necessarily appear more frequently in text than the relatively marked member, whether the consideration is diachronic or synchronic. This does not follow, because the sound-meaning pairing is arbitrary for the vast majority of morphemes in any human language, and because, as a result of this, a marked member of a phonological opposition can accidentally appear in morphemes which will be of extremely high frequency for non-phonological — i.e., grammatical/semantic — reasons. This fallacious argument form will be referred to as the Type-Token Fallacy.

For example, the voiced interdental fricative in English would be considered marked relative to the voiceless interdental fricative on the basis of its greater articulatory complexity, but because of the fact that it appears in the English definite article, the demonstrative pronouns and adjectives, and the third person plural pronoun, its text frequency is significantly higher than that of the voiceless interdental fricative (Cf. Roberts 1965).

Similarly, in German, although on the basis of both articulatory complexity and neutralization, the voiced dental stop would be considered marked relative to the corresponding voiceless dental stop, because [d] appears in the German definite article, a morpheme with a high text frequency, the absolute frequency relationship between [t] and [d] cannot be a logical consequence of the set-subset relations of their distributions in terms of the phonological environments in which they appear. This is because for the environmental distribution of members of an opposition to be the determining factor in their relative text frequency, in that environment where either member may appear, they would have to appear at least equally frequently in text; however this is not the case in this instance — [d] is the most frequent initial sound in text, while [t] is only the ninth most frequent (Cf. Meier 1967: 267).

It must be concluded, therefore, that whatever effect the diachronic factors of marked phoneme development have on text frequency of marked and unmarked phonemes, that effect is not sufficient to deduce their relative text frequency, because of two non-phonological factors which intervene. First, if the sound-meaning pairing is arbitrary, the gross number of lexical items in a language which have a particular sound configuration may vary. Second, text frequency of individual lexical items is dependent on their grammatical and semantic function. Thus, it should be expected that instances like the German and English examples could be found. This is not to deny that the environmental restrictions (diachronic or synchronic) on the marked phoneme have an ultimate effect on text frequency, but rather to attempt to put this into perspective relative to other factors. The calculation of text frequency must be a function of total number of lexical entries with the "subset environment" and the chance factors involved in one of this subset of lexical forms being chosen from the total lexicon for a high-frequency morpheme, i.e., being paired with a syntactic/semantic meaning with a high frequency of occurrence. It would be expected, for example, that for languages with an overt definite article, that morpheme would have a high frequency of occurrence, etc.

To summarize, ease of articulation alone is not sufficient to account for the assumed text frequency relations of marked and unmarked sounds, since while language change to facilitate paradigmatic ease produces articulatorily simpler segments, language change to facilitate syntagmatic ease produces articulatorily complex segments. Nor is the range of (diachronic or synchronic) environments of occurrence of marked members of a phonemic contrast relative to the unmarked members sufficient to account for the relation between frequency and complexity of articulation, because range deals with distribution and text deals with tokens. Since the sound-meaning pairing is essentially arbitrary, token frequency is dependent on grammatical/semantic factors as well as phonological factors.


3.0 We now return to the question of text frequency in relation to the other criteria in (1) in syntax and to an investigation of possible explanations for why frequency is a correlate of these criteria in those cases where this seems to be true. This will be done by examining a number of specific instances where the relevant text frequency statistics are available and where other markedness criteria can be brought to bear on the issue, concentrating on the logical and explanatory relations between relative frequency and the specific structures being considered. Most examples are drawn from Modern Spanish, with frequency statistics from Julliand & Chang-Rodriguez (1964).

3.1 In Spanish, all nouns belong to one of two gender-classes, distinguished by the form of the definite and indefinite articles with which they occur. In cases where an animate plural consists semantically of members of both genders, the masculine form of the article is used, and where the noun varies, the masculine form of the noun is used, e.g., *el padre* 'the father,' *la madre* 'the mother,' *los padres* 'the parents/fathers,' *las madres* 'the mothers; *nosotros* 'we, masc. & fem./masc.,' *nosotras* 'we, fem.' In addition, the masculine form is used generically, as in *el hombre* 'the man/Man.' Thus, the masculine gender is characterized as unmarked relative to the feminine gender by the criteria of dominance and *par excellence* expression.

Also, for some noun stems the masculine form has zero expression, while the feminine is marked with an overt suffix (e.g., *profesor* 'teacher/male teacher' vs. *profesora* 'female teacher'), but the converse situation, where the feminine has zero expression but the masculine has an overt gender suffix does not occur.

In addition, in noun-adjective agreement (as in noun-determiner agreement mentioned above), the masculine plural has dominance over the feminine, e.g., *El hombre y la mujer son simpáticos* 'The man and the woman are nice + masc. pl.'

Thus, zero expression, *par excellence* expression, and dominance jointly converge to characterize the masculine gender as unmarked relative to the feminine gender. If the Relative Frequency Hypothesis stated in (2) is correct, then it should be expected that masculine nouns should show a higher text frequency than feminine nouns. I used as a means of determining the relative text frequency of masculine and feminine nouns the combined frequency of the uses of all forms of the Spanish article in the Julliand Chang-Rodriguez study, and determined that of the total use of all articles, masculine forms appeared 54.6 % of the time, and feminine forms 45.4 %.[5]

We know ask why such a correlation should be expected to exist in this kind of situation. It is not possible to use the parallel of the phonological distribution argument here to deduce text frequency, for the same reasons that it couldn't be used in phonology. For while it is true that the masculine gender has a wider range of usage than the feminine gender with respect to animate nouns (i.e., the *par excellence* and domi-

---

[5]  I might point out that these statistics show the two genders as being much closer together than the statistics on Spanish gender given in Greenberg (p. 40) — his statistics were taken from the 100 most frequent adjectives in Spanish, which represents neither a complete text nor a random sampling.

nance usage), this cannot explain the greater text frequency without committing the Type-Token Fallacy.

We might add an additional hypothesis to avoid the Type-Token Fallacy, such as the one given in (3).

(3)  *Semantic Range Hypothesis*
     Human beings, in communicating, refer/tend to refer equally to all points within a semantic range.

Specifically, this hypothesis applied to the point under discussion would say that in human communication, equal reference is made to masculine and feminine animate referents. From this hypothesis it would necessarily follow that the specific gender which had a wider range of usage in the category of animate nouns must also have a greater frequency of usage for animate nouns. To my knowledge, there are no current statistics available on which this hypothesis can be tested in a relatively straightforward way. Note, however, that reference to such a hypothesis would be possible to explain frequency data in syntax but impossible in the corresponding situation in phonology, because in syntax — at least in instances such as this — the meaning will determine the range of usage. That is, given that one gender (masculine) covers a larger area of the joint semantic range than the other in that it can be used to refer to the full range 'animate being' as well as to the sub-range 'male animate being,' while the other gender covers only the sub-range 'female animate being,' the syntactic distribution of the first gender is greater.

But even if this hypothesis should turn out to be true, the particular gender system which we are examining consists of inanimate as well as animate nouns, though the zero expression criterion applies only to animates, as well as *par excellence* expression and dominance-(i).[6]

If we assume that inanimate nouns are (synchronically) arbitrarily assigned to one of the gender classes, there is no way of knowing whether a disproportionately large number might not be accidentally assigned to the marked gender,[7] thus possibly influencing text frequency in favor of that gender. Several hypotheses suggest themselves that could either prevent or neutralize this situation; these are given in (4) and (5).

---

[6]  This situation raises the question of whether, in inanimate nouns, either gender is to be considered marked. However, I see no syntactic reason apart from not fitting these criteria to distinguish, say, animate masculine from inanimate masculine, because their syntactic behavior is the same with respect to determiner, pronoun, and adjective agreement, which are the only syntactic processes that depend on gender-class in Spanish.

[7]  Since this would be possible, though not probable, in random gender assignment, the effect discussed here bears only on the strong form of the Relative Frequency Hypothesis.

(4) *Hypothesis of Unmarked Gender Assignment*
Assignment of inanimate nouns to a gender class is skewed in favor of the least marked gender.
(5) *Animate Interest Hypothesis*
Human beings tend to talk more about animate entities than inanimate entities.

The hypothesis in (4) could be tested by either an extended sampling of the Spanish lexicon or by a count extending over the total lexicon. I have thus far done only a small-scale sampling of the inanimate nouns on 20 pages of Cassell's *Spanish-English Dictionary,* and found that out of 921 inanimate houns, 453 or 49.2 % were masculine, and 468 or 50.8 % were feminine. Should such a minimal difference occur on a larger scale, we could conclude that gender assignment does not tend to favor either gender to a significant degree.

The hypothesis in (5) was checked on the data from the Julliand & Chang-Rodriguez study, and no evidence was found there to confirm it; in fact, the opposite seemed to be true, in that in the first 500 most frequent words, inanimate nouns outnumbered animates by approximately four to one (specifically, animates accounted for only 20.6 % of the nouns in the 500 most frequent words). Should this finding be borne out on a larger scale, the Animate Interest Hypothesis would be shown to be false.

Some conclusions on how arbitrary class assignment does work in languages can be reached on the basis of class shifts, however. For example, Latin inanimate nouns moved into the masculine or feminine gender class in Spanish mainly on the basis of whether their endings in Vulgar Latin were the same as the gender inflection for most masculine animates (i.e., *-o)* or as the gender inflection for most feminine animates (i.e., *-a)* — that is, the new grammatical classification was based on phonological rather than semantic similarity; e.g., Latin *úlimus* 'elm' fem. > V. Lat. *olmo* > Spanish *olmo,* masc. Also, a number of doublets occur in the Spanish verb system, where borrowed forms, being phonetically closer to Latin from which they were borrowed, were systematically placed in a different conjugation class than the corresponding vulgar terms, which had undergone sound change, e.g., *rumpĕrĕ* 'break' > *romper* (2nd conj.) but *interrumpir* 'interrupt,' (3rd conj.). Again, no semantic generalization would seem to account for this particular situation. If it is true, then, that so-called arbitrary gender assignment tends to be at least in part phonologically conditioned, then it would seem that the Hypothesis of Unmarked Gender Assignment is not tenable as the only principle of gender assignment.

Thus, while it seems that in the Spanish gender system, the criteria of *par excellence* expression, dominance, and zero expression weakly correlate with text frequency data in determining the relative markedness relations between masculine and feminine gender, the hypotheses examined here for why the frequency relation should be as it is have been seen to be either false (on the basis of the limited data available) or untested (though in principle testable).

3.2 An instance where at first glance the relative frequency of marked and unmarked categories seems to follow from other characteristics of the language is found in case-marking systems. It has been claimed (Hjelmslev 1935, Greenberg 1966) that the case which includes among its uses that of marking subjects of intransitive sentences is universally unmarked relative to all other contrasting cases in a case system. It would follow from this assumption and the Relative Frequency Hypothesis that this case (which will be refered to as 'nominative' following traditional terminology) must also show the highest test frequency. This is in fact true in three of the four languages with nominal or pronominal case systems which I have examined:[8] the personal pronoun system of Spanish (Julliand & Chang-Rodriguez 1964), the French personal pronoun system (Etudes Statistiques sur le Vocabulaire Français 1971), the German nominal system (Meier 1967), and the Russian nominal system (Šteinfeldt 1969) — I will return to a discussion of the fourth case. These studies were chosen because they were readily accessible, used as text a large corpus, and could be used in such a way as to derive statistics relevant to the issues discussed here.

We now raise the question of why this case should be the most frequent, if indeed it invariably is. Considering first only texts made up of simple sentences, if we assume that in all languages, some sentences will have no other nominal arguments besides subject (i.e., some sentences will be like 'The boy fell'), it will follow that in any representative text, some sentences will have only nouns inflected for nominative case, while other sentences will have at least one noun inflected for nominative case, plus some nouns inflected for other cases. Still, in actual case systems, even intransitive sentences may have prepositional phrases in which the nouns are case inflected — e.g., Modern German, where locative phrases contain dative or accusative inflection, or Classical Latin, where locative phrases contain accusative or ablative inflected noun phrases (or the ablative alone). But in such cases (except for the non-prepositional Latin ablative), it is not clear that these prepositional cases should be taken as tokens of the same type as the correspondingly inflected non-prepositionally marked nouns, although tradi-

---

[8] I should emphasize that I do not mean to imply here that a pronominal system of case inflection should be considered comparable to a nominal system; rather, these systems were chosen solely on the basis of accessibility of frequency data.

tionally they have been so considered. The reason why this is doubtful is that the case-inflection does not function alone to specify the relation of these noun phrases to the verbal predicate. Rather, that relation is carried by a combination of the preposition and the case-inflection, and this combination should perhaps itself be considered a discontinuous relation-marker distinct from the non-prepositional inflection which stands alone as a relation marker.

At first glance, the syntactic situation discussed thus far does not seem to represent an instance of the Type-Token Fallacy because, while in phonology the sound-meaning pairing is essentially arbitrary, in syntax the structure-meaning pairing is in significant ways non-arbitrary. Specifically, in this instance, if we assume that natural language semantic structures consist of a predicate and one or more arguments, one-place predicates will almost all be realized syntactically as intransitive sentences with subjects which are nominally inflected, and multi-place predicates will be realized syntactically as complex structures one argument of which will be subject.

However, when we consider other kinds of simple sentences and also complex sentences — sentences with conjoined objects, subordinate clauses, nominalizations, etc. — it is clear that even though each sentence may have at least one nominative-inflected argument, it may have more than one objective case-inflected noun phrase in the same case — e.g., the sentences in (6) to (8):

(6) Der Kaufmann kauft den Wein und den Apfel.
    nom.              acc.            acc.
    The merchant buys the wine and the apple.

(7) Hoc mihi magnō dolōrī est.
    nom./dat.        dat.
    acc.
    This is a great sorrow to me.

(8) Tē impēratōrem appelō.
    acc.    acc.
    I call you emperor.

(6) demonstrates that compound non-subjects in a language like German with case-inflection will produce more than one non-nominative case-inflected form in some syntactic structures; this will be true whenever non-subject noun phrases are conjoined. The Latin sentence in (7) shows that because some cases have multiple uses, sentences with arguments in more than one relation to the predicate may also produce structures where the nominative case is out-numbered. (8) shows that this may also result from possible complex sentence sources. It therefore does not follow from the fact that because nominative is the case of the subject of intransitives and of one of the arguments of a transitive

sentence — that is, that each grammatical sentence contains a nominative — that it will necessarily be more frequent; thus, again, such
reasoning does in fact commit the Type-Token fallacy.

We might suggest an additional hypothesis, which, in conjunction
with the definition of nominative, would be sufficient to infer that the
nominative would be the most frequent. Such a hypothesis might be
something like that stated in (9).

(9)  *Multiple Case Hypothesis*
     Sentences with multiple occurrences of the same case are used
     less than sentences with single occurrences of any one case.

I know of no available statistical data which can be examined to attempt
to prove this hypothesis; however, it can be tested in principle, by counting number of uses of the same case in a sample of sentences. Should it
be demonstrated to be consistent with the facts in a sufficient sample, the
relative frequency of nominative vs. all other cases would be deducible
from the definition of nominative and other facts about the syntactic
structures of human languages and thus would not be considered axiomatic.


3.3 In examining actual case systems, a problem can immediately be
seen in considering the nominative as the unmarked case with respect to
frequency of occurrence, in that not all languages with case systems
require an overt subject. A further problem may also arise in those
languages which require an overt subject, where the nominative has zero
expression in at least some instances. Here the problem is whether a ∅
inflection can legitimately be counted as an instance of a case —
certainly the traditional position has been that it can. On the other hand,
it is also true that in many languages inanimate nouns do not contrast
nominative and accusative forms, but animates do (case systems of some
Indo-european languages, for example). The zero expression situation
seems different in an essential way from a system where a subject is not
required, however, in that zero expression preserves the opposition
between nominative and accusative, while in the other, no contrast
occurs. Thus, for our purposes, it would seem legitimate to count zero-
expression nominatives as instances of nominative case, but not legitimate to count functional accusatives and functional nominatives as
instances of those respective cases when they are not in opposition.

This is a non-trivial problem in evaluating the Russian and German
case counts, however, because each language has noun classes which do
not show morphological opposition between nominative and accusative,
and it is unclear whether the counts refer to function or to inflection.

To elucidate the problems of how to interpret the cases in an actual
system, we will consider the criteria characterizing markedness with

regard to nominative and accusative cases in the Spanish personal pronoun system.

Besides the universal claim that nominative is unmarked, one might argue that the nominative pronouns are unmarked in Spanish relative to the accusative forms in that the gender distinctions made in the first and second person plural for the nominative are syncretized in the accusative, e.g., *nosotros* 'we,' nom. masc. & fem./masc. vs. *nosotras* 'we,' nom. fem. but *nos* 'us' acc.; *vosotros* 'you' nom. pl., familiar, masc. & fem./masc. vs. *vosotras* 'you,' nom. pl., familiar, fem. but *vos* 'you' acc. pl. familiar.

For all third person pronoun forms, nominative case appears in 11.2 % of the instances in the text, and accusative case in 32.6 %. These figures go even higher in favor of the accusative in non-third person forms, where the accusative syncretizes with the dative and reflexive; these figures are summarized in the table in (10).

(10) *Person/Case*                  *Percentage* (for each person)

|   |                  |         |
|---|------------------|---------|
| I | Nominative       | 26.6 %  |
|   | Acc./dat./reflex.| 65.9 %  |
|   | Other[9]         | 7.4 %   |
| II| Nominative       | 28.5 %  |
|   | Acc./dat./reflex.| 67.3 %  |
|   | Other            | 4.2 %   |
| III | Nominative     | 11.2 %  |
|   | Accusative       | 32.6 %  |
|   | Dative           | 13.1 %  |
|   | Reflexive        | 43.1 %  |

As these statistics show, the Spanish frequency count represents an apparent counter-example to the hypothesis that text frequency is inversely correlated with degree of markedness. The reason why this should be so is evidently because Spanish uses subject pronouns only when emphasis is intended (e.g., to function contrastively, to disambiguate reference, etc.). An alternative, then, would be to consider the subject pronouns as being emphatic pronouns, and the subject agreement inflection on the verb as the true nominative pronouns. In support of this analysis is the fact that it would make subject and object pronouns parallel in that each would have a non-emphatic form cliticized to the verb, and an emphatic, non-clitic form (the traditional subject pronouns and the prepositional object forms (*a él, a ella,* etc.)).

In addition, analyzing the subject agreement inflections and the object clitics as belonging to the same class allows one to state at least

---

[9]  "Other" for first and second person forms refers to the prepositional forms *mí* and *tí;* for third person, the nominative form is used with prepositions.

one generalization which is independent of the issues addressed here. Moravcsik (1974) investigates a large number of languages with subject- or object-marking on the verb and concludes that the following implicational universal holds:

(11) If a language marks any direct objects on the verb, then it marks some subjects on the verb.

Spanish was one of the languages in Moravcsik's sample, and she considered both subject inflection and object clitics to be verbal markings.

Should we choose to analyze the subject inflections as subject clitic pronouns, the particular frequency statistics in (10) are irrelevant because they compare emphatic nominatives with non-emphatic accusatives. Furthermore, the Julliand & Chang-Rodriguez count does not provide the relevant data from which to derive new statistics, as it does not break verb usage down by person inflection.

Also, this alternative presents its own problems to the characterization of markedness; for example, in the past imperfect, the conditional, and all subjunctive verb forms, the first and third person subject inflections do not contrast (i.e., are syncretized) — e.g., *cantaba* 'I/he, she sang' imperfect; *cante* 'I/he, she sing' pres. subjunctive, etc. — while in no tense/mood/aspect combination are the first and third person object clitics syncretized, nor do any other person neutralizations occur in the object clitics. In addition, in the object clitics masculine and feminine gender contrast in the third person, while in the subject inflections, no gender contrast occurs. Thus, by the criterion of syncretization, the subject inflections are characterized as marked relative to the object clitics. This goes against the claim that the nominative is universally unmarked, if the appropriate comparison for Spanish is between the subject inflections and the object clitics.

On the other hand, if we take the criterion of range of morphological variation to determine markedness, then the object clitics are characterized as more marked in that they are more regular than the subject inflections, which vary depending on tense, mood, aspect, and conjugation class of the verb to which they are attached.

It seems, then, that a number of criteria which Greenberg suggests to characterize syntactic markedness are in conflict in this instance. The criterion of morphological variation characterizes subject inflections as less marked; conversely, the criterion of syncretization characterizes the object clitics as less marked than the subject inflections. To my knowledge, there are no available frequency data to bear on this issue, but those data are certainly obtainable. Should they be obtained, one would have to question the weight that facts about text frequency should receive in judging the markedness relations relative to the other criteria considered. If a valid text sampling were to show that the subject inflections are more frequent than object clitics, must we then conclude that syncretism does not always correlate with the other criteria in (1) and thus should be eliminated from the predicates used to characterize markedness? Or if frequency investigations show that object clitics are more frequent than subject inflections, then should we conclude that morphological variation should be eliminated from the predicates used to characterize markedness? The point is that either way, not all of the suggested markedness criteria converge in this instance to characterize the same markedness relations between subject inflections and object clitics, while on the other hand, if we consider the overt pronouns to be the appropriate representatives of nominative case, then the frequency data available clearly goes against the universal claim that nominative case is unmarked relative to all others. Without more clear cases of correlation or non-correlation among these criteria, it is not clear to me what the significance of this situation is, whether it reflects on the inadequacy of present notions of how to characterize markedness relations, or whether it should be interpreted as signalling a state of non-equilibrium in the Spanish system.

3.4 If we eliminated from our count a certain class of items, say Class X, and the relative frequency relations of the various categories we were investigating remained constant, we would conclude that whatever function Class X served, that function was not a factor in determining the relative frequency of these categories. On the other, if, by subtracting Class X from our count, the frequency proportions between categories should vary, then we would conclude that some function of Class X is relevant to determining these frequencies, and if we would determine what function Class X has which is a factor in determining the frequency proportions, we would have isolated one of the factors which determines the frequency of one category relative to the others.

The Russian frequency count in Šteinfeldt (1969) provides some interesting data concerning the possible interaction of case frequency and semantic function of syntactic relations; specifically, the frequency variation in case which occurs in a text depending on the inclusion or exclusion of proper nouns in the count. This information is given on the chart in (12):

| (12) Case | % without proper nouns | % with proper nouns | Difference |
|---|---|---|---|
| Nominative | 28.3 | 33.6 | +5.3 |
| Genitive | 26.0 | 24.6 | −1.4 |
| Dative | 5.0 | 5.1 | +0.1 |
| Accusative | 21.8 | 19.5 | −2.3 |

| Instrumental | 8.6 | 7.8 | −0.8 |
| Prepositional | 10.3 | 9.4 | −0.9 |

An inspection of this chart will show that when proper names are included in the count, the nominative case shows the most gain, with the dative case showing a very small gain, while the genitive, accusative, instrumental and prepositional cases all show a loss, the largest loss being in the accusative case.

Consideration of animacy is not sufficient to account for the increase in the nominative, because if animacy were the main characteristic of proper nouns to influence the relative precentages of case usage, there should be no significant difference in in the frequency increase between nominative and dative cases, as the nominative has among its uses the agentive role, while the dative has among its uses the animate receiver role. However, if we consider the function of subjects, particularly with respect to the discourse notion 'topic,' the fact that subjects tend to be definite is a consequence of the fact that they tend to be topics. Then, since proper nouns are by definition definite, it follows that if we do not count a large subset of definite elements, the frequency of the case(s) with uses most highly correllated with definiteness will be the most affected. Thus, it appears that the difference in frequency for nominative case when proper nouns are included and excluded from the count is predictable on semantic grounds, on the basis of the definiteness of proper nouns and the semantic functions associated with subjecthood. If this is indeed true, it would be expected that in any language the case whose frequency would vary most with the inclusion and exclusion of proper nouns would be the case which marks a syntactic function which is highly correlated with the notion of topic. Thus, in this particular instance, it seems possible that at least one of the variables which controls syntactic frequency is the semantic function of the various categories.[10]

4.0 In this last section, we turn to a general examination of the relationship among the various criteria assumed to characterize syntactic markedness which we enumerated in (1).

4.1 Greenberg (p. 68) mentions the relation between frequency and degree of morphological irregularity and suggests that it is the high

---

[10] Two additional Russian-specific alternatives have been suggested to me which would skew the statistics somewhat in favor of a nominative/proper noun correlation: one is that this count includes the formally non-distinct vocatives as nominatives, the other is that in Slavic culture, syntactic structures are preferred which avoid assigning an accusative function (correlated with semantic "thingness") to a human object. I am grateful to J. Ard and A. Raun respectively for pointing these possibilities out to me.

frequency which allows irregularities to be preserved by virtue of their constant usage, while the less regular forms succumb to analogy and syncretism. If this is true, and there seems to be sufficient documentation of this in facts about diachronic change (Cf. Hockett (1958), pp. 396—97), then morphological irregularity and frequency are not two independent criteria converging to determine relative markedness, but rather morphological irregularity is a diachronic consequence of frequency, and we would expect these two factors to covary.

4.2 It would further seem reasonable that those categories which are referred to most frequently in human communication would tend to be those for which more distinctions are made because of either the universal importance which they have in human communication or their importance within a given culture; thus the many distinctions among types of snow expressed lexically in Eskimo or the lexical distinctions among kinds of fish-catching activity in Tongan vocabulary.

Also, it may be that frequency supports multiplicity and sublety of distinctions for much the same reason that it apparently supports morphological variation — by keeping the distinctions fresh in linguistic memory through constant performance. If this is true, then syncretism is also not logically independent of frequency in syntax, but rather is like morphological regularity produced through analogy in that it has the effect of leveling out the distinctions and making those patterns which are less used (and therefore less automatic) the more regular and general.

4.3 We may also question the independence of the zero expression criterion. If we consider that the main goals of language as a human communication system are efficiency in sending and clarity in perceiving the message, then certainly one aspect of efficiency is the time which it takes to send the message. Thus, although zero expression is not necessary, if it should occur, we would expect it to occur on the most frequent items rather than the least frequent — that is, those tokens which are used most often should tend to be shortest; then zero expression coulc also be considered to be a consequence of frequency. As a parallel case, I refer again to the differing cultural value placed on particular objects, distinctions, or activities and the correlation with whether these categories and distinctions are expressed lexically or syntactically.

4.4 In Schwartz (1977) I examined two means of signalling grammatical relations, one being morphological marking and the other being fixed word order. I concluded that morphological marking attached to the more marked member (determinable from other markedness criteria) and that fixed word order was always the unmarked order (also determinable by use of other markedness criteria). If we take frequency to be a prime factor in determining some facts about differences between categories in opposition, these seem like two extremely natural results. In disambiguation by use of a morphological marker, the strategy is to mark the less frequent function, leaving the more frequent — and therefore the more expected — function unmarked. Disambiguation by fixed word order reduces to a strategy to interpret unspecified relations as instances of the most frequent — and hence most expected — relations expressed in that syntactic form.

4.5 Returning to the definition of markedness, it is thus no longer necessary to consider the predicates 'frequency,' 'zero expression,' 'syncretization,' and 'degree of morphological variation' to be part of that definition, because frequency is seen as a consequence of deductions based on the range of distribution-determining factors of neutralization, dominance, and *par excellence* expression in conjunction with other hypotheses about the general nature of human communication, while zero expression, syncretization, and degree of morphological variation can be deduced from relative frequency in conjunction with general principles of human cognition and communicative efficiency. Further examination is required to determine whether the remaining predicates of 'neutralization,' 'dominance' and '*par excellence* expression' are independent and independently sufficient to characterize markedness relations in syntax.

# Bibliography

Greenberg, Joseph A. 1966. *Language Universals.* The Hague: Mouton & Company.

Hockett, Charles. 1958. *A Course in Modern Linguistics.* New York: The MacMillan Company.

Householder, Fred W. 1960. "First Thoughts on Syntactic Indices," *International Journal of American Linguistics* 26: 195—7.

Hjelmslev, L. 1935. *La categorie des cas.* Aarhus.

— 1953. *Prologmena to a Theory of Language.* Baltimore.

Imbs, Paul. 1971. *Dictionnaire des fréquences.* Nancy: Centre de recherche por un trésor de la langue français.

Jakobson, Roman. 1939. "Signe Zero," *Melanges de linguistique, offerts a Charles Bally.* Reprinted in *Readings in Linguistics II,* E. Hamp, F. Householder, R. Austerlitz, eds., Chicago: The University of Chicago Press, pp. 109—115.

— 1957. *Shifters, Verbal Categories, and the Russian Verb.* Cambridge.

Julliand, Alfonse and E. Chang-Rodriguez. 1964. *Frequency Dictionary of Spanish Words.* The Hague: Mouton & Company.

Meier, Helmut. 1967. *Deutsche Sprachstatistik.* Hildesheim: Georg Olms Verlagsbuchhandlung.

Moravcsik, Edith. 1974. "Object-Verb Agreement," *Stanford Working Papers on Language Universals*, pp. 25—140.

Roberts, A. Hood. *A Statistical Analysis of American English*. The Hague: Mouton & Company.

Schwartz, Linda J. 1977. "Ambiguity Avoidance and Syntactic Markedness," *Proceedings of the 1976 Mid-America Conference*, Kathleen Houlihan, ed. Minneapolis.

Šteinfeldt, E. 1969. *Russian Word Count*. Moscow: Progress Publishers.

Trnka, B. 1958. "On Some Problems of Neutralization," *Omagiu lui Jorgu Jordan*, pp. 861—6. Bucharest.

Trubetzkoy, N. S. 1939. *Grundzüge der Phonologie*. Prague.

# Qualitative vs. Quantitative Analysis in Linguistics*

Esa Itkonen

The nature of the data that a science is meant to account for determines the nature of the science. So far there is no unanimity as to the true nature of the data of grammar.[1] This state of affairs has several consequences. On the one hand, the methodological status of grammar remains in doubt; on the other, the nature of socio- and psycholinguistic data, which must be delimited against grammatical data, remains equally in doubt. From this latter fact it follows, in turn, that the methodological status of socio- and psycholinguistics is not quite clear either.

In this paper I intend to give, first of all, an explicit and consistent account of grammatical data and of its relation to socio- and psycholinguistic data. As a consequence, I shall be able to show, at a relatively abstract level, what precisely is the relation of grammar to socio- and psycholinguistics. Secondly, I shall consider questions of linguistic methodology in more detail. Grammar or autonomous linguistics will be shown to be methodologically similar to philosophy and logic. The distinction between non-autonomous and autonomous linguistics is that between causality and the lack of it; moreover, the adequate notion of causality must be here, as in social science in general, the probabilistic one. Causal models for socio- and psycholinguistics will be outlined in the remaining part of this paper. The view of the relationship between qualitative and quantitative analysis, as it emerges here, is directly generalizable to human sciences in general.

## I Data

### A. Grammar

There are two principal views concerning the nature of grammatical data: Either the grammarian investigates sentences invented by himself

* I wish to thank Professor Raymond Boudon for his advice on topics connected with Sect. II B below.

[1] By "grammar" I mean Saussurean autonomous linguistics. It follows, somewhat awkwardly, that e.g., "performance grammar" is not a type of "grammar." I use the term "science" in the sense of the German "Wissenschaft." Consequently, e.g., logic and philosophy are (nonempirical) "sciences."

or he investigates a corpus of actual utterances. It is also often thought that even if the former alternative is the case, it is the latter which *ought* to be the case. This conflict of opinions can be summed up as a conflict between intuition and observation. I shall review here first some proposed solutions.

Bloomfield and Harris are usually identified with the view that all one has to do is to describe a given corpus. This is false in a twofold sense. First, a cursory reading of Bloomfield (1935) and Harris (1961) shows that, whatever their methodological statements, in their descriptive practice these authors use *only* self-invented examples, i.e., reject observation and espouse intuition. Second, even their methodological statements contradict the view that corpus-description is all that counts. Bloomfield clearly recognized the creative and open-ended nature of language; for him this fact was "obvious" and in no need of special emphasis:

> ". . . it is obvious that most speech forms are regular, in the sense that the speaker who knows the constituents and the grammatical pattern, can utter them without ever having heard them; moreover, the observer cannot hope to list them, since the possibilities of combination are practically infinite" (Bloomfield 1935: 275).

Thus, transformational grammar (= TG) did not invent the creativity of language. What it did invent, were recursive rules to describe creativity. However, this is a mistake in two ways. First, sentences which natural speakers can and do utter, i.e., which constitute (the output of) their competence, contain a minimal amount of recursivity. Second, the theoretical considerations which seem to allow an infinite application of recursivity in the "ideal speaker's" competence are based on the assumption of an analogy between logical induction and what might be called "grammatical induction." However, there is no such analogy (cf. Itkonen 1976 a).

Bloomfield also recognized that because of the conventional or normative nature of language, quantitative analysis is not needed in grammar:

> "However, there is another and simpler way of studying human action in the mass: the study of conventional actions. . . . Here the linguist is in a fortunate position: in no other respect are the activities of a group as rigidly standardized as in the forms of language. Large groups of people make up all their utterances out of the same stock of lexical forms and grammatical constructions. A linguistic observer therefore can describe the speech-habits of a community without resorting to statistics" (Bloomfield 1935: 37).

The same argument to show the irrelevance of statistical considerations to grammar recurs in Chomsky (1957: 16). What Bloomfield and Chomsky are trying to do here is to justify the actual descriptive practice of most modern grammarians. In my opinion their position is entirely correct with respect to that particular type of data with which they are concerned. When one has to do with a set of reasonably well-established rules, one can perfectly well describe *possible* correct (results of) actions

without paying attention to which actions are in fact performed in space
and time, and how often. However, one can be interested in more than
one type of data, and different types of data require different methods
of description. Performance grammar is a perfectly sound concept, and
it requires taking statistical and probabilistic aspects of language into
account (cf. below).

Harris notes explicitly that although, in his opinion, the grammarian
must start from a corpus, his description necessarily goes beyond it:

> "The interest in our analysis of the corpus derives primarily from the fact that it can
> serve as a *predictive* sample of the language" (Harris 1961: 244; emphasis added).
> "When a linguist offers his results as a system representing the language as a whole,
> he is *predicting* that the elements set up for his corpus will satisfy all other bits of
> talking in that language" (op. cit.: 17; emphasis added).

Harris carries out his morphemic analysis with the aid of such theoretical constructs as "frames of substitution;" these are selected on
account of their contribution to the over-all simplicity of the description:

> "The criterion which decides for -*ing*, and against *un-*, as the relevant environment
> in determining substitution classes [for verbs] is therefore a criterion of usefulness
> throughout the grammar, a configurational consideration" (Harris 1957: 143, n. 6;
> also 150).

The same argument recurs in Chomsky (1957: 55): "the only ultimate
criterion in evaluation is the simplicity of the whole system."

Neither Bloomfield nor Harris presents a coherent and acceptable
account of the nature of grammatical data. Yet, at least in my opinion,
their positions were better than they are today made to appear. In particular, TG has seriously misrepresented Harris's grammar-conception,
characterizing it as non-predictive and non-theoretical description interested merely in matters of "observational adequacy."

Chomsky's view of the nature of grammatical data has been explicitly
self-contradictory from the start: In Chomsky (1957: 13) he claims that
grammar explicates an intuitive concept whereas elsewhere (op. cit.: 49)
he claims that, just like physics, grammar explains and predicts observable events. In Chomsky (1965) he emphasized the intuitive aspect, but
recently he has returned to the observational, physicalist conception:

> "... our scientist S ... studies language exactly as he studies physics, taking humans
> to be 'natural objects'" (Chomsky 1976: 315).

In this context linguists' capacity for self-contradiction seems almost
unlimited. Chomsky has never studied speakers as natural objects. All he
has ever done is to study his own intuitive knowledge of English with the
aid of self-invented sample sentences; and this is something that natural
objects cannot do. Similarly e.g., Lieb (1976: 198) and Wunderlich
(1976: 81) claim that grammatical descriptions must absolutely be based
on a corpus; and yet they themselves not once make use of a corpus in

their own published work. Sampson (1975) has tried to give a consistently observational account of grammatical data. Significantly, even he manages to present his case without the help of any actual corpus (for criticism, cf. Itkonen 1976 c and d).

Unlike the linguists mentioned so far, Labov has *actually* investigated real corpora, and therefore he can recommend the use of observation at least without being guilty of any obvious self-contradiction. Labov's position here is not quite easy to pin down. He generally seems to identify use of intuition with investigation of idiolects, which he considers methodologically unsound (e.g., Labov 1972: 191—202). Elsewhere, however, he admits that use of intuition is indispensable (op. cit.: 227 and 234). More recently he has come to explicitly entertain the view that in Chomskyan "clear cases," where results of intuition, observation, and experimentation coincide, or can safely be assumed to coincide, intuition suffices all alone, and insistence on the use of observation/experimentation results from misunderstanding (Labov 1975: 7—14). This view is, as it were, extensionally identical with mine; yet I find it unsatisfactory because it fails to indicate the precise relation between intuition and observation, or what it means for the two to "coincide."

Thus Labov no longer advocates a wholesale rejection of intuition in favor of observation/experimentation, or the replacement of grammar by socio- and psycholinguistics. However, such a position seems to be gaining ground, in spite of the fact that it stands in stark conflict with the descriptive practice of the majority of today's linguists, notably generativists and Montague-grammarians. Therefore I shall explicitly refute it in Sect. B and C.

So far we have been dealing with a straightforward dichotomy between self-invented sample sentences and a set of actual utterances, i.e., a corpus. The study of the latter type of data is quantitative in the sense that it must take relative frequencies of (different variants exemplifying) grammatical categories into account; moreover, in experimental-psycholinguistic research the data may be quantifiable also in the sense of containing several degrees of correctness or acceptability. The former type of data is that investigated by Saussure, Bloomfield, Harris, Chomsky, and Montague, among others. Its study is non-quantitative, i.e., qualitative, in a twofold sense. First, it has nothing to do with relative frequencies. Second, the data is discrete (= categorical, two-valued): these are the "clear cases," which are (known to be) definitely correct, and are contrasted with all other, less than clear cases. Consequently, observation is connected to the quantitative analysis of actual utterances whereas intuition is connected to the qualitative analysis of conceptual possibilities, i.e., either correct or less than correct sentences which may or may not be exemplified by actual utterances. In my opinion this dichotomy, as here characterized, is perfectly justified.

This simple dichotomy has been challenged by Ross (1973), who, with his notion of "squish," wishes to introduce a grammar-conception which is at the same time intuitive and quantitative. Notice, first of all, that Ross is primarily interested in establishing the non-discrete, quantifiable nature of *theoretical* concepts like "noun phrase." This leaves open the possibility that the questions or criteria which are used to rank particular words as to their "nounphrasiness" admit only of a discrete, yes-or-no answer, as in the genuine Guttman scale (cf. e.g., Mayntz et al. 1976: 57—63). However, since Ross wishes to fill as many slots of his implicational scale as possible, he subjects his noun phrase candidates to a set of "NP tests," i.e., lets them undergo definite transformations or inserts them into definite contexts, and comes out with a huge number of sentences, prefixed with one or two stars and/or question marks, which no one would ever have reason to utter. It is only natural that, as Ross's battery of stars and question marks so eloquently demonstrates, there can be no clear and reliable intuitions here. Yet it is possible that the data, in spite of its general unreliability, exhibits some kind of hierarchy of correctness, and is hence quantifiable. Now it seems reasonable enough that in experimental psychology, where we are interested in discovering the "profile" of the subjects' capacities, we must move them to do what they would not normally do, e.g., utter incorrect or outlandish sentences, and to try to do what they are not quite able to do, e.g., evaluate in a precise way the (in)correctness of outlandish sentences. But all this must be carried out in conformity with a general experimental methodology. It is certainly a mistake to rely here on one's intuition alone, as Ross is doing. As a consequence, pairing intuition with qualitative analysis and observation/experimentation with quantitative analysis remains a valid principle.

In the remaining part of this section I shall present, somewhat schematically, my own conception of the nature of grammatical data. A more detailed account is to be found in Itkonen (1974) and (1978).

Grammar traditionally concentrates upon the concept "correct sentence (or speech act) of L." A corpus consists of exemplifications of the concept "factually uttered sentence of L." These are two different concepts, as can be seen from the fact that, on the one hand, there are indefinitely many *correct* sentences of L which have never actually been uttered (but must, by definition, be described by grammar) and, on the other, there are indefinitely many actual utterances of *incorrect* sentences of L (i.e., sentences which, by definition, must not be described by grammar). Observation pertains only to space and time; and a corpus consists of spatiotemporal occurrences. Since grammar is not, and could not be, based on a corpus (cf. above), observation is incompatible with grammar. It is convenient to call the act of knowledge pertaining to "correct sentence" by the name of "(linguistic) intuition."

The distinction between "correct sentence" and "factually uttered sentence" is a special case of the general distinction between normativity and factuality, or between what one ought to do and what one does in fact. It is a well-known philosophical truth that this distinction cannot be eliminated by reducing one of its terms to the other. In particular, trying to derive "ought" from "is" means committing the "naturalistic fallacy."

Analyzing the concept "correct sentence" means analyzing those *rules* (or norms) which make sentences correct. Each correct sentence can be analyzed into a set of quite trivial rules — ultimately rules connected with particular words (i.e., word *-types)* and constructions — which make it correct. Such rules are potential objects of *conscious* knowledge. Just as an action contains a physical "substratum" without being identical with it, a rule could not exist without its own substratum, i.e., a regularity of actions, but is not reducible to it. Attempts at such a reduction, which amount to attempts at eliminating (linguistic) normativity altogether, are criticized in Itkonen (1976 b, c, and d).

Rules are not spatiotemporal entities and therefore cannot be observed but only intuited. The notion of correctness is inseparable from the notion of rule. Consequently, when one is observing a correct utterance, one's observation (of space and time) is in fact *subordinated* to one's intuition (of rule). This is the general relation, in linguistics, between intuition and observation (cf. also Friedman 1975). It parallels the general relationship between a rule and the actions conforming or failing to conform to it: the former is a *conceptual precondition* of, or a priori vis-à-vis, each of the latter. Analogously, Durkheim (1938: 57) insists that "social facts" must be analyzed in themselves, isolated from their individual manifestations. On the other hand, it is clear that, taken as a whole, the domain of non-normative actions is presupposed by the domain of rules and institutions.

Due to the normative, conceptual nature of the data, data-gathering in grammar does not consist in looking for new occurrences in new spatial and/or temporal regions, as in empirical science, but in *reminding oneself* of what one knows already (i.e., after one has learned the language in question). More precisely, the grammarian does not remind himself of what he or someone else has said as a matter of fact, but what one ought to say. In other words, the situation is here the same as in philosophical analysis, as characterized by Wittgensteinian philosophers of language (cf. e.g., Hare 1971 and Specht 1969: Sect. 9).

In each type of scientific data-gathering a subjective act of knowledge takes hold of something objective. In physics, the act is observation, and it pertains to measurable events. In logic, the act is logical intuition, and it pertains to inference rules and/or to the concept "valid formula." In grammar, as we have seen already, the act is linguistic intuition, and it pertains to rules of language. Rules of language exist *qua* objects of (three-level) *common knowledge* (cf. Lewis 1969: Ch. II). One's (subjective) intuition is identical with one's (three-level) contribution to common knowledge: one's intuition both pertains to a rule and, in part, creates it (for details, cf. Itkonen 1977).

There is only one possible way in which incorrect observations and intuitions, whatever their cause, can be corrected, namely through the intervention of others. If this possibility did not obtain, we would have a solipsistic, private-language universe. However, such a universe is logically impossible (cf. Itkonen 1974: Ch. II). Because observation and intuition are subjective by nature, they are necessarily fallible. Thus I emphatically reject the view that intuitions are somehow "incorrigible." However, I do claim that linguistic intuition is (objectively) *certain* to the same extent as logical or philosophical intuition.

Ringen (1975) recognizes that the role of intuition is, in principle, the same in grammar, logic, and philosophy. In addition, he requires, in particular in Ringen (1977), that in all these cases the use of intuition must be somehow philosophically justified. A similar claim is also forwarded in Cohen (1976). Now, it could be pointed out that Wittgenstein's refutation of private languages guarantees at least a modicum of intersubjective validity for those rules (of language or of logic) which our intuition pertains to. Moreover, our world happens to such that, as even Labov is willing to admit, there *are* "clear cases" about which we do possess a rather secure knowledge. The world might have been otherwise; but it is not. I do not think that there is anything more one can say. As Wittgenstein (1958: 136 and 180; 1969: 18 and 23) points out, a doubt or a need for justification which does not come to an end sooner or later is not even doubt. I think one must let the chain of justifications stop here, but Ringen and Cohen would apparently like to go one step farther.

## B. Sociolinguistics

In Sect. A I made a precise claim concerning the relation between grammatical data on one hand and socio- and psycholinguistic data on the other. In Sect. B and C I intend to show that my claim is in fact true.

Grammar could be replaced by sociolinguistics only if it could be shown that the sociolinguist makes no reference, either explicitly or implicitly, to those normative phenomena which constitute the data of grammar or, equivalently, if it could be shown that the sociolinguist can dispense entirely with intuition and rely solely on observation (as well as on his capacity for theory-construction). If, as I claimed in Sect. A, grammatical data constitute an indispensable precondition of sociolinguistic data, then of course the sociolinguist could not possibly give up the use of intuition.

Social behavior exhibits no strictly deterministic or nomological regularities and can therefore be described and explained only statistical-probabilistically. It is often claimed that linguistic behavior is practically unpredictable, but this claim cannot be taken seriously. It is clear that probabilities for predicting actual utterances are extremely low. However, if one refers only to the general semantic content of potential utterances, it is not at all difficult to predict that people will say such and such under such and such circumstances. Furthermore, and more importantly, if we resort to *conditional* probabilities, i.e., if we ask what is probably the case, given that an utterance — either any utterance or more specifically an utterance containing such and such material — has been made, we can establish perfectly reliable probabilities with which different grammatical categories or constructions will occur (cf. Sect. II B). This characterization holds true independently of whether grammatical categories are exemplified by one invariant or by two or more variants. In the latter case we have the standard data for the Labov-type analysis of variation.

The question is now, whether it is possible for the sociolinguist to state the relative frequencies and to infer the corresponding probabilities without any reference, explicit or implicit, to the normativity of language. To show that this is not the case, it is enough to point out that there are in fact *two* types of probability of occurrence here, and that the sociolinguist's descriptive practice is adjusted to this fact. First, there is the occurrence of either one correct invariant exemplifying the grammatical category X or of two or more correct (or at least plausible) variants exemplifying the category Y. Second, there is the occurrence of variants, whether correct *or* incorrect, exemplifying the categories X and Y. It is with the *first* type of (probability of) occurrence that the sociolinguist is dealing. This can be seen from the fact that he operates with the notion of invariant or categorial rule, and may even regard such rules as representing the *normal* state of language (cf. Labov 1969: 738 and 1972: 223; Bailey 1973: 33 and 84); but in connection with the second type of (probability of) occurrence there could be *no* invariant or categorial rules, because there always can, and do, occur incorrect variants contradicting them, i.e., making them less than invariant.

What I just said, can be illustrated by considering Labov's descriptive practice. He states explicitly that sociolinguistic data is not described as such but is, rather, processed in accordance with "certain universal editing rules;" after the editing, "the proportion of truly ungrammatical and ill-formed sentences falls to less than two percent" (Labov 1972: 203). Now, it is clear that Labov edits his original data and evaluates the edited data as either correct or as "truly ungrammatical and ill-formed" on the basis of his *intuitive* knowledge about the *rules* of language. He cannot be relying just on observation, because what he is doing is precisely to evaluate his observations as either correct or incorrect. Furthermore, it would not help if Labov, instead of just relying on his own intuition, would try to experiment with the intuitions of his fellow sociolinguists, i.e., their reactions to the data at hand. Not only utterances, but also reactions to utterances are either correct or incorrect, and it is only on the basis of intuition about linguistic rules that an incorrect reaction can be recognized as incorrect. On the other hand, it is reasonable to say that Labov can *consult* (rather than experiment with) the intuitions of his fellow sociolinguists. This kind of consulting (which is always possible, although normally unnecessary) is located at the level of intersubjective, *pre-experimental* understanding.

The preceding argument involves an apparent difficulty. The learning of rules necessarily starts from observation, but in the course of this learning process there occurs a "leap" from observing actual occurrences to (intuitively) grasping the rule, which subsequently serves as a *criterion* for evaluating what is observed. Because the gap between factuality and normativity can be neither bridged not eliminated, as we know from philosophy, one has to leap over it. That one is in fact able to do so, is, if you wish, a proof of the creative nature of learning (cf. also Itkonen 1976 b).[2]


## C. Psycholinguistics

The inner logic of TG has led its practitioners to base their descriptions on more and more outlandish sentences (cf. the discussion of Ross in Sect. A). It is only natural to assume that in such cases there are no reliable and intersubjectively valid intuitions, and this assumption has in fact been experimentally verified, e.g., in Spencer (1973). This state of affairs has, perhaps understandably, provoked a backlash: It has been claimed, e.g., in Derwing (1973), that the use of intuition is always unscientific and should be replaced by experimental methods. For instance, whether something is or is not a correct sentence, can presumably be established only as a result of experimentation. I have already explained, on general grounds, why I consider such a view as inadmissible. In this section I

---

[2]   This kind of "leap" is closely similar, although perhaps not identical with what Rescher calls "imputation." For instance, causal or nomic necessity cannot be inferred from mere regularities of observable events. Rather, it is something that the human mind "imputes" upon observable events, and cannot help doing so (Rescher 1973: Ch. II). This explication of causality can, in turn, be shown to be practically identical with von Wright's (1974) "manipulative" or "interventionist" notion of causality.

shall show in detail that, rather than a result of experimentation, the concept of "correct sentence" is built-in into the experimental design and therefore constitutes one of its conceptual preconditions. I shall base my discussion on Greenbaum & Quirk (1970), which is one of the most thorough investigations in the field.

The central concept in Greenbaum & Quirk's study is "relevant noncompliance" (= RNC). In the present context we can ignore why they consider this concept so important. The test person is given a sentence, i.e., a "test sentence," on which he is instructed to perform an operation to reach a new sentence, i.e., a "target sentence." If he fails to carry out the instruction, i.e., if the sentence he produces is not the target sentence but an "evasion" of it, then his behavior is a case of RNC (op. cit.: Ch. II). To illustrate:

| Test sentence | | Target sentence |
|---|---|---|
| | negation | |
| He can certainly | → | He cannot cer- |
| drive a car | | tainly drive a car |
| non-deviant | RNC? — big | deviant |
| | question | |
| She has mentioned | → | Has she mentioned |
| it at all | | it at all? |
| deviant | RNC? — small | non-deviant |

Now, it is immediately clear that the deviant or non-deviant, i.e., incorrect or correct, nature of test or target sentences is known on the basis of intuitive, *pre-experimental* knowledge: it is a fact which precedes the experiment and determines its character.

Notice also that the pre-experimental concept of correctness is a built-in component of the very concept of RNC. A target sentence may have several variants, or as the authors put it, "we may *decide in advance* that the target sentence may have more than one form" (op. cit.: 20; emphasis added). Whether a sentence is merely a variant of the target sentence or an evasion of it, and hence a token of RNC, depends on whether it is, again pre-experimentally, known to be (in)correct like or unlike the target sentence (op. cit.: Ch. III). To illustrate:

| Test sentence | | Variants of the target sentence |
|---|---|---|
| | question | |
| | → | ⎧ Will he probably ⎫ |
| He will probably | | stay late? |
| stay late | | Will he stay late |
| | | probably? |
| non-deviant | | deviant |

|                    | question       | Evasion of<br>the target sentence |
|--------------------|----------------|-----------------------------------|
| He will probably   | →              | Is it probable that               |
| stay late          |                | he will stay late?                |
| non-deviant        |                | non-deviant                       |

A change which in one context produces a variant may in another context produce an evasion. In the above example, changing the place of "probably" did not affect the status of the new sentence. However, when the test sentence is "He deeply admires X," moving "deeply" to the end of the sentence upon questioning it produces an evasion of the (deviant) target sentence "Does he deeply admire X?"

Actually the way in which the intuitive notion of correctness determines the experimental design can be demonstrated even more directly. Greenbaum and Quirk note that there is simply no point in setting up experiments when there is "no reason to believe that we would have much less than 100 per cent acceptance" (op. cit.: 18). In such a case, experimentation is "a slightly absurd exercise, with the results a foregone conclusion" (Wason & Johnson-Laird 1972: 78). To me it seems clear enough that people who wish either to eliminate or to "justify" intuition even in the clear cases are engaged precisely in such "absurd exercises."

To think that the concept of "correct sentence" emerges as a result of experimentation is to commit a fallacy analogous to thinking that the concept of "centimetre" *results* from measuring the height of a person and from noting that he is, e.g., 185 centimeters tall.


D. Conclusion

Clear cases, i.e., well-established rules, can and must be investigated by means of intuition. Unclear cases, i.e., less than well-established rules, as well as actual linguistic behavior in general, must be investigated by means of observation. There must obviously be an area which *mediates* between intuition and observation, or between rule and action. Not surprisingly, this area is diachronic/geographical/social *variation.*

Grammatical data is a conceptual precondition of socio- and psycholinguistic data. Therefore grammar is a "transcendental" science in relation to socio- and psycholinguistics in precisely the same way as Husserl's "phenomenological psychology" and Winch's "aprioristic sociology" are transcendental sciences in relation to experimental psychology and empirical sociology, respectively. The following characterization of phenomenological psychology applies, *mutatis mutandis,* to grammar as well:

"Although it is true that empirical psychology is able to bring to light valuable psychophysical facts . . . , it nevertheless remains deprived of . . . a definite scientific evaluation of these facts so long as it is not founded on a systematic science of conscious life which investigates the psychical as such with the help of 'immanent' intuitive reflection. . . . The experimental method is indispensable . . . But this does not alter the fact that it *presupposes* what no experiment can accomplish, namely, the analysis of conscious life itself" (Kockelmans 1967: 425; emphasis added).

Thus phenomenological psychology is interested primarily in the necessary a priori of every possible empirical psychology" (op. cit.: 447).

Notice also the following justification of the Winch-type sociology:

„Thus when we elucidate concepts we are elucidating the possibilities of social life, and conversely when we explain social life we elucidate the concepts available to members of that society. . . . We now see that the social sciences are permeated by conceptual considerations" (Ryan 1970: 145).

A science need not be transcendental in relation to a human or social science only. Lorenzen's (1969) "protophysics," which investigates the hierarchically-orded norms of measuring length, time, and mass, is a transcendental science in relation to physics (cf. also Böhme 1976). That is, it investigates the concept "possible physical event" just as grammar investigates the concept "possible correct utterance." Interestingly, in his "Amsterdam Lectures" Husserl clearly anticipated protophysics as a "general aprioric science of nature."

## II Methods

—

## A. Grammar

Each scientific grammar-conception aims at describing the similarities and differences between correct sentences of L in a maximally systematic or general way. TG tries to achieve this by generating all and only correct sentences of L with their "correct" structural descriptions by means of as few grammatical rules as possible. Instead of representing rules of language by a *list* of corresponding rule-sentences, a scientific grammar represents them by a *system* of grammatical rules. This amounts to replacing piecemeal atheoretical certainty (about the existence of rules and the truth-value of rule-sentences) by systematic theoretical uncertainty (about the truth-value of scientific hypotheses expressible in terms of grammatical rules).[3]

---

[3]  In other words, the following entities must be carefully distinguished: a) rules of language, which may or may not exist; b) rule-sentences, which purport to describe single rules of language and are true or false in a self-evident, "necessary" way (cf. below); c) grammatical rules, which are used to make theoretical hypotheses (e.g., the "complex NP constraint") about large sets of rules of language.

In Sect. I it already became evident that, due to the non-spatiotemporal nature of its data, grammar must be, at least in some general sense, similar to logic and philosophy. This methodological similarity can be demonstrated in considerable detail. Generative grammars and systems of logic are interested in correctness and validity of sentences, respectively, not in their empirical truth. Correctness and validity are properties whereas empirical truth is a relation. That is, unlike the criteria for empirical truth, the criteria for correctness and validity do not lie outside of the sentence, but in the sentence itself. As an "extended axiomatic system" (Wall 1972: 197—212), a generative grammar is neither true nor false, and cannot of course be taken as an axiomatic theory. However, it has its own metagrammar which does make either true or false claims about the generative capacity of the grammar, in precisely the same way as the metalogic of a logical system makes true or false claims about the latter's generative capacity.

The requirements to generate *all* and *only* correct sentences of L have their counterparts, within logic, in the requirements of completeness and soundness, i.e., the requirements to generate all and only valid formulae expressible in the relevant formal language. Even if a system has been proved as *formally* sound and complete, it can still be (nonempirically) falsified by showing that it either generates an *intuitively* invalid formula or fails to generate an *intuitively* valid formula. For instance, although von Wright's original "monadic" system of deontic logic with the two axioms "$\sim (Op \,\&\, O \sim p)$" and "$O(p \,\&\, q) \equiv (Op \,\&\, Op)$" was formally sound and complete, it was nevertheless falsified, because it generated the intuitively invalid formula "$Op \supset O(\sim p \supset q)$," which says that doing something forbidden, i.e., $\sim p$, commits one to doing anything whatever, i. e., $q$. This system was also open to the criticism that it did not generate the intuitively valid formula "$P(p \lor q) \supset (Pp \,\&\, Pq)$," which says that if one is permitted to do $p$ or $q$, then one is permitted to do $p$ and one is permitted to do $q$ (for details, cf. Itkonen 1975 b). On the other hand, there is an important difference between the *research interests* of grammar and logic, and this has clear (although little-noticed) repercussions on how the formal structure of grammars should be conceived of (cf. Itkonen 1976 a).

Furthermore, philosophical analysis too is structurally similar to grammatical analysis. For instance, the analysis of the concept "knowing that one knows," as presented in Hintikka (1962), consists in postulating a "basic" or deep meaning from which several "residual" or surface meanings are derived. Generality is achieved, once again, by replacing a list of (apparently) disconnected items through a system which shows in a perspicuous way their similarities and differences (cf. Itkonen 1975 b). To give another example, the analysis of the concept "virtue," as presented in Plato's *Meno,* consists in looking for a definition which would capture the "essence" of virtue or the *basic* virtue, of which all cases of virtuous behavior are mere (surface) exemplifications. Although the analysis remains uncompleted, it nevertheless offers many clear instances of falsification in philosophy (cf. Itkonen 1978: Ch. XI).

The above-mentioned types of analysis can be identified as cases of *explication*, as defined in Pap (1958). According to Pap, explication consists in replacing intuitive necessity by formal necessity. Now, it can be shown that rule-sentences, i.e., sentences describing single rules[4], can be falsified neither by incorrect actions nor by correct actions. Briefly, they are unfalsifiable, or necessarily true or false (cf. e.g., Itkonen 1975 b: Sect. 2). It is clear that what we have here is *intuitive* necessity. On the other hand, it is natural to interpret the TG-type analysis as attempting a systematic translation of sentences about (e.g.) "correct in L" into sentences about "generable by $G_L$." Insofar as such a translation cannot be made, in either of the two directions, the grammar $G_L$ has been falsified. It is a *formally* necessary truth (or falsity) that a grammar generates or does not generate a given sentence. Consequently, grammatical analysis does translate intuitive necessity into formal necessity. Analogously, von Wright transforms the intuitive necessity of, e.g., the sentence "If one ought to do $p$ and is not forbidden to do $q$, then one is permitted to do both $p$ and $q$" into the formal necessity of "(Op & ~ O ~ q) ⊃ P(p & q)" by constructing his monadic system of deontic logic. The same holds true of philosophical analysis as well, as Pap himself has shown. Hence, explication functions as the common denominator of grammar, logic, and philosophy.[5]

The data of grammar, logic, and philosophy is not spatiotemporal (even if, to repeat, it has its spatiotemporal "substratum"). *A fortiori*, these sciences are not concerned with matters of causality, i.e., with discovering cause-effect relationships in their data. Indeed, the word "autonomous" in the expression "autonomous linguistics" could be understood as meaning "autonomous vis-à-vis causal influences." On the other hand, it is well known that the causalist terminology makes

---

[4] My rule-sentences are what Leech (1974: Ch. 5), for instance, calls "basic statements." The important thing here is that unlike the basic statements of natural science, the basic statements of grammar are not about particular spatiotemporal occurrences. One can easily convince oneself of this by looking at Leech's examples. My claim is that, here as elsewhere, the basic statements of grammar are about (maximally simple) *rules of language*.

[5] Of course, this is not to deny that there are important differences between logic and philosophy on the one hand and grammar on the other. In particular, logic and philosophy have a *prescriptive* research interest: they intend to *improve* our rules of inferring and thinking. By contrast, grammar (as it exists today) is content to describe rules of speaking as they are.

frequent intrusions into grammar. For example, it might be said that in German [g] becomes [k] *because* it occurs in the word-final position. The causal mechanism which is vaguely implied here must be of psychological nature. The investigation of such mechanisms is a useful accompaniment of grammatical analysis (cf. Sect. II B). However, it must be clearly understood that, as an empirical-experimental undertaking, investigation of causality is qualitatively different from grammatical analysis, which, as we have seen, is a case of explication, or conceptual analysis. It is also impossible that the former might replace the latter (cf. Sect. I C).

Chomsky has never really grasped the relationship between grammar and psychology. He makes an elementary mistake when he tries to explain grammatical data extragrammatically, i.e., psychologically, but refuses to consider any extragrammatical evidence, i.e., facts of linguistic "performance," preferably elicited under experimental conditions. This procedure has been rightly accused of circularity, e.g., in Botha (1971) and Derwing (1973). Surprisingly, Chomsky fails to see the point:

> "Some have argued that the approach outlined here is 'circular,' failing to see that if this were true, the various empirical principles postulated within theories of generative grammar would be irrefutable, whereas they are, in fact, all too refutable and have been repeatedly modified in the light of new discoveries and observations" (Chomsky 1975: 11).

Chomsky is here guilty of two confusions. First, he confuses "circular," in the sense intended by his critics, with "tautological" or "unfalsifiable." Secondly, he confuses "falsifiable" with "empirical." Grammatical and logical descriptions are equally "circular:" In both cases descriptions of data of the type X are tested against (new) data of the type X, and in both cases descriptions are falsifiable (cf. above). There is nothing wrong with this kind of (non-tautological) circularity. However, Chomsky's "psychologism" exhibits a wrong kind of circularity: He makes the hypothesis that descriptions of *grammatical* data have *psychological* relevance, but he "tests" this hypothesis only against more grammatical data. The fact that grammatical (or logical) descriptions are falsifiable proves absolutely nothing about their psychological relevance, or about their allegedly empirical status.

To be sure, Chomsky occasionally pays lip-service to the investigation of performance data, e.g., in Chomsky (1976: 306), but he never follows this advice in practice. In *op. cit.* he still maintains the myth of the psychological reality of transformations and simply ignores all *experimental-psycholinguistic* evidence, reviewed, e.g., in Fodor et al. (1974), which clearly points in the other direction. The confusion between grammar and psychology (of which the pre-Chomskyan autonomous linguistics was entirely free) has been made complete by Chomsky's (1976: 304—305) proposal to eliminate altogether the distinction between conscious knowledge and unconscious psychological mechanisms and to refer to both uniformly by the term "cognizance."

Since grammatical data is not spatiotemporal, it goes without saying that Hempel's (1965) deductive-nomological model of (empirical) explanation is inapplicable in grammar. However, it is significant that it is precisely the D—N model, and not any of the statistical models of explanation, which has been proposed as an adequate model of grammatical explanation, e.g., in Wunderlich (1974). This choice recognizes, at least, the discrete nature of grammatical data (cf. Sect. I A), but then mistakes it for the discreteness of a fully deterministic *spatiotemporal* mechanism. It should be self-evident, however, that (macro-)explanation of actual social, including verbal, behavior can be of *statistical* character only (cf. Sect. B).

This section sums up the general argument of Itkonen (1974) (cf. also Itkonen 1975 a and 1976 c). Its more philosophical implications will be mentioned in Sect. C. Congenial grammar-conceptions have been presented in Ringen (1975) and Lass (1976).

## B. Socio- and psycholinguistics

Sociolinguistics, as this term is currently understood, is an empirical science, and therefore its methodology cannot be discussed without explicit reference to the philosophy of empirical sciences. The latter was dominated, until recently, by the hypothetico-deductive conception of science, as expounded, e.g., in Popper (1965), Nagel (1961) and Hempel (1965). These authors regarded the construction of axiomatic theories as the ultimate goal of science. Significantly, they accorded at most a heuristic role to the concept of *causality*. For instance, Hempel (1965: 352—353) emphasized that D—N explanations include also functional, non-causal explanations.

This conception of science has been increasingly criticized for its lack of concern with the *actual* practice of empirical scientists. One of the most forceful criticisms has been presented in Harré (1970). He notes that physicists, for instance, are not primarily interested in setting up systems of sentences, consisting of axioms, inference rules, correspondence rules, and operational definitions. Rather, they are interested in discovering the actual constitution of the universe, i.e., those *causal mechanisms* which make things happen in the way they do happen. Consequently, the notion of causality and the models for (hypothetical) causal mechanisms acquire a central importance. From a rather different perspective, von Wright too has been arguing for the theoretical, not-just-heuristic importance of causality. In von Wright (1974: 70), for instance, he notes that "the basis of functional laws [like Ohm's law] are causal relations between (variations in) determinate states." What is more, if it is said, e.g., that a definite change happens as a function of time, such a formulation actually *conceals* the real state of affairs, because time as such (just as little as place as such) could not bring about any changes.

It is very interesting to note that Hempel has come to accept the correctness of such and similar criticisms:

> "And as for the claim that formalization makes explicit the foundational assumptions of the scientific discipline concerned, it should be borne in mind that axiomatization is basically an expository device, determining a set of sentences and exhibiting their logical relationships, but not their epistemic grounds and connections. A scientific theory admits of many different axiomatizations, and the postulates chosen in a particular one need not, therefore, correspond to what in some more substantial sense might count as the basic assumptions of the theory; . . ." (Hempel 1970: 152).

> "Thus, a model in the sense here considered is not only of didactic and heuristic value: The statements specifying the model seem to me to form part of the internal principles of a theory and as such to play a systematic role in its formation" (op. cit.: 158).

I state as a desideratum of any adequate methodology of empirical linguistics that it should provide causal models of linguistic behavior. One type of model will be described in what follows. Attempts at axiomatization are commendable, but nevertheless of secondary importance only.

Speaking is a form of social behavior. It is an undisputed fact that each type of social behavior, including rule-governed or normative behavior, exhibits a larger or smaller amount of unpredictable variation. Therefore description and explanation of actual linguistic behavior must be of *statistical* nature. It can even be stated as a geral principle that if a linguistic description is not statistical, then it cannot be empirical, i.e., it cannot deal with regularities in space and time. (However, statisticalness does not entail empiricalness.)

For some time, Hempel's (1965) inductive-statistical ($= I-S$) model, which for convenience is presented here together with his $D-N$ model, provided the standard model of statistical explanation:

$$
\begin{array}{ll}
\text{D}-\text{N} & \text{I}-\text{S} \\
(x)\,(Fx \supset Gx) & P(Gx \mid Fx) = r \\
Fa & Fa \\
\hline
Ga & \overline{\overline{Ga}} \qquad r
\end{array}
$$

In the $D-N$ model the explanandum "Ga" follows logically from the explanans. By contrast, in the $I-S$ model the explanans only confers the probability $r$ upon "Ga." Moreover, according to Hempel, the event *Ga* can be said to be explained only when $r$ is relatively high.

Salmon (1971) presents a different, process-like notion of statistical explanation. According to it, we start with a probability statement "P(G| F) = r," which states that if anything is a member of the reference class F, it is a member of the attribute class G with the probability *r*. F is said to be homogeneous with respect to G if no attempts to further specify F affect the probability *r*. Next, we choose a category H and form, with it, a new reference class F & H, which is hopefully more homogeneous with respect to G than F alone was. If this is the case, the probability of G will increase, relative to F & H. On the other hand, relative to the other new reference class F & H̄, the probability of G will decrease. For this reason (and some others) I agree with Stegmüller (1973: 330—350) that in the present context the term "statistical explanation" should be replaced by a more neutral term like "statistical analysis." This kind of analysis consists, then, in changing the prior weight *r* into the posterior weights *s* and *t*, irrespective of whether *r* is high or low:

$$P(G|F \& H) = s > P(G|F) = r > P(G|F \& \bar{H}) = t$$
2. stage                    1. stage                    2. stage

In a situation like this, H is said to be *statistically relevant* to G. Statistical relevance may in turn be an indicator of *causal* relevance.

Reference classes may be homogeneous as far as we know, i.e., epistemically homogeneous, but still ontologically inhomogeneous. The two types of homogeneity undisputably coincide in (well-confirmed) D—N explanations, where "P(Gx|Fx) = 1," i.e., "(x) (Fx ⊃ Gx)," holds true: here F is literally included in G. For dogmatic determinists, the use of statistical analysis is always, e.g., in microphysics, a sign of ontological inhomogeneity.

It will be seen that Salmon's notion of statistical analysis corresponds rather well to the descriptive practice of social scientists in general, and sociolinguists in particular.

Actual linguistic behavior is described by performance grammars. Suppes (1972) develops a context-free performance grammar in which rules are given constant probabilistic weights in the following way:

$$r: \ X \to \left\{ \begin{array}{c} Y \\ Z \\ W \end{array} \right\} = \begin{array}{l} r_1: X \to Y \\ r_2: X \to Z \\ r_3: X \to W \end{array} \quad \text{and } P(r_1) + P(r_2) + P(r_3) = 1$$

In other words, the rules in any block must have probabilities the sum of which equals 1. What, precisely, each $P(r_i)$ is, must be determined empirically. The probability of a definite utterance or, more realistically, of an utterance exemplifying definite (high-level) grammatical categories, can be computed, relative to other utterances, simply by multiplying the probabilities of the rules figuring in its derivational history.

Suppes-type grammars may be useful first approximations. However, giving fixed probabilities to rules is quite unrealistic because rules of natural language grammars obviously apply with a higher or lower probability depending upon their (linguistic and/or extralinguistic) contexts (cf. also Klein 1974: Ch. 4). What is needed, is obviously a method of ascribing *conditional* probabilities to rules. Salomaa (1969) develops a grammar in which the probability of a rule is made dependent on the immediately preceding rule. This is an improvement vis-à-vis the Suppes-type grammar, but even from the intralinguistic point of view there is no reason why we should restrict our attention to the influence of the immediately preceding rule. Moreover, concepts like "preceding" and "following" cease to be meaningful when we take, as we must, the influence of extralinguistic factors into account.

A performance grammar operating with conditional probabilities makes statements of the type "$P(A|B) = r$." It is natural to interpret B as an independent, causally effective variable vis-à-vis A and to start looking, in the way suggested by Salmon, for additional independent variables C, D, etc. If B, C, D, etc. are linguistic variables, a causal interpretation can be achieved only by postulating a psychological (or perhaps physiological) mechanism which connects them with A. Thus, for instance, if A is the application of the devoicing rule and B is the word-final position, then in order to say that B *causes* A (with a certain probability), we obviously need to assume a (stronger or weaker) disposition to do A which is, under some circumstances, triggered by definite factors, including B.

Performance grammars deal indifferently with outputs of obligatory and optional rules. As is well known, Labov's notion of "variable rule" concentrates solely upon the latter. Labov's merits in arousing the general interest in sociolinguistics are beyond dispute. In what follows, however, I shall argue that the notion of "variable rule" is open to two objections, at least one of which is decisive. First, it is hardly satisfactory from the viewpoint of the philosophy of science to merely refer to a computer program when it should be explained how the probabilistic weights connected with different variable constraints are arrived at (cf. e.g., Cedergren & Sankoff 1974). It also follows that the corresponding notion of *causality* remains opaque, at the very least. Secondly, and more seriously, Labov and his associates explicitly base their notion of variable rule on the assumption that there are no *interaction effects* between variable contraints or independent variables. In other words, they assume that the force with which B influences A in "$P(A|B)$" remains the same in all contexts, e.g., in "$P(A|B \ \& \ C)$" or "$P(A|B \ \& \ D)$." Now, it is quite easy to show, with Labov's own data, that this is not the case (cf. below). Consequently, Labov-type variable rules must be rejected. — This very simple argument has been presented already in Klein (1974).

Here I shall outline what I take to be a more adequate causal model for linguistic behavior. In particular, it is able to handle cases of interaction. It is taken directly from Boudon (1974), which I recommend to linguists' attention. Blalock (1968) has been used as background information.

The significant linguistic variables are of nominal or qualitative nature, i.e., their values cannot be ordered on a quantitative scale. (The only quantitative aspect of values of such variables consists in their frequencies of occurrence.) Usually there is no upper limit to the number of the values of a (linguistic) qualitative variable. Unfortunately, Boudon's models deal, primarily, only with dichotomous variables like $x_a = A/\bar{A}$. However, this restriction can be overcome, to some extent at least, by noting that, e.g., the trichotomy A/B/C can be transformed into the two dichotomies A/BC and B/AC.

We are developing *causal* models here. Causality is normally an asymmetric notion, in the sense that the effect of a sufficient cause is not a sufficient, but a necessary condition of that cause; and the same holds, *mutatis mutandis,* of the effect of a necessary cause. Only effects of sufficient *and* necessary causes are sufficient and necessary conditions vis-à-vis those causes, but such cases of *equivalence* are seldom met in practice. Now, our models are restricted to equivalence between causes and effects. Boudon points out (op. cit.: 35) that some work by Guttman, for instance, bears indirectly upon the possibility of constructing (more realistic) models of *implication.*

As has been noted before, no strictly deterministic regularities exist in social science. Therefore, once the formulae *p* and *q* are replaced by the classes A and B, we notice that instead of the truth-functional notion of equivalence, we have here the following type of *weak* equivalence:

|        |        | q     | ~ q   |
|--------|--------|-------|-------|
| Not:   | p      | true  | false |
|        | ~ p    | false | true  |

|        |        | A      | Ā      |
|--------|--------|--------|--------|
| but:   | B      | often  | seldom |
|        | B̄      | seldom | often  |

In other words, it is never the case that A and B on the one hand and Ā and B̄ on the other would totally coincide. Instead, they overlap to a larger or smaller extent:

fig. 1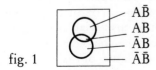

AB̄
AB
ĀB
ĀB̄

We are dealing, so far, with two dichotomous variables $x_a$ and $x_b$ with, respectively, two values $A/\bar{A}$ and $B/\bar{B}$. Our data consists of cross-tabulated frequencies, e.g.:

|     | A  | Ā  |     |
|-----|----|----|-----|
| B   | 35 | 20 | 55  |
| B̄   | 15 | 30 | 45  |
|     | 50 | 50 | 100 |

We make the following notational convention:

|     | A        | Ā         |         |
|-----|----------|-----------|---------|
| B   | $n_{ab}$ | $n_{\bar{a}b}$ | $n_b$   |
| B̄   | $n_{a\bar{b}}$ | $n_{\bar{a}\bar{b}}$ | $n_{\bar{b}}$ |
|     | $n_a$    | $n_{\bar{a}}$  | N       |

fig.2                                                          fig. 3

Now we can define: $\dfrac{n_{ab}}{n_a} = \dfrac{n_{ab}/N}{n_a/N} = \dfrac{p_{ab}}{p_a} = p_{b,a}$

"$p_{b,a}$" is identical with "$P(B|A)$," except that the former deals with frequencies while the latter deals with probabilities.

Next we define a suitable coefficient of correlation ($=$ phi-coefficient):

$$f_{ab} = p_{b,a} - p_{b,\bar{a}} \; ; \quad f_{ba} = p_{a,b} - p_{a,\bar{b}} \; ; \quad \varphi_{ab} = \sqrt{f_{ab} \, f_{ba}}$$

$f_{ab}$ can be transformed into $\dfrac{p_{ab} - p_a \, p_b}{p_a \, p_{\bar{a}}}$. Given that the numerator is identical, in the probability notation, with "$P(A \,\&\, B) - P(A) \times P(B)$," it is clear that if the difference does not equal 0, then there must be a (positive or negative) correlation.

For instance, with the data of fig. 2 we get:

$$f_{ab} = \frac{0.35}{0.50} - \frac{0.20}{0.50} = 0.7 - 0.4 = 0.3 \; ;$$

$$f_{ba} = \frac{0.35}{0.55} - \frac{0.15}{0.45} = 0.64 - 0.33 = 0.31 \; ; \quad \varphi_{ab} = 0.3$$

The $\varphi$-coefficient measures the strength of the correlation between $x_a$ and $x_b$. As such, it says nothing about the degree of the certainty or the probability that such a correlation does in fact obtain. As usually, this question is decided by a significance test. A chi-squared test would be applicable here. However, I can dispense with discussing significance tests, because, as e.g., Labov (1972: 49) points out when referring to the "extreme generality of linguistic behavior," any moderately large sample can be safely taken as representative of its speech community.

Next we have to define a *causal* coefficient ($=$ d-coefficient). It must be mentioned that in connection with dichotomous variables the talk of causality is the most natural when $\bar{A}$ is not just the complement of A ($=$ "anything but A"), but has a well-defined status of its own (e.g., "female" as the opposite of "male"). It is a well-known truth that numerical, non-experimental analysis cannot as such tell us the *direction* of causality. This can be decided or assumed only on the basis of additional considerations. — Let us take the same data as in fig. 2, and let us assume that there is reason to believe that the causal influence goes from $x_a$ to $x_b$. Now the group of those 35 units which are both A and B among those 50 units which are A, is divisible into two subgroups: either they are B *because* they are A ($= a_{ab}$), or they are B for some other reason ($= e_b$). It is natural to think that $e_b$ can be measured by the proportion of the 20 ĀB-units among the 50 Ā-units, since the ĀB-units are B although there is no causal influence $a_{ab}$. Presumably the same proportion among AB-units would be B, even if they were not A, i.e., they would be B for some other reason ($= e_b$).

We get the following equations:

$$p_{b,a} = a_{ab} + e_b$$
$$e_b = p_{b,ā}$$

Therefore:

$$a_{ab} = p_{b,a} - e_b$$
$$= p_{b,a} - p_{b,ā}$$
$$= 0.7 - 0.4 = 0.3$$

So we see that in this maximally simple case f-coefficients and a-coefficients coincide.

We can equally calculate the $a_{ba}$-coefficient (which, to be sure, conflicts with the assumed direction of causality) and then the symmetric d-coefficient:

$$d_{ab} = d_{ba} = a_{ab} \sqrt{\frac{p_a\, p_{ā}}{p_b\, p_{b̄}}} = a_{ba} \sqrt{\frac{p_b\, p_{b̄}}{p_a\, p_{ā}}}$$

In practice it is often convenient simply to use f- and a-coefficients instead of φ- and d-coefficients.

The equation "$p_{b,a} = a_{ab} + e_b$" can be transformed into "$p_b = a_{ab}\, p_a + e_b$," i.e., "$0.55 = 0.3 \cdot 0.5 + 0.4$." When the decimal numbers are converted into integers, the equation can be read as saying that the 55 B-units consist of three groups: first, those 15 AB-units which are B *because* they are A; second, those 20 AB-units which are B for some other reason; third, the 20 ĀB-units which, of necessity, are B for some other reason.

If we assume that both A and Ā are causally effective, the following picture emerges:

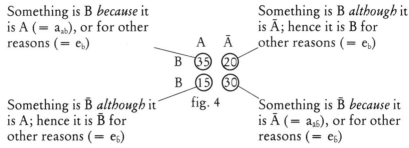

Something is B *because* it is A (= $a_{ab}$), or for other reasons (= $e_b$)

Something is B *although* it is Ā; hence it is B for other reasons (= $e_b$)

Something is B̄ *although* it is A; hence it is B̄ for other reasons (= $e_b̄$)

fig. 4

Something is B̄ *because* it is Ā (= $a_{ab̄}$), or for other reasons (= $e_b̄$)

Here I have defined the meaning of (probabilistic) causality of our models. As far as I know, Labov-type sociolinguistics has given no corresponding definition.

Next, let us consider cases with three variables. Let the initial numerical data be as follows, with $x_c$ as the dependent variable:

|     | B   | B̄   |      |
|-----|-----|-----|------|
| C   | 374 | 120 | 494  |
| C̄   | 206 | 300 | 506  |
|     | 580 | 420 | 1000 |

We get:
$$f_{bc} = a_{bc} = P_{c,b} - P_{c,b̄}$$
$$= \frac{0.374}{0.580} - \frac{0.120}{0.420} = 0.36$$

fig. 5

To put it differently, B is statistically relevant to C:
$$P(C) = 0.49 < P(C|B) = 0.64$$

That is, the probability of the joint occurrence of B and C is more than random: $P(B \& C) = 0.37 > P(B) \times P(C) = 0.26$

Now we take into account a third variable $x_a$, which we assume also causally influences $x_c$, and cross-tabulate the data accordingly:

|     | A   |     |     | Ā   |     |     |      |
|-----|-----|-----|-----|-----|-----|-----|------|
|     | B   | B̄   |     | B   | B̄   |     |      |
| C   | 294 | 72  | 366 | 80  | 48  | 128 |      |
| C̄   | 126 | 108 | 234 | 80  | 192 | 272 |      |
|     | 420 | 180 | 600 | 160 | 240 | 400 | 1000 |

$f_{ac} = 0.29$
$f_{ab} = 0.30$
$f_{bc} = 0.36$

fig. 6

Next we compute the (assumedly) causal a-coefficients. In a case with more than two variables this presupposes that we have in mind a definite model depicting the causal relationships that we assume to obtain. In the present case the most simple model would be this:

fig. 7

$x_a$   $x_b$
$\searrow \swarrow$
$x_c$

The a-coefficients are computed as before, except that this time they are identifiable as *conditional* correlation coefficients. For instance, if we consider the influence $a_{bc}$, there are this time *two* situations where it can obtain, namely either with the positive or with the negative value of $x_a$. (Of course, the same is true, *mutatis mutandis*, of the influence $a_{ac}$.) Consequently, we get two values "$p_{c,ab} - p_{c,a\bar{b}}$" and "$p_{c,\bar{a}b} - p_{c,\bar{a}\bar{b}}$." If the values are identical, we have proof that the influence of $x_b$ upon $x_c$ is constant, or independent of any other factors. Models with constant a-values are called *disjunctive* models. If, on the other hand, we have "$(p_{c,ab} - p_{c,a\bar{b}}) \neq (p_{c,\bar{a}b} - p_{c,\bar{a}\bar{b}})$," then we have proof that $a_{bc}$, i.e., the influence of $x_b$ upon $x_c$, is itself influenced by, or dependent upon the variable $x_a$. If this is the case, we have to do with a *conjunctive* or *interaction* model.

My argument here can be summed up as follows. Labov assumes that disjunctive models are sufficient in sociolinguistics. I am going to show that Labov's own data require the use of conjunctive models. To repeat, the notions of disjunctive and conjunctive model are directly taken from Boudon (1974).

We get the following a-values:

$$a_{ac} = p_{c,ab} - p_{c,\bar{a}b} = \frac{0.294}{0.420} - \frac{0.080}{0.160} = 0.2$$

$$= p_{c,a\bar{b}} - p_{c,\bar{a}\bar{b}} = \frac{0.072}{0.180} - \frac{0.048}{0.240} = 0.2$$

$$a_{bc} = p_{c,ab} - p_{c,a\bar{b}} = \frac{0.294}{0.420} - \frac{0.072}{0.180} = 0.3$$

$$= p_{c,\bar{a}b} - p_{c,\bar{a}\bar{b}} = \frac{0.080}{0.160} - \frac{0.048}{0.240} = 0.3$$

The first noticeable thing here is that the f-values and the a-values are seen to differ:

$$f_{ac} = 0.29 ; \quad a_{ac} = 0.2$$
$$f_{bc} = 0.36 ; \quad a_{bc} = 0.3$$

We are primarily interested here in the causal influences of $x_a$ and $x_b$ upon $x_c$. But we also notice that there is a correlation between $x_a$ and $x_b$:

$$p_{b,a} - p_{b,\bar{a}} = \frac{0.420}{0.600} - \frac{0.160}{0.400} = 0.3$$

Hence, assuming that it is $x_a$ which influences $x_b$, we must replace our original model with the following one:

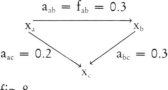

fig. 8

With these values we are able to distinguish between the *direct* and the *indirect* influence of $x_a$ upon $x_c$. It can also be seen that the correlation coefficient $f_{ac}$ consists of these two influences in the following way:

$$\begin{aligned} f_{ac} &= a_{ac} + f_{ab} \cdot a_{bc} \\ &= a_{ac} + a_{ab} \cdot a_{bc} \\ 0.29 &= 0.2 + 0.3 \cdot 0.3 \end{aligned}$$

The value $f_{bc}$ can be computed in a similar way, but it is intuitively less natural.

To sum up, we have here the following three disjunctive models, which are interrelated through simple algebraic transformations:

$$\begin{aligned} p_{c,ab} &= a_{ac} + a_{bc} + e_c \\ p_c &= a_{ac}\, p_a + a_{bc}\, p_b + e_c \\ f_{ac} &= a_{ac} + f_{ab} \cdot a_{bc} \end{aligned}$$

These models could be called "proportion model," "multiple regression model" (in a figurative sense), and "correlation model," respectively.

Our present case is the prototype of a disjunctive model. All more complex disjunctive structures can be generated from it by a simple recursive rule. That is, the f-values of, e.g., a disjunctive structure with four variables can be analyzed in the same way into simpler f-values and ultimately into a-values:

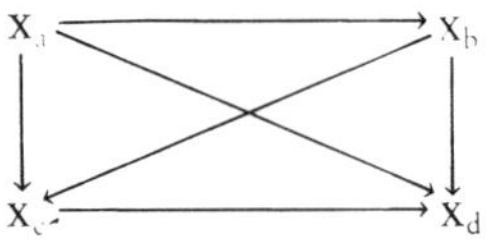

For instance:

$$\begin{aligned} f_{ad} &= a_{ad} + a_{bd} \cdot f_{ab} + a_{cd} \cdot f_{ac} \\ &= a_{ad} + a_{bd} \cdot a_{ab} + a_{cd} \cdot (a_{ac} + a_{bc} \cdot f_{ab}) \\ &= a_{ad} + a_{bd} \cdot a_{ab} + a_{cd} \cdot a_{ac} + a_{ac} \cdot a_{bc} \cdot a_{ab} \end{aligned}$$

fig. 9

Notice that the above equation exhausts all possibilities of going from $x_a$ to $x_d$. It is of course a different question whether such pure disjunctive structures are ever found in reality.

Our simple model with three variables represents a clear case of Salmon-type statistical explanation: $P(C|A \,\&\, B) = 0.7 > P(C|B) = 0.64 > P(C|\bar{A} \,\&\, B) = 0.5$. Moreover, it already suffices to illustrate the sense in which hypothetical models can be said to be constructed and tested in non-experimental social and psychological research. If we have assumed, for instance, that there is no (causal) relationship between $x_a$ and $x_b$, then this assumption is — temporally at least — refuted by the existence of the correlation $f_{ab} = 0.3$. Remember, however, that statistical relevance may, but does not have to, be an indicator of causal relevance. On the other hand, (genuine) lack of statistical relevance entails lack of causal relevance.

Our model can also be used to illustrate the distinction between frequency and probability. If our data exhibits a near-perfect agreement with the assumption of a disjunctive structure, it may be legitimate to infer that the values ascribed to our model represent objective probabilities, i.e., "real" properties of our subject matter, whereas our observational values are partly due to chance.

Let us take one more example of a disjunctive structure. Let the data be as follows:

|   | B | B̄ |   |
|---|---|---|---|
| C | 32 | 24 | 56 |
| C̄ | 18 | 46 | 64 |
|   | 50 | 70 | 120 |

$f_{bc} = 0.3$
$P(C) = 0.45 < P(C|B) = 0.64$

fig. 10

Thus $x_b$ is statistically relevant to $x_c$, and we assume that this is a sign of causal relevance as well. Suppose, however, that we take a third variable $x_a$ into consideration and obtain the following data:

|   | A B | A B̄ |   | Ā B | Ā B̄ |   |   |
|---|---|---|---|---|---|---|---|
| C | 30 | 15 | 45 | 2 | 9 | 11 |   |
| C̄ | 10 | 5 | 15 | 8 | 41 | 49 |   |
|   | 40 | 20 | 60 | 10 | 50 | 60 | 120 |

$f_{ab} = 0.5$
$f_{ac} = 0.57$
$f_{bc} = 0.3$

fig. 11

We have been assuming that we have the same type of model as in fig. 8. But when we compute the a-values, we get the following:

$a_{ab} = 0.48 \sim 0.5$
$a_{ac} = 0.53 \sim 0.57$
$a_{bc} = 0 \sim 0.02$

In other words, in spite of the statistical correlation $f_{bc} = 0.3$, there is no causal influence between $x_b$ and $x_c$. The same thing can be expressed in the probability notation as follows:

$$\left[ P(C|A \ \& \ B) = \frac{30}{40} \right] = \left[ P(C|A) = \frac{45}{60} \right]$$

In a case like this, the statistical relevance of $x_b$ to $x_c$ disappears, or "$x_a$ screens off $x_b$ from $x_c$," as Salmon (1971) would say.

The present data is compatible with two entirely different interpretations, namely these:

fig. 12                                                          fig. 13


Figures 12 and 13 correspond, respectively, to Lazarsfeld's notions of "explanation" and "interpretation." In both cases the original connection between $x_b$ and $x_c$ is made to disappear, but in differing ways. "Explanation" means the discovery of a common cause. "Interpretation" means, in social science, the discovery of an intervening variable which makes the original connection psychologically understandable. A good example of sociolinguistic "interpretation" is Labov's discovery in his study of the centralization of vowels at Martha's Vineyard, that the correlation between the centralization and the social group "middle-aged fishermen" was mediated by the variable "positive attitude towards staying in the island."

Now we can finally take up a sociolinguistic example. Our data is taken from Labov (1972: 222). We can identify here the following four variables:

$x_a$   (= dependent variable) = —t, d disappears (= A) or not (= Ā)

$x_b$ = The following word begins with a consonant (= B) or not (= B̄)

$x_c$ = A morpheme boundary does not precede (= C) or does precede (= C̄)

$x_d$ = Lower working class (= D), upper middle class (= D̄)

The data can be presented in the following way:

|     |         | C   |     | C̄  |     |
|-----|---------|-----|-----|-----|-----|
|     |         | B   | B̄  | B   | B̄  |
| D   | A       | 97  | 72  | 76  | 34  |
|     | Ā       | 3   | 28  | 24  | 66  |
| D̄  | A       | 79  | 23  | 49  | 7   |
|     | Ā       | 21  | 77  | 51  | 93  |

fig. 14

The above numerical data has been achieved by converting percentages into frequencies. This is of course an illegitimate procedure, but I have no other choice, since the data has not been properly cross-tabulated. What is important, however, is that the presence or absence of interaction effects is evident even from data that has been manipulated in this way. As a further consequence of this manipulation, no dependencies between the independent variables $x_b$, $x_c$, and $x_d$ can become apparent.

When we compute the coefficients $a_{ba}$ and $a_{ca}$ separately with the two values of $x_d$, we get the following results:

$$\text{D:} \quad a_{ba} = 0.27 \sim 0.42 \quad \left.\begin{array}{c} \text{with C} \quad \text{with C̄} \\ \\ \text{with B} \quad \text{with B̄} \\ \\ a_{ca} = 0.21 \sim 0.38 \end{array}\right\} \quad \text{negative interaction}$$

$$\text{D̄:} \quad a_{ba} = 0.56 \sim 0.42 \quad \left.\begin{array}{c} \text{with C} \quad \text{with C̄} \\ \\ \text{with B} \quad \text{with B̄} \\ \\ a_{ca} = 0.3 \sim 0.16 \end{array}\right\} \quad \text{positive interaction}$$

In other words, we have here *two* levels of interaction: First, the influences $a_{ba}$ and $a_{ca}$ depend upon variables $x_c$ and $x_b$, respectively. Second, the interaction $a_{bca}$ is dependent upon the variable $x_d$. That is, Labov assumes that we have the structure of fig. 15, whereas the structure of fig. 16 is what we have in fact:

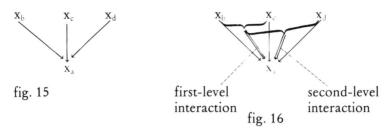

fig. 15                        first-level              second-level
                               interaction             interaction
                                        fig. 16

The computation of interaction values is rather laborious (cf. Boudon 1974: Ch. 9). It requires, among other things, redefining $a_{ba}$ and $a_{ca}$ as $a'_{ba} = a_{ba} + a_{bca} \cdot p_c$ and $a'_{ca} = a_{ca} + a_{bca} \cdot p_b$, respectively. Finally we get:

$$D: \quad a'_{ba} = 0.34 \qquad \bar{D}: \quad a'_{ba} = 0.45$$
$$\phantom{D: \quad} a'_{ca} = 0.3 \qquad \phantom{\bar{D}: \quad} a'_{ca} = 0.23$$
$$\phantom{D: \quad} a_{bca} = -0.17 \qquad \phantom{\bar{D}: \quad} a_{bca} = 0.14$$

Notice in particular that the positive value of $x_d$ brings about the negative interaction $a_{bca} = -0.17$ whereas the negative value of $x_d$ brings about the positive interaction $a_{bca} = +0.14$.

The interaction value $a_{bca}$ can be defined as follows:

$$p_{a,bc} = a_{ba} + a_{ca} + a_{bca} + e_a, \quad \text{hence}$$
$$a_{bca} = p_{a,bc} - (a_{ba} + a_{ca} + e_a)$$

This last equation can be transformed into the following form:

$$a_{bca} = (p_{a,bc} - p_{a,\bar{b}c}) \quad - (p_{a,b\bar{c}} - p_{a,\bar{b}\bar{c}})$$

the influence    the influence
of $x_b$ upon $x_a$    of $x_b$ upon $x_a$ in
in the case of C    the case of $\bar{C}$

the influence of $x_c$ upon the
influence of $x_b$ upon $x_a$, or:
$$x_c \to (x_b \to x_a)$$

We get the identical value for the second-level influence $x_b \to (x_c \to x_a)$. We can check our definition (cf. fig. 14):

$$\bar{D}: \quad a_{bca} = (0.79 - 0.23) - (0.49 - 0.07) = 0.14$$

The interaction value as here defined has the disadvantage of ranging from 2 to $-2$. When converted into a d-value, however, it will remain within the limits of 1 and $-1$. For simplicity, this conversion is not carried out here.

The causal efficacy of $x_b$ and $x_c$ is based on psychological mechanisms while that of $x_d$ is based on social mechanisms (which, to be sure, must always be psychologically mediated in each individual case). Consequently, our model is applicable in non-experimental psycholinguistics as well as in sociolinguistics. Furthermore, our model obviously conforms to Salmon's model of statistical analysis because consideration of new variables gives us more specific knowledge of the probability of the dependent variable $x_a$. As Salmon himself emphasizes, his model is that of empirical, not of theoretical, explanation (or rather analysis). In the present state of sociolinguistics, however, more theoretical models would hardly be realistic.


## C. Conclusion

The variables of natural science, i.e., length, time, and mass, are inherently quantitative or measurable. By contrast, linguistic variables are typically non-measurable or qualitative. Their only quantitative aspect consists in the *frequencies* with which units exemplifying their values occur. Since such units occur with a fair amount of unpredictability, any models purporting to represent the causal mechanisms which make them occur must be of statistical-probabilistic nature. Unlike in natural science, in social science the (relative) unpredictability of the data is due to the historicality, the culture-dependence, and the (limited) free will of the research objects. Apart from this, however, the construction of causal models is largely similar in social science and in natural science.

Linguistic variables are subordinated to the notion of normativity: units exemplifying or failing to exemplify their values are (aspects of) correct or incorrect actions. Rules of language determine (the values of) the linguistic variables as conceptual possibilities; they constitute conceptual preconditions of actual bits of (correct or incorrect) linguistic behavior. Analysis of linguistic rules is a qualitative, conceptual undertaking, technically speaking a case of "explication." As such, it is similar to logical or philosophical analysis, and fundamentally different from the construction of (probabilistic) causal models. Explication, characteristic of grammar, and causal analysis, characteristic of socio- and psycholinguistics, stand in a relation of complementarity to each other; the one cannot be replaced by the other. The study of linguistic variation mediates between the two.

The philosophical tradition which claims that methods of natural science, ultimately methods of causal analysis, must be applicable in all sciences, is identifiable as *(neo-)positivism.* Logic and philosophy are prime exceptions to the positivistic program, and, as we have seen, grammar too is an exception to it. The basic similarity of grammar, logic, and philosophy consists in the fact that in all these cases people investigate, or reflect upon, the rules of their *own* behavior, that is, rules of speaking, inferring, or thinking. More precisely, people reflect upon what they know that they ought to do. This type of knowledge, "agent's knowledge," is to be distinguished from the "observer's knowledge" characteristic of natural science and, to some extent, of empirical sociology and psychology as well. Intuition and (self-)reflection, which are characteristic methods of explication, are qualitatively different from observation and experimentation, which are characteristic methods of natural science. To this extent the results achieved here vindicate the standpoint of *hermeneutics* which is a philosophical tradition claiming that it makes a difference whether one investigates physical phenomena or human phenomena.

## References

Bailey, Charles-James, 1973: *Variation and linguistic theory*, Arlington: Center for applied linguistics.
Blalock, Hubert, Jr., 1968: "Theory building and causal inferences," in H. Blalock Jr. & A. B. Blalock: *Methodology in social research*, New York: McGraw-Hill.
Bloomfield, Leonard, 1935: *Language*, London: Allen & Unwin.
Böhme, Gernot (ed.), 1976: *Protophysik*, Frankfurt a/M: Suhrkamp.
Botha, Rudolph, 1971: *Methodological aspects of transformational generative phonology*, The Hague: Mouton.
Boudon, Raymond, 1974: *The logic of sociological explanation*, Penguin Books.
Cedergren, Henrietta & David Sankoff, 1974: "Variable rules: performance as a statistical reflection of competence," *Language*.
Chomsky, Noam, 1957: *Syntactic structures*, The Hague: Mouton.
— 1965: *Aspects of the theory of syntax*, Cambridge, Mass.: MIT Press.
— 1975: *The logical structure of linguistic theory*, "Introduction," New York: Plenum Press.
— 1976: "Problems and mysteries in the study of human language," in Kasher 1976.
Cohen, Jonathan, 1976: "How empirical is contemporary logical empiricism?", in Kasher 1976.
Derwing, Bruce, 1973: *Transformational grammar as a theory of language acquisition*, Cambridge: Cambridge University Press.
Durkheim, Emile, 1938 (1895): *Les règles de la méthode sociologique*, Paris: Alcan.
Fodor, J. A. & T. G. Bever & M. F. Garrett, 1974: *The psychology of language*, New York: McGraw-Hill.
Friedman, H. R., 1975: "The ontic status of linguistic entities," *Foundations of language*.
Greenbaum, Sidney & Randolph Quirk, 1970: *Elicitation experiments in English*, London: Longman.
Hare, R. M., 1971: "Philosophical discoveries," in C. Lyas (ed.): *Philosophy and linguistics*, London: Macmillan.
Harré, R. M., 1970: *Principles of scientific thinking*, London: Macmillan.
Harris, Zellig, 1957: "From morpheme to utterance," in M. Joos (ed.): *Readings in linguistics*, Chicago: Chicago University Press.
— 1961 (1951): *Structural linguistics*, Chicago: Chicago University Press.
Hempel, Carl, 1965: *Aspects of scientific explanation*, New York: The Free Press.

— 1970: "On the 'standard conception' of scientific theories" in M. Radner & S. Winokur (eds.): *Minnesota studies in the philosophy of science* IV, Minneapolis: University of Minnesoty Press.
Hintikka, Jaakko, 1962: *Knowledge and belief,* Ithaca: Cornell University Press.
Itkonen, Esa, 1974: *Linguistics and metascience,* Kokemäki: Studia Philosophica Turkuensia II.
— 1975 a: "Transformational grammar and the philosophy of science," in E. F. K. Koerner (ed.): *Transformational-generative paradigm and modern linguistic theory,* Amsterdam: Benjamins.
— 1975 b: "Concerning the relationship between linguistics and logic," Indiana University Linguistics Club.
— 1976 a: "The use and misuse of the principle of axiomatics in linguistics," *Lingua.*
— 1976 b: „Die Beziehung des Sprachwissens zum Sprachverhalten", in H. Weber & H. Weydt (eds.): *Sprachtheorie und Pragmatik,* Tübingen: Niemeyer.
— 1976 c:„Was für eine Wissenschaft ist die Linguistik eigentlich?", in Wunderlich 1976 b.
— 1976 d: *Linguistics and empiricalness: answers to criticisms,* Publications of the General Linguistics Department of the University of Helsinki, 4.
— 1977: "The relation between grammar and sociolinguistics," *Forum Linguisticum.*
— 1978. *Grammatical theory and metascience,* Amsterdam: Benjamins.
Kasher, Asa (ed.), 1976: *Language in focus,* Dordrecht: Reidel.
Klein, Wolfgang, 1974: *Variation in der Sprache,* Kronberg: Scriptor.
Kockelmans, Joseph (ed.), 1967: *Phenomenology,* New York: Doubleday.
Labov, William, 1969: "Contraction, deletion, and inherent variability of the English copula," *Language.*
— 1972: *Sociolinguistic patterns,* Philadelphia: University of Pennsylvania Press.
— 1975: *What is a linguistic fact?* Ghent: The Peter de Ridder Press.
Lass, Roger, 1976: *English phonology and phonological theory,* Cambridge: Cambridge University Press.
Leech, Geoffrey, 1974: *Semantics,* Penguin Books.
Lewis, David, 1969: *Convention,* Cambridge, Mass.: Harvard University Press.
Lieb, H.-H., 1976: „Kommentare zu Kanngiesser, Ballmer und Itkonen", in Wunderlich 1976 b.
Lorenzen, Paul, 1969: *Methodisches Denken,* Frankfurt a/M: Suhrkamp.
Mayntz, R. & K. Holm & P. Hoebner, 1976: *Introduction to empirical sociology,* Penguin Books.
Nagel, Ernest, 1961: *The structure of science,* New York: Harcourt.
Pap. Arthur, 1958: *Semantics and necessary truth,* New Haven: Yale University Press.
Popper, Karl, 1965 (1935): *The logic of scientific discovery,* New York: Harper & Row.
Rescher, Nicolas, 1973: *The primacy of practice,* London: Oxford University Press.
Ringen, Jon, 1975: "Linguistic facts," in D. Cohen & J. Wirth (eds.): *Testing linguistic hypotheses,* New York: Wiley.
— 1977: Review of Itkonen 1974, *Language.*
Ross, John, 1973: "A fake NP squish," in C.-J. Bailey & R. Shuy (eds.): *New ways of analyzing variation in English,* Washington: Georgetown University Press.
Ryan, Alan, 1970: *The philosophy of the social sciences,* London: Macmillan.
Salmon, Wesley, 1971: *Statistical explanation and statistical relevance,* Pittsburgh: Pittsburgh University Press.
Salomaa, Arto, 1969: "Probabilistic and weighted grammars," *Information and control.*
Sampson, Geoffrey, 1975: *The form of language,* London: Weidenfeld.
Specht, Ernst, 1969: *The foundations of Wittgenstein's late philosophy,* Manchester: Manchester University Press.

Spencer, Nancy, 1973: "Differences between linguists and non-linguists in intuitions about grammaticality-acceptability," *Journal of psycholinguistic research.*

Suppes, Patrick, 1972: "Probabilistic grammars for natural languages," in D. Davidson & G. Harman: *Semantics of natural language,* Dordrecht: Reidel.

Wall, Robert, 1972: *Introduction to mathematical linguistics,* Englewood Cliffs: Prentice-Hall.

Wason, P. & P. Johnson-Laird, 1972: *Psychology of reasoning,* Cambridge, Mass.: Harvard University Press.

Wittgenstein, Ludwig, 1958 (1953): *Philosophical investigations,* Oxford: Basil Blackwell.

— 1969: *On certainty,* Oxford: Basil Blackwell.

von Wright, G. H., 1974: *Causality and determinism,* New York: Columbia University Press.

Wunderlich, Dieter, 1974: *Grundlagen der Linguistik,* Reinbek: Rowohlt.

— 1976 a: „Kommentar zu Itkonen", in Wunderlich 1976 b.

— (ed.), 1976 b: *Die Wissenschaftstheorie der Linguistik,* Frankfurt a/M: Athenäum.

# Author Index

# Subject Index